PENGUIN BOOKS

HAIG'S COMMAND

'This well-researched and important book brings to life the polemics
and controversies of a past generation over Field Marshal Haig ... The
fresh documentary evidence produced by Winter makes it difficult for
historians in future to take up the cudgels for Haig' – Richard Lamb in
the *Spectator*

'Only by reading unweeded copies of British documents held in
Canada and Australia ... was the author able to expose a remarkable
rewriting of history. It makes fascinating reading' – Julian Thompson in
the *Observer*

'A major contribution to Great War history ... It has long been known
that the British Official History was painstakingly sanitized, and that
Haig had a hand in the process. How exactly it was done Winter
explains in detail' – John Keegan in the *Weekend Telegraph*

'This is history on several levels, human, technical and, in the end,
moral. Haig does not come at all well out of this work; but Winter
does, for he demolishes, piece by piece, the version that was served by
the Official Histories ... This is among the score of books on
1914–1918 which will live' – Norman Stone

'[An] impressive work of radical revision ... the author's indefatigable
exploration of the sources and impassioned presentation
of the case for the prosecution should ensure that his study is taken
seriously by all future historians of the First World War' –
Brian Bond in *History Today*

D0767738

DENIS WINTER

_____

HAIG'S COMMAND

A REASSESSMENT

PENGUIN BOOKS

PENGUIN BOOKS

Published by the Penguin Group
Penguin Books Ltd, 27 Wrights Lane, London W8 5TZ, England
Penguin Books USA Inc., 375 Hudson Street, New York, New York 10014, USA
Penguin Books Australia Ltd, Ringwood, Victoria, Australia
Penguin Books Canada Ltd, 10 Alcorn Avenue, Toronto, Ontario, Canada M4V 3B2
Penguin Books (NZ) Ltd, 182–190 Wairau Road, Auckland 10, New Zealand

Penguin Books Ltd, Registered Offices: Harmondsworth, Middlesex, England

First published by Viking 1991
Published in Penguin Books 1992
1 3 5 7 9 10 8 6 4 2

Copyright © Denis Winter, 1991
All rights reserved

*For my mother
and in memory of my father,
1583 Sergeant H. Winter, MM,
who fought in the front line at
2nd Bullecourt, St Julien, Chipilly
and the Canal du Nord*

Contents

Contents

List of Illustrations

ILLUSTRATION ACKNOWLEDGEMENTS

The author and publishers are grateful to the following for permission to use the following photographs: The Trustees of the Imperial War Museum for nos. 2–6, 9–31, 33, 35–44; Liddell Hart Centre for Military Archives, King's College, London, for nos. 32, 34, 46; Hulton Picture Library for no. 7; Topham Picture Library for nos. 1, 8, 47, 48; Australian War Memorial for no. 45.

List of Maps

Acknowledgements

It is a pleasure to acknowledge support from Canberra, Oxford and London. A five-month Visiting Fellowship at the Australian National University (Research School of Social Sciences) gave a hard-pressed schoolmaster breathing space. It also permitted a period of uninterrupted work in one of the world's great military archives – the Australian War Memorial. Anne Lu was in charge of the Memorial's documents at the time and a more helpful or knowledgeable guide it would be hard to imagine. Professor Norman Stone made time within a busy schedule to read the manuscript and make a number of constructive comments and criticisms. Eleo Gordon and the editorial staff at Penguin Books have again been the acme of efficiency and support. My special thanks to her and to David Duguid, who acted as copy editor.

A Summary of the Chief Events of Haig's Life

1861 Born
1875 Clifton College
1880 Brasenose College, Oxford
1884 Sandhurst
1885 Lieutenant, 7th Hussars
1886 Embarked with 7th Hussars for India
1896 Staff College, Camberley
1898 Staff Officer in the Sudan campaign
1899 Staff Officer in the Boer War
1901 Commander of the 17th Lancers, Boer War
1903 Inspector General of Cavalry, India
1905 Marriage during leave in England
1906 Director of Military Training, War Office
1907 Director of Staff Duties, War Office
1909 Chief of the General Staff, India
1912 The Aldershot command
1914 Commander of the 1st Corps (August)
      Commander of the 1st Army (December)
1915 Commander in Chief (December)
1916 The year of the Somme
1917 The year of Arras, Messines and Passchendaele
1918 The great German offensive (March)
      The allied counter-offensive (July–November)
1919 Commander in Chief, Home Forces
1920 Command of the Home Forces terminated
1928 Death

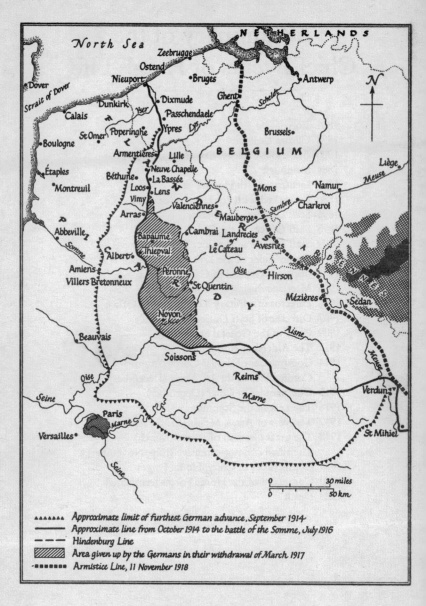

1

Introduction

Until the 1960s, Britain's contribution to the Great War seemed clearcut, the roles of her chief players generally accepted.

Haig campaigned consistently for concentration of effort against Germany's main army. The politicians, on the other hand, preferred to look for short cuts to victory in Italy, the Balkans or the Middle East. Tactically, Haig urged a major battle in the Belgian province of Flanders from the start. The politicians procrastinated, plotted and favoured action anywhere but Flanders.

When it came to the actual fighting, the traditional view was that Haig had pounded the Germans with a string of attrition battles, worn them down and in the end won that sweeping victory he always predicted. There was room for heated argument over his methods, but when the small size of Britain's pre-war professional army was added to its lack of experience in recent European wars, the slow, costly progress towards the relative efficiency of 1918 seemed inevitable.

In the 1960s, Cabinet papers and War Office records were opened to researchers for the first time and traditional assumptions began to shift. At about the same period, a large number of private collections became accessible, and the documentary record could then be compared with the published books which had monopolized discussion of the Great War for fifty years. It became obvious soon enough that radical adjustments were necessary.

In matters of high policy, Lloyd George emerged from the re-examination much more of a 'Westerner' than had previously been thought. Key soldiers like William Robertson and Henry Wilson also appeared in a new light, as strategists well aware of the eastern Mediterranean's vital importance for the British Empire. The whole strategic context of the war became, in fact, larger and more blurred. Russia and the United States came out every bit as important as France in their influence on British foreign policy, while persistent friction in the British Cabinet began to make better sense in the context of a traditional difference of opinion between the continental school (Marlborough, Wellington) and the amphibious empire grabbers (Clive, Wolfe) which went back to the Pitts, father and son, if not further.

The Western Front received a more cursory re-assessment. Politics and strategy rate higher than battles and tactics when questions of academic promotion arise. Documentation for the battlefield also proved more difficult to work with than the records of Cabinets and Cabinet Ministers for simple, geographical reasons. Students of politics can get most of their raw material within strolling distance of the Public Record Office's excellent cafeteria. Analysts of battle must chase their documents in Record Offices and archives throughout the British Isles – and abroad.

My personal interest in the relatively unworked area of the Great War's generalship and battles dates from 1980, when a Visiting Fellowship at the Australian National University's Research School coincided with the opening of Charles Bean's papers at the Australian War Memorial (Australia's equivalent of the Imperial War Museum). In his capacity as Australia's official war correspondent and her official historian, Bean gathered working notes which fill thirty yards of box files today. A first glance through these files revealed unusual range and detail, but that was hardly a surprise. Anyone who knows Bean's six massive volumes of official history would expect no less. What did startle was a collection of GHQ and Army Command material which had no counterpart in the Public Record Office in London. Much of it had apparently been copied by Bean's representative in London during the 1920s and nearly all of it was important. The possibility that important material had been withheld in Britain suggested itself at once and the private papers of Keith Murdoch, the journalist, reinforced the impression. Murdoch had been a go-between for Lloyd George and the Australian Prime Minister during the war and some of his reports in that capacity were given to Bean after the war. Since the quality and range of Murdoch's information was far in excess of anything available to researchers in Britain in our time, further inquiry was clearly indicated.

Moving on to Canada, I discovered Cabinet minutes fuller than transcripts available in London and covering meetings which never took place – according to British records.

Checking Haig's diary in Edinburgh next, I noted a substantial discrepancy between the typed version (invariably used by historians) and the handwritten original. On top of that, entries in both sources were sometimes at odds with contemporary documentation elsewhere. This meant that it was unlikely that all Haig's entries had been written when they were supposed to have been.

The one conclusion making sense of these anomalies was that falsification on a considerable scale must have taken place for so many documents to have been held back – or even re-written. It was unlikely that the various authorities involved in Britain would admit to past fraudulence. I therefore adopted Liddell Hart's 'indirect approach' and began to track down sources less likely to have been doctored. The national archives of countries allied to Britain during the war offered a promising source and the collections of private papers which had passed more rapidly through Whitehall's filter, another.

The end result of my work was a large quantity of new documentation, extracted from nooks and crannies in Canberra, Ottawa, Washington and local archives in Britain, together with another mass of material from the private papers of a hundred or so individuals ranging from generals and Cabinet Ministers through Staff Officers and Cabinet Secretaries down to press proprietors, official historians, socialite busybodies and an assortment of liaison officers. (Appendix 1 lists them and evaluates them in more detail.)

Three conclusions emerged after processing this material. The first was that Haig had systematically falsified the record of his military career, underpinning the most important years with a diary written for circulation in his own cause during the war and re-written in his own favour after it.

The second conclusion was that the official record of the war – political as well as military – had been systematically distorted both during the war as propaganda and after it, in the official history.

A corollary was that all documents passed on to the Public Record Office were carefully vetted so as to remove those which contradicted the official line. A similar procedure was followed before the private papers of leading soldiers, politicians and public figures were opened to researchers. Using its influence and a network of informers, the Cabinet Office (which came under the umbrella title Committee of Imperial Defence in the post-war period) was usually able to vet those collections in advance and either impound what was embarrassing or return particular documents to the families concerned, advising that they should be withheld.

The third conclusion was that huge gaps in the war's documentation remain. Some of the most important in this area include the record of Britain's preparation for war with Germany which began with the setting-up of the Committee of Imperial Defence (the CID) a decade or so before the war. A miserably thin fragment of the CID's papers at the Public Record Office continues to distort our understanding of that crucial institution. Another gap covers political discussion in the Cabinet during the war and the memoranda on which that discussion was based. A glimpse of how much we are missing in this area is offered by the National Archives at Washington, which hold a magnificent collection of documents copied by the American Official History team during the 1920s. The changing structures and procedures of the British Expeditionary Force are also poorly documented. What we are missing is suggested by the records of the Australian and Canadian Corps, retained by those bodies from 1916 and therefore immune from the Cabinet Office's mincing machine.

The book which follows represents an attempt to re-work a cross-section of newly available documentation with a view to finding out more of Haig's background as a soldier, discovering what his masters were trying to hide and suggesting a narrative which matches available documents better than the old fictions of Haig's command.

The value of these objects is self-evident, but it presented considerable difficulties of balance and proportion. If new documents pointed towards interpretations different from glosses long established and widely held, what of the perversity of the historian or the unrepresentative nature of the documents he was presenting? My checks here were of two sorts. If the same event was described in the papers of, say, the British ambassador in Paris, one of GHQ's liaison officers, a Cabinet Minister and a reliable corps commander, and if these in turn could be compared with the minutes of a Cabinet session and of Haig's weekly army commanders' conferences, any interpretation straying from the facts was likely to be thrown into relief. The quantity of sources used and the number of cross-checks made possible was my litmus test at every stage.

The second check was external. Within a year of starting work, my documentation began to assume the elusiveness of Alice's world through the looking glass. A newly bound set of Imperial War Cabinet minutes mysteriously appeared in the Public Record Office when I pointed out discrepancies between the Cabinet Office's offering and what was available in Ottawa. The resources of the Scottish Record Office proved unable to locate the transcript of an important legal case concerning the ownership of the Haig diaries in the 1930s. Staff College conference minutes, available to other historians, would abruptly disappear when I requested access. The Earl of Derby's diary appeared and disappeared within a few weeks, while Lord Rawlinson's diary in the Army Museum, which I and several other historians had consulted, de-materialized with an assurance that the museum had never held it. And so it went on, complications of this sort cropping up constantly, both in Britain and Australia, throughout the ten years of researching, processing and writing. Few historians have the good fortune to receive such clear indication that their research is proceeding on the right lines.

Several technical points in the text require explanation. The various sub-divisions of the British Army are the most intricate of these. The name of British Expeditionary Force was given to all soldiers in France and Belgium commanded first by Sir John French and, after December 1915, by Haig himself. The BEF was divided into a hierarchy of formations, best explained in tabular form:

Approximate number of men	Name	Officer in command
200,000	army	general
50,000	corps	lieutenant-general
12,000	division	major-general
4,000	brigade	brigadier
2,000	regiment	colonel
1,000	battalion	major
250	company	captain
60	platoon	lieutenant
15	section	lance-corporal

Haig's Command refers frequently to corps and to the Australian and Canadian Corps in particular, since they were much the most effective fighting units in the BEF from mid-1917 to the end of the war, and their semi-independent status allowed them to claim their own unit war diary material for record purposes, thus side-stepping most of the document shredding or withholding which was customary with British war records.

The army, the largest unit, was a flexible entity. For much of Haig's command, the five armies were distributed in the order 2nd, 1st, 3rd, 4th, 5th from north to south and centred on Ypres, Armentières, Arras, Albert and Amiens respectively. But an army was where its commander set up his HQ. Thus when Gough moved from the Somme to Ypres in 1917, the men already in Flanders simply became the 5th Army. Likewise, when the battle of Passchendaele began, units from all the other armies were rotated through Gough's battle area and styled 5th Army men for their tour of duty.

The structure of the BEF remained the same from the start to the finish of the war, but the number of units in each category increased with the expansion of the British Army. The best indication of the scale of that expansion is a check on the number of officers and men in France each November of the war:

260,000	1914
938,000	1915
1,530,000	1916
2,000,000	1917
1,860,000	1918

Two other technical terms crop up frequently. The 3rd Bureau was the French equivalent to Haig's Operations section at GHQ and the reader will come across it regularly, since an intelligent, well-informed and garrulous American liaison officer worked in it and described its response to events from the latter part of 1917.

Haig's Operations section sent out directives prefixed OA. His personal orders went through the section and were distinguished with the prefix OAD. The OAD sequence is obviously of fundamental importance in piecing together the story of Haig's command, and the miserable quantity which has reached the Public Record Office (the full quota would run into several thousand) offers the strongest possible evidence of falsification by the Cabinet Office. British researchers wishing to read the fullest sequence of OADs must refer to it in Canberra.

The large number of individuals named in the text reflects the number of document collections consulted. Any reader wishing to know more about the men behind the names must refer to the biographical sketches section at the back of the book.

Two particular omissions in *Haig's Command* require an explanation. The first is the relative scarcity of secondary sources or learned articles cited in the bibliography. My judgement was that a reconstruction of the Great War from documents which became available in the 1960s was likely to prove more valuable than yet another regurgitation of well-worn secondary sources. I was encouraged in that assessment by the fact that most books tapping recently opened documents relied heavily on the Public Record Office and Haig's typed diary. My own conclusion was that both sources were suspect. An interpretation based on a much wider range of previously unused material was therefore likely to be of value.

German sources are another omission. The generally accepted view is that German military archives covering the Great War failed to survive the bombing of Berlin in the forties. I was unconvinced. Sir James Marshall-Cornwall told me that he had been in Berlin with Sir John Wheeler-Bennett shortly after its capture. Both had been authoritatively told that these records had been moved to safety before the serious bombing began, and even if they had stayed put could Harris's bombers really have destroyed the building which housed them? In 1934 Hitler ordered that a special annexe be added to the Reichsarchive for all military documents referring to the Great War. It was to be six storeys high, of reinforced concrete and fire-proof. One would have thought such a structure bomb-proof. But whatever the facts of the case, German military documents available to a researcher today are inadequate and, rather than lean on official histories or published documents (my own work had given me a particularly jaundiced view of both sources), I concentrated on the British dimension.

HAIG'S CREDENTIALS

2

Personal Credentials

Shortly before Christmas 1915, Haig received a letter marked 'Secret'. It was enclosed within three envelopes, written by the Prime Minister in person and phrased with Asquith's usual economy:

'Sir John French has placed in my hands his resignation of the office of Commander in Chief of the forces in France. Subject to the King's approval, I have the pleasure of proposing to you that you should be his successor.'

Leo Rothschild, an old friend, had already alerted Haig, so the offer didn't take him by surprise. It must have been intensely satisfying nevertheless to be formally offered what he had coveted for half a lifetime, and so with a slight delay for the sake of decorum, Haig sent his formal acceptance. In doing so, he took charge of one million soldiers and seventy miles of the Western Front. No British general had ever commanded so many men. Only Marlborough and Wellington had shouldered comparable responsibility. What sort of man was he then and – the million-dollar question – how far did his personality match the requirements of such a massive job?

A steady flow of visitors passed through GHQ in the early days of Haig's command looking for the answers to those questions, and most were surprised by the man they found. They expected a stiff, haughty soldier. They met instead a self-confident gentleman who greeted them with old-world courtesy and grave ease of gesture. Photographs emphasized the greying hair, thickening waistline, rounded shoulders and forward stoop of a fifty-five-year-old, but in the flesh visitors found that traces of the remarkably handsome young Hussar Haig had once been made a stronger impression.

John Masefield's impressions can be taken as typical of many who passed through GHQ. 'Going to GHQ,' he wrote, 'we stuck in the mud and had to get soldiers to pull us out so we arrived forty minutes late and covered with filth. Owing to this, I barely saw Sir Douglas but he was like Ian and Lord Methuen and these other wonderful men rolled into one. No enemy could stand against such a man. He took away my breath. I don't know what it is in such men. It is partly a very fine delicate gentleness and generosity and then partly a pervading power and partly a height of resolve. He makes me understand Sidney and Fairfax and Falkland and all these others, Moore and the rest. He is a rather tall man with grey hair, a moustache and a delicate, fine, resolved face and a manner at once gentle and eager. I don't think anyone could have been nicer and I don't think any race but the Scotch could have produced such a one.'[1]

The second quality which made an immediate impact was Haig's poise. After serving him for many years as a Staff Officer, Clement Armitage told one of Haig's biographers: 'He had a very quiet manner. I never remember him to raise his voice in discussion.'

And so it remained on the battlefield. Late in summer 1918, when success lay in the balance in front of the Hindenburg Line and the Australian Corps commander, Monash, had worked himself into a state of high agitation, Haig appeared at the critical moment and steadied things. Monash later described the episode to his wife: 'Haig was kind enough to come and have a talk with me but I can say with unreserved candour that the reverse was far more often true. It was a source of immeasurable relief to find him calm, resolute, buoyant and hopeful in the face of irretrievable chaos and disaster.'

Dignity and calm are therefore beyond dispute, but getting at the real man beneath the formal exterior was quite another matter. Taciturnity alone saw to that. As Haig's private secretary put it, 'Haig disliked speaking freely in the presence of anyone he did not know well and trust. He preferred to stay silent rather than run the risk that what he said might be misunderstood or misrepresented.'[2]

Even when Haig did open out, his notorious inarticulacy darkened any meeting of minds. Desmond Morton served Haig as an ADC before rising to third position in MI6's hierarchy between the wars, and his description of the tongue-tied Commander in Chief brings out the point perfectly. 'Haig was a silent man,' wrote Morton, 'but such silence was babbling compared with what he said when he gave an oral instead of a written order. You had to learn a sort of verbal shorthand made up of a series of grunts and gestures. After the battle of Cambrai when the tanks under Hugh Elles were used, he sent me forward to see and report what was going on, giving me what he would have described as a full personal briefing of the plan, the situation on the second day as reported by telegram and telephone, what he wanted to know and where best I should go to find out for him. Actually, the briefing lasted about twenty minutes and consisted of Haig with a pointer in front of a large-scale map of the battle pointing at various spots and making grunting noises with a few words interspersed. "Never believed . . . petrol . . . bridge gone . . . where cavalry?" and so on. Fortunately I knew the cipher by this time. I am sure Haig felt he had given me a long and lucid lecture on the whole affair. When I got back, I had an hour with him. I talked, interrupted occasionally by a grunt, interrogative or otherwise. When I had run dry and he had ceased to grunt, it seemed clear that he was wrestling with something else he wanted to say and couldn't get the words. I waited. Eventually, he waved a hand in a certain manner and managed to get out, "Thank you very much indeed. Good." This was a very long speech for him in the circumstances.'[3]

Others remarked on Haig's remarkable inability to communicate. 'Dined with Haig and Braithwaite,' wrote Guy Dawnay, GHQ's Deputy Chief of Staff in 1918. 'Chief in good humour. He is, however, the most inarticulate man I ever met.' And Dawnay was supported by Monash, the distinguished commander of the Australian Corps. On one occasion, Monash told Australia's official war correspondent that even after half an hour's discussion with Haig, he was quite unable to see what the Commander in Chief was driving at.

The combination of constraint and inarticulacy in this degree bewildered most men who had to deal with Haig. Even acquaintances of long standing had to admit that if respect for the man deepened with time, their understanding of his personality remained where it had been at the start. Desmond Morton put it well when he told Liddell Hart: 'Haig remained no little of a mystery to me. I have rarely met so self-contained a man. Everyone said so. Noel Birch [Haig's artillery adviser] warned me that Haig was a rum 'un and that although he had known him for many years in the army and socially, he didn't really know him.'

Contemporaries like Birch who tried to form any sort of picture of Haig had, of course, to depend on the speech and writing of a man always reluctant to project any sort of image in public. Three generations later, it is a good deal easier to penetrate Haig's defences. Books on the Great War have been coming out continuously since 1918 and the opening of the archives for the Great War period in the 1960s added a mass of additional information. Using these sources, the conundrum confronting Haig's personal staff is easier to unravel and resolves itself into a personality with a single core but three distinct facets.

The first of these facets was Haig, silent and aloof. John Charteris, who served on Haig's staff for nearly twenty years, went on to write a fine biography of him after his death which captures this aspect beautifully. 'His manner to those who were intimate with him,' wrote Charteris, 'though completely courteous, was cold and formal. He appeared to treat those with him rather as a doctor would a patient. If he perceived undue depression, he would go out of his way to provide encouragement. If he perceived undue elation, he would take steps to provide an antidote.'[4]

Did Haig deliberately slip on a cold, impersonal disguise to create distance between himself and his subordinates and thus safeguard his own status? Eric Geddes, Haig's transport organizer, thought so and suggested that 'Haig had a full sense of the dignity of his position and of the need for formality.'[5]

If Geddes was right, Haig was certainly successful. 'Even officers of high rank who were seeing him regularly entered his presence with a certain feeling of nervousness,' Charteris recalled. 'His personal staff used to note with amusement the little symptoms of anxiety in those waiting to be ushered into his room – the distrait manner, the large number of matches used to light a pipe or cigarette.' Lord

Esher, a patron of Haig and an old friend, agreed with Geddes, adding that Haig's 'aloofness of mind strengthened his hold on officers under him'.[6] And yet, for all this agreement between acquaintances of long standing, professional calculation offers only a partial explanation. Colleagues had noted Haig's reserve long before he occupied military commands of any importance. Nor did he have any need to defend himself against loyal friends. The icy barrier stayed firmly in place nevertheless. As Charteris put it in the *British Legion Journal* when Haig died, 'He was not one with whom real intimacy was possible. In moments of greatest confidence, one felt the ice of his self-reliance and reserve was always there.'

The second facet was astonishingly different. Open, direct and boyish, this was the Haig that Stephen Butler encountered when he became Haig's (temporary) Intelligence chief in 1918. 'The other day I had to see the Commander in Chief,' Butler wrote to his father. 'I told him all the information of importance and then he asked me about myself and got me yarning with him about East Africa, Sudan and Arabia and got very interested. When I left, he said he'd like to go on talking for a long time but he had much to do. Next day, I received an invitation to dinner. I was the only guest and he yarned away like a schoolboy and seemed so interested in my travels and was very nice when he said goodnight. He had such a fine, straight, strong face and kind eyes. He's a big man and everyone out here thinks the same.'

In such a mood, Haig might even display quiet humour. 'He looks you straight in the face with a pleasant, kindly smile which has a slightly ironical twinkle to it,' Frederick Oliver recalled. And that irony could even go beyond a twinkle. Lady Haig described such an occasion in a book on her husband. Fire had broken out in the Commandant's house at Aldershot shortly before the war but was quickly brought under control. 'Captain Charteris then appeared in rather dirty looking pyjamas and when the fire was extinguished, the flooring was burnt and we could see anyone passing beneath. Douglas spied Charteris just below and out of pure mischief, seized the largest jug he could find and poured the contents over Charteris's head saying, "A very good shot and that will clean him up." Captain Baird and myself who were looking on could not help roaring with laughter.'[7]

On paper, this mood was expressed by Haig's quirkish use of the exclamation mark, which signalled a double meaning to the reader. The mockery implied is always barely perceptible, but for a man supposedly literal-minded (Charteris thought that no man told fewer jokes than Haig), his grave whimsy surprises. An example given in Haig's official biography features Trenchard's personal assistant, with a whimsical exclamation mark followed by a signature of ironic formality. 'Haig christened Maurice Baring "Nicodemus". For what reason Baring never knew. After the war he once attended a levee at the Court of St James's in court dress. Haig was standing beside the throne. After Baring had made his bow but before he left the Palace, a note was handed to him which ran, "Nicodemus. Your stocking is coming down! (signed) Haig F.M."'

Haig could therefore seem cold and remote. He could with equal ease switch to a relaxed, almost whimsical mood. But between these two and seldom far below the surface was a third Haig, indicated by a number of mannerisms and punctuated by outbursts of the bottled-up emotion which generated them. Frequent tugging at his moustache was one of these. A brisk forward jab of the arm as if throwing away a match when he was emphasizing a point was another. Flaws in breathing and digestion are good barometers of stress and Haig was always blighted in both areas. His breathing seizures were usually attributed to hay fever or asthma in his diary, and a sensitive stomach is reflected in a self-imposed ban on oily or fatty foods since his days at Brasenose.

Those biting comments, which are such a feature of Haig's diary, are another indication of tension. They invariably mark out those who threatened his position (Lloyd George, Plumer, Allenby, Maxse) or dared to criticize him (George V, Joffre, Derby).

Tears came from the same root. Thomas Blamey, as the Australian Chief of Staff, described a typical outburst during a conference after the battle of Amiens in August 1918. 'Gentlemen,' Haig had said, 'you may not realize what you have done for the Empire, you Australians.' At that point Haig's tears flowed in such profusion that, according to Blamey's record, he had been unable to go on with his address.[8] In his private diary, Currie, the Canadian Corps commander, recorded another tearful spasm when Haig told him of his relief at having Canadians in reserve during the dark days of April 1918. These are unexpected emotions indeed in a man characterized by Jan Smuts among many as 'the most outstanding instance I ever came across of a strong, silent man'.

The relaxed, amiable side of Haig's personality requires no explanation. It is the man beneath the defensive barriers. What then of the tense, silent character which contrasts so strongly with it?

Lord Geddes, who may have had inside information from his brother Eric, Haig's transport organizer, dated it back to Haig's youth in Edinburgh. In a review of Blake's 1952 edition of the Haig diary, he blamed it on whisky and snobbishness, suggesting that 'at the core of Haig's being, there was always a sense of the existence of powers opposing him. He had a persecution diathesis and was always suspicious that someone was plotting against him. The origin of this dates from the 1860s. John Haig, father of Douglas and a wealthy whisky distiller, established himself at 24 Charlotte Square, the heart of Edinburgh's West End, and the neighbours of the whisky Haigs were not appeased by any suggestion that some 250 years before, these Haigs had sprung from an ancient line of Bemersyde. To them, he was just a whisky tradesman. In consequence, Douglas Haig was not educated at a Scottish school and even in 1885 he was not posted to the Scots Greys, the regiment of regiments for a Haig of Bemersyde.'[9] But if social resentment had bitten so deeply, the only sign of it during the war was a long letter, written on the eve of the battle of Messines and featuring Haig's defence of the Clackmannan Haigs against heraldic authorities who claimed to have found breaks in the succession.[10] The point here was that when James Haig died in 1854, unmarried and pre-deceased by his brother, the obvious link through direct succession with the thirteenth-century Haigs of Bemersyde was broken. James Haig's sisters, themselves unmarried, passed the family home to a 'cousin' of uncertain ancestry – Lt.-Col. Arthur Haig, equerry to the Duke of Edinburgh – and if these Haigs from Clackmannan were in fact parvenus, the Commander in Chief's own claim to aristocratic status would have been revealed as fraudulent.

How then can the three facets of Haig's personality be understood? Drawing on the reflections of Haig's elder brother, Charteris probably put out the best explanation when he emphasized Haig's family backgound and his early years.

Paternal influence during those years seems to have been minimal. Absent abroad for long periods, nominally on account of ill health, his father paid brief visits to Edinburgh which left little more than the memory of foul temper and the bad language that went with it. What the boy missed from his father's side was however more than compensated for by his mother, who withdrew into her family and transferred all her emotions on to her children. She visited their bedrooms at four in the morning, prayed with each child and supervised all educational matters in detail. Douglas, her youngest, seems to have suffered most from this stifling regime (her photograph hung over his bed to the end of his life), and when she died, sister Henrietta took over the mothering role, financing Douglas, introducing him to friends at Court and nursing his career at every turn. Douglas responded warmly, writing to her regularly throughout his life. He was to die in her house. She followed him within months.

Brought up by doting women as the centre of attention and as one of whom much was expected, Haig had just the sort of early life to produce a thoroughly spoilt child and, according to Charteris, it did just that. 'We leave his childhood days,' Charteris wrote, 'with a picture in our minds of a small, bad-tempered, bekilted child with a crop of bright yellow curls, secured to the pannier of a pony and bearing in his hands a drum with the inscription, "Douglas Haig – *sometimes* a good boy".'

Haig's years at Clifton College (1875–9) and Brasenose College, Oxford (1880–83), have left few traces of social tension. On the contrary, he was a capable and active games player at both places and was elected a member of the socially exclusive Bullingdon Club at Oxford. But he was under no pressure during these years. Percival, Clifton's first headmaster, was the originator of compulsory games, and in Haig's time there competition was frowned on and academic excellence placed well below 'character formation'. Nor did he have to compete at Brasenose. He was only reading for a Pass degree and failed to achieve even that humble distinction.

From Oxford, Haig moved to Sandhurst and a military career. The Army, with its introverted, competitive atmosphere, exacerbated his childhood problems and reinforced many of his peculiarities. When he was looking for an explanation of the vitriolic comments in Haig's diary, Lord Geddes drew particular attention to the Old Army, with its private feuds and long-sustained animosities. 'In the pre-Boer war Army, most regimental officers retained an almost schoolboyish way of talking about officers of other units. No real criticism was implied when the other fellows were called cads and bounders, rotters and stinkers. It only meant that in the ferociously tribal Army of the 1890s, they belonged to a different tribe. It would all have been quite normal in the lower fourth and was part of the persistent adolescent characteristics of many regimental Messes.' Geddes was adding a charitable gloss to an unpleasant business, but the tensions were real enough. Haig's personality, resentful of competition from the nursery, bore a permanent scar from the Army's reinforcement of that flaw.

Even before he joined a regiment, the degree of savage intensity in Haig's competitiveness had been noted by colleagues as something quite unusual. 'We were a cheerful, sociable lot except for Haig,' wrote one of his Sandhurst contemporaries. 'Haig worked harder than anyone else and was seldom seen at Mess except for meals.' And on one occasion when he did appear, a colleague who was to become Britain's official historian of the Western Front noted a fine example of Haig's abrasiveness. Thus Birkbeck to Haig: 'Nice day!' and Haig's typically surly reply: 'What's that to you?'[11]

He sustained this level of abrasiveness through Staff College (1896–7) and fellow students registered their disapproval pointedly when they elected Allenby to the Mastership of the Drag Hunt even though, as one of them later told Allenby's biographer, 'Allenby's fat arse and big thighs made him an abominable horseman.'[12]

When he left the Staff College, Haig was seconded to the Egyptian Army and served as a Staff Officer in Kitchener's campaign of 1898 against the Dervishes. He saw action in the skirmish of Atbara and the decisive battle of Omdurman and described both in long contemporary letters to Sir Evelyn Wood, the Adjutant General, who had requested Haig to keep him briefed. The sharpness of Haig's criticism was characteristic. 'Really,' he wrote in a typical passage, 'I cannot think that the Promotion Board fully appreciates the re-

sponsibility which rests with them when they put duffers in command of regiments.'

Haig's next campaign was in South Africa from 1899 to 1902
against the Boers. Beginning as a Staff Officer with the Cavalry
Division, he took command of a cavalry force in the final phase of
guerrilla warfare, ending the war as commander of the 17th Lancers.
This should have been a very acceptable progression for an ambitious
soldier but, once again, the tone of his letters to England remained
tetchy and querulous. At the start of 1900, for example, he told his
sister: 'So many Colonial Skallywag Corps have been raised that the
horses of the whole force could not have a full ration. The Colonial
Corps raised in the Cape Colony are quite useless; so are the recently
raised Mounted Infantry. They can't ride and know nothing about
their duties as mounted men . . . You will thus see that the success of
the Cavalry Division has been in spite of these ruffians . . .'

Peace, promotion and the retention of his command of the 17th
Lancers worked little appreciable change in Haig's angry, suspicious
nature. He messed alone and made a point of keeping his distance
from the officers and men of his command. Nor did he soften when
he went out to India as Inspector General of Cavalry in 1903.
Charles Bean, Australia's official war correspondent, questioned an
old Indian Army man serving on the Australian staff during the
Great War and was told: 'Haig was as clean and determined a man as
I have ever met. No man I knew inspired regular soldiers with as
much fear as Haig, not even Kitchener. They were panic-stricken in
his presence. He was most heavy-handed in telling off officers whom
he criticized.'[13] John Charteris, who was Haig's Intelligence chief
during the Great War, remarked on this aspect during the period
when he first joined Haig's circle in India: 'Lack of effort or the
slightest variation from straightforwardness were like sparks to tinder
and could be followed by an explosion of ire. Holding himself
perfectly rigid as if with difficulty restraining himself from physical
assault on the culprit, his eyes blazing, Haig would administer
reproof in a tone so hard and words so forcible that even the most
callous winced.'

Haig only began to moderate with the acceleration of his own
promotion. As a friend of both George V and Haig and an inter-

mediary between them throughout the war, Sir George Arthur watched Haig closely when he returned from India to a staff position at the War Office in 1906. He noted a gradual transformation. 'Those who worked near Haig during those three years noted a mellowing difficult to define but impossible to deny. The constraint which had been felt, if it was never meant, was to disappear. To all that he said or did was now added a degree of charm hitherto unnoticed if not unsuspected.'[14]

In 1909, Haig returned to India for a three-year tour as Chief of the General Staff, and Charteris described a continuation of this thawing process. 'The mellowing that had begun at the War Office was proceeding apace through his wife's influence [Haig had married the Hon. Dorothy Vivian, Maid of Honour to Queen Alexandra, during a spell of leave from India in 1905]. He took to tennis. He played polo regularly at Annandale and spent many weekends golfing on the miniature course perched precariously on the side of a Himalayan mountain at Naldera, a few miles from Simla. He entertained largely if not lavishly. A fancy-dress ball had the remarkable result of displaying the reserved and somewhat unbending Chief of Staff arrayed as Henry VIII and, to all appearances, enjoying himself as much as the youngest of Simla's Staff Officers.'

With a position protected by the social standing of his patrons, Haig even began to relax a little and took the first steps in mixing with juniors. Charteris approved the development, noting that 'Haig now learned to utilize sympathetically those with limitations. His reserve and shyness took a softer tone. Brusqueness of manner gave way to dignified courtesy in his dealings with others which later in France gained comment from all strangers meeting him for the first time.'

Ivor Maxse, an able corps commander, described one of Haig's switches into this softer mood during the war. He was visiting a corps earmarked for the right wing at Passchendaele and, as Maxse wrote, 'Haig was in great form. Better than I have ever seen him. He was full of confidence and, for him, genial. He consented to go round my staff and cracked jokes with the humbler members, including NCOs. Some were in shirt sleeves and none was standing too rigidly to attention.'[15]

Monash told his wife of a similar encounter. Haig's relations with the Australians were always a shade uneasy (as the caustic comments in his diary demonstrate) but they were a powerful command and, in the later stages of the war, semi-independent. Tact was therefore required and Monash described Haig's exercise of that quality on the eve of the Australian thrust against Passchendaele village in October 1917. 'He put his arm round my shoulder and with much feeling and warmth said, "You have a very fine Division. I wish you all sorts of luck, old man."' Both men were riding side by side at the time, in full view of the division.

Haig may have mellowed as his professional standing increased. He stayed close to his defences nevertheless, always on the lookout for threats – and with good reason. The way he had been able to ease Sir John French from the position of Commander in Chief in 1915 could only have sharpened that old instinct for danger which had been such a strong feature in earlier years.

Rumours that Kitchener, as Secretary of State for War, planned to sack French had already reached Haig in December 1914 via Rawlinson. A month later, everything seemed set for Haig to replace French. A letter from the king's assistant secretary went so far as to congratulate him, adding the hope that 'from time to time you will write to me freely and in the strictest confidence'.[16] An intervention by Joffre, the French Chief of Staff, saved French, but by June 1915 he was wobbling again and Haig resumed his destabilizing efforts. Arthur Lee, a thruster from Munitions, described an example of Haig's tactics at the time with a suitably dry pen. 'Each time Haig received me,' wrote Lee, 'we might have been perfect strangers and his demeanour was one of chromium-plated correctness. Then, unexpectedly, in the privacy of his sanctum, he would dissolve into the man with a grievance whose services were unappreciated and whose career was being prejudiced by the jealousy and even malice of an effete and incompetent Chief. It was obvious that he did not take me into his confidence in order that I might transmit his views to Sir John French. His hope, undoubtedly, was that I might direct the arrow in the direction of Kitchener and the Cabinet.'[17]

Haig's nerves must have worn thin during that year-long struggle to take the final step of his career. Men close to him sensed a new intensity in his suspicious nature and a reinforcement of a Manichaean tendency to divide the world between the good men who supported him and the bad who intrigued against his just claim to the Army's top job.

Edward Spears, an articulate and mischievous liaison officer with the French, noted the symptoms of Haig's dualism with his usual perceptiveness when he wrote: 'Haig had a warm heart and showed great affection for those whom he considered his friends. His wide-set, level, blue eyes under their straight eyebrows seemed to question any newcomer as if considering whether or not he was to be trusted. To those he knew and liked, that clear look could be very warm and friendly. But it took some time to overcome his reserve.'[18]

Haig's saints were a diverse group, but two particular types were always warmly regarded by the Commander in Chief. Personal staff were the first of these. 'Tommy' Thompson, an ADC, gave an example: 'My reason to go to the 9th Division was met by Haig with a firm refusal. He said it was absurd as I should only get in the way of younger men. He told me to think it over. If he was a music-hall general and made a habit of thoroughly ramming his entourage occasionally, I shouldn't hesitate to insist on going but he is such a very humane person and so thoughtful of others.'[19]

Young soldiers formed a second, favoured group. Desmond Morton noted the pleasure Haig took in the company of handsome young officers when he told Liddell Hart that 'private soldiers and officers adored him when they knew him'. A letter in the *Toronto Globe* offers support. Signed 'Old Mac', it referred to an incident in summer 1917 when the Canadians were about to attack Lens. Coming from rest, 'Old Mac's' battalion was marched to a narrow, hedged cart track near the front for inspection. Haig arrived with an escort of 17th Lancers, chatting first with Colonel Saunders, then turning to the men. Facing Goodchild, 'Mac's' company commander and 'a fine, clean young Canadian', Haig raised a finger to his cap and smiled, 'just as any middle-aged man would to a son'.[20]

A pleasing recollection reinforces the point. Haig, visiting the headquarters of the Australian Corps during the Somme, had found occasion to criticize Birdwood's dispositions and organization. Brude-nell White, a Camberley-trained Australian, was Birdwood's Chief

Staff Officer at the time. 'I felt myself getting hot all over,' he told Bean later. 'At last I could stand it no longer. In spite of Birdie's protest, I dragged Haig back to the map and said, "Look here, sir. I may be a damned interfering colonial but you were wrong." And I took him back over the accusations and showed him that it was not Birdie's fault at all. I was in such a state that I didn't really care. But Haig was splendid. He just looked at me with his kindly blue eyes and said, "Perhaps you're right, young man!" '[21]

Haig was less spontaneous with older men, but once a candidate had passed the test (after much scrutiny), Haig was forthcoming. 'My dear Birdie, I return to France tomorrow,' runs one postcard in the Birdwood papers. 'My dear Harrie, Just a line to say how astounded I am to hear of five major-generals being promoted over your head' (this is to Rawlinson, a general promoted by Haig each time he lost a battle). 'It is a great help in difficult times to feel one has a few loyal friends about one,' Haig told his wife after dining with Byng, an army commander invariably addressed in Haig's private correspondence as 'Bungo' and his wife, 'Mrs Bungo'.

These were the sheep, and Haig's trust in them was almost boundless. John Headlam, Haig's gunnery adviser until the Somme, was much struck by the extent of a confidence which contrasted so strongly with that cold eye Haig cast over so many others. 'It is very curious,' he remarked to Charteris, 'that intense confidence in everything belonging to him (Gort, Vaughan etc.) and the reverse feeling regarding everything else.'[22]

And what of the goats? Generals were the most immediate threat to Haig's position and he always searched the higher ranks of the Army for potential rivals. Desmond Morton noted the point in a penetrating memoir written for Liddell Hart, contrasting Haig's 'kindness' to subordinates with his stance as 'holy terror to equals, superiors and possible competitors'. Morton went on to suggest that Haig's only political interest was in searching for the first signs of moves to remove him from command.

Politicians formed a second group of goats. Charteris indicated Haig's feelings in the first months of the war when he told his wife: 'Sir Douglas hates all politicians and does not like to see me talking to them. He says you can't trust anyone who has ever been in parliament.'

'Three years later, distrust had turned to loathing. As Haig told his wife, 'To be a successful politician requires practice and training like every other profession. There are depths of insincerity and almost dishonesty in politics to which no soldier could stoop.'[23]

The practical consequence of this venom was Haig's reluctance to supply the Cabinet with accurate statistics at any time or keep them fully briefed over his negotiations with successive French Commanders in Chief. But even more damaging than Haig's fractious working relationship with the politicians (who had plenty of alternative sources of information) was an inability to work with the Chief of the Imperial General Staff, William ('Wully') Robertson, who to Haig was nothing more than a politician in khaki and to be treated as such. It was obviously important that the Army in the field and at home should speak with one voice, so that Cabinet decisions might be based on the best possible information, but with relations between Haig and Robertson as they were, this could never happen.

The particular reason for Haig's dislike was a combination of suspicion ('You want to champion my cause by wringing the necks of those intriguers at the War Office? That would do no good because Robertson is very necessary for the country now. Besides, I expect his neck will be very tough'[24]) and social disdain ('Robertson talks too much of "I". He means well and will succeed, I feel sure. How much easier though it is to work with a gentleman'[25]).

The result was that Haig told Robertson as little as he could get away with, resented his visits to the front line and kept up his end in a dialogue of cat and mouse which ran through the wartime correspondence of the two men. 'It is necessary you should keep me acquainted with your views,' ran a typical letter from Robertson. 'If I have to depend entirely on press communiqués, my opinion is not much more valuable than anyone else's and, indeed, it is almost impossible to give an opinion.'[26]

It was quite in line with Haig's bloody-mindedness that when a Supreme War Council was established towards the end of 1917 as that coordinating body unanimously recommended by the alliance's leading generals in July 1917 (and commended to Haig by Esher and Lord Derby), Haig insisted on perceiving another hostile set of 'politicians' in khaki and did what he could to make their work more difficult.

The British ambassador in Paris gave the Foreign Office a practical example of the difficulties created by Haig's attitude when he wrote in January 1918: 'These feminine jealousies between the generals are very absurd. GHQ will not recognize Versailles. Versailles wants to give GHQ the go-by, the result being that a Versailles warrant does not run in the war zone and Haig's officers between Paris and the Channel ports refuse to recognize the validity of Henry Wilson's messengers' certificates and the embassy is asked to get the messengers passed on their way to London. This we are happy to do but how ridiculous it is! Why do not the proper authorities in London give such instructions to Haig as will ensure his issuing the requisite orders to his officers to let the King's Messengers pass along?'[27]

Foreigners in general and the French in particular formed the third group of Haig's goats. Dislike and contempt were graphically recorded by the medals and ribbons on his chest. Though Haig had seventeen foreign decorations and five and a half rows of foreign ribbons by the end of the war, he normally wore only British ribbons, adding foreign medals representing the countries of men he was scheduled to meet on a particular day.

In his diary, Haig's references to foreigners were usually dismissive, and his text is shot through with caustic comment. Three examples suffice to give the flavour of Haig's dislike:

'I must say that I feel disgusted with our allies who have succeeded in putting us in these straits. We almost seem to be fighting against the laws of nature in trying to keep alive races who are obviously of an inferior kind and who themselves feel inferior to the Germans, so England has a burden to carry.'[28]

'The Italians seem a wretched people, useless as fighting men but greedy for money. Moreover, I doubt whether they are really in earnest about this war. Many of them, too, are German spies.'[29]

'I thought Mme Junot's memoirs would interest you [his wife]. Napoleon was such a scoundrel and so capable and unscrupulous, one never tires of reading about him. I fancy the French are much the same now as then. Few realize the difference between right and wrong, between honest, straightforward dealing and low cunning.'[30]

Maxse told Liddell Hart that Haig's loathing of the French pre-dated the war and had been particularly noticeable whenever Haig was sent to observe Foch's field exercises. Maxse went on to mention a comment made when Haig and he were organizing the occupation of the Rhineland after the Armistice: 'The French! They're the fellows we shall be fighting next.'

Since France and Britain were never more than allies of convenience, Haig's xenophobia was particularly unhelpful during the war. It is hard to believe that episodes such as the Nivelle offensive in spring 1917 or the dialogue with Pétain during March 1918 would have generated quite the friction they did generate if a man of greater maturity and balance had been in charge of the British Army. Human engineering was, after all, a vital aspect of high command. As Commander in Chief, Haig was committed to constant communication with all manner of politicians and foreign allies. Cajoling them towards consensus on strategy and manipulating both parties to get the best possible allocation of battle frontage and mechanical raw material was a necessary part of the job.

Closer to his own headquarters, Haig was required to coordinate those thrusting *condottieri* who had pushed themselves to the top of the Army and, with subtle blend of stick and carrot, bend 'the Barons' (as they were called by men like Oliver and Esher who had close knowledge of the BEF's dynamics) to his own will.

All details of organization fell to GHQ's staff. The Commander in Chief's job here was to fit a mass of assorted pegs into holes of approximately the right shape and integrate the final ensemble in such a way that it delivered the fullest possible information in the most accessible form to his desk before translating his orders into the smoothest administrative shape.

These were skills demanding the highest intelligence, the most awesome degree of personal maturity and the diplomatic finesse of a Renaissance Pope. Could Haig – suspicious, embattled, inarticulate – ever have been a suitable man for this complex job? Or did the strength of Haig's purely military credentials compensate perhaps for his deficiencies in the field of personal relationships?

3

Professional Credentials

When Churchill reviewed Haig's official biography in the 1930s, he expressed a widely accepted view of Haig's qualifications when he wrote: 'He was, when he became Commander in Chief, head boy and prize pupil of the military school. He had fought as a cavalry squadron leader, served in the field as a Staff Officer, held an important military appointment in India, commanded the Aldershot Division before the outbreak of the war and valiantly led the 1st Army Corps and the 1st Army for nearly eighteen months of Armageddon. He had no professional rivals at the time.'[1]

One would have thought Churchill well qualified to pronounce on the matter. Cabinet Minister before the war, Minister of Munitions during it and Minister of War immediately after, he must have known Haig's background well, but most documents contradict his judgement.

Haig's Sandhurst days, for example, are invariably described as an auspicious beginning to a distinguished career – he passed out first in order of merit and won the Anson Sword as a bonus. Those facts have been repeated like an incantation over fifty years, but the record fails to support either claim. The custom of Sandhurst was for cadets to be gazetted in order of merit, top of the list going to the senior regiment and so on down the order. The fact that Haig passed into the 7th Hussars hardly suggests that he came near the top, even after getting a 20 per cent mark bonus 'from the professors' without explanation.

The Anson Sword presents a similar problem. Compared with

today's Sword of Honour, the Anson was a prize of strictly limited value. Captain the Honourable Augustus Anson, VC, had been a strong opponent of those Victorian Army reforms which abolished a rich officer's right to buy a commission. His sword had therefore been intended as a protest against the invidious principle of promotion by merit, and only gentlemen cadets were eligible – which meant the Anson had nothing to do with the sort of merit demanded by the battlefields of the Great War. The year in which Haig is supposed to have won it is anyway blank in the records today. If he had invented his award of the Anson Sword, it wouldn't have been the only fabrication in the *curriculum vitae* he put together to further his own career.

Haig's years at Camberley Staff College pose further difficulties. He failed the entrance exam – 'This beastly exam' as he described it in a letter to his sister – and, checking War Office records, Edmonds discovered that royal influence had been used to squeeze him in, Haig's sister Henrietta being the moving force. Married to a whiskey Jameson, she was able to use her husband's position as Keeper of the Prince of Wales's racing yachts to get Douglas into those Court circles which lubricated the rest of his career. The immediate result of Henrietta's lobbying was that the aggregate mark qualifying for a royal nomination dropped by 15 per cent – the exact amount Haig needed to get into the Staff College.

James Edmonds, the sharp-tongued official historian, was an exact contemporary of Haig at Camberley and the two men were quickly forced into each other's company. Noting that Haig would not work out schemes in detail, Professor Henderson used the weight of his reputation to order Edmonds, the star pupil, to work with Haig. 'He said I was a man of detail and Haig was inclined to take too general a view and we might correct each other.' On one occasion, Henderson even instructed Edmonds to dictate examination answers to Haig. It was to be the start of a long association but one which proved uneasy in the short term. Edmonds deserted Haig during the final practical examination. 'I can't afford to be handicapped by you and Baird any longer,' he explained. Haig's Staff College years were thus undistinguished and he later withheld the private diaries which covered them.

His early military performance was equally undistinguished. Serving with Kitchener in the Sudan campaign of 1898, he was awarded the brevet rank of major for steadying an Egyptian cavalry force which had been taken unawares by the Dervishes, but the facts are by no means certain. The only record of the incident is in a book written by Haig and published anonymously in 1910.[2] When it is compared with the letters he wrote during the campaign, there are surprising discrepancies. Were the guns involved in the incident Maxims or light field artillery? And was the order halting the retreat of those guns Haig's or had it been sent previously by General Broadwood? During the Great War, those who knew about the Sudan campaign commented drily on the slowness of Broadwood's promotion despite fine performance in the field.

Haig's contemporary reputation as a Staff Officer was certainly a solid one. After the Boer War, he presented the war diaries he had written to the Staff College, where they served as models of clarity, tidiness and detail. But the effectiveness of his command of the 17th Lancers in the final stages of the war had been altogether more questionable. Just after he took command, the 17th Lancers were defeated by Jan Smuts on Elands River, and in later years Haig's valet noted his master's reluctance to discuss any aspect of the Boer War.

Against this thin evidence of outstanding military capacity or achievement, why did Haig rise so far and fast in the Army? At the age of thirty-seven he was still a captain, while many who had started their careers with him were already senior in the service. Five years later, he was Inspector General of Cavalry in India and had overtaken all his contemporaries, attaining the rank of major-general and a position as ADC to Edward VII, with the Order of the Bath as a mark of the king's special favour. Since Haig's intellectual and military achievements had been so thin, what were the other ingredients in this rapid rise?

Determination of a formidable order was undoubtedly among them. 'He was a glutton for honours,' Lord Esher observed, and Charles Bean underlined that point after talking with an old Indian Army officer who served on the staff of the Australian Corps. 'Carruthers told us what he knew of Haig in India. He was a tremendously ambitious man and a most painstaking student.' Edmonds made the same point more briefly when he wrote from the personal knowledge of many years, 'He was dominated by an unrelaxing pursuit of his own ambition.'

Astute diplomacy reinforced this ambition. Early in his career, he borrowed £2,000 from Henrietta and lent it to Sir John French. This may have represented an act of spontaneous generosity, but if it did it was out of character in a man who parted notoriously hard with coin. French's latest biographer points out that 'less generous souls might suggest that it was hardly ethical for a junior officer to make what was in fact, if not in theory, a substantial gift – worth say £30,000 at today's prices – to a senior, knowing that the senior was responsible for initiating reports which could determine his immediate military future.'[3]

Haig continued to demonstrate a sure political touch as Inspector General of Cavalry in India. His tour of duty coincided with a violent struggle between Curzon (the Viceroy) and Kitchener (the Commander in Chief) over the issue of whether or not civilians should be in a position to veto the soldiers' proposals for military expenditure. Charteris noted Haig's active involvement in the debate, remarking that 'Haig had given his own opinions in his letters to Edward VII and it may have been owing to his representations that the Sovereign expressed complete approval of the final decision' – in other words, total victory for Kitchener. Haig preferred to refer more obliquely to this campaign: 'We soldiers certainly owe the King a good deal of gratitude for the important share he has taken in bringing about this satisfactory change.'

Many officers were as ambitious as Haig and a few may have been as politically acute, but the most important single element required to get to the top in the Old Army was skill in the manipulation of patronage, because, as Edmonds put it in correspondence with Bean, 'You must remember that before 1914 the Army was still very feudal in its status and that great personages still exercised the higher patronage.'[4] There were plenty of examples of that fact. Robertson began his rise from trooper to Field Marshal only after a push from Field Marshal Nicholson, who in his turn had been propelled by Field Marshal Roberts as the man on his staff best able to translate his own inarticulacies into the book *Forty-One Years in India*. Among Haig's contemporaries, Henry Wilson and Ian Hamilton were Roberts men and Birdwood was a protégé of Kitchener. Where Haig excelled all these rivals was in the number and social standing of the patrons he enjoyed.

Sir Evelyn Wood, Adjutant General in the 1890s, was the first of these patrons. His attention had been drawn by a report Haig had written on military manoeuvres abroad. Wood probably appreciated the evidence of professional commitment in that report. He was certainly attracted by the striking physique and blue eyes of a young Hussar who scattered copies of his report like the biblical sower of seed. As a consequence, Wood saw to it that Haig was attached to Sir John French's manoeuvres in 1894, then chosen to accompany Kitchener in the Sudan. Haig's appreciative comment was conveyed in a letter to Henrietta: 'Sir E.W. is a capital fellow to have on one's side as he always gets his way.'

Wood continued to keep an eye on his man's progress. Writing to Lady Haig in 1919, he told her of his involvement in her husband's early career. 'I doubt you are so young if you knew Douglas in 1895 but the enclosed [photograph] explains part of the attraction that your man had for a keen soldier like yours sincerely . . .'

The encounter with Kitchener was to prove a fateful one. With an ear well placed and sharply tuned to inside information, the lawyer–politician F. E. Smith (Lord Birkenhead) remarked tartly: 'In 1898 Haig was able to bring himself under the notice, not afterwards relaxed, of Kitchener' and it was Kitchener who gave Haig his first field command and went on to insist on promotion so that Haig would qualify for the Inspector General's position in India. Kitchener was never the sort of man to explain what qualities he was looking for in his protégés, but a combination of professional zeal, bachelor status and a handsome appearance linked most of the young men whose careers he favoured.[5]

Lord Esher was Haig's next patron. Promiscuously homosexual and a friend of the king, Esher had been one of the architects of the Committee of Imperial Defence, that secretive body which organized Britain's part in the war with Germany a decade before it began. He was therefore one of the most influential power-brokers of the

Edwardian age, and from Haig's point of view a potent patron whose regard was recorded in a memorandum written after the annual manoeuvres of 1906 and filed in his private papers. It drew a lively picture of his Arab horse loose and cropping the downland turf while an orderly held Haig's pony. As the two men lay overlooking the panorama of the war games, side by side, Haig analysed dispositions, criticized tactical movements and named each company without reference to notes. In a letter sent to Haig in 1915 requesting weekly access to GHQ, Esher referred to the impression this episode had made on him: 'I never can forget our talks on a certain hill in Buckinghamshire from which date many things. Bless you, dear Douglas.'

Esher's recommendation carried great authority at the time, but it was not yet sufficient to push so young a candidate into the post of Chief of the Imperial General Staff, as Esher had requested in 1906. Frustrated over that prize, Esher settled for a position in the War Office with Haldane, where Haig helped to work out the BEF's schedule. It was to prove an important step. On the one hand, it brought Haig to the attention of the Liberal Party's hierarchy. On the other, in the opinion of Lord Geddes, it gave him a break from the barrack square and offered him a chance to acquire social graces, so conspicuous by their absence at the time.

Thus Haig's rapid promotion owed little to proven professional competence and much to good fortune with patrons. Wood, Kitchener and Esher were all men of substance and their support had pushed Haig far ahead of his rivals – but at a price. The *frisson* of homosexuality attaching to each of his patrons gave ammunition to jealous rivals, all the more because of a strong dislike of women which he made little effort to conceal. As a middle-aged bachelor, Haig realized that he was in a potentially embarrassing position and his marriage must be seen in this context. With his tour of duty in India moving towards its end in 1905, Haig dealt with the conundrum by meeting a suitable wife, making a proposal of marriage and clinching the deal – all within seventy-two hours. 'I have often made up my mind on more important problems than that of my own marriage in much less time,' he said. Nor did it harm Haig's career prospects to have married the queen's favourite attendant and become the first man outside the royal family to be married in Buckingham Palace's private chapel in the process.

After the period of rapid ascent between the Sudan campaign (1898) and his move to the War Office (1906), Haig's career progressed at a slower but steady rate. As the Director of Military Training moved up to Director of Staff Duties, Haig became involved with the creation of the Imperial General Staff, the organization of the British Expeditionary Force and the composition of *Field Service Regulations* in the version that would underpin the Great War. From his own point of view, however, it was probably more important that he became known to Haldane, the Minister of War, and Asquith, the Prime Minister, who was to appoint him Commander in Chief during the war.

Between leaving the War Office in 1909 and the outbreak of war, Haig occupied two more positions. From 1909 to 1911 he served as Chief of the General Staff in India, then came home to take up the Aldershot command which carried with it the field command of one of the two corps which made up the BEF should war be declared. Haig was therefore perfectly placed for the events of July and August 1914. But his advancement had owed everything to good looks and ambition, good fortune and skilled diplomacy. How then did such fortuitous promotion stand the test of war in the two years before Haig became Commander in Chief?

The Great War in the West began with two great offensives. On 4 August, the Germans commenced their sweep through Belgium with a view to encircling Paris and fighting a decisive battle with the French. The French, in their turn, launched a direct attack on Germany at the other end of what was to become the Western Front on 14 August. At first sight, British involvement in these two great manoeuvres might seem small. The Germans, after all, were manipulating eighty-seven divisions, the French sixty-two, the British a mere six. But the fortunes of war decreed otherwise, and the BEF found itself in the direct path of the main German attack. Thus four British divisions confronted the 1st German Army at Mons on 23 August; Smith-Dorrien's 1st Corps had to fight a brave rearguard action at Le Cateau on 26 August against intolerable odds during the BEF's retreat; and the British found themselves advancing into the gap between the two German armies at the start of September when the French counter-attacked in the battle of the Marne, along a front of 100 miles.

What of Haig's role in these events as commander of one of the two corps into which the BEF was divided?

At Mons, Smith-Dorrien's 2nd Corps had confronted the main German attack. During the battle's crisis that day, he sent an urgent message to Haig requesting reinforcement and, although the 1st Corps was under little pressure, Haig sent just two battalions. It required a personal visit by Smith-Dorrien to prise adequate reinforcement from Haig.

At Le Cateau, Haig was even more disobliging and Smith-Dorrien was left to fight his rearguard action alone. After the war, the British official historian told Liddell Hart about von Kuhl's comment at German GHQ during the battle: 'One corps stands to fight; the other walks away.'

During this phase of the retreat Haig, with many other officers, was in a state of nervous exhaustion. Unable to sleep, he was suffering a severe bout of diarrhoea. In that condition, his corps rested one night in the small settlement of Landrecies. News of German troops approaching broke Haig's nerve and, as the Cabinet Minister Walter Long was told by one who took part in the skirmish, Haig ordered his men to sacrifice themselves so as to save the remnants of the British Army. But the German force turned out to be a skirmishing detachment, repulsed at a cost of just 150 casualties. The main force had moved north-west instead of coming straight on.

On the Aisne, Haig's response was again faulty. His orders were to seize the crossing points of the river Aisne and thus widen the gap between the two retreating German armies. And Sir John French's orders were sound. British aircraft had reported that only rearguards held the ground in front of Haig's corps. He ordered a halt nevertheless. As the official historian drily put it to Liddell Hart in 1934, 'Haig didn't like discussing the delay at the Aisne and put the blame on Smith-Dorrien. He had not history in mind or he would have

ordered the 1st Corps to push over the Aisne, well knowing it would
be too tired to get there . . . His usual Scots caution!'

Sir John Fortescue, the Royal Librarian who wrote the first
volume of the interim official history during the war, exposed many
of these shortcomings in Haig's conduct during the war's early days.
He put them into an article for the *Quarterly Review*[6] and all were
cheerfully endorsed by Edmonds as official historian in the course of
correspondence with Liddell Hart. Haig had indeed looked on at
Mons, walked away at Le Cateau and panicked at Landrecies. 'He
didn't like discussing the delay on the Aisne, well knowing that the
men were too tired to get there,' wrote Edmonds. 'His later excuse
was that the 3rd Division on the left were not keeping up and the
French 18th Corps on the right were not to be relied on.'

The battle of 1st Ypres (October–November 1914) was the BEF's
first major engagement and marked the end of the war's fluid
opening phase. A bitterly fought defensive battle, it is often presented
as a highpoint in Haig's war, and his ride down the Menin Road on
31 October as a critical event at the crisis of the battle. A report had
come through that the 1st Division had cracked. There was therefore
nothing between the Germans and Ypres. Haig mounted his horse
immediately and, according to the Official History, 'His appearance
moving up the road at a slow trot with part of his Staff behind him
did much to restore confidence.'

The events of the day were, in fact, less simple and discrepancies in
the various versions of Haig's celebrated ride suggest that the whole
story was first distorted, then blown up by Haig to advance his own
career. According to Duff Cooper's official biography of Haig, the
confidence-restoring ride took place shortly after midday, with Haig
about to ride to the front a second time when Sir John French arrived
at 2 pm.[7] The second ride was therefore postponed. Haig's typed
diary, on the other hand, puts the crucial ride at 3 pm. Odder still is
the letter Haig sent Edmonds in 1923 to clarify events.[8] In this letter,
Haig put the first ride after breakfast at 8 o'clock. During it, he
claimed that he had fixed all positions in case of retirement, assisted
by his Chief of Staff, John Gough (elder brother of Hubert Gough,
who would command the 5th Army two years later). On returning
to HQ, Gough told Haig that the 1st Division had been broken by

the Germans. This must have been between 2 and 3 pm, because Haig was about to mount his horse in response when French's arrival cancelled that ride. Haig's 1923 line thus contradicted both the Official History's version and his own typed diary. Edmonds was obviously perturbed and contacted Neill Malcolm for his memories of that day. 'Haig is extraordinarily accurate,' Malcolm replied. 'It is very unlikely he made any mistake in what he wrote down at the time.' Edmonds's initial letter is missing from his papers today, but the gist of his questioning and the strength of his doubts can be inferred from Malcolm's wording. Edmonds obviously believed Haig had invented the whole story and, from the various accounts, it would seem that he had. A routine ride early that day, before any danger had developed, was converted by Haig into a ride into the heart of the danger zone that afternoon. Haig's staff would have known the facts, of course, but they were too loyal to make them known. Others, deeply involved in a critical moment of the battle, were unlikely to know where Haig was or be able to check on his movements after the event.

1st Ypres had been a defensive battle. In March 1915, Haig took charge of the first major British offensive, at Neuve Chapelle.[9] Outnumbering the Germans three to one, with a field gun each five yards and heavy artillery every nineteen yards, Haig announced in his pre-battle conference that 'the advance to be made is not a minor operation. We are entering on a serious offensive with the object of breaking the German line. It is very likely that an operation of considerable magnitude may result.'

What happened subsequently was outlined by a renegade official historian using inside knowledge. 'The 48 battalions of the corps were arrayed in two columns like a battering ram of about 30,000 men facing the German breastworks held by six infantry companies – about 800 men. So strong is modern firepower that these six companies might well have held that massed manpower in check but surprise was gained, an accurate bombardment blew the breastworks to pieces and at 8.05 am a great part of the two columns burst through on a front of 1,600 yards. They were to fan out at once behind the breastworks, but for about 400 yards on both flanks the assault had not been successful. At 9 am the leading battalions were halted until the flanks of the battering ram could get forward. This check to the general forward movement caused a great block to the battalions moving up in the rear. The strength of the battering ram was limited to the firepower of its leading companies – a maximum of about 800 rifles on the 1,600 yards of the break-in's frontage. The remainder of the 48 battalions were useless cannon-fodder until they could fan out behind the German position – if such an operation was at any time possible.'[10]

The end product of Neuve Chapelle was therefore an advance of 1,000 yards at a cost of 12,000 casualties. By any standards, the figures represent failure if not fiasco.

Loos, in September 1915, was Haig's next battle and one of considerable importance for several reasons. French strategy was to nip the flanks of the Noyon Salient (that great bulge in the Western Front, extending close to Paris), drive the Germans back on the Ardennes and split their army in two, while the British played a minor role on the north flank. Loos was thus part of a dress rehearsal for Nivelle's offensive in spring 1917 and Foch's in autumn 1918. On the British side, participation was the first indication of a decision to pull out of Gallipoli and concentrate on the Western Front. From Haig's personal point of view, Loos supplied the pretext for sacking Sir John French. It was therefore much the most important battle in which Haig participated before he became the new Commander in Chief. It was also the most controversial, being followed by a fierce debate on the way in which GHQ's reserve was deployed and used.

Haig's version of the battle, which enjoyed wide support at the time, was set out in a letter he sent to Kitchener four days after the start of the battle. 'You will doubtless recollect how earnestly I pressed you to ensure an adequate reserve being close in the rear of my attacking Divisions and under my orders,' Haig wrote. 'My attack was a complete success. The enemy had no troops in the second line which some of my plucky fellows reached and entered without opposition. The two reserve divisions, under the Commander in Chief's orders, were directed to join me as soon as the success of the 1st Army was known at GHQ. They came on as quickly as they could, poor fellows, but only crossed our trench lines at 6 pm. We had captured Loos twelve hours previously and the reserves should have been at hand then. We were in a position to make this the turning point of the war and I feel annoyed at the lost opportunity.'[11]

This letter raises several points. It was an accepted principle of the period that a commander should keep about 20 per cent of his force in reserve. Sir John French held a reserve of that size at Loos. Haig was to keep a similar proportion in his own hand on the first day of the Somme. At Loos a substantial reserve had been all the more necessary since the French attack on the British right flank was only to be delivered hours after the British attack and at an eccentric angle. This meant that a gap was bound to appear between the British and French if the offensive enjoyed any degree of success, and a German counter-attack (a feature of German tactics by spring 1915) could be expected.

A second point brought out in Haig's letter concerns the movements of the 21st and 24th Divisions. Writing from GHQ on 16 October, Robertson pointed out that when the battle started these divisions were exactly where Haig had wanted them — four and a half miles from the front line.[12]

In reply, Haig appeared to accept Robertson's claim but insisted that the crisis of the battle had been between 9 and 11 am 'when, if the reserves had been available, they could have pushed through with little opposition'.[13] Haig's claim raises several difficulties. Men moving forward towards the battle front during the war seldom covered more than one mile an hour, heavily laden with equipment as they were. The inference is that Haig's calculations before the battle had been mistaken. Even if he had been able to assess the degree of success within minutes of his attack going in and then pass the message to GHQ promptly — and this would have needed a good telephone line which had survived horses' hooves, shell bursts and souveniring soldiers — his reserve would have been unable to fight before 11 am. But even that time was ruled out, because Loos was scheduled for the first use of chlorine gas by the British (the Germans had first used it at 2nd Ypres in April). All timings depended on the exact moment of release. This in turn hung on a meteorologist's judgement of when a wind of the right force and direction could be expected (he was the man who later told Haig that he might expect a spell of drier weather when Passchendaele began on 31 July 1917). In the event, meteorologist Gold was able to produce a favourable forecast only at 3 am on the morning of the battle. Haig immediately set zero for 5.50 am,[14] but the accumulation of delays meant that it had never been possible to keep GHQ informed on timings before the battle began or for GHQ's decisions to be dovetailed into arrangements for the first day. Haig's contentions can therefore be dismissed as the special pleading of a man terrified at the thought of the possibility of losing his life's ambition through an eleventh-hour blunder.

Another contentious aspect of that day was the exact moment Haig took charge of the reserve. As a junior commander, Rawlinson told Kitchener five days after the battle that the divisions had come under Haig's orders at 9 am.[15] French's Chief Staff Officer put that time at 9.30 in a letter to Haig,[16] and five days after receiving it Haig admitted to 10.45. Sir John French's own figure, put in a letter to Kitchener shortly after the battle, was between 11 and midday.[17] Richard Haking, the corps commander who had been in charge of the divisions, recorded a time of 1.20 pm.[18] Haig's position in this area was therefore a good deal less clear than he later chose to make out.

Argument as to whether or not French should have handed over the reserve earlier or located it differently tends anyway to divert attention from the use Haig made of it.

An order to attack was sent from Haig's HQ at 11.30 on the first morning of the battle, but such was the confusion that the order did not reach the two divisions until 1 o'clock next morning. The attack specified by Haig was to commence at 11 am, cross 1,000 yards of open downland and approach the Germans over a forward-facing slope in full view of their machine-gunners.

The corps commander involved realized the danger and saw that the key positions on the flank (Hill 70 and Hulluch village) would have to be taken before the men could advance. As it turned out, neither position was taken. Nor was any information passed on to the attacking divisions to suggest that the final objective was still strongly held by an enemy line thick with machine guns. Indeed, many of the troops involved were under the impression that they were only moving into reserve behind the British line. To cap the shambles, early morning mist meant that the guns which had been allocated to prepare the attack had taken up faulty positions and were of no assistance to the attack at all.

The result of all this was that the two divisions lost 8,000 men in the first hour[19] and would have lost more but for the fact, recorded in the history of the 15th German Reserve Division, that the Germans were 'nauseated by the sight of the massacre of the *Leichenfeld* (field of corpses) of Loos'. When the British retirement began, 'No more shots were fired at them for the rest of the day, so great was the feeling of compassion and mercy after the victory.'

One finds nothing of this in Haig's letters at the time. Indeed, a letter to his brother on 5 October suggests that the quality of the reserves had been Haig's chief problem. 'They weren't much good as they had only just landed or we would have been through the second line.' Haig developed the point four weeks later in another letter to his brother. 'We actually broke the enemy's line on 25 September but French insisted on keeping the reserve under his own hand so long that they did not arrive in time to be of use and then, although divisions which had experience of war were available, the reserves consisted of two new arrivals. Then, when they did come up, they were worn out with fatigue and fled at the first shelling.' Haig's reasons for blaming the reserves and the accuracy of his analysis require no futher comment.

Haig became Commander in Chief three months after the blunderings of Loos. His period of command, first of a corps, then of an army, had exposed grave professional weaknesses in a man whose rise had always owed more to intrigue and patronage than to any evidence of talent as a soldier. Was it possible for his professional ability to grow in his new command? Fine war leaders like Foch and Mangin on the French side or Maxse and Monash on the British developed prodigiously after early disasters. Currie, the most effective commander in the British Army during 1917–18, had been utterly bewildered by 2nd Ypres in April 1915, deserting his command in questionable circumstances. But if development on such a scale was required of Haig, time was not on his side. Currie had used all of 1916 to develop his craft and Monash most of 1916 and 1917. Haig's first major test was to come within six months of his blunderings at Loos, played out before the eyes of the the world on the chalk downs of Picardy.

THE ATTRITION BATTLES
OF 1916–17

4

The Somme

Haig's first task in 1916 was to organize a battle where the French and British sectors met on the river Somme, and one of the first decisions he made as Commander in Chief was to put Rawlinson's 4th Army in charge of the main thrust.

Rawlinson immediately made a personal reconnaissance of the prospective battlefield and he liked what he saw. 'The country resembles Salisbury Plain,' he told the king's assistant secretary, Clive Wigram. 'It is large, open country with any number of partridges which we are not allowed to shoot. It is a great improvement on the flat, muddy plains of Flanders. It is capital country in which to undertake an offensive when we get a sufficiency of artillery for the observation is excellent and we ought to be able to avoid the heavy losses which infantry have suffered on previous occasions.'[1]

Disillusionment was to come quickly and the battle's statistics make intolerable reading even three generations later. The most revealing figures relate to artillery, the number of shells fired on the Somme telling more of the battle's nature in a sentence than most books written about it. Thus, a battle fought from July to November 1916 saw the British and German armies fire thirty million shells at each other and suffer a million casualties between them in an area just seven miles square.

This staggering fact means that no other battlefield in the Great War witnessed more killing per square yard. Verdun remains a byword for slaughter with the French, and was left just as it had been when the battle ended – an entire battlefield turned into a national symbol of loss. Yet in comparison with the Somme, the same number of shells at Verdun were dropped into an area twice as large and for a period twice as long (from February to November 1916). The British sector on the Somme was always a more savage affair.

What was the immediate impact of a shellburst every five paces? Aerial photos of Passchendaele in its final stages show grass and even trees. By autumn 1916, on the other hand, there was no vestige of grass on the Somme. Twenty years later, the battlefield remained a treeless wilderness, and in the 1980s no other part of the old Western Front remains so rich in the fragments of that killing time. Bullets, dud shells and smashed helmets lie thick round the edge of fields, and the first ploughing of the year still has to be done with a thick steel plate behind the plough.

The impact of shells on men was another matter and one quietly acknowledged by the commander of Haig's 5th Army four weeks after the start of the Somme when a Routine Order laid down that all burials were to be in trenches rather than individual graves. The first layer of corpses was to be buried four feet down, with quicklime separating it from the next layer. Gough's requirements were a blunt acknowledgement of the fact that men on the Somme were usually killed faster than grave-diggers could process them.

Even four months after the battle had finished, John Masefield was astonished by the quantity of human litter still scattered about the battlefield. 'The first thing I saw in High Wood,' he told his wife, 'were two German legs sticking out of the ground. Just inside the wood, there was a skull high up in a tree and helmets with bits of head in them and legs galore. From there, I walked on to Delville Wood which is nothing to High Wood, it has been so nicely tidied up. Still, the north west corner must have had more shells on to it. The dead lay three or four deep and the bluebottles made their faces black there.'[2]

Slaughter on this scale left an enduring impression, and the 60,000 casualties sustained on the battle's first day remain a potent symbol of the Great War in Britain. For many years, 1 July was to remain a time of particular remembrance – blinds were drawn and black armbands worn on the sleeve. So too the four months of fighting

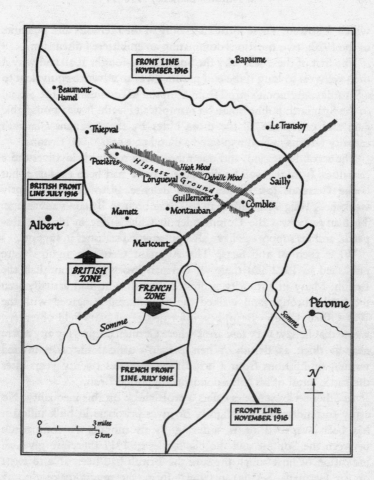

Map labels:
FRONT LINE NOVEMBER 1916 · Bapaume · Beaumont Hamel · Thiepval · Le Transloy · Pozières · Highest Ground · High Wood · Delville Wood · Longueval · Sailly · BRITISH FRONT LINE JULY 1916 · Guillemont · Mametz · Montauban · Combles · Albert · Maricourt · BRITISH ZONE · FRENCH ZONE · Péronne · Somme · Somme · FRENCH FRONT LINE JULY 1916 · FRONT LINE NOVEMBER 1916 · N · 0 3 miles · 0 5 km

2 THE BATTLE OF THE SOMME, July–November 1916

Haig's aim on 1 July was to attack with just sufficient force to pin the Germans down along the front running due south from Beaumont Hamel. His main thrust was to be in front of Mametz. It aimed to reach the dominating ridge at Pozières and then swing east along the high ground to Combles. This would enfilade the German second line. The French and English could then combine to move on Bapaume and destabilize the whole German position in the area. As events turned out, a plan for several days took several months and then was only partially achieved.

which followed. These featured vividly in the memoirs and polemics of the 1920s, two questions dominating an embittered discussion.

The first of these was why the Somme was fought at all and why it then went on so long if the end product was an advance equivalent to a Saturday afternoon's stroll from Simpson's Restaurant in the Strand to the Spaniards public house on Hampstead Heath. It was a miserable gain and one made all the more bitter by the Adjutant General's casualty returns, which registered a blood cost of 600,000 Britons.

The second question, and one more easily resolved, involves those casualties. It might well be that little ground had been captured, but if the Germans lost so heavily ˙in defence as to be permanently weakened, Haig's tenacity may still have been to Britain's advantage. That anyway was the Commander in Chief's line in his final dispatch, and his supporters have always spawned statistics in support.

What then of the facts? The Adjutant General's figures were published in 1922 and these set German losses at just one half the British. Many in authority protested, but all who had actually seen the battle through and walked the field during it agreed with the War Office. Charles Bean, best informed of all battlefield observers, wrote that he saw very few areas where German corpses lay anywhere near as thick as British. When Britain's official historian invited written submissions from a host of eyewitnesses twenty years after the battle, most of his correspondents supported Bean.

Another set of statistics offers a cross-check on this inequality. No army surrenders its guns lightly or gives prisoners in bulk unless it has been surprised or is suffering in its morale. A comparison between the Somme and the big battles of 1917 therefore gives an indication of how much pressure the British had been able to exert on the Germans. Set out in tabular form, the results make gloomy reading:

	German prisoners	German guns captured
Arras, first day	13,000	200
Messines, first day	5,700	67
Cambrai, first day	7,500	120
Somme, 130 days	31,000	125

Whether in terms of ground gained or damage inflicted, the Somme has all the appearance of a disastrous experience for the British Army, why was the battle fought? What went wrong? Why did Haig persist from July to November?

The conventional answer to all these questions involves the French. It was they, according to the traditional view, who insisted on British involvement in a big battle during 1916. When Haig wanted to fight in Flanders, it was the French who forced him to fight on the Somme. Haig had wanted to start in August. The French used the superior size of their army to impose July. Haig's plans were based on the assumption of substantial French support. Verdun not only took away most of that support but obliged Haig to carry on fighting to ease the pressure on his ally.

Argument over the Somme has always revolved around this French connection, but the injection of a mass of fresh evidence in the sixties changed the whole context of the 1916 campaign. This evidence not only clarified the matter of responsibility; more urgently, from the British viewpoint, it opened up the much larger problem of logistics.

Two papers, both written by Haig during 1915, are crucial here.[3] These were filled with detailed calculation of what was required to fight a major battle 'with good prospects of success' on a twenty-five-mile frontage. Translating his conclusions into the frontage finally adopted on the Somme, Haig's requirement was of thirty-six divisions backed by 828 medium and heavy guns. On 1 July, the British had just half that number of men and guns.

It was the same with transport. Haig's calculations in November 1915 were that twenty-nine roads and seven broad-gauge railway lines were essential. In the event, the Somme kicked off ahead of three broad-gauge and a single metre-gauge track, with road capacity just as inadequate if not more so. Even the official historian conceded the point. 'The main roads were not suited for heavy traffic,' Edmonds admitted. 'Metal thickness was only three inches on a foundation of chalk and broke if the surface was cut. The side roads were little better than tracks. Nor was there any building, since calculation that a battle might require from 59 to 128 trains daily for basic supply meant that to reach the figure, it was agreed to cut out carrying road stone.'

What sort of battle could Haig have been contemplating if his preparation was so minimal? The answer is stated at many points in contemporary writings, most bluntly in a lengthy analysis written at Haig's direction four days after he received formal notification that he was to become Commander in Chief.[4]

The first point established in this analysis is that the story of the Somme having been imposed by the French on a reluctant Haig is complete poppycock. Haig's paper of 14 December 1915 stated bluntly that, since the British had been forced to conform with the French in 1914–15, a change was necessary. The French idea of success in a single battle had been found wanting. A major battle on the Somme could therefore be imposed on the French as a result of their failures in 1915, the more so since 'they were probably rather at a loss what to do'.

The paper went on to suggest that 'The main lesson of the battle of Loos as of all previous attacks is that, given adequate artillery preparation or some form of surprise like chlorine gas, there is no insuperable difficulty in overwhelming the enemy's troops in front and support lines but there is the greatest difficulty in defeating his reserves who are not subject to the strain of a long bombardment and come up in good order to meet our troops at a time when they are exhausted, in confusion and out of hand.' The solution was obvious. 'The basic principles of the battlefield, which are unaltered' meant that the enemy's reserves had first to be worn down before a decisive attack could be delivered at another point.

The deficiency in guns, divisions and communications suggests that the Somme had been planned as Haig's wearing-out battle. Where then did he propose to launch his breakthrough battle? His correspondence leaves no doubt.[5]

On 30 December 1915, the new Commander in Chief visited Plumer, who commanded the 2nd Army, in the Ypres Salient and gave orders to continue preparations for 'a serious attack' in 1916. A fortnight later, he was more specific. The big attack was to be at Ypres and directed at the key rail junction of Roulers via the Houthulst Forest with diversionary thrusts against Lille and the Messines Ridge (Maps 4 and 5, pp. 89, 93). In other words, Haig was preparing to fight the battle of Passchendaele a year earlier than it was actually fought and hoping to make the job easier by a feint on the Somme which would pull German reserves away from Flanders in the north.

Rather surprisingly, Haig made no secret of his intentions, telling Joffre on 20 January that 'the decisive attack of the British will be made with a view to capturing the Belgian coast'[6] and, despite repeated denials in the British Official History, preparations for this big battle in the north were continuous from that moment. Indeed, they were even enlarged. A second army was added for a breakout round the whole perimeter of the Ypres Salient.

At the end of February, the Germans attacked at Verdun and, according to the traditional story, all these plans were upset. Haig had to take more of the front line from the French and fighting on the Somme had to be prolonged to relieve pressure on them. According to this view, offensive operations in the Ypres Salient were promptly shelved. Haig's papers imply the fact. The Official History spells it out. But again the documents require a drastic revision of the old fables.

The first myth which has to go is that the French were severely weakened by Verdun. At the start of that battle, Henry Wilson had reported that 'the French were never so rich in guns and men' and the facts backed him. Whereas the Germans had put all their '1916 Class' (men aged twenty in 1916) into the ranks, the French were under so little pressure that they had been able to hold their twenty-year-olds back and keep the option of feeding them in during the year. Even after four weeks of savage fighting at Verdun, the French maintained a reserve of fourteen fresh divisions. A month later, that number had risen to eighteen.

During June they were certainly under pressure, and disturbances at Verdun led to the shooting of some officers and men; but so far as actual losses went, the French were not suffering unduly by the standards of the Western Front. On 4 July, Clive told Esher that the French were losing 110,000 men monthly.[7] Since the much smaller British Army reckoned to lose 41,000 each month even when no big battle was on, Haig was fully justified in taking a light view of Verdun. On 10 April he therefore told his army commanders that the battle in Flanders would go ahead. 'I have under consideration an offensive on a large scale on the front Armentières–Dixmude,' he said. 'The general direction will be towards Roulers and Lichtervelde.'[8] In other words, Haig had seen nothing at Verdun to alter his initial plans. In a minuted conversation with King Albert of Belgium, Haig even suggested that Verdun might wear the Germans enough for the Somme to be dispensed with altogether.[9] Ypres would thus be the first major British battle of 1916, and Haig went on with his preparations on that assumption well into the summer. Final orders for the Flanders battle were issued on 15 June, a fortnight before the Somme began.[10] Plumer had about 100 heavy and medium guns at the time. Haig ordered him to make preparations to fit 400 more into the Salient during the next six weeks. Nor was Plumer's to be the only attacking force. On 12 June, a special conference between GHQ and the Admiralty finalized preparations for a specially trained division to land behind German lines on the coast near Ostend.[11] What all these plans meant, of course, was that though Verdun remained an embarrassment, it was never thought to pose sufficient threat for Haig's planning in January 1916 to need much of an overhaul.

How was the feint on the Somme to be fitted in with the main thrust at Ypres? The key here is the figure fourteen. Haig told Rawlinson on 27 May that he would be given only enough shells for a preliminary bombardment and battle lasting fourteen days[12] and the figure had obviously been around for some time. When Plumer inquired with some irritation during March 1916, 'What I should like to know is are we to prepare for all the operations ordered by Haig and by what period should preparations be complete?'[13] GHQ replied promptly that the first thrust would be at Messines on 15 July and the chief attack north of Ypres at the end of July. The Flanders battle, in other words, was to start fourteen days after a short-lived diversion on the Somme, hence the meagre scale of preparation for the Somme.

Piecing together the orders and conference minutes which have come down to us, the battles Haig wanted to fight in July 1916 can now be described in detail and fixed to a definite timescale:

1 July: A limited Somme offensive with fifteen divisions fighting fourteen days to draw enemy reserves from the north. If successful, cavalry were to pass through the gap, destabilize the rear and permit Allenby to make a limited advance to the north of Rawlinson's 4th Army with his own 3rd Army.

15 July: Nine divisions to attack Messines and another four to assault the German canal line north of Ypres.

17 July: A thrust by six divisions against Lille to allow guns to move forward north of Ypres for the next stage of the battle there.

20 July: End of the Lille diversion.

22 July: Nine divisions to attack the German second line at Pilckem Ridge, north of Ypres.

24 July: Once Pilckem Ridge had been taken, Gough's 5th Army to move north from the Somme on its own line of communications. On reaching Ypres, Gough was to check on Plumer's success at Messines. It was hoped that a fresh army would be able to press beyond the Ridge and on to the river Lys before swinging north towards Roulers. Rawlinson's 4th Army was meanwhile to wait on the Somme until Pilckem Ridge fell, since Haig did not wish to draw attention to the key point of Houthulst. If things went with a swing, Rawlinson was to move rapidly from the Somme and drive north from Pilckem. The objective was a Gough–Rawlinson pincer movement which, hopefully, would link with a push inland from a coastal landing planned by the old Gallipoli hands at GHQ.

All these plans added up to a bold strategic conception. We know today that it broke down at an early stage, but could Haig's plan of a double-headed battle have worked? Was it within the capacity of the British Army?

Using documents recently opened, there are good grounds for believing that the scheme would have been bound to fail even if the Somme had managed to deceive the Germans and pull their reserves from Flanders. The chief analysis here was provided by Plumer, who commanded in the Ypres Salient. Arthur Currie, the very capable Canadian commander, spoke for most of the British Army when he wrote of Plumer, 'He was such a solid, sensible man and having been an infantryman and Quartermaster General, he had an appreciation of what troops required by way of preparation. He never planned his battles by drawing lines across a map and putting dates on those lines.' Plumer's assessments, in other words, carried weight with the best soldiers of the time and his analysis in January 1916 began with the opinion that 'No strategical breakthrough is recommended on the 2nd Army's front owing to the successive lines of defence open to the enemy. He is very strong against direct advance on Houthulst Forest in infantry, artillery and entrenchments. It is advisable to capture the Zandvoorde Ridge on the right first and that is a big operation in itself.'[14] Plumer drew Haig's attention in particular to that mass of concrete pillboxes, growing in number all the time and more numerous in the Salient than anywhere else on the Western Front.

He went on to highlight the difficulty of trying to concentrate two separate armies in an area bounded by flooded land next to the Channel on one flank and by the Lys marshes on the other. There probably wasn't enough room for the men of two armies; there certainly wasn't for the guns they would require.

Plumer concluded with a reference to transport. Roads were few in the Salient, led either to Ypres or Armentières and were impassable before the muds of winter firmed up in April – in a dry year. If it was difficult to move troops within the Salient; it was even more difficult to move them towards it, since the Germans enjoyed the use of a rail network three times as dense as the British in the region. These were formidable disadvantages in 1916. They were to remain so a year later.

Even if tactical expedients had been found to neutralize the enemy's advantages in Flanders, the difficulties involved in moving the number of men necessary to fight a big breakout battle would almost certainly have beaten the British Army in 1916. The best evidence for this proposition is the breakdown of transport before the battle of the Somme even began.[15] By 1 July, eighteen stationary trains stretched back from Amiens station for six miles. Lorries and cars had been brought in to salvage the most urgently needed material, but in so doing destroyed the surface of roads leading to the front.

The scale of this transport crisis was nicely registered when Lloyd George appointed Eric Geddes, a civilian rail expert, to size up the problem. Geddes worked fast. The bottleneck was traced back to the marshalling yards of Abbeville, and Geddes demanded that the officers responsible be sacked on the spot. He then put in an order for 200,000 tons of railway track, 60,000 wagons and 1,000 miles of light railway – which raises the question how a railway system so deficient could have supplied two separate armies in a massive breakout battle when they couldn't even feed a single limited offensive on the Somme.

A battle in Flanders had been the third link in Haig's battle strategy and transporting an offensive force from the Somme to Flanders the second link. The first and most vital stage which had to start the chain reaction was the battle of the Somme. A fortnight's fighting was vital to draw German reserves away from Flanders on a scale sufficient to give the Ypres thrust a real prospect of success. Could it ever have done so?

The German reserve in Flanders during February 1916 was assessed at twenty-three divisions.[16] By May, the number had risen to thirty. If the British intended to hit the Germans on the Somme with just fifteen divisions, the scale of French cooperation was therefore bound to be a key factor.

Joffre's promise of forty-five divisions made when planning began must have seemed promising, and forty-five plus fifteen might have seemed enough to accomplish what Haig hoped. Unfortunately for his hopes, all the indications are that Joffre was never serious about committing a large French force, that his promises were pure deception and that they were made only to get the British fighting on a large scale, somewhere in France.

When optimism seemed the best way to sustain his deception, Joffre therefore served it up cheerfully. 'I do think the French mean to deal fairly with us,' Haig wrote to Robertson. 'Foch hopes to employ thirty-eight divisions and told me that even if the Germans take Verdun, they would not allow their plans for the summer to be disorganized.'[17]

On the other hand, when Haig mentioned that mid-August would be the best starting time for the Somme, presumably hoping that Verdun would divert German reserves and allow the British to go straight into the Flanders battle without a Somme preliminary to weaken it, 'Joffre at once got very excited and shouted that the French Army would cease to exist if we did nothing till then.'[18] Haig gave way, but obviously had suspicions of his own and asked Lord Bertie, the British ambassador, to check French intentions from Paris,[19] having already suggested to Robertson that 'French pessimism may be due to some idea of urging our preparations for the offensive.'[20]

Joffre's fears disappeared magically as soon as Haig got back to the original date of 1 July. 'Spoke to Joffre,' wrote Haig just a fortnight after Joffre had foreseen the disappearance of the French Army. 'He said the fighting at Verdun was severe but expressed no wish to change 1 July. A carelessly organized and hurried development of our attack would seem unlikely to have the desired effect.'[21]

The final crushing announcement by the French came on 2 June, after four months of deception. On that day, Foch told Rawlinson that the French contingent on the Somme would be substantially less than the twenty divisions promised on 20 May – which meant that the Somme offensive ceased to have the capacity to draw enough German reserves and wear them down before Haig struck in Flanders.

There remained one last gamble. If Haig was able to hit the enemy position on the Somme with a first strike of great force, the Germans would be bound to send reinforcements to an area so close to that vital lateral rail line which ran from Metz to Valenciennes via Hirson (Map 1, p. xviii). The problem here was that, to pose a real threat, the British would have to get all objectives fast and maintain a threat of real penetration.

The pressure Haig put on a reluctant commander suggests that he was fully aware of this. When Rawlinson planned to omit most of the enemy's second line from the initial attack, Haig insisted on him going right through to the enemy gun line along the whole front. 'I think we can do better than this,' he had told Rawlinson. 'It is usually wiser to act boldly and secure at the outset points of tactical value. The first advance should be pushed as far as the furthest possible objectives of tactical value which we can reasonably hope to retain after capturing.'[22]

Rawlinson was more successful in resisting Haig's desire to attack after a brief bombardment, but Haig once again had the last word. 'The zone to be prepared by the artillery should be as deep as possible,' he ordered.[23]

Nor did Haig leave the occupation of ground prepared by the artillery to chance. He specified that 'assaulting columns must go right through, above ground to distant objectives in successive lines or waves, each line adding impetus to the proceeding line'.[24] A fortnight before the attack, Haig repeated and reinforced his requirement of successive infantry waves: 'Isolated advances by detachments pressing forward beyond the reach of support should be avoided. In the advance of infantry, we should aim at such uniformity as will ensure mutual support.'

Later generations were to blame the disasters of the Somme's first day on the depth of the objectives and the linear conception which Haig insisted on. In retrospect it is less easy to be certain.

The possibility of inflicting a shattering blow by deep penetration at the outset and with a relatively light attack had been clearly established by mid-1916. In May 1915, for example, the Germans used a twenty-four-hour barrage to break twelve miles of Russian front at Gorlice. They hinted at the same possibility on the Western Front in their Verdun offensive of February 1916. Haig had been quick to see the danger and he studied Verdun, discussing his conclusions in one of his weekly army commanders' conferences.[25] The meeting focused on the overwhelming impact of a hurricane bombardment which had allowed the Germans four miles of penetration on a nine-mile front and all but captured Verdun.

The French agreed with Haig on this possibility of deep penetration. Foch's directives in April 1916 stated that 'The offensive can only maintain a superiority over the defenders on condition that it prevents them from re-organizing and collecting their means of resistance. The second position must be reached with all accessories of attack without delay. The defensive position needs to be seized with one effort.'[26]

With these words, Foch endorsed Haig's plan of going straight through to the guns – and stopping there. Even Haig, optimist though he was, issued orders a fortnight before the battle that no attack must go beyond the enemy's third position and the cavalry were given orders equally specific.[27] They were 'to take Bapaume and establish a good position in the neighbourhood'. Cambrai was therefore put out of bounds even if the Germans disintegrated – and it should be remembered that there was a distinct possibility of that happening. Haig's fifteen divisions faced only five German divisions and GHQ's Intelligence correctly predicted that it would take the Germans at least five days to get five more divisions into the battle area.[28] Haig stuck firmly to the concept of a rapid, limited advance nevertheless. The aim of a battle on the Somme, after all, was to threaten the Germans and draw them to the area, not to try and beat them there. There were dangers, too, in trying to do more, and Haig stated them in a document put out by GHQ: 'The lessons of the war to date are that carefully planned attack causes more loss to defence than attack in the first stages. Then, owing to the depth of defence, the enemy gains time and organizes a counter-attack. Provided he has the necessary reserves, he is likely not only to stop the attack but fully counter-balance his early losses. Thus operations calculated just to cause loss must not be pushed beyond artillery support.'[29]

What of those ponderous lines, stacked together and advancing like a German machine-gunner's dream? Rawlinson explained the thinking behind them in a lecture he gave to several HQs after the battle of Loos in September 1915. 'Experience has shown that what we gain in the first rush is the easiest gain and very often much more than we are finally left in possession of. The amount of risk involved depends very much on whether the first rush will reach the last German line before it can be manned by reserves. A panic, such as occurred at Loos, renders the chance of reaching the last line in time very favourable. But victory is almost as disorganizing as defeat and no victory more so than when the attack is "All out", with units intermixed and becoming exhausted. Unless we have sufficient reserves to follow up and make good what they have won, a more modest plan must be adopted. The reserves must be close up when the flag falls and must follow at once. What is required is depth in units so that there will be no unnecessary intermixture.'[30]

The concept of linear advance was thus based on the British experience of battle in 1915 and it enjoyed French benediction too, at the time. Laffargue's study on the subject, which was widely read in both armies during autumn 1915, prescribed slow, linear advance with men at five-pace intervals 'to keep them to their duty and combat the terrible selfishness of the battlefield'.[31] At the root of this 'selfishness' was the fact that 'infantry burn away in this furnace like bundles of straw'. Fear could thus be combined with confusion to confound the attackers and undermine their morale. Foch agreed, predicting 30 per cent losses in the first wave of any attack, adding that 'Go as you please' spelt disaster. His answer in April 1916 was linear advance, with a pause at the enemy's first position to allow time for the second line to fill gaps in the first. The attack could then move slowly to the enemy's second position. Depth in attack with men disposed in lines thus represented the best thinking of the day.

Nevertheless 1 July was a day of two battles. The French in the south gained all their objectives at a cost of 7,000 casualties. The British to the north failed to make any significant impression and lost 60,000 men in their failure. What was the difference between the two allies?

Artillery stands out as the most striking contrast. Since the British were hoarding guns and shells for Flanders, the French had been able to deploy twice as many guns and four times as many shells in proportion to their frontage.[32] But the discrepancy went beyond simple quantities.

The Old Army's assumption before the war was that the next European war would be fought at short ranges over open sights. There had been a fierce debate on the matter at the Staff College, but the short-range men had won.[33] In 1914, British gunners had therefore virtually no experience of night firing, counter-battery work, wire cutting or long-range indirect fire. Artillery had in fact been relegated to a sideshow, and appalling backwardness for the first three years of the war was the result.[34]

This was carefully hidden from outsiders at the time – and even from insiders. When Birch was appointed Haig's chief artillery adviser four weeks before the start of the Somme, he found it hard to believe the situation he inherited at GHQ. 'I was told that I was the Artillery Adviser and was ushered into a room containing two Staff Officers. There was not even a list of the guns in France in the office and very few books of reference on artillery matters. There was no department to collect the technical expertise of other nations and nobody watched the tactical development of artillery or issued detailed instructions for guidance. Ammunition in France was under a GSO2 and altogether, I may say, there was no artillery office at GHQ – which was the situation in France above division at that time.'[35]

One consequence of this backwardness was to have fatal results on 1 July. It had nothing to do with quantity of guns or shells or even of the failure to produce specialist trench-war weaponry like the heavy mortars which the French installed at 100-yard intervals, or the high-velocity field guns which they used to knock out machine-gun positions from their own front line. The great weakness was an utter lack of concern with accuracy or, as GHQ's printed 'Artillery Notes' put it in January 1916, 'accuracy is a new demand in this war'.[36]

Two results followed from the gross inaccuracy of British artillery work. Since it was reckoned that 100 eight-inch howitzer shells were needed to be sure of hitting an enemy gun emplacement and because 'Artillery Notes' laid down that British shells could not be used with safety less than 300 yards from their own men,[37] the German front-line trench with its multiplicity of concreted machine-gun posts remained virtually untouched along most of its length. When the British infantry advanced on that first dreadful day, they were therefore taking on a defensive position in prime condition.

Nor could they expect their own artillery to support them as they attacked. A Staff College conference in 1908 had been disturbed to discover that Japanese troops in the Russo-Japanese war had been able to advance behind a creeping barrage bursting just 100 yards ahead of them. British inaccuracy in 1916 and the 300-yard requirement meant Rawlinson had to state bluntly that a British creeping barrage was 'too difficult'. It was a dreadful admission, but not one

which apparently gave GHQ or the artillery much concern. 'In
trench warfare,' ran 'Artillery Notes' in April 1916, 'the arrangements
for covering the actual assault are comparatively simple owing to the
proximity of the actual lines. The infantry will, in most cases, start
from within assaulting distance.' Put more bluntly, this meant that
in addition to being unable to neutralize the enemy's front line,
British artillery lacked the skill to shepherd their own men towards it
or, if they were successful at the start, take them to the second
position.

French infantry, by way of contrast, were preceded to within sixty
yards of the enemy's front line by a creeping barrage which beat the
ground ahead.[38] At that point, so the French had bloodily discovered
in 1915, the value of shells was cancelled out by the weight of small-
arms fire through the shell curtain. The French artillery barrage
therefore jumped forward to isolate the enemy's front line and the
infantry changed from lines into small, flexible formations which
could manoeuvre independently over the last few yards. These half-
section units were naturally well provided with light machine guns,
rifle grenades, hand grenades and rifles in a pre-planned ensemble
whose effectiveness was as much the result of training as of firepower. This followed from a uniform training system which gave basic
skills in three months and went on to battalion work for another
three. Recruits were supervised and trained throughout by the
officers and NCOs who would lead them in battle. These, in their
turn, had been specially selected from the front line on the basis of
proven effectiveness in battle.

The British were absolutely unable to reproduce this tactical
sophistication. It wasn't just that changes from lines to groups and
back to lines had never been practised or even contemplated by the
British Army. It was rather that the whole philosophy of British
preparation assumed war in the eighteenth-century style – or as the
4th Army's training booklet put it on the eve of the Somme, 'The
men must learn to obey by instinct without thinking. The whole
advance must be carried out as a drill.'[39] It was a guideline which
would kill thousands in July 1916. Though it has been customary to
blame Rawlinson for the 4th Army's 'Red Book' on training, he
had in fact only expanded Haig's detailed instructions, issued over

the signature of his Chief of Staff, Launcelot Kiggell (standard army practice, since Haig signed his own name only when communicating with his superiors).

The combined result of faulty training and inadequate artillery work was dreadfully plain on the day. In the course of writing the British Official History, Edmonds received a graphic letter describing that first attack: 'At 7.30 am there were two minutes of free advance. Then with a stabbing clatter, the Boche machine guns opened up. The line of our men fell in swathes and lay as they fell, about 100 yards from the German front trench. I could not see a single German machine gun but several German soldiers leapt on top of their trench with their bayonets ready. They were shot down by our infantry as one knocks down ninepins. I saw a small party gather and enter the German trenches. After five minutes they were driven out. All this time, our artillery fire was moving away according to the programme – perfectly useless. The wounded kept writhing and raising their arms and legs but the slightest movement brought a burst of fire.' [40]

Translating the slaughter into statistics, the Queen Victoria Rifles suffered 76 per cent casualties, the Queen's Westminsters 76 per cent, the London Scottish 70 per cent. 'I will never forget the scene in No Man's Land when I walked across it some days later near Tara Hill,' one artillery officer told Edmonds. 'Line after line of dead men lay where they had fallen, literally in hundreds.'

Those men lying in such numbers so close to their own lines represent one of the great tragedies of the war. They represent, too, the final failure of Haig's double-headed battle strategy for 1916. The tiny gains made by the first attack meant that the Germans had no need to move reserves down from Flanders. Nor did they do so at any time during the next five months. Confidential GHQ material in the Buchan papers confirms that point. It meant, in turn, that none of the requirements of a big battle in Flanders had been met. Haig's best policy after the 1 July failure was therefore to reduce the scale of his diversionary attacks on the Somme and begin to transfer men to Flanders for a battle at some time in the future, and this Haig tried to do. On 3 July he met Joffre in a conference on strategy in the immediate future and, according to his own diary, came out of the negotiations well. 'Joffre exploded in a fit of rage' when Haig proposed reducing battle frontage to that area alone in which British progress had been most favourable. 'He ordered me to attack Thiepval and Pozières. If I attacked Longueval, I would be beaten etc. I waited calmly till he had finished. His breast heaved and his face flushed. The trùth is, the poor man cannot argue nor can he easily read a map. I soothed old Joffre down. He seemed ashamed of his outburst and I sent him and Foch off to Amiens.'

From this account, one might infer that Haig had won his point, and his diary entry that day went on to add triumph to victory: 'I quietly explained what my position is relative to him as the Generalissimo. I am solely responsible to the British government for the action of the British Army and I had approved the plan and must modify it to suit the changing situation as the fight progresses.'

But Haig's was not the only account of the crucial meeting. Lord Bertie, the British ambassador in Paris, had a very different story to tell. 'Haig counselled delay while Joffre insisted on taking advantage by dealing a smashing blow. The discussion became very heated. Joffre told Haig that it would be dishonouring to the British Army if he did not continue the attack' – and went on to threaten placing Haig under Foch and Castelnau. 'Whether the British Army is to join in an immediate continuation of the offensive is a question not decided,' wrote Bertie, 'but Haig has asked for the services of some French Staff Officers to assist his own staff.' [41]

A letter from Robertson, Chief of the Imperial General Staff, to Haig on 7 July supports Bertie's implication that Haig had planned to stop the British attack and transfer it to Flanders. 'Liaison officer Castelnau said that the French desired to exploit success,' Robertson wrote. 'They wished our assistance to reinforce the north-east corner of the bulge. They hesitated to make this proposal on Monday as it would appear to be regarding the original plan as a failure. They think to exploit to the south was the best plan which would be impossible if we go north' (i.e. to Flanders). [42]

The final decision at this conference was anyway a foregone conclusion. Kitchener's instructions obliged Haig to defer to Joffre. [43] He therefore issued orders on 4 July naming Pozières as the chief British objective and stating the necessity of 'continuing operations relentlessly and allowing the enemy no respite'. The immediate result of that order was the rapid transfer of the Australians (already regarded as an elite attacking unit) from Messines in Flanders to Pozières, the highest point on the Somme battlefield and the key to the German second line.

The four months of fighting which followed were never going to be easy. Haig was committed to fighting a major battle in an area whose infrastructure had been prepared for a fourteen-day battle. But even taking this into account, there was a strong feeling in the British Army that Haig's performance in directing the battle fell short of what experienced soldiers expected. Evidence of this can be seen today in confidential letters sent to Edmonds while he was writing the Official History.

Correspondence over Guillemont offers a good example. It seemed to be a tiny farming village of brick cottages, stinking manure heaps and rutted tracks. German diligence had changed it into a fortress of concreted buildings and bunkers, impossible to identify with the naked eye. Capturing positions like Guillemont posed problems to the end of the war, but these could be magnified many times by inept leadership on the spot and inadequate direction from above. As Edmonds's correspondent put it, 'No one in Corps or Divisional HQ understood why our attacks failed. Everything seemed to go well up to a point. Then, in some unexplained way, the Germans got their old positions back again. In the end Congreve assembled a corps conference at which the evidence of survivors was pieced together. The conference concluded that the Germans had camouflaged machine guns somewhere near map reference S24D.5. These caught the support and reserve waves once the leading waves had got through. Before anything could be done, we were replaced by the 14th Corps.'

The result was that the British hammered away at Guillemont for a month, but 'As soon as the first spark of originality was shown,' Edmonds's correspondent recalled with bitterness, 'Guillemont was taken. Success was simply due to avoidance of a completely frontal attack.'

Where had Haig been while Guillemont's resistance embarrassed the southern flank of the British battle? Even Joffre was stung into delivering a formal protest at Haig's failure to get a grip on the battle, to which Haig replied that he was in full agreement with the principles set out in Joffre's Directive 8162 of 11 August (inevitably missing from Britain's public records). Haig concluded with the observation: 'Isolated engagements as a means of developing success and preparing the way for each further step on a large scale are, to some extent, unavoidable. But combined simultaneous attacks on as wide a front as the means at our disposal admit should certainly remain the guiding principle of our action.'

Could Haig have done better? Was the sophistication of staff work or battle tactics sufficient by summer 1916 to have fought more efficiently? Comparison with the French suggests that it was.

In his excellent and little-known book on the war, Lt.-Col. Head contrasted the two armies as a front-liner saw them (by chance near Guillemont, where the sectors met). 'For a long time I fought alongside the French on the Somme so had opportunity of comparing their methods and performance with ours. While we struggled painfully through the mud, they progressed in clean jumps and finally got far ahead of us across the Bapaume–Péronne road while we never got within a mile of it. Our weight of metal was heavier than theirs; our regimental officers and men at least as good. Why was there such a discrepancy in our performances? As we took over ground to our right gained by the French, I twice took over newly-made gun positions. We always liked getting hold of French positions. They were so much better than ours. Good roads to them, good gunpits, comfortable dugouts for officers and men. The French in their attacks did not shoot the ground to bits before they moved over it. A short, intense bombardment followed by a rush of men gave them the position clean and intact. Then a labour battalion arrived hotfoot to construct the necessary shelter and prepare roads. We had labour battalions but I never saw them at the front. We would shoot our ground into a quagmire and then send troops slowly forward over it and expect them to provide their own cover from the enemy's retaliation.' [44]

There is plenty of evidence to support Head's impression of British backwardness both at the front and at those rarefied command levels invisible to an officer in the trenches. The most pungent support, ironically, comes in Haig's diary at the end of the battle, when he put British casualties at 361,000 (against the War Office's more reliable 600,000) and French casualties at 181,000.[45] Traditionalists would reply that since the French were fighting at Verdun as well as on the Somme, they would have used fewer troops and met fewer enemy divisions on the Somme, but that was not the case. John Buchan wrote GHQ's communiqués in the second half of the battle and his private papers still contain a sample of GHQ's data which he used for the purpose. These demonstrate that the French sent as many troops to the Somme as the British and took on about the same number of German divisions.

The comparison between the French and British is therefore a deadly one for Haig's credibility in 1916, but it is an abstract comparison, and events in November 1916 allow us to give Haig's ineptness a more human face.

The last skirmish of the year was a direct assault on the fortified village of Beaumont Hamel. It has always been the custom to register satisfaction at the evidence it afforded of how much the British Army had learnt during its bloody apprenticeship. The real story is, however, very different. In 1926, Kiggell explained to Edmonds why a position of such limited tactical value had been assaulted too late in the year for there to have been any possibility of exploiting success: 'I noted in the last batch of your history that it was written that when I first saw Gough on the subject of the attack, I mentioned that success would have a good effect at the approaching Paris conference. Sir Douglas spoke to the same effect at his interview with Gough a little later. I hope you will agree to omit this. The full story is that there was a favourable tactical opening here so I suggested the attack to Haig whereupon he sent me to Gough for his opinion. At the time, I heard rumours that Lloyd George meant to make trouble for Haig over the Somme and the chance of a good, cheap success from that point of view just before the conference came to me as an afterthought. Whether I mentioned this at first to Haig I don't remember and much doubt. At any rate, the responsibility is mine and, if it is to stand at all, I hope that Haig's mention of it to Gough will be omitted at any rate as giving his enemies an opportunity to allege that his decisions were influenced by such considerations.'[46]

It was a fitting finale to Haig's management of the Somme. The year had begun with his plan for an ambitious double-headed battle far beyond the capacity of his Army. It ended with another of those inconsequential little attacks, fought without purpose and unrelated to anything else that was happening on the mud-bound wilderness of the Somme battlefield.

5

Passchendaele: The Roots

The tiny village of Passchendaele stands on the crest of a ridge which curls round the Ypres Salient like a giant pruning hook. Its grim brick cottages make little impression on tourists hurrying through it to Ypres today, but to the generation which lived through the Great War Passchendaele ('3rd Ypres') was synonymous with a battle which dominated 1917 as completely as 1916 had been dominated by the Somme. For those at home who read the names of the dead in daily newspapers, Passchendaele seemed a killing-ground with a biblical resonance to its name – like Calvary. For those who fought, mention of Passchendaele produced an angrier response.

Cyril Cruttwell, an Oxford don and old soldier, put the fighting men's view when he wrote: 'All the combatants on either side regarded it as the culmination of horror. The rain was pitiless, the ubiquitous mud speedily engulfed man and beast if a step was taken astray from the narrow duckboards upon which descended a perpetual storm of shells and gas. Some of the pictures in the Imperial War Museum preserve an aspect of the macabre grotesqueness of this blasted and mangled land. Long-distance gun-fire and the art of night-bombing had developed so much during the last year that reserves and resting troops were kept in a fever of perpetual apprehension. Men's nerves were badly frayed before they took part in the fighting and had little chance of healing when they were withdrawn from it.'[1]

With these words, Cruttwell seems to be describing a unique battle. Certainly it had been so for him. But was Passchendaele really so different from earlier battles?

The Somme had been fought over the chalk downlands of Picardy at the southern extremity of the British line in 1916. Passchendaele was to be fought on the wet clay pasturelands at the northern extremity of the Western Front in 1917. In most other respects, the two battles were like as twins. Each began in July. Both pulled the greater part of the British Army over a lunar shellscape in a slow rotation. The two battles ended in mid-November. Neither advanced the British line more than half a dozen miles or came within a gunshot of breaking the German Army. Of the two, whatever the popular feeling, the Somme was the more savage. Shelling had been more concentrated and, even on Cruttwell's accounting, casualties 25 per cent more numerous.

Why then did Passchendaele make the deeper scar on the public mind and why did it generate a debate whose bitterness has endured three generations while the Somme remains, in public memory, the disaster of a single day?

The answer lies in a combination of reasons. Passchendaele's conscripts were, for a start, less highly motivated than the volunteers of the Somme and less likely to accept their hardships with patriotic discretion. Those at home were also less accepting of the war's cost after another year of food shortages, another year of seeing the wounded returning or the bereaved mourning without an end in sight. But practical factors alone fail to explain the degree of ferocity which debate over Passchendaele has maintained for so long. Only a handful of those who fought it remain alive, and the sour temper of Britain at war is long past. Anyone wishing to grasp the significance of the battle must therefore look to symbols, not facts; to 1922 rather than 1917, for in that year two books appeared which offered an interpretation transforming a complexity of tactics and strategy into a simple view which seemed to summarize the chief issues of the Western Front and make Passchendaele a pivotal moment. Nominally a statement of Haig's case in preparation for the long-running shouting match with Lloyd George and his supporters, Haig's stance over Passchendaele in those two books was immediately perceived as something more important than the rights or wrongs of a single battle five years earlier. Soldiers versus politicians? Tories versus Liberals? The force of tradition as embodied by Haig against

Lloyd George and the force of change? At whatever level men debated, Passchendaele and therefore the Western Front became an extension both of internal politics and of that divide between left and right which had bubbled beneath the Edwardian age and was given massive impetus by the Russian revolution.

Sir Douglas Haig's Command by George Dewar (a journalist) and John Boraston (a Staff Officer at GHQ and, for a time, Haig's private secretary) was the bulkier of these publications,[2] but Frederick Maurice's wafer-thin 6d pamphlet hit harder and reached a wider audience.[3] Carrying the authority of Robertson's right-hand man at the War Office and the notoriety of an intervention in high politics at a critical time during the war (see Appendix Two), Maurice wrote with the simplicity and force implicit in his title – *Intrigues of the War. Startling Revelations Hidden until 1922. Important Secrets now Disclosed.*

Maurice's thesis was a straightforward one. Joffre and Haig had met at the Chantilly conference of November 1916. They had agreed on a big attack early in 1917 and if that attack had gone in, so Maurice argued, the Germans would have been hit hard during their retreat to that formidable defensive position just completed behind the crucial central section of the Western Front – the Hindenburg Line. The allies would have caught them cold and probably ended the war in 1917. Enter Lloyd George, who had pushed Asquith aside and made himself Prime Minister in December 1916. Fearing another Somme as fiercely as he distrusted Haig's ability, Lloyd George set about castrating the soldiers' plans for an early offensive.

His first attempt at sabotage involved diverting a mass of Haig's heavy artillery to Italy. A conference in Rome on 7 January blocked that scheme, but on his journey back to London Lloyd George met Nivelle, the new French Commander in Chief. In the improvised setting of a Parisian railway station, Nivelle outlined an alternative offensive scheme, claiming it would win the war in forty-eight hours – but only if Haig joined the offensive in a subordinate capacity.

Lloyd George must hardly have believed his luck. With Frenchmen dying in the place of Britons and Haig operating as Nivelle's poodle, his two dearest wishes came together. For that reason, Lloyd George committed the British government to Nivelle's offensive at the

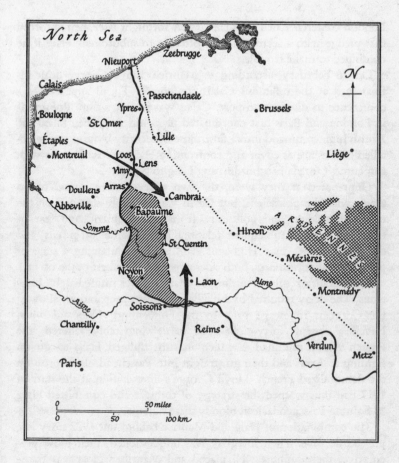

3 NIVELLE'S PLAN FOR THE SPRING OFFENSIVE, 1917

The strategic idea behind Nivelle's scheme was the limited one of nipping off the German salient closest to Paris with the British moving on Cambrai, the French on St Quentin. When Foch presented maps to the allied commanders in July 1918, he marked the ground the Germans could afford to surrender without significantly weakening their position. His line ran through Lille, Hirson and Metz, effectively demonstrating the limited scope of Nivelle's plan. Whatever hopes Nivelle might have had of panicking the Germans into a retreat towards the Ardennes were check-mated when the Germans evacuated the shaded area just before Nivelle's attack, taking the steam out of the French push.

London conference of 15–16 January. A fortnight later, he reinforced that pledge with a secret message offering to subordinate Haig if he continued to make trouble.

On 26 February, according to Maurice, Lloyd George dealt his final card at the infamous Calais conference. To all appearances a conference to discuss transport, Calais was in fact a trap. Politicians in London and Paris first coordinated plans in secret, then lulled the British high command into a false sense of security by using an inter-allied conference as cover and confronting Haig and Robertson with a document formally subordinating Haig to Nivelle.

Unprepared as they were, the two soldiers were bound to go along with the politicians, but Calais was indelibly stamped on the minds of soldiers and politicians from that moment, and fear of treachery marked subsequent relations between the 'brass hats' and the 'frock coats'. Like Highland clans, each maintaining a state of permanent war readiness, both sides expected the worst of the other.

The military result, according to Maurice, was immediately disastrous. The delay required by Nivelle's complex preparations allowed the Germans to escape back to the Hindenburg Line and when Nivelle's absurd 'forty-eight-hour battle' inevitably faltered, the French Army mutinied – which in turn obliged Haig to go on fighting at Arras and then go straight into Passchendaele to prop up the demoralized French. Lloyd George's intervention at the start of 1917 had thus warped the strategy of the war and committed Haig to fighting Passchendaele at bloody disadvantage.

The combination of Haig and Maurice behind this 1922 story line proved decisive. Their integrity was unquestioned, their blow pre-emptive, their support well placed and Maurice's gloss was transformed into historical orthodoxy, reinforced by the support of a cooperative official historian. Only when official archives were opened to researchers (and that was over forty years after the event) could outsiders check this story and expose it for the fiction it always was.

Since high policy was initiated in Downing Street, Cabinet papers make the best starting point, in particular the series of submissions from leading politicians which put forward policy proposals for 1917 during the autumn of 1916.[4] These all show remarkable unanimity.

Germany was winning the war. Italy and Russia were on the verge of revolution. France was contemplating peace, and war weariness in Britain was held to be undermining the national effort, reinforced by the possibility of a collapse of financial credit within six months. Surveying this wreckage, the Cabinet supported Balfour's conclusion that premature peace would mean the resumption of war within ten years against a Germany reinforced by the resources of the Russian Empire and provided with so many U-boats that the British Empire would be strangled.

After considering the options, the Cabinet's final decision was set down in a formal policy statement.[5] Many have been deceived by its title ('The Hankey Memorandum'). Lloyd George's initials show that it in fact represented the Cabinet's view, with Hankey's heading a naïve and not uncharacteristic bid for a place in the history books. The contents anyway were unambiguous, aggression on all fronts being the common denominator. Naval supremacy remained the chief priority, but guns were to be sent to Italy and a major offensive was mooted for the Middle East, with Aleppo the target, so that Britain would have a bargaining counter if the French made peace prematurely.

The Cabinet was also in agreement that 'a very powerful offensive on the Western Front' was necessary to head off a pre-emptive strike by the Germans, but how and when the offensive was to be made the Cabinet was undecided – at least on paper. Discussions on 3 November had concluded that a resumption on the Somme would lead to nothing.[6] The Germans could always retreat fifteen miles (as they were to do in spring 1917) and even give up Bapaume and Cambrai without serious disadvantage. When Joffre and Haig announced a few weeks later that they proposed to resume on the Somme in May, the Cabinet was therefore doubly displeased. May was too late to forestall a major German attack, and the Somme was the wrong venue.

When Nivelle replaced Joffre and changed everything, the Cabinet was therefore pre-disposed to favour a plan fitting its own ruminations more closely and Nivelle's did just that. It was given to the Cabinet on Christmas Day, 1916 (so much for the fiction of the Parisian railway platform!)[7] and Haig was promptly notified of the Cabinet's favourable response – long before the Rome conference.

What the politicians liked above all was Nivelle's timescale.[8] The Chantilly agreement in November 1916 had not visualized a major offensive until May 1917, when melting snow would allow both Italy and Russia to join with attacks of their own. Nivelle's plan proposed a start on 15 February instead and would therefore hit the Germans before their best divisions could get back from their winter campaign in Romania.

As a bonus, Nivelle guaranteed a major French commitment which had not previously been certain. In his Chantilly address, Joffre had spoken of the French making just one more attack before handing the chief burden on the Western Front to the British. There were rumours too that Painlevé the peacemonger might succeed the bellicose Briand as Prime Minister. In August 1916, Robertson had submitted a memorandum on that possibility: 'Each day I become more anxious over our position in the event of negotiations for armistice or peace. I fear we may be caught unprepared. We may be sure that Briand will have very decided views carefully worked out for him by the clever people who surround him. These views will probably have been communicated to the Russians as old allies of the French – but not to us.' These fears were confirmed in December 1916 when Esher revealed that the French had indeed been offered generous terms and were carefully considering them.

There was therefore no element of personal pique in the welcome Lloyd George gave to Nivelle's proposals. The new plan offered the simultaneous prospect of supporting Russia, keeping the French war party in power and sustaining the Anglo-French alliance. Nor was the plan accepted without the most detailed examination by the Cabinet.

The Nivelle offensive has usually been presented as an absurd scheme drawn up by an inexperienced soldier and imposed on gullible amateurs. It was, after all, only natural that naïve politicians should have been over-impressed by an articulate English-speaker who promised to win the war in forty-eight hours. Photographs of Nivelle in a fancy dress uniform and wearing the twisted smile of a cheerful lunatic seemed only to reinforce the impression of a charlatan, and yet there was always more to Nivelle than that. Brigadier (1914), corps commander (1915) and army commander (1916),

Nivelle had shown the highest ability in coordinating artillery and infantry at Verdun and, though British document weeders have done their best to prevent us studying the details, it is clear that Nivelle's battle plan was discussed by soldiers and politicians at length and found attractive on solid military grounds.

Robertson, for one, produced a balanced synopsis of Nivelle's scheme for the Army Council in January 1917.[9] Nivelle, he suggested, wished to start early so that German reinforcements would still be in Romania, before the German munitions programme outlined by Hindenburg began to bite and to make the most of French drafts before their numbers began to dwindle later in 1917. Nivelle's plan, Robertson went on, was for an initial attack lasting between six and fourteen days. The main blow would then be delivered elsewhere and reach the German gun line within forty-eight hours, thus repeating on a larger scale what had been achieved in Nivelle's 15 December attack at Verdun.

Haig's gloss on Nivelle's plan, equally favourable, was set out for the Cabinet in May 1917. 'The normal process of battle follows three stages. Fighting until the enemy's power is weakened; dealing a decisive blow when his power of resistance is weakened; then reaping the fruits of victory. The present allied operations [Nivelle's scheme] were based on the theory that by careful artillery preparation, the advance of the infantry could be so accelerated that the first two stages would merge into one and that the fruits of victory would be reaped in the course of a few weeks, if not days. The capture of Laon and Cambrai as a result of one operation, the turning of the Hindenburg Line by this and the cutting of the enemy's parallel railway lines along the whole of his front would probably have produced a state of disorganization such as would have admitted large strategical results to have been obtained.'[10]

Briefly, the Noyon Salient, pointing at Paris like a stubby howitzer barrel, was to be nipped on its flanks, with powerful attacks driving through to key rail junctions. These thrusts would deprive the Salient of nourishment, push the Germans back on the Ardennes and compel a withdrawal from France unless the enemy was willing to fight on with its army fragmented. It was the same attractive proposition as that which Foch tried to implement in autumn 1918, but was it practicable in spring 1917?

Haig was impressed by the possibilities. After meeting Nivelle for the first time, he told the king: 'We talked for two hours. I formed the opinion that he is a practical soldier who knows his work as a general in the field. My own plans are not really altered from what had been agreed on with Joffre except that as a temporary measure, it will be necessary to take over more line.'[11]

The Cabinet were more critical and arranged a full-scale investigation. Within a week of the Rome conference, Nivelle had to present his case to the Cabinet in person. The first meeting on 15 January took the form of a lengthy interrogation, with Ministers obviously keen to make up their own minds after the painful lesson of giving *carte blanche* to the military in 1916.[12] In the course of this inquisition, Nivelle explained that his trump cards were the new 155 mm guns which were coming off the production line at the rate of forty-eight monthly. Six months earlier, Nivelle admitted, he would have thought it impossible to break the German line, but with the new 155s he could reach 4 km further than the best guns of the Somme period and destroy positions 8 km deeper than their gun line. Absent from the minutes but known to the Cabinet were new infantry tactics, linked to the 155s and based on specially trained platoons delivering a body blow by penetrating down the avenues cut by the 155s. The concept was pure *Blitzkrieg,* and a few months later the Germans used Nivelle's methods successfully at Riga on the Eastern Front and again at Caporetto on the Italian Front. There was therefore nothing quixotic in Nivelle's tactical thinking.

The Cabinet liked what Nivelle had told them anyway and all the more since the parlous state of the British Army after the Somme was well known. 'The old British Army was extraordinarily good,' said Lloyd George. 'It could be entrusted operations of manoeuvre. Now, practically all the officers are gone. In the Welsh Division, few below lieutenant-colonel are trained officers. The rest are boys from the Public Schools with no experience of manoeuvre at all. Nivelle has told us that from captain downwards, one third of French officers are professionally trained and most have been fighting for two and a half years. I have no hesitation in saying that the British should hold the trenches and the French take the offensive.' Cabinet minutes indicate that Curzon was following Lloyd George and speaking for the rest of his colleagues – 'The Prime Minister is preaching to the converted.'

When the Cabinet accepted Nivelle's scheme, one might have thought the discussion at an end. They had backed Lloyd George's lack of confidence in Haig and opted instead for a French scheme. But things weren't what they seemed.

Minutes for the Cabinet's closed session on 16 January have been severely pruned and many speeches cut from their context by the censor's pencil. But enough remains to show that Cabinet plans for 1917 were anything but that straightforward acceptance of Nivelle's plan which is usually assumed. Lloyd George, for example, observes at one point in those minutes that he could never understand why one million soldiers were kept back in Britain. When Robertson pointed out to him that he had often explained the situation while Lloyd George was Minister of War, the Prime Minister came back at him to urge that at least 300,000 should be sent to France. 'I think the CIGS might advise the Cabinet to take the risk.' An unexpected stance indeed for a Prime Minister supposedly hostile to major battles on the Western Front!

At another point in proceedings that day, Lloyd George came out with a statement that he inclined to Haig's view that Nivelle's offensive would not succeed completely, but that there would anyway be time for another plan if the French scheme did not accomplish all that was hoped. What was this other plan and was it related to the 300,000 men Lloyd George wished to send to the Western Front?

The answer is given by Haig's contribution on 16 January, in which he stated that by landing a sizeable force on the Flemish coast, a French division would be relieved. The censor's prunings have removed Haig's interjection from its context, but what remains makes no sense unless it was part of the detailed examination of some big battle in Flanders. The final directive which ended proceedings that day bears this out by ordering Haig to make preparations for an offensive in the north as well as the south. Lloyd George's scheme for an offensive later in 1917 (a scheme requiring at least 300,000 reinforcements) was therefore the 1916 double-headed battle revived, using the French to soften up the Germans where the French and

British sectors met, then dashing north to fight a big battle which aimed at bursting out of the Ypres Salient.

It was a daring strategy and quite probably as unsound militarily in 1917 as it proved in 1916, but the Cabinet backed it. On 9 February, Robertson was even required to send a formal message to Haig reinforcing the Cabinet's decision of 16 January. 'Lloyd George wishes Haig to consider combined operations after the termination of the Franco-British operations. His Majesty's Government has also decided that the plan for the coming summer should embrace a scheme for further offensive action after the main operations have taken place on another part of the British front.'

In the context, 'combined operations' must mean an Army–Navy combination and that was possible only in Flanders. Whether 'further offensive action' meant the Cambrai plan, which was to be put into operation in November 1917 but which was originally devised for September 1916 (Haig left written instructions for his wife that the passage in his diary referring to it should not be copied), or whether Lloyd George intended a push in Italy, Salonika or the Middle East, remains unclear.

But whatever the small print, the message of the London conference in January 1917 was clear enough. The Cabinet proposed to make 1917 a year of all-out British effort on as many fronts as possible. The Western Front was scheduled for a major push, starting as early as possible in the year and going right through the summer, with the French used as *hors d'œuvres*. Nivelle's offensive might perhaps push the Germans out of France; probably it wouldn't. Either way, British plans focused where they always had done – on the security of Britain and the presence of weak powers on the other side of the Narrow Seas. Nivelle's scheme, whatever its outcome, was therefore seen in London as nothing more than a preparation for a battle to guarantee British security the other side of the Channel.

The immediate problem with this devious strategy was that it made Haig responsible for hiding Passchendaele up his sleeve and appearing to offer Nivelle stronger assistance that he ever intended to deliver. It would have been a difficult business for a nimble-footed diplomat. Could a slow-thinking professional soldier, moulded by the strict hierarchy of the barrack square, fight that particular corner

1 Haig and his family outside the small house on Kingston Hill, London, which was the family home during the war. The Charteris family were neighbours, and a golf course, Haig's basic requirement at the time, was close at hand.

2 Château Beaurepaire, which served as Haig's base from March 1916 to April 1919. It stood in isolation just a few miles from GHQ at Montreuil, directly accessible over cornfields on horseback.

3 Haig stands with the king of Montenegro on the steps of Château Beaurepaire.

4 Holding his withered arm characteristically behind his back, the Kaiser is flanked on his right by Hindenburg, on his left by Ludendorff.

5 On the left, Kitchener at an allied conference, Paris.

6 Chief of the Imperial General Staff Sir William Robertson, pipe firmly clasped in his right hand, stands next to a splendidly dignified Foch.

7 Asquith leaving the War Office, October 1915.

8 Haig and Joffre explain their strategy for the battle of the Somme to Lloyd George in July 1916. The photograph corrects an impression often given by that statuesque pose which was *de rigueur* for military men in the period. The subordination of generals to politicians and the need for deference in their importunity is made clear.

9 Lloyd George visits the front. On his right is French munitions expert Albert Thomas. The civilian to his left is Lord Reading. Lloyd George's wary alertness comes across strongly. Stance, dress and length of hair indicate a man who thought himself an outsider.

10 Charteris, Haig's Director of Intelligence, is presented to the Queen in June 1917. The stooped back belongs to Kiggell. Philip Sassoon, private secretary to Haig and brother of Siegfried, looks at the camera.

11 Pétain about to be awarded the baton of a Marshal of France. Behind him, from left to right, stands Joffre, Foch, Haig and Pershing. Chief of Staff Weygand stands immediately behind his master, Foch.

12 Haig reviews a Canadian unit, escorted as always by the 17th Lancers. From spring 1917 to the Armistice, the Canadian Corps was the most effective fighting force in Haig's Army. Young officers like Montgomery and Alan Brooke who served in it would have noted how much could be achieved by tight organization and promoting the best men.

13 Haig during one of the innumerable tours of inspection which occupied so many of his afternoons. The troops on display here are Canadian. Haig's Chief of Staff Lawrence is in the raincoat with the walking stick. Immediately to Lawrence's left is the bulky figure of Canadian Corps commander Currie. Horne, who commanded the 1st Army, stands behind Currie.

14 Haig with Lawrence, his Chief of Staff. Behind them are Haig's four ADCs. On the extreme left is Desmond Morton, one-time gunner but shot through the heart near Arras and lucky to survive. Between the wars, Morton was one of Churchill's confidential advisers.

15 Sir William Orpen's portrait of Haig, painted at GHQ in May 1917. A distinguished painter of portraits, Orpen's discreet brush usually managed to eliminate jowls, grey hair and signs of fatigue from the finished canvas.

successfully? The answer was hardly unexpected, and the real story of the first three months of 1917 features the British Cabinet desperately trying to recover from a succession of gaffes committed by its Commander in Chief.

The first of Haig's blunders came at the end of January.[13] The setting was a conference convened to discuss a rail crisis which had been brought to a head by Haig's demand that the Nord railway carry 200,000 tons weekly for the British in addition to its usual 100,000 for the French. Nivelle took inevitable umbrage. Haig's statistics meant that an army half the size of the French was claiming the use of three and a half times the number of railway wagons each day. 'No doubt it could be explained,' Robertson lamented. 'Unfortunately it was not explained. Subordinates have a way of putting forward outside figures' and Nivelle would have seen very quickly what those figures meant (he later told Henry Wilson that he had been unable to speak with Haig for fifteen minutes during the planning period without Haig's attention wandering off towards Flanders): 200,000 tons made sense only if Haig was preparing two separate battles. Nivelle therefore protested. Concentration of effort was fundamental to his own scheme and he told Haig as much. 'Once battle is engaged, it cannot enter your thoughts to cease to fight and leave me alone at grips with the enemy in accordance with your appreciation of the operations. If we engage, then it must be with the intention of going through to the end and engaging all forces.'

For the sake of the alliance, Lloyd George had to intervene speedily and it was with the intention of soothing an angry Nivelle after the transport conference that Lloyd George told the French attaché in London that he was prepared to issue secret instructions subordinating Haig. Since Kitchener had ordered Haig to treat Joffre as the allied Commander in Chief from December 1915 and since the Cabinet intended to fight in Flanders that summer, Lloyd George's words to the attaché were nothing more than diplomatic window-dressing, and for that reason he had been careful to speak in front of witnesses. The secret instructions of 1 February which Maurice made so much of were therefore nothing more than diplomatic courtesy to cover a short-term difficulty.

What transformed this sensitive situation was another blunder by Haig on the very day Lloyd George met the French attaché. In one of the most remarkable episodes of the whole war, Haig made a public announcement about Nivelle's battle, indicating where it was going to be fought and outlining its general scope. The occasion was an interview given to three French journalists. Haig told them that after the initial assault, trench war would give way to open war and lead to a military decision in 1917. The German defensive system round Bapaume would be pulverized and the German front would undoubtedly be broken by a decisive attack which would be delivered by the French.

When this interview was published in the French press, reaction in Britain was strong. The king contacted the Earl of Derby at the War Office, regretting 'that Haig has allowed himself to be interviewed by press correspondents and still more that the Field Marshal, whom he has hitherto regarded as of a peculiarly reticent and uncommunicative nature, should have given expression to opinions so positive and, indeed, confidential as those recorded in the press last evening. The king is further under the impression that by King's Regulations officers are forbidden to make utterances of this nature to the press.'[14]

Derby replied ruefully: 'I am afraid there is no doubt the interview took place. If he said what is reported, it is going to get us into endless trouble as in addition to being impolitic, it gives certain information which we could have wished to keep secret. I can't understand how a man as reticent as Haig is should have given such an interview.'

Haig's own response was one of apparent astonishment: 'I gave no interview. I merely talked platitudes and stated my confidence in victorious termination of the war. By some mistake, a summary of one of these talks has slipped past the censor. I am much annoyed as I hold it quite wrong for the Commander in Chief's views to be published by the press at all.'[15]

By 19 February, Haig had changed his line, claiming that he had met 'distinguished Frenchmen' as requested by the propaganda department of the Foreign Office.[16] He had received them as Deputies rather than journalists 'and had consequently spoken to them quite freely without intending that the subject of conversation would appear in the press or, indeed, supposing that it would be published.' Later that day, Haig wrote to his wife: 'It should never have appeared in the papers. The fault is due to the Foreign Office's desire for "propaganda" – and then, certain individuals at home were anxious to get something to go at one about.'

Despite these changes of tack, there seems little doubt that Haig knew exactly what he was doing. The published interview in *Le Journal* had been spotted by the Press Bureau, who got in touch with MI7. That same day, the Admiralty intercepted a cable transmission to the USA and sent the transcript of Haig's interview to Derby. GHQ was immediately contacted and confirmed the authenticity of the text, adding its opinion that the interview should be published. When the transcript was scrutinized in London a little later, Kiggell's signature was discovered on it and whatever Kiggell's many virtues, independence of decision wasn't among them – nor indeed was it desirable in a Chief of Staff. If Kiggell signed documents, it was only after previous authorization by Haig.

Whether Haig's interview represented an unfortunate error of judgement on his part or a serious attempt to undermine the Nivelle offensive, the publication of a sanitized version in the London press on 13 February coincided with Haig's second depth charge. On that day, he cabled to the Cabinet: 'If the French commence operations on 1 April, I can only comply with War Cabinet instructions as to combine with them to the extent of a very modified attack. This course, so far as British arms in France are concerned, could have no more than a very local and temporary effect on the enemy and would use up resources which would prejudice the success of subsequent operations.'[17]

The Cabinet replied on 14 February, ordering Haig to meet Nivelle and sort out the problem. A conference was duly arranged in which Haig stated that the difficulties confronting him with rail transport had become so acute that the British attack on 1 April would have to be a limited one. The first German trench system might fall, but the second line could be captured only on a small front and would be followed by a delay of several weeks. Only if the rail situation improved dramatically and the attack was deferred fourteen days was a breakthrough possible.

Lloyd George had to act fast. Not only was Nivelle's fundamental principle of a violent first strike under threat but the date suggested by Haig meant that he hadn't shifted his stance one iota from the one he had taken at the policy-making conference three months earlier at Chantilly. The Franco–British alliance was at stake and the Calais conference of 26 February was the immediate result.

Although it is invariably presented as the combination of an ambush and a conspiracy, the plain fact is that the Calais conference had been Haig's idea in the first place. He made the proposal on 14 February and Robertson had scented danger at once. 'I knew we should have trouble,' the CIGS later told Esher. 'If there had been no Calais conference, there would have been none of the recent trouble.'[18]

After dealing with a series of difficulties over allied war plans during the previous fortnight, the Cabinet seized on Haig's idea at once. Matters had to be resolved in writing and a conference was the obvious setting, with discussions leading to a written statement which should cover not only transport but the whole plan of operations, the division of responsibility and relations between Haig and Nivelle. Nothing less would do after a succession of damaging squalls. The Cabinet therefore discussed their tactics at meetings on 20 and 22 February.

Robertson later claimed that he had been deliberately kept in the dark on all this and excluded from the Cabinet. Possibly his memory was at fault. Perhaps he was lying. He was certainly present at the meetings on both days[19] and when Haig asked him for the Calais agenda forty-eight hours before the event, Robertson was able to give him a detailed briefing: 'The British government suggested the chief object of the conference should be to discuss and definitely decide upon the plan of forthcoming operations on the Western Front. It is suggested that the French government should clearly define the assistance and cooperation which they desire the British armies in France to afford and the British government, for their part, should state clearly the extent to which it was possible to meet the French request.' This reply meant that Haig and Robertson knew exactly what was in the minds of the politicians before the conference, despite their claims to the contrary over the next ten years.

If Haig or Robertson still had any doubts, Hankey was able to dispel them on the morning of the conference. As he told the king's secretary later, 'I gave Robertson and Maurice what struck me at the time as a very fair and full statement of the case, making it quite clear that Lloyd George had full power from the War Cabinet to take any decision he considered necessary, specifically a free hand to decide between Nivelle and Haig.'[20]

The consequence of rushed preparations and imperfect coordination were quickly apparent at the conference. When the French presented the central point of their case – a written request defining 'the assistance and cooperation which they desired' – Lloyd George pronounced their paper 'absurd' (Blake misquotes Haig, substituting the milder 'excessive' in his edition of the diary) and in a letter to Leo Rothschild immediately after the conference, Haig confirmed the spontaneity of Lloyd George's interjection. 'The French put forward a terrible scheme for putting the British under a French commander in chief. Thank goodness even Lloyd George thought it went too far.'

Indeed, the whole tone of Haig's contemporary correspondence reinforces an impression that what transpired at Calais was very different from the story put out by Haig and Maurice later. The day after Calais, for instance, Haig told his wife: 'Today we came to a compromise which my diary will show you. The decision regarding the command should work without difficulty provided there is nothing further behind it.' On that same day Haig informed the king that 'so far, this document merely defines in words what I have, in accordance with the spirit of the Instructions received from Kitchener, been trying to do, viz. "Closest cooperation". I think as the actual document stands, no great difficulty should occur in carrying out what I have been doing, provided there is not something behind it.'[21]

This was hardly the language of a man who had just passed through one of the great crises of the war and been mugged in an ambush. Nor was his subsequent conduct that of a man traumatized by unexpected and dangerous changes. When Nivelle sent a letter requesting copies of all GHQ orders as well as two bi-lingual British Staff Officers for liaison work, Haig sat on the letter six days before stonewalling on all Nivelle's points.[22] In his reply, he doubted whether he could be ready on 8 April, questioned the value of a battle in the Vimy–Arras area and suggested that preparation to fight in the Ypres Salient should be hastened. Haig then sent Nivelle's original letter to the Cabinet, naïvely asking whether it wished 'the British Commander in Chief to be subjected to such treatment by a junior *foreign* [Haig's emphasis] commanding officer?'

This clash was resolved only by a second conference in March. All points were decided in Nivelle's favour and a sharp letter from George V warned Haig that he would get no more support from the Palace unless he showed greater willingness to cooperate with the French.

After two months of fumbling, details of Nivelle's offensive had thus been sorted out at last. The British attack was to start on 8 April, with Cambrai the British objective and with Gough's 5th Army fighting at Arras rather than going north to the Ypres Salient as Haig intended.

But even if the details of Nivelle's offensive were settled, a big question still remains – and it is one which interests historians today as much as it did Cabinet or GHQ at the time – to what extent was the battle of Passchendaele thrown out of joint by the Nivelle offensive? Maurice was adamant that the disruption had been critical. Was he correct?

A key point in the Maurice thesis was an insistence that the six-week gap between the starting date visualized at Chantilly (February) and the one finally adopted by Nivelle (April) allowed the Germans to escape to the formidable defensive position of the Hindenburg Line.

Documents accessible today (and which Maurice must have known well) show that his point was nonsense, since Joffre's intention at Chantilly had been to delay battle until May at the earliest. A day before the Chantilly meeting,[23] Haig thus told his army commanders that Joffre was proposing a coordinated allied offensive for 1 May. 'The enemy may attack so there might perhaps be a premature call for operations,' Haig added, suggesting that four small attacks should be held in readiness. He then sent a brisk note to Joffre listing all the reasons why the British could not be ready for a big battle before 1

May at the earliest. The conclusion is clear enough. Of all the attacking schemes on the table at the end of 1916, only Nivelle's original plan would have caught the Germans in retreat, and the mid-January conference in London killed that possibility. Disagreement between Nivelle and Haig meant that the Cabinet had compromised between February (Nivelle's choice) and May (Haig's preference) by selecting 1 April.

Did Nivelle's April battle delay Passchendaele and were the six weeks trumpeted by Maurice instrumental in fixing the start and finish of Passchendaele in a period of torrential rain and deep mud? A paper produced by GHQ on 3 December 1916 and headed 'Very secret. Notes on Operations, 1917' is conclusive on the point.[24] The paper began with a summary of the Chantilly agreement. 'The offensive on the West Front is to consist of a prolonged battle of usure [wearing-down or attrition] as a preliminary to the attack to achieve decisive results.' The paper concluded with an estimate of just how long the wearing-out battle would have to last before 'the British portion of the decisive battle' began 'north of the river Lys to secure the coast'. The experience of 1916 proved that two months of fighting was required to wear out a German reserve of 127 divisions. Since Haig reckoned to start Arras on 1 May, the paper shows that Passchendaele was planned for the start of July at the very earliest.

The date actually visualized is more clearly defined in the working papers of the Macmullen committee which had been set up in January 1917 to work out details of the Passchendaele battle. These show that the function of Messines was to pull German guns away from the north of the Salient. To do that, Messines was timed for 15 June, with Arras in full swing (so much for the later claim that Arras had been prolonged to ease pressure on the French!) Since Macmullen's team calculated that it would take six weeks to get men from Arras to Passchendaele, a battle which actually began on 31 July did so only a fortnight or so later than originally planned.

Nor did the force visualized differ very much from what had been planned at the end of 1916. In a secret meeting at the Admiralty just ten days before the Nivelle scheme was first heard of, Haig specified thirty-five divisions for Flanders. When the battle actually got under way, Plumer had thirteen divisions and attacked with five; Gough had sixteen, attacking with ten; the French had six and used two, making a total of thirty-five divisions with seventeen utilized for the initial thrust. In guns, likewise, Haig had demanded 2,988 back in December 1916. On 31 July, he was using 3,091.

Then there was the matter of German reserves. Already at the start of 1916, Haig had realized that no thrust in Flanders stood much chance unless German reserves had been severely battered in advance. The defences built by the enemy round the Salient were simply too strong for a frontal offensive to stand any chance of success. When he addressed the Cabinet on 1 May 1917, Haig showed he had not forgotten that fact when he said: 'For the dwindling British force alone to continue the offensive would assuredly result in the enemy massing against us in such strength as not only to make it impossible for us to gain any real advantage over him but to place it in his power to assume a dangerous offensive against us when our strength was exhausted. We are not strong enough to continue a vigorous offensive alone and we cannot rely on adequate French cooperation.'[25]

Was Haig right? Did French passivity prevent effective wearing-down of the Germans and did the weakened, mutinous condition of the French after Nivelle's failure reinforce this effect and compel the British to attack despite the enemy's strength?

Statistics bearing on the first question are clearcut. Even at the height of their troubles, the French were perfectly capable of repelling strong German attacks. Between April and June, with the French Army supposedly disintegrating, the Germans sent 105 of their 157 Western Front divisions against the French and by the end of July (so the War Office told the Cabinet) the Germans had used forty more divisions and made seventy attacks on the French at Chemin des Dames, east of Soissons.[26] The wearing-out process had therefore gone according to GHQ's most favourable calculations.

The condition of the French Army was another matter. According to majority opinion after the war, French passivity stemmed from Nivelle's failure and the consequent mutinies. In fact, Haig and Lloyd George each knew the real situation. On 25 April, Haig had written to Robertson: 'If Nivelle is replaced by Pétain, I understand it is doubtful that the latter would maintain vigorous offensive.'[27] A month later, Esher confirmed this assessment after a meeting with Pétain. He told Haig that Pétain's policy was based on three principles – to take over as little line as possible, to avoid attacks on a grand scale and to lose no men. French caution was therefore based, not on personal whim, but on specific instructions from the French government to wait on the Americans.

Nor did 'mutinies' contribute much to this new French policy. In the third week of May, there had been a measure of disorder in those units which had fought in Nivelle's Aisne battle, but Charteris was able to re-assure Haig on 25 May that 'Things are better in the French Army.' A week later, Charteris's assessment was confirmed by GHQ's liaison officer at Pétain's HQ. The peppery judgement which Edmonds gave Liddell Hart in the 1930s was therefore substantially correct. 'No one in the German or British Army, not even Haig, heard of the "Mutinies" at the front. There was grumbling at better pay, rations and leave of the British. The French made the "Mutinies" a convenient excuse for doing nothing in the latter half of 1917.'[28]

When Passchendaele began on 31 July, the date, location and the relative strengths of the opposing forces were thus in full accord with Haig's requirements at the start of 1917. The smoke-screen of lies and fictions put out by Haig, Maurice and the military faction in the 1920s were just that – a smoke-screen, a cloud of poison gas. If Passchendaele, like the Somme, failed to produce the results expected by either the Cabinet or GHQ, explanations must be sought outside those dastardly plots which have been allowed to dominate discussion of 1917 for too long.

6

Passchendaele: The Battle

Few battles look simpler on a large-scale map than Passchendaele. None offered the prospect of such glittering prizes. If the British Army could break out of the Ypres Salient, drive the Germans from the Belgian coast and link up with the Netherlands, the German position in Belgium would be outflanked and Germany's industrial heartland in the Ruhr put under direct threat. A successful offensive in Flanders therefore offered a real possibility of speedy victory.

There was no serious argument over these possibilities. GHQ papers had analysed them in depth. Haig had demonstrated their feasibility with sweeps of his forefinger over the Cabinet's wall map in June 1917. The Cabinet had set up a special committee to examine the battle and decided to sanction it after prolonged discussion, and three months of fighting by the whole British Army followed. At the end of it the British had conquered a patch of mud Haig could have walked round in a day.

The discrepancy between the effort and the achievement suggests that something went radically wrong, and if the Haig–Maurice version which put all the blame on Lloyd George can be discounted where then did the fault lie? A number of possibilities have been discussed over the years, analysts agreeing that separate discussions were required for the battle's two phases. The first phase was the attempt to break through fast on a narrow front and capture the rail junctions of Roulers and Thourout by *coup de main*. When failure became obvious in the middle of August, a broadening of the attacking front signalled the start of the second phase, with Plumer's

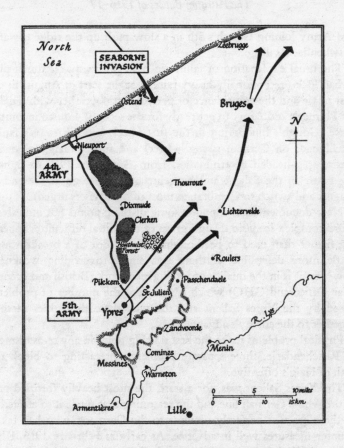

4 THE STRATEGIC IDEA BEHIND THE BATTLE OF PASSCHENDAELE

Right through the war, the War Office and Cabinet were agreed that a thrust from Ypres to the Netherlands would bring the Dutch into the war. The crucial rail junction of Liège would then be outflanked and the Ruhr industrial area threatened. But flooded marshes either side of Dixmude and the marshy Lys posed major difficulties by limiting the attacking front. Two counter-measures were planned in 1916: a coastal thrust from Nieuport and an amphibious landing at Ostend, using landing craft and tanks dispatched from a purpose-built, secret port at Sandwich. In the event, a German counter-attack three weeks before Passchendaele began scuppered the first and the failure to win a quick success in the main battle, the second.

2nd Army joining Gough's 5th in a slow push up the ridge towards Passchendaele village.

The usual explanation of failure in both phases makes much play of bad luck (exceptionally heavy rainfall at the start of August in the first phase and the coincidence of perfect battle weather with a delay for Plumer's 2nd Army to get ready for the second), human incompetence (Gough's blundering in the first attack and Charteris's faulty Intelligence on German strength later) and finally Haig's obsessive nature (pig-headed determination from December 1915 to fight a big battle in the Salient and his reluctance to let go at the end of August and switch to Cambrai, as most of his advisers urged).

New documentation supports some of these points but indicates a more complex scenario, Haig's grasp of the initial difficulties appearing firmer than used to be thought and his idea of a breakthrough battle more defensible. If there is a single, overriding weakness, however, it is in the quality of Intelligence work (British and French, War Office and GHQ) which overlooked the number of problems posed by the Ypres Salient and the way these difficulties meshed together to the enemy's advantage.

Physical problems make the best starting point in any re-assessment of Passchendaele, three separate problems interacting to block the path of Haig's offensive.

The Ypres Salient was, for a start, the most heavily fortified part of the whole German line and the reasoning that made it so attractive to the allies was perfectly obvious to the Germans, who had taken counter-measures well in advance. As early as February 1916, King Albert of Belgium gave Haig and Curzon an opinion that the strength of German defences ruled out any chance of a breakout in Flanders [1] and from that time, the deepening of those defences was painstakingly recorded in the reports of the 2nd Army's brilliant Director of Intelligence, Charles Mitchell: [2]

22.11.16 Continuous work in the Salient. Many concrete strongpoints being built.

11.1.17 Considerable increase in the number of German working parties in the Salient.

24.3.17 Very active work on rear defences.

25.6.17 Shellhole posts echelonned in depth. Our patrols unable to locate exact lines. There is no easily located forward position.

The meaning of this was firmly grasped at GHQ. Charteris, as head of Intelligence, visited Mitchell regularly at 2nd Army HQ and was able to check Mitchell's observations against half a million aerial photos taken over the Salient between March and June 1917. Haig might therefore talk about going through the German lines with pigs' bladders to keep up the morale of his entourage, but the maps in his study showed six separate German defensive zones stretching back well beyond the Passchendaele Ridge when the battle began.[3]

It was Haig's misfortune that the strength of these defensive zones wasn't just a matter of concrete and steel. Geology and the foul climate of Flanders reinforced those barriers because of the measures Haig was bound to take in preparing his assault. Massed blockhouses and great sweeps of wire meant that the British had to use a powerful barrage even though the Salient was close to sea level and had a water table near the surface even at the height of summer. There was no escaping the dilemma and no obvious solution to it. Without shelling, German defences could not possibly be penetrated; with shelling, the ground would become a morass. In an off-the-record conversation with Liddell Hart many years later, Edmonds admitted the result: 'The ground was impassable for tanks after 31 July, not by rain but by shelling which converted the ground into cheesecake.' Edmonds went on to suggest that a shell-crater zone half a mile wide and covered by four feet of slime had proved a greater barrier to British advance than all the barbed wire laid by the Germans.

The combination of cream cheese and heavy rain was another matter and one Haig had long been aware of. 'Operations are liable to the danger of interruption by bad weather,' ran a GHQ paper in May 1917. 'A few hours of rain brings the brooks into flood which only subsides within periods varying up to twenty-four hours. A few weeks' rain may make the whole country impracticable for prolonged operations for at least one week.'[4]

Did GHQ know in advance about the likelihood of rain and the amount likely to fall in the period chosen for the battle? The papers of Plumer's Intelligence section are conclusive.[5] Studies based on all available records from the previous thirty years demonstrated that July and August were the most unpredictable months of the year, with heavy thunderstorms possible at any time. September was the best month. It was dry one year in four (1917 was to be one of those years) and the ground dried out completely after rain. October was dry only one year in ten (1914 was such a year) and usually marked the change to winter conditions. Over thirty years, October had proved the wettest month of the year, a wet spell in the middle of the month invariably marking the onset of winter.

No commander could have been better informed about the defences facing him, the terrain over which he proposed to fight or the weather he was likely to encounter – and Haig acknowledged the fact. Briefing his army commanders before issuing final operation orders on 5 July, Haig warned them: 'The progress of events may demand modifications, especially in view of the comparatively short period of fine weather which we can count on.'[6]

One segment of the battlefield in particular demanded an accurate weather forecast and that was the Steenbeek valley, which ran right across the front of the main attack. If rain swelled the stream before the advance, impenetrable swamp would be added to the half-mile belt of porridge created by British shells. Yet Haig always knew that the accuracy of prediction which he needed for the Steenbeek region was out of the question. GHQ's meteorological adviser was Ernest Gold, a Wrangler and Fellow of St John's College, Cambridge. His personal papers are preserved in the Meteorological Office's archives today and their primitive contents startle the reader. 'N.E. winds usually indicate dull weather,' runs a typical comment in the margin of Gold's notebooks. 'Strong east winds at Valencia when a depression appears to be coming quickly usually means it will not affect Flanders for twenty-four hours.'

Gold acknowledged these limitations and always refused to make any predictions more than twenty-four hours in advance. Even then, he might run ahead of his data. His forecast a day before the start of Passchendaele was that 'The weather is likely to improve generally but slowly.' In fact, 76 mm of rain fell during the first four days of the battle, as against an average 8 mm for those four days over the previous thirty years.

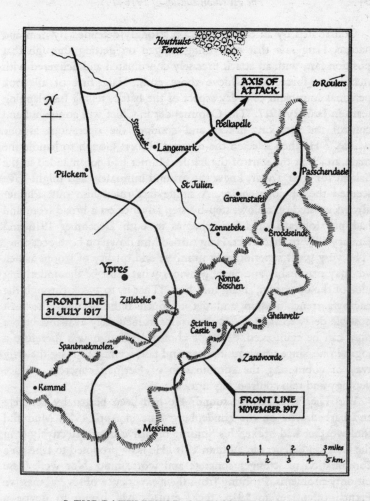

5 THE BATTLEFIELD OF PASSCHENDAELE

The Ypres Salient is a low-lying, gently undulating pastureland, liberally sprinkled with copses. Two features stand out. The low ridge from Kemmel to Passchendaele seems to dominate the battle area. It was, in fact, of little significance in 1917, since artillerymen had detailed maps and used aeroplanes to observe their shooting. The Steenbeek, an apparently insignificant little stream, was much more important. Shelling transformed it into an almost insurmountable barrier across the axis of attack.

Confronted by an enemy position strongly defended by man and nature, Haig saw that everything hinged on getting through that position fast, with an attack precisely coordinated and delivered with maximum force. To achieve those ends, Haig first of all took personal command of every aspect of the battle, telling his planning team in January 1917: 'The Commander in Chief will command and control the attacking forces and conduct the operations as one whole.'[7] He then selected the dashing Hubert Gough to handle the main attack at the start of the battle. Plumer had commanded in the Salient for over a year, knew the ground intimately and might have seemed the obvious choice. A single fact ruled him out. Plumer always insisted on a slow, step-by-step advance on a broad front and had put forward offensive schemes in both December 1916 and January 1917 to that effect. Haig turned him down on both occasions. 'The very great superiority in numbers and quality of troops which we may reasonably anticipate provides what must be the underlying idea of the operation,' Haig told him. 'That is, to break through the enemy's trench system and get to open fighting with the least possible delay so as to defeat the troops immediately available before they can be reinforced.'[8] Haig's choice of Gough was therefore a logical one, since penetration, deep and fast, seemed to Haig the only way of countering the combination of German concrete, surface geology and rain confronting him.

Was Haig's judgement sound? He had been beaten by concrete and barbed wire on the Hindenberg Line in April 1917. Mud and foul weather had broken his Somme offensive more effectively than the German defences in autumn 1916. He now proposed to take on a combination of stronger concrete and worse mud. Nor were these his only problems. Profiting from their experience of several massive French offensives in 1915, the Germans had begun to devise a number of defensive expedients which were deployed in the Salient to such effect that, even if the sun had shone every day and the German position been protected by sandbags alone, the Passchendaele offensive would almost certainly have foundered at the outset.

The first of these expedients was artillery usage. Although the Germans had only a quarter the guns which the French and British deployed in the Salient, they were always in a position to disrupt

Haig's preparations with a crushing weight of artillery fire. This was partly the result of a position on the outside of a salient, with all the possibilities of concentrated convergence. Even more important was the technological edge they enjoyed. Streamlined, clip-on nose cones and superior propellants gave German guns greater range. Aerial domination by faster and better-armed planes allowed them a free run of the skies too and therefore the superior accuracy which aerial photography and direct observation of shooting gave.

The Germans also kept the novelty of mustard gas up their sleeve and it came as a complete surprise.[9] The liquid was carried in shells marked with a yellow cross, and it stained the ground like sherry. Samples were immediately sent to Porton Down for analysis and scientists there identified a sulphur derivative with a high percentage of chlorine which boiled at 223 degrees centigrade. But exactly what it was they did not know. Its effectiveness in blistering the skin of anyone walking through the area of evaporation came to the scientists as a matter of report, but they were unable to reproduce the yellow-cross shell for another twelve months and they never found an antidote.

The impact of mustard was so great that British records were all but wiped clean to conceal the degree of embarrassment it caused. The 5th Army's war diary makes a brief reference to one man in six becoming a mustard casualty in a single division after the barrage of 26 July,[10] and the private diary of Pershing, the American Commander in Chief, reinforces that point. (The Americans had declared war on 6 April after the sinking of some of their ships by the Germans.) After watching operations, Pershing noted 26,000 British mustard gas casualties in the fortnight before the battle began. It was an intolerable loss, but the nearest GHQ ever came to acknowledging the degree to which their preparations had been disrupted by mustard was a single cryptic reference in a report dated 16 July: 'This gas was certainly a very effective weapon.'[11]

The combined effect of mustard and high explosive on Haig's battle plan was very specific. Zero had originally been set for 19 July. As a result of artillery fire, the date had to be pushed forward twice.[12] In his diary Haig blamed the French for these delays and, since the postponements led to the first assault coinciding with torrential rain, the French have been blamed over seventy years for sabotaging Haig's first thrust, but the facts are against this view. On 16 June, Gough told an army command conference that the weight of German shelling ruled out the 19 July date. Zero was therefore put back to 28 July. On 23 July, Gough requested another extension for the same reason as before. The French had certainly arrived late and refused to dig in their own guns (men too old to fight did that sort of work in the French Army, so New Zealanders had to be brought in to prepare French gun positions), but enemy shelling had been the underlying problem throughout.

The quantity and quality of German artillery work had cut deeply into Haig's hopes. On the eve of battle, the Germans went on to play a second tactical card with even more effect. On the eve of the Nivelle offensive, they had pulled back to the Hindenburg Line and thrown the whole allied timetable out of joint, and they had given a repeat performance on the eve of Messines in June 1917.[13] The British had dug huge mines under the German front line and coordinated their attack to coincide with their detonation. A week before the battle, the Germans pulled back. A baffled Haig asked for Plumer's opinion, suggesting that Plumer should attack at once, without mines. In the event, the plan was left intact. Mines laboriously dug were therefore wasted on an almost empty German position and the much-trumpeted victory of Messines was little more than the capture of a few scattered pillboxes. The British then advanced into a killing-ground on which pre-ranged German artillery smashed the attackers. There was therefore little talk of victory among those who knew the facts, and Haig posed the vital question at the army commanders' conference which followed Messines – had the Germans known of the British offensive in advance and had the withdrawal of the guns been a sign of strength or weakness?[14]

The Germans answered both questions in July. Four days before Passchendaele began, they pulled back to leave a zone of marshland between their new forward position and the British front line. GHQ's communiqué put the blame on a Welsh sergeant who betrayed the date and time of attack under interrogation as a prisoner.[15] This was complete nonsense. Robertson had written to GHQ from Paris on 27 July with a wry observation: 'Everybody in my hotel knows the date of the offensive down to the lift boy.'[16] If the British were caught out by a speedy German retreat for the third time in 1917, garrulous Celts had nothing to do with it.

The Germans held one more tactical surprise in store for Haig. High explosive and mustard had delayed him. Tactical retreat had confronted him with even more mud than he expected. The third surprise lay in the sophistication of the enemy's defensive deployment once the zone of mud had been crossed. Ever since the Champagne battles of spring 1915, the Germans had been deepening their defences. A full-blown second position appeared in summer 1915, and by the autumn a third had been added so far back that it lay beyond the range of French and British guns. Between these defensive lines, concrete troop shelters and machine-gun nests formed an additional hazard, scattered like peppercorns to slow an attacking force and pose an impossibly irregular puzzle for allied artillerymen who might try to neutralize the defensive system. By the summer of 1917, the thinning and deepening process had reached its highest level of sophistication. Barbed wire funnelled attackers into zones swept by the interlocking arcs of carefully positioned machine guns and pulverized by crippling concentrations of shells.[17]

The British response at the higher command levels was as one might expect. Gough had been disconcerted by new German tactics in April 1917 but he had been careful to give no hint of the fact in writing. 'Though the Germans are increasingly hard to find,' he wrote in a typical report, 'their tactical changes involve no new principles. It is better to use too many troops than too few. It is better to use them too soon than too late. When in doubt, go ahead. When uncertain about your tactics, kill Boches quickly. Get going at once. Don't wait for orders to do so. Make mistakes and thus learn not to make the same ones again. Don't waste time.'[18]

Haig's appreciation was equally obtuse if more polished in style. At the start of 1917, observers had been sent to report on the lessons drawn by the French from their Somme experience. They returned with glowing reports of storm troops, progressively and uniformly trained, and rifles being replaced by machine guns. French infiltration methods won particular praise, since they appeared to mesh well with the decreasing density of German defences. Haig refused to budge nevertheless. Only after pressure from London did he make the small concession of issuing a directive which standardized attacking formations.[19] Massed linear advance was to remain basic, but the density of men and distribution of weapons within those formations was at least standardized. What Haig should have been working towards, as the French and Germans perceived by 1917, were flexible barrages, infiltration methods and training in small groups. Haig's orders demonstrate that all were beyond his grasp.

Concrete, mud and rain supplemented by an immensity of shells, a novel gas and a strategy of retreat within a deep defensive position would have baffled generals better briefed and more talented than Haig. When the British attack was launched on 31 July, the result was therefore not unexpected. In the run-up to battle, British artillery had prepared for the advance by depositing five tons of shells on to each square yard of a thinly occupied German forward position. These shells had inflicted only 5 per cent casualties and in doing so created a bog which slowed the British advance and set up a perfect target for German machine-gunners and counter-attack battalions, each of them protected by concrete shelters of massive thickness during the preliminary bombardment. Charteris recorded the result in a letter home twenty-four hours after the first attack. 'The Germans succeeded in turning back our centre by counter-attacking on the right flank in considerable strength.'

On the second day, Haig sent an equally gloomy report to the Cabinet: 'The enemy is fully prepared for our attack. He has several positions in the rear and has several divisions in reserve. No rapid progress is therefore to be expected.'[20]

Ninety-six hours into the battle, Haig's second dispatch reinforced that initial impression. 'As rain continues, I cannot say when it will be possible to continue the offensive. There will have to be a struggle for aerial and artillery supremacy before the attack is launched. Ground is reported to be as bad as last winter on the Somme and Ancre.'[21] It was a surprisingly candid admission of failure and Haig's bewilderment was shown in a plaintive circular sent to army commanders a week later: 'Is it not necessary to consider the capacity of infantry training and discipline as well as artillery?'[22]

A quick breakthrough had been Haig's only real chance of success.

Once German counter-measures eliminated that possibility, Haig was facing a prolonged slogging match. What of the condition of his Army when the slogging match began and which side was likely to outlast its opponent?

There was general agreement on the state of the Germans. In February 1917, the War Office suggested that the Germans had one million men in training depots and another two million available for military service if required.[23] By shortening their front line that spring, the Germans added forty-five divisions to this reserve (a German division held 12,000 men) and Charteris suggested that if the Germans defeated Russia in summer 1917, as seemed possible, twenty more divisions could be sent to the Western Front by the end of the year.[24]

The British had no answer to such abundance. After telling the Cabinet on 1 May that he was 60,000 below establishment, Derby informed Haig that home reserves were 'down to the bedrock'. He was therefore under no illusion and at the start of July told army commanders, 'The drafts available to replace casualties are limited in number. It is essential we shall conserve the energy of officers and men so that we may outstay the enemy.'[25]

Nor did the situation improve at any time during the battle. Many British divisions had begun the battle 4,000 men short of their 13,000 strength, and when losses mounted Haig was driven to stop-gaps like clearing VD hospitals for front-line duty. Even the War Office became uneasy, and Robertson sent a query to GHQ about its low casualty returns. Haig's reply conceded that many British divisions were down to half their establishment by September 1917.

The big question which has always been asked of Passchendaele confronts the reader forcibly at this point. The only hope for the British had been a clean breakthrough, achieved early and fuelled by bountiful reserves. In the first week of August, it was clear to everyone that the possibility of victory no longer existed. There had been no breakthrough. Men were short. Why then did the Cabinet allow Haig to press ahead and why was he so keen to do so?

The need to confront the U-boat danger and destroy German bases on the Flemish coast is usually offered as the key factor, supported by an assertion that U-boat activity came within measurable distance of starving Britain into submission in 1917. This argument must now be discarded. In May 1917, Esher had a personal briefing from the Quartermaster General and discovered, to his surprise, that Britain held a vast stock of potatoes and had sufficient meat to last two and a half years.[26] She was getting 110,000 of the 130,000 tons of grain required daily, and if there were any shortfalls in grain the deficiency could be made up from the 6½ million tons of barley and 21 million tons of oats which were produced each year. Haig's own comment on the situation was therefore terse. Describing a meeting of the Cabinet's War Policy Committee on 20 June, he told his diary: 'Jellicoe was feeble and vacillating. No one shared Jellicoe's views and all were satisfied with the food situation.'

By May, it appeared that a U-boat threat, which seemed critical at the end of 1916, had become equally insignificant. Sims, an American admiral with authority to open any drawer at the Admiralty, noted the breakthrough in spring 1917.[27] Electronic eavesdropping on the nightly position reports which U-boats had to send home, together with the invention of the depth charge and the fact that they were building only three U-boats weekly, meant that the Germans could keep only twenty of them at sea at any moment. If they had realized the potential of U-boats and built them as ferociously as howitzers and machine guns, things would have been different.[28] As it was, the only serious problem facing the Cabinet in autumn 1917 was the reluctance of the Admiralty to accept either the convoy system or the electronic Intelligence it was offered. Once again, human obtuseness rather than enemy machinery posed the gravest threat to Britain.

The need to bolster faltering allies is another pretext frequently put forward – and with more substance – for pressing on towards Passchendaele village. The condition of France gave London little concern after June 1917, since the Cabinet knew that French passivity was the result of a considered policy of waiting for American troops to arrive in sufficient numbers. Russia was a different matter, and the possibility of German divisions being transferred from Russia to the Western Front generated moments of panic. Political and military opinion was divided over whether Britain should fight a big battle to distract the Germans or evacuate the BEF, but there was no easy solution and the dilemma was often discussed up to August 1918.

In April 1917, for example, Esher gave Haig his personal opinion. Delaying Passchendaele might lead Russia to make peace and the disintegration of the Entente before the Americans appeared. On the other hand, might not it be better 'To look after our own narrow interests and secure our own safety re your enormous army cooped up in an angle of French territory'?

The king pondered the same conundrum in August. His judgement was often simplistic and expressed in language which would bring a blush to the cheek of a Smithfield meat porter – or so Lord Geddes thought – but he was an earnest man, a compulsive reader of State papers and the recipient of a massive correspondence from commanders on all fronts. He was therefore among the best informed of men and when he heard that Haig planned to extend his battle front in the Salient during the fourth week of August, an anxious monarch checked with the Earl of Cavan, who was commanding the 14th Corps at the time. His letter is not in the public domain, but its contents can be inferred from Cavan's reply: 'I thank Your Majesty for the haunch of venison. If the surface at Langemarck were dry, we would just get over it. If not, we would sink to our armpits. I assure Your Majesty that the decision of the Commander in Chief to press the right forward by the help of the next army was a very sound one though it must take a little time to prepare. Even if Russia made peace and France did the same, I am convinced that the navy could get us home and could, in conjunction with the Americans, absolutely forbid the sea to any German merchantman for ever.'[29]

The British were therefore concerned about their allies and, more particularly, with the possibility of débâcle in Russia, which would threaten the BEF with the full weight of the German Army and the possibility of a permanent German presence in the Low Countries.

A letter Charteris sent his wife in April 1917 showed that GHQ were thinking along the same lines. Lloyd George, he wrote, accepted his suggestion that the Germans would make a seductive peace offer within a few months with the object of splitting the allies. Charteris's was a far-sighted point and one he elaborated for the Cabinet (with Haig's endorsement) in a GHQ paper later that month. 'On the allied side, the pressure of war is becoming very acutely felt,' Charteris argued. 'It seems probable that whatever the outcome of operations this year, the desire for peace will decide the war before it is fought to a military decision. If this is so, the bargaining at the conference would decide who is to gain the fruits of the war. For this reason, in all our military operations we must bear in mind the desirability of depriving Germany of her assets in bargaining' – in other words, get hold of the coastline of the Narrow Seas quickly.[30]

There was nothing new here. The Low Countries had been a central preoccupation of the Pitts. Grey had constantly urged the importance of the region at the start of the war,[31] and in June 1917 Milner suggested to the Cabinet's War Policy Committee that the coast of Belgium was worth the lives of half a million soldiers.[32] It was a patriotic calculation and one which underpinned the basic reason for pressing on at Ypres long after the possibility of deep penetration had disappeared. A tempting peace offer by Germany might end the war before the Narrow Seas were in the bag. What that meant Kitchener had already told Haig in January 1916: 'Unless we can impose peace by force of arms this year, we shall run a terrible risk of an unsatisfactory stalemate peace which will certainly necessitate hostilities again in about five years when we shall have few allies and be unprepared.'[33]

In September 1917, the much feared peace offer was indeed made and Lloyd George went immediately to France to brief Haig in person.[34] 'The offer is known to be *bona fide*,' said Lloyd George. 'It would leave Germany stronger than at the start of the war. If the public knew of it, the allies might stop fighting.' In that sentence lay the root of the last bloody push on Passchendaele village. The American ambassador sensed as much and wrote to President Wilson: 'Confidential. The British Foreign Office has had this telegram from the ambassador at Madrid for a fortnight. Balfour remarked that he thought too prompt an answer would be bad diplomacy. I have no doubt that another reason for waiting so long to reply to it was the wish to see the result of the battles in France which Haig has won and that these victories make a reply now more opportune.'[35]

The terms which gave such a fright to British politicians were a free hand in Russia in return for the restoration of Germany's gains in the West and the Balkans. There was certainly much to be said for accepting the offer, and after examining the terms pragmatically

Balfour pronounced them 'so favourable that I am suspicious there must be a sinister objective'. Hankey agreed, noting with surprise how 'extraordinarily reasonable' they were.[36]

It was a crucial moment in the war. A secret meeting was called at Lloyd George's Welsh retreat on 24 September to discuss the response. The cover story was that the meeting had been convened to discuss the sacking of Haig, but the date fits the peace offer too closely, the more so since a full Cabinet meeting discussed the German proposals within a week.[37] As a researcher might expect, no record survives of that session. It would hardly have done to put on record a discussion which balanced blood and profit so nakedly. The Cabinet's shorthand writers had therefore been ordered out of the room.

The final decision should surprise no one. The Cabinet was always likely to favour going on with the war and pressing ahead with a battle which seemed to offer the best prospect of getting hold of the North Sea coast.

Haig's reasoning, on the other hand, is less easily fathomed, since the tone of his correspondence at the time verges on mental derangement. One letter to Robertson gives an example: 'The only point I am not in accord with you is the desirability of issuing such pessimistic estimates from your Intelligence branch. They do, I feel sure, much harm. This being the decisive point, the only *sound* policy is for the government to support me *wholeheartedly* and concentrate all possible reserves here. In this Army, we are convinced we can beat the enemy provided we are kept up to strength. Our opinion is based on the actual *facts*, viz. the poor state of the German troops, the high standard of efficiency of our own, the power of our artillery to dominate the enemy's fire etc. An occasional glance at our daily Intelligence summaries would convince even the most sceptical of the truth of what I write. Moreover, I have been in the field now for three years and know what I am writing about. The foreigners have constantly misled our government. The views which I have always held and expressed as to the decisive effect on the enemy of a blow north of the Lys are daily shown to be sound. In my opinion, the war can only be won in Flanders. If the war were to end tomorrow, Britain would find herself the greatest power in the world. The chief

people to suffer would be the Socialists who are trying to rule us all
the time when the right-minded of the nation are so engaged on the
country's battles that the Socialists are left free to work their mischief.' [38] One might perhaps add Roman Catholics to Haig's bestiary
of foreigners and Socialists, since other writings at this time show
him assured that Macdonogh's Intelligence work at the War Office
formed part of a Catholic–pacifist conspiracy which spanned Europe.

And yet, beneath these absurdities, two solid reasons bolster
Haig's urge to continue the battle through October and even into
November. The first had been supplied by Kitchener, who was one
of the few men whose judgement Haig always respected. Kitchener
had made his point during a discussion with Charteris in 1915:
'Never let me hear from the Intelligence services of piercing the line.
You are not fighting the troops in front of you. You are fighting the
manhood of a great power. Lean against the line. Press it hard and
press it continuously. After some time, you will find the line will
move backwards. But you will never pierce it.' [39]

In January 1916, Kitchener had developed this idea for Haig and
fitted it with a timescale: 'We shall want a whole year of fighting to
bring about a state of things under which Germany will be obliged
to sue for peace. To push Germany backwards may very probably
take till August if we start in March. You must allow three months
after that to make them accept terms of peace that will be satisfactory
to the French and to ourselves.'

Haig's correspondence suggests that he accepted Kitchener's
opinion. In July 1917, for example, Kiggell, Haig's Chief of Staff,
told the king of Haig's view: 'If the weather does not prove very
unduly unkind and if we get two or three months of straight, hard
fighting in on this front before the winter, the results may well be far
greater than many people dare allow themselves.' [40] Three weeks into
the battle, Haig repeated that view for his army commanders: 'By
making one great effort and continuing it for the next few months,
it is possible a decision may be reached this year. It is essential to
keep going till November.' [41]

The best military Intelligence available reinforced Haig's thinking
and gave him a second solid reason for pressing on. The Intelligence
services, both British and French, believed that the Germans were

planning a big retreat and would put it into effect if only they were kept under sufficient pressure. Rumours to that effect had begun when Hindenburg replaced Falkenhayn in command of the Western Front during the Somme, and right through 1917 a continuous flow of information seemed to support the credibility of those rumours. Examples can be taken from many sources, but the following are representative:

1 July: Rawlinson wrote in his diary that Humbert (on the staff at Pétain's headquarters) stated that if the Nivelle offensive had succeeded, the Germans would have gone right back to Hirson for the winter.

12 July: Neville Lytton, a press officer at GHQ, told Bean that if the Nivelle battle had succeeded, the Germans would have gone right back to the Meuse.

27 August: American Intelligence reported that factories were being dismantled within 40 km of the German front line.

30 August: Clive (one of GHQ's men with the French) noted Pétain's belief that the line would not be broken in 1917 but that the Germans would shorten it voluntarily.

31 August: The Cabinet's War Policy Committee concluded that Germany had 620,000 reserves, which meant that maintenance of fighting at a Somme level would force their '1920 Class' to the front by January 1918, thus obliging a retreat between Lille and Verdun – a conclusion in line with Charteris's supposedly 'optimistic' analysis.

1 September: American Intelligence reported the evacuation of Roulers and the strengthening of fortifications around Eccloe, ten miles north-west of Ghent.

3 September: Esher noted information from Belgium and Holland suggesting that a twelve-mile retirement was in preparation.

2 November: Haig wrote to the War Office that French Intelligence had reported German withdrawal in Flanders. Haig stated that he did not believe it would happen so soon and that he was preparing a battle at Cambrai to force this retreat.

Though official records passed to the Record Office have been scrupulously sanitized and references to the possibility of any German withdrawal extracted, politicians were certainly aware of Intelligence reports at the time and were obviously attracted by them. Imperial War Cabinet minutes are generally fuller than British Cabinet records during the war and they let the cat out of a bag which Hankey, the Cabinet Secretary, must have believed claw-proof. The key passage comes from the Imperial War Cabinet minutes for August 1918. Lloyd George told the Dominion representatives: 'In September 1917 the government had done its best to stop the Passchendaele attack. We must not be led again into operations on the bright anticipation of the enemy running away.' [42]

Cabinet and GHQ thus combined to set up that crowning blunder of 1917 – the final push up the slope to Passchendaele village itself.

Haig's plan for that final advance was based on an injection of Dominion troops to give extra push. [43] The Australians were thus scheduled to capture Passchendaele village on 12 October. The Cavalry Corps and Canadians would then push on to the vital rail junction of Roulers and cut off the Germans on the coast.

The preparatory work for this big attack was scheduled for two British divisions, and on 10 October Plumer reported to Haig that the job had been done to his complete satisfaction. 'I am of the opinion that the 49th and 66th Divisions carried out today an assembly which will afford the Australians a good jumping-off line on the 12th.'

The facts were different. The 66th had never been in battle before and had moved forward under the impression that they were going into support. [44] Without food or water for twenty-four hours, the division arrived so late on the battlefield that the covering barrage had to be brought back. Since the gunners were not in direct contact with the front line, they opened fire on their own men and cut the 66th to pieces. Birdwood brought this tragedy to GHQ's attention, but the divisional commander involved countered by demanding the name of Birdwood's informant (he was in fact one of the Tasmanian Maxwells, a family distinguished by a vast array of military decorations won in the field) and threatened to block all promotion within the Australian Corps unless he withdrew his witness. This episode, with its mixture of chance and gross ineptitude, would have been lost to us but for the eye witness of Charles Bean, and no doubt that caustic observer of military folly relished the Tolstoyan twist which promoted the 66th's commander to the post of Chief of Staff, GHQ, within three months.

Despite the failure of the 66th Division, Haig sent in the Australian attack with confidence. 'I expect we will have Passchendaele village tonight all right,' he told his wife. 'The New Zealand and Australian 3rd Division are to put the Australian flag in the church there.' That attack was, of course, a fiasco, and at the end of the day the Anzacs were back where they started after taking 60 per cent casualties. 'I stopped the attack early in the day,' Haig wrote laconically. 'The ground was quite impossible.'

The Canadians were next ordered to replace the Anzacs and they sent two Staff Officers to report on the position. One of them was William Ironside, a giant who served Buchan as a model for Hannay and later became a Field Marshal. His report was damning. 'I found the front quite indefinite. There were wounded and dead Australians all over the place and nobody was doing anything. I had to organize the line and place machine guns myself. No German was to be seen. There was no firing [Ironside was writing forty-eight hours after the battle]. One could walk anywhere in the front. No Australian brigadier had been up. Hopeless confusion. The single road to Zillebeke was being mended and used at the same time. Continuously shelled.'[45]

Ironside's colleague was Morrisson, the Canadian artillery chief who damned 'the camouflage of misinformation and the pose that everything was all right' after he discovered that 60 per cent of the Salient's guns were either clogged with mud or knocked out from excessive wear. They were also too far back, concentrated in two groups and out of communication with each other. In the course of a last effort to locate the number of guns he was supposed to have, Morrisson paused to watch sixteen Gotha bombers lumber across the sky in double column, drop 150 bombs and depart at their own pace without a single shot from British anti-aircraft guns.

The result of such chronic disorganization was that Haig had to allow the Canadians an extra week of preparation, which incidentally gives us a valuable insight into Haig's state of mind through the jottings of the Canadian Corps' chief artillery Staff Officer, Lt.-Col. Alan Brooke (he was to become 1st Viscount Alanbrooke, Field Marshal, late in his career). After listening to one of Haig's briefings in October 1917 he wrote: 'I attended a conference which Haig ran at Canadian headquarters. I could hardly believe that my ears were not deceiving me. He spoke in the rosiest terms of our chances of breaking through. I had been all over the ground and, to my mind, such an eventuality was quite impossible. I was certain that he was misinformed and had never seen the ground himself.'[46]

The final attack on Passchendaele village was described by Borden, the Canadian Prime Minister, in a speech lasting an hour at the Imperial War Cabinet on 13 June 1918. He spoke with mounting anger and concluded his denunciation by striding up to Lloyd George, seizing his lapels and shaking him. 'Since our last meeting,' Borden had said, 'I sent for General Currie and ordered him to tell me the truth so far as he understood it with respect to the occurrences of the past few months. Whenever the Canadian Corps was called upon to attack, Currie always had his attacking troops in the trenches at least thirty-six hours before the time fixed for the attack in order that officers and men might become acquainted with the nature of the ground and learn precisely where the objective lay. On one of his flanks, a British battalion came into the trenches the night before the attack. Four companies wandered over to the Canadians in the morning and asked if the Canadians knew where they should go. Two of these companies stationed themselves at a point which proved to be about 100 yards ahead of the barrage. When the barrage lifted, these two companies became non-existent. The two supporting companies, in their confusion, attacked the Canadians. Currie was informed he was supported by 364 guns but he found only 220. When he asked for more guns, he was asked to send indents. He said he could not fight the Germans with indents. He wanted guns and he could not get them . . .'

According to severely pruned Cabinet minutes, Massey, the New Zealand Prime Minster, was next to speak. 'I was told last night by a reliable man – a man I knew years ago before he joined the Army – that the New Zealanders (he was one of them) were asked to do the impossible. He said they were sent to Passchendaele, to a swampy locality where it was almost impossible to walk and where they found themselves up against particularly strong wire entanglements which it was impossible for them to cut. They were, he said, simply shot down like rabbits. These are the sort of things that are going to lead to serious trouble.'

Currie described conditions in the front line graphically, but in that final thrust conditions in the rear were little better. A young gunner subaltern, John Mortimer Wheeler, later to become one of the most distinguished archaeologists of his generation, described them in a letter home on 29 October which was typical of many in October–November 1917: 'I cannot attempt to describe the conditions under which we are fighting. Anything I could write about them would seem an exaggeration but would, in reality, be miles below the truth. The whole battlefield for miles is a congested mess of sodden, rain-filled shell holes which are being added to every moment. The mud is not so much mud as a fathomless, sticky morass. The shell holes, where they do not actually merge into one another, are divided only by a few inches of this glutinous mud. There is no cover and it is of course impossible to dig. If it were not for the cement pillboxes left by the Boche, not a thing could live for many hours. The guns are all in the open and – most phantastic of all – many of them are in full view of the Boche. I must not say much about my own battery's position but to give you some idea of it, our gun was in water up to its breech and when it recoiled, the breech splashed under water. The gunners work thigh-deep in water.' [47]

By the second week of November, it was all over. The village of Passchendaele had been captured and fighting in the Salient had come to an uneasy end. The Canadians went into rest. Mortimer Wheeler went on leave. So what had been gained by the crucifixion at Passchendaele?

If success in battle is measured by the value of ground, the final position had little to commend it. Nine days after taking Passchendaele, even Haig admitted that 'The positions we hold fall far short of what we wished and would be costly to hold if seriously attacked.' [48] Hunter-Weston, who took charge of the Salient when fighting ceased, agreed with Haig's assessment: 'If the Germans think it worthwhile to put in an attack in force against this silly Salient, I fear we would be certain to lose it.'[49]

Casualties suffered on each side have been the customary measure of success in battle, and the debate over Passchendaele has been bitterly contested for seventy years.

The British Official History put British casualties at 238,000, but there are many indications that Edmonds's figure was much too low. The War Office's calculations, published in 1922 and based on the weekly returns of the Adjutant General's department, recorded a figure of 775,000 British casualties for the whole Western Front during 1917. Since the number of divisions thrown into Passchendaele was 40 per cent of the total committed to battle in 1917,[50] one would expect casualty statistics close to 350,000, and several well-informed sources support such a figure. Bean, for example, was able to use his privileged position as Australian official historian to make inquiries during the 1920s. The statistic Edmonds gave him in confidence for Passchendaele was 332,432, specifically excluding the 45,000 British casualties of Cambrai in November 1917.

Jan Smuts proposed an even higher figure when he replied to Borden's accusations in the Imperial War Cabinet during June 1918.[51] It would hardly have been in the Cabinet's interest to exaggerate losses, yet Smuts told the Dominion representatives: 'It is remarkable that with a change in our naval policy, the situation from the naval point of view has been largely retrieved. What the Army could not do in six months [Smuts includes Messines with Passchendaele] at a loss of half a million men, the Navy in two nights achieved completely and Ostend and Zeebrugge were sealed up [Smuts was referring to the Zeebrugge raid on 23 April].' That same figure of half a million was mentioned by Sidney Clive when he recorded Haig's quiet comment at the end of Passchendaele – 'Have we really lost half a million men?'

The gap between a quarter and half million suggests that an accurate figure will never be established, but it is clear enough that the official historian's 238,000 is insufficient. What of the Germans?

Edmonds's own calculations began with the statement of Kuhl, the Chief Staff Officer involved, that sixty-three divisions had been withdrawn from the German battle area. Edmonds therefore suggested a figure of 310,000 casualties on the assumption that German divisions were not extracted from battle until they had lost 50 per cent of their attacking strength. He then added an extra 25 per cent to cover the lightly wounded, which he believed to have been omitted from German records.[52]

If Edmonds was right, the Germans had lost more heavily than the British, but his figures have many defects. The Cabinet Office spotted the most obvious when they checked his figures and discovered the true total should have been 362,000 – using Edmonds's own criteria correctly.[53]

Other weaknesses were of a more military nature. The 50 per cent figure, for example, was lifted straight out of Charteris's work papers and based on a study Charteris made of German casualty lists back in 1916. The problem is that, by autumn 1917, the Germans were rotating their divisions fast and keeping them in the line for less than a week. On 6 August, even Haig remarked that 'Charteris thinks there must be some underlying reason for this rapid rotation of divisions other than casualties'. Nor is it easy to see how the Germans could have suffered more heavily than the British, since they were spread out thinly, at great depth, and were supported throughout by more effective artillery.

As regards the 25 per cent added by Edmonds for the lightly wounded, Bean gave his researcher specific instructions to check German statistics in Potsdam in the early twenties and find out whether or not German casualty figures had included this category. His researcher duly discovered that they had, as did Swinton, who was researching for Lloyd George at the time.[54]

What conclusion is the reader to draw? Milner, probably one of the best-informed Cabinet Ministers at the time and Lloyd George's right-hand man during Passchendaele, stated bluntly that the Germans had lost far fewer men than the British. He thought their loss two thirds of the British, probably less.[55] It was a judgement about as near to finality as we are likely to get three generations later, with the Cabinet Office sitting tightly on the statistics which could resolve the matter in a few minutes.

If German losses were substantially less, what of the possibility that British pressure during Passchendaele weakened the German Army to a greater degree than raw casualty figures might suggest?

Surviving statistics give cold comfort.[56] Captures of men and weaponry give a rough indication of the amount of pressure applied and for the big battles of 1917 these read:

	Prisoners	Guns
Arras, first 35 days	21,000	252
Messines, first 5 days	7,200	67
Passchendaele, first 99 days	20,000	55

Figures for the rotation of German divisions through Passchendaele reinforce the impression of an opponent able to meet the demands of the battle with relative ease. These are in a confidential memorandum from GHQ's Intelligence branch which give the monthly total of enemy divisions serving a first and second time in the Salient.[57] The final results were set out in tabular form:

	First time	Second time
August	35	0
September	14	5
October	21	9
November	8	11

The remarkable fact emerging from this table is that the Germans put only half the number of divisions through Passchendaele proportionate to the total number in their army and none of them more than twice. In comparison, 25 per cent of British divisions fighting in the Salient did so more than twice, and 20 per cent served four times or more. Nor did any German divisions go in for a second spell before they had rested at least two months. Charteris unearthed the fact and reckoned that German divisions were restored to full establishment within fourteen days of leaving a battle, which meant that German divisions, unlike their British counterparts, had time to rebuild, train and maintain some sort of *esprit de corps*.

Most of Passchendaele's statistics have been withheld from the Public Record Office, but the implications of those we can read are as clear to us as they were to those in a position to know the facts at the time. Josiah Wedgwood, a radical MP related to the Cecils by marriage, was one of those who did know what was happening. His memoirs describe a graphic eyewitness account of the battlefield he delivered to the House of Commons. On leaving the Chamber, Bonar Law came over from the government's front bench and said to him, 'You did right to say what you did but never let any of that be known outside. The public could not bear it.' [58]

7

Cambrai

The battle of Cambrai began on 20 November 1917. Early that morning, nineteen British divisions and three tank brigades attacked six German divisions with the idea of breaching the Hindenburg Line. Given the relatively small numbers involved, the attack must have seemed more a large-scale raid than a battle, but two features gave the action disproportionate importance in the history of the war.

Liddell Hart had one of these in mind when he described Cambrai as 'one of the landmarks in the history of warfare, the dawn of a new epoch'. Previous battles had been preceded by weeks of shelling before the infantry set off and advanced over a lunar landscape for months on end. Cambrai was different. There was no preliminary bombardment (Haig's diary shows him ignorant of the fact!) and 381 tanks began the battle by advancing over a virgin landscape which might have been the best grazing land in Oxfordshire. On the first day, the British advanced five miles. Ten days later, the Germans drove them back in a fierce counter-attack marked by small groups of specialist infantrymen supported by low-flying aircraft. From start to finish, Cambrai lasted less than a fortnight and, in many ways, it looked forward to the *Blitzkrieg* battles of the Second World War.

The second feature was Haig's role in the battle. Censorship meant that few knew the facts at the time, but Milner had been touring the front during the battle and he returned with a lurid outline of events and the information that Haig had taken command in person throughout. This meant that the battle offers an unrivalled opportunity to discover what Haig had learnt from two years as Commander in Chief, since it was fought by British troops throughout, had been subject to minimal interference from politicians or allies and was the last battle before Foch took charge as Generalissimo.

There was certainly nothing of improvisation or haste about Haig's original conception. That went back to September 1916, when a push on Cambrai had been part of his scheme to exploit German panic after the second big push on the Somme. In the event, the September battles misfired and Cambrai was shelved. A year later, Haig picked up the old scheme as part of a wider exploitation of that big German retreat he hoped for in Flanders, but by that stage he was alone. Byng, Commander of the 3rd Army, and Davidson, Haig's Director of Military Operations, had urged Cambrai upon him during August without success, and when the short days and heavy rains of winter began both men gave up their advocacy.[1] Haig's belated decision therefore met strong opposition from the generals and staffs who had to work up the battle at short notice.[2]

Speaking to the Canadian Corps after the battle, Byng was one of many who recalled Haig's decision with bitterness. 'In the second week of October, I saw the C. in C. and he made then what I think and I am sure history will agree was a very great decision. He said that in spite of having to send troops to Italy; in spite of not going ahead in the north as much as he wanted; in spite of only being able to give me divisions which had been over the top a great many times, he was determined to carry out the operation. This is a decision to which only history will be able to do justice.'[3]

Brigadier Tandy, a GSO1 in GHQ's Operations section, witnessed the same response at GHQ when he was summoned to the initial planning conference. He was asked what men were available. Haig suggested the Australians. Tandy reminded him that Dominion forces could only be used with all their divisions fighting together. Haig next mentioned two or three other units which he had offered to Byng. Tandy again ruled them out. None would have had time to absorb its drafts. 'I thought he would eat me,' Tandy recalled, 'and he would have if I had been one of his Chief Staff Officers but he was too big a man to bully a humble member of the band. That evening he said that only Kiggell, Davidson, Birch, Vaughan [the 3rd Army's Chief Staff Officer] and Elles [i/c Tank Corps] knew. When the others were told, I have never seen a more horrified bunch of generals – twenty or thirty of them. All agreed they needed double the time and three times the available resources.'4

Not content with forcing a major battle on unwilling subordinates and giving them just four weeks to prepare, Haig went on to overrule Byng on matters of depth and frontage.

In September, Byng had offered to capture Cambrai if he was given the Canadian Corps. Haig accepted these terms, but the Canadians were sent away to Flanders after an unexpected Australian failure at Passchendaele in mid-October. Byng's immediate response was to scale down his offer, telling Haig that he could guarantee only the capture of two bridges across the Canal du Nord (a massive barrier across his front) and pass a small cavalry force over those bridges and on to the crossing points of the river Sensée, due west of Cambrai. If these were taken, British infantry could advance next day and occupy Bourlon Wood – a dominating height in the battle area. A raid of this sort might well force the Germans to retreat between the Sensée and Arras to the north, thus registering a small victory and raising British morale at the end of a disastrous year.5

Haig disagreed and put forward his own proposal on 3 November. The whole Cavalry Corps was to be pushed through the breach on the first day. It would surround Cambrai and allow the infantry to capture it. The cavalry would then gallop off to the distant rail junction of Valenciennes. The infantry were to seize Bourlon Wood meanwhile as part of their first-day assignment and then go on to Douai, another distant rail junction.6 It was a wildly over-ambitious plan, assuming a deeper advance by larger bodies of men than had been seen on the Western Front since stalemate set in at the end of 1914.

Confronted by Haig's grandiose vision, Byng countered by revising his assessment of the battle frontage he could manage. Boxed in by the Sensée marshes to the west and a sharp southward bend in the German line to the east, his mind turned to those monstrous traffic jams which marked most previous battles. He therefore urged that

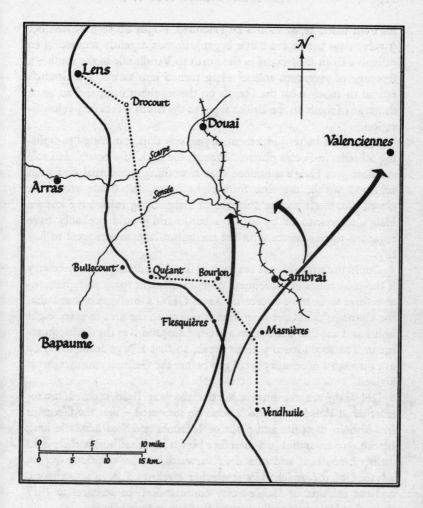

6 THE STRATEGIC INTENTION AT CAMBRAI

As on the Somme, Haig's plan was to use a kink in the German line to lever it open. The important rail junctions of Douai and Valenciennes were rich prizes. Crossing points over the river Sensée made a suitable intermediate objective because capture would threaten the enemy's line of supply to the Drocourt–Quéant position, otherwise all but impregnable, as the allies discovered in autumn 1918.

his own battle front should be extended. Right up to 8 November (twelve days before the battle began), he was urgently requesting an offensive from Bullecourt in the north to Vendhuille in the south – a frontage of seventeen miles.[7] Haig turned him down. De Goutte's refusal to attack with the French on the southern flank and an acute shortage of shells on the British front to the north were cited in justification.

Against his better judgement, Byng was thus committed to fighting a battle, in Foch's phrase, 'through the neck of a bottle'. His sole comfort was Haig's assurance that if nothing substantial had been achieved within the first forty-eight hours, the battle would be closed down. As a close associate of Haig, Byng must have known Haig's reluctance to let go of a battle and would probably have regarded this assurance with the pessimism later events were to justify.

Could the gamble have succeeded? Two conditions were necessary if the constraints of inadequate time, insufficient space and questionable force were to be overcome. Since GHQ's Intelligence knew that the Germans could get four fresh divisions to the area in forty-eight hours and another ten within a week,[8] surprise was the first requirement. The second was a clean break, so that a large force could be got through a necessarily small gap before the German reinforcements arrived.

Did Haig achieve surprise? After the war Bean ordered his researcher at Potsdam to check what he suspected – that the Germans had known the time and place of Messines and Passchendaele long before zero hour and had therefore been able to withdraw their own artillery, re-site it and thin their forward infantry positions well in advance of the attack. His researcher confirmed Bean's suspicions, and the minutes of Haig's army commanders' conferences in 1917 show that Haig was well aware of that fact at the time.

If the Germans knew about past battles in advance, how could they have possibly remained ignorant of 100 guns and 400 tanks moving towards the Cambrai sector? Not only was their electronic eavesdropping well ahead of that of the allies but, as Byng later told the Canadians in his address, 'Train movements are a subject of conversation for a lot of people in the back areas and train movements for Cambrai were rather complicated owing to the fact that we had to rail up 460 tanks. Our own carrying power for them was under sixty so we had to borrow, largely from the French. People on the railways saw this procession of tanks and it was rather difficult to stop them talking . . .'

The Germans were given additional assistance through information leaked at high level. 'There is no doubt that some people in England may have talked far more than was wise,' Byng told his audience. 'But as to this, I have nothing to say.' The discreet Byng was equally reluctant to mention leakage at a lower level. Just ninety-six hours before zero, the Germans captured four prisoners from the 16th (Irish) Division who gave away details of sufficient importance to reach the private diary of Aylmer Haldane, a corps commander.

The Germans were therefore well primed and took counter-measures, moving men back from the front line and bringing up reinforcements[9] – though a reader will find no mention of this in the Official History or any of the standard accounts. The result was the British bumped up against a German force, estimated by Charteris at four divisions and by Haig at five,[10] on a front normally occupied by one and a half German divisions. German front-line positions were also thinned down as they had been ahead of Messines and Passchendaele. Writing to Edmonds later, Brigadier Burn commented on the fact, recalling his surprise at the scarcity of enemy wounded and dead.[11] Walking the line that first evening, he had been able to find only thirty German corpses on his divisional front.

Surprise, one of the two prerequisites for success, had not been achieved. Haig's intervention made it certain that a clean break followed by a swift forward movement was equally certain to fail.

Whatever post-war histories may say, there had been no great problem in getting an attacking force of the right size together, despite Passchendaele. Byng demanded seven infantry divisions for the attack and Haig arranged to give him that number in conjunction with Pétain.[12] Byng went on to ask for seven divisions in the second wave and Pétain obliged with five infantry and three cavalry divisions.

After getting the right number of troops for the attack, Haig went on to make two important blunders. He insisted firstly that the

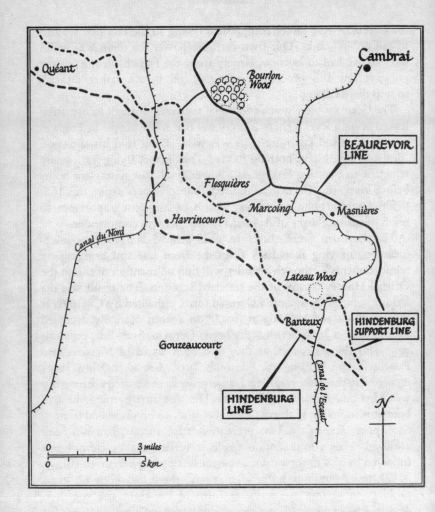

7 THE CAMBRAI BATTLEFIELD, November 1917

Cambrai, like Passchendaele, was an attack (in Foch's phrase) 'through the neck of a bottle' with two deep, wide canals limiting the attack's frontage. The switch trenches linking the Beaurevoir and Hindenburg support lines further strengthened the German hold on this bottleneck and served as an outpost for the commanding height of Bourlon Wood. The canal bridge at Masnières seemed to offer an easy way round the tough nut of Flesquières – on the map, at least.

whole Cavalry Corps must pass through the breach on the first day,[13] which in turn meant that the cavalry had to be close to the front and near the key bridges over the Canal du Nord. Since the French refused to take extra line on the southern flank, the troops Pétain offered had to be placed where they were directly linked to their own supply line and would not disrupt Byng's back area.[14] This meant putting them behind the British Cavalry Corps.

It was a dangerous conjunction. The postulate 'If something should happen, then something else can happen' had brought disaster throughout the war, from the notorious August offensive at Gallipoli onwards. Now everything hinged on a fast breach in the German line so that cavalry could move and make space for the French to advance. Haig made his second blunder at this point.

Even before 1914, he knew that cavalry had no offensive power against unbroken infantry and had stated the point in his pre-war manoeuvres.[15] This lack of bite meant that in planning the first attack Haig had to make sure that the final German line would be captured early in the battle, and it was the provision he made for capturing that Beaurevoir Line, just the other side of the Canal du Nord, which was to prove a particularly costly error.

The British divisions which had been selected to start the battle had to advance in six bounds, stopping twice for half an hour to re-group. This movement would bring them to the Beaurevoir Line if everything went according to plan, but Haig suspected a big advance like that would be exhausting. To make sure of it, he therefore added an extra division for the critical assault on the Beaurevoir position itself. It was an imaginative idea, but the orders given to this division were to play a key role in the battle's failure.

De Lisle's 29th Division had always been regarded as an elite unit, from the Helles landing at Gallipoli to the assault of Pozières on the first day of the Somme.[16] Haig now chose it to replace the Canadians and gave the news to De Lisle on 9 October. There seems to have been no further communication until 15 November when, just five days before the battle, De Lisle was formally notified that his men were to form the spearhead at Cambrai. Their job was to march south from Ypres over five days and make a final approach by night so as to deceive German reconnaissance aircraft.

The end result was predictable. A division weakened by fighting at Passchendaele went straight into another major battle without a break. The night before the battle, the 29th Division marched ten miles to the edge of the battlefield in full battle order before marching another three miles at dawn and going straight into action. It was an astonishing piece of planning on Haig's part. A cavalry officer who saw them that day told Edmonds later that 'the 29th marched through our forces. They looked very tired. Marcoing was their objective and they did not look like men about to take it.'[17]

Tiredness was not their only problem. At one point during the first morning, the division was ordered to halt because of enfilade artillery fire from a wood at the north-east corner of the battlefield. The gun involved was quickly crushed by an unmanned tank, but no further orders arrived. Sensing unnecessary delay, De Lisle on his own initiative issued orders to move. A second lengthy delay then followed when the division reached the ruins of Marcoing village and stopped for thirty minutes for tired men to fill their water bottles in a deserted brewery.

These delays were the straw which broke the back of the battle plan. Fighting in the third week of November meant eight hours of practicable daylight. The depth of enemy defences was about three miles and the town of Cambrai six miles from the closest point on the British line. Set against Edmonds's calculation that the average rate of advance in successful battles was, at best, one mile an hour, Byng had been given only the finest of margins within which to work. An exhausted spearhead division arriving late failed to breach the Beaurevoir Line. Since the line was unbroken, the cavalry were unable to move and if the cavalry couldn't move, the French were blocked. Observing the battle on behalf of the Americans, Pershing summed it all up laconically: 'The British cavalry spoiled the plan of cooperation with the French.' The spearhead had proved blunt. The cavalry had stumbled like blind men. The French had been unable to move. Confronted by a still-born battle, what was Haig to do?

When he made his first personal reconnaissance of the battlefield forty-eight hours after zero, it was obvious there had been no breakthrough and that the Germans were reinforcing fast. On the other hand, as Haig wrote in his confidential report a month later, there were signs of German withdrawal both south of the river Scarpe near Arras and to the north of Bourlon village.[18] GHQ's Intelligence branch also passed on the news that the Germans had only one division in reserve. Perhaps Haig was badly informed. More probably he was lying. Either way, he made the decision on 22 November to override his promise to terminate the battle if it failed to break the German position early on.

When Davidson read the watered-down treatment of that crucial episode in one of Edmonds's drafts, he sent a critical letter. 'You have made little or no reference to the major issue at stake. The main facts and cause of losses at Cambrai were, I think, quite clear. In my recollection, they were as follows: (1) The fighting power and morale of the German Army were higher than was supposed. There had been miscalculation in that respect. (2) We had been fighting the greater part of the German Army for a long period. Our troops were tired and not adequately trained for open warfare. The weather was bad. Some of our divisions, trained for this particular operation, had been removed to Italy. Under these circumstances we had not the requisite force to persist in the operation after the first serious check. (3) The delay and hold-up caused by the Flesquières Ridge on the first and second days was so serious as to warrant the abandonment of the operation as soon as its effect was realized, i.e. when the Commander in Chief rode over the battlefield. I was with him and remember it well. (4) The operation was based on a surprise break clean through. When that was out of the question, it should have been called off.'[19] This from Haig's Operations Director was authoritative criticism of Haig's decision to fight on, and the events which followed came straight from Alice in Wonderland.

Byng had insisted in the first draft scheme for the battle that it could go ahead only if the Germans were fighting hard in Flanders and therefore unable to send sizeable reinforcement to Cambrai. Haig's rush into a major battle at short notice meant that difficulties in preparation delayed zero from 10 November until the 20th. This, in turn, meant that Passchendaele had already been captured and the Flanders offensive ended when Cambrai began. Within a week of Cambrai starting, the Germans had therefore been able to move twenty divisions and 700 guns into the battle area.

Counter-attack had been standard German procedure since mid-1915. With Passchendaele closed down and the enemy able to concentrate on Cambrai, it should have been obvious what would happen and, in his handwritten report to the Cabinet on 18 December, Haig insisted that it had been obvious.[20] He described an abnormal degree of rail activity behind German lines, together with low-flying reconnaissance aircraft forty-eight hours before the Germans delivered their counter-attack. Pre-warned, so Haig claimed, his troops had been re-disposed to meet the counter-attack and had that been the case Haig's responsibility would have been much reduced, but the documents are against his claim. Writing to his wife on the day of the counter-attack, Charteris recorded the simple fact that the British had been taken by surprise: 'Such a bore. I was just going to telegraph you that I was going on leave tomorrow when the Boche attacked. It was very unexpected and he's had some measure of success and so my leave had to be postponed. It may be the beginning of a long battle.'

De Lisle's diary backs Charteris on the point with all the weight of a first-class soldier whose fate had been to command where the German counter-attack was strongest. 'On 30 November we were surprised,' he wrote. 'It is useless to disguise the fact. The Germans made a secret concentration and at dawn advanced in three columns against our three divisions. Just as we had finished breakfast at 8.45 am, machine-gun fire opened at close range. My staff thought this was anti-aircraft fire but I had heard Mauser fire too often in Africa to accept this and ran up the quarry steps to see what could be happening. My worst fears were confirmed. The Germans were within 300 yards of us. There was only time to give the alarm, seize my writing case of important papers and run. It was a most uncomfortable situation. The nearest cover was at Gouzeaucourt about 1,200 yards away. Behind us were the German machine guns; in front of us a thick barrage of high explosive shells and above us, three aeroplanes firing at us from 150 feet. On such occasions personal fear is eliminated by more important things but the physical fatigue of running at speed over ground cut up by shell craters was the worst item. Captain Croome, one of my staff officers, was killed. My servant Piddington and our valued cook Kettley were captured.'

What of the condition of the British who came under attack? Astonishingly, Haig had dismissed all the troops Pétain put at his disposal just five days before the counter-attack (further proof, if any were needed, that he was taken by surprise). Nor had he made any attempt to re-distribute his own force, which was bunched on the left-hand side of the battlefield as a result of prolonged battering at Bourlon Wood.

When the Germans attacked on the right, the inevitable result was a heavy casualty bill – the South Wales Borderers were not untypical in losing 540 men and coming from the line just eighty strong. Indeed, it could have been worse. Pershing witnessed the German counter-attack and thought 'an enormous disaster was only narrowly avoided'. Milner, too, briefed Lloyd George on 'the real and very bad state of affairs'.[21]

Today we can read the sort of thing Milner would have told the Prime Minister in the private notes Maxse made as president of GHQ's inquiry into the débâcle. Among them is a statement from Fuller that 'British defences in the rear did not exist.' Byng agreed: 'Even if we had secured their best service I am not sure that the barrage we had on our defensive lines was sufficient to stop an enemy attack. Our guns had to be in such depth that rear guns can assume the work of breaking up formations that have penetrated our forward lines and I don't think that the odd row of eighteen pounders in line, unless they have very good luck, will stop a heavy attack.' Perhaps Byng was right here, but was he really unaware that machine guns distributed in depth were the best stoppers of any attack?

If there was little support in the rear, the front line was pure Heath Robinson, the disposition of the 55th Division being representative.[22] Although it had suffered 50 per cent casualties at Passchendaele, the 55th received no reinforcements during the ten-day lull which followed the initial attack and was instead spread thinly along a wider front than the one occupied by the six divisions which started the battle off. To hold that vast stretch of line, it almost goes without saying that the 55th were given neither barbed wire nor extra machine guns.

Compounding absurdities like these was a complete failure to establish intelligible unit boundaries. Corps demarcation lines before the battle were simply projected as straight lines into the battle area. In the case of the 55th Division, this meant that another division occupied their rear area and that 600 yards in the northern part of their area was unclear. When the 7th Suffolks went into the zone of uncertainty, they were told they were in reserve and should under no circumstances take any notice of what was happening to the east. As it turned out, the Suffolks were in the front line astride the axis of the strongest German thrust – delivered up the Banteux ravine, due east.

A modern reader will find little of this in the Official History, and though Haig took personal charge of the battle (as he had done of all the big 1917 battles) the Official History hardly mentions his name. Posterity has therefore been left with the impression that Cambrai was Byng's battle – quite apart from a large number of false impressions on the tactical level which Edmonds and his team had fed into their narrative.

The failure on the left flank, for example, was attributed to a series of blunders for which junior commanders alone were responsible. Harper's 51st Division had rejected the attacking formations ordered by Byng. A solitary German artilleryman behind the Flesquières Ridge had knocked out tank after tank in a single-handed action (wheel marks in the ground showed, in fact, that a whole battery had been involved). A cavalry division which might have ridden straight into Cambrai had been handed over for use as dismounted infantry by an aged commander safely positioned ten miles to the rear.

All this was the purest humbug. Trench maps recently made available in the Public Record Office show that the hold-up on the left was due, not to human error, but to a well-fortified trench extending in an arc round the Flesquières position. It was to mark the precise extent of British advance that first day.[23] Linear jump barrages proved inadequate to deal with a curved defensive position, and when a French Staff Officer visited Byng on Pétain's behalf later, Byng's chief suggestion was that, in future, artillery should be concentrated on key points and open breaches for armoured cars and tanks towing artillery. Byng was recalling the Flesquières trench and his own painful memory of it in this advice.

The Official History went on to attribute failure on the right flank to the combination of a vital bridge at Masnières collapsing under the weight of a tank and a German division, previously unlocated, arriving in the nick of time.[24] Collapsed bridges had in fact little to do with the course of the battle and much with official myth-making. The 5th Cavalry Division had been allocated to Masnières, but owing to a scarcity of trench maps and barbed wire charts they took an hour to negotiate twenty-two belts of German barbed wire. By the time the rest of the division caught up with the vanguard, it was 3.30 pm, dusk was falling and further advance was necessarily halted. The Canadian Fort Garry Horse elected to advance and were duly cut to pieces. All the while, the bridge at Marcoing, a short distance to the north, lay open – unknown to Byng because the carrier pigeon used to give him that information failed to get through. Bad luck and worse planning rather than collapsed bridges thus lay behind the failure on the right, and whether one or ten German divisions had arrived to defend the Beaurevoir Line, they would have been confronted by few British troops, fewer cavalry and no artillery or tanks.

The outcome was anyway an indictment of Haig's professional expertise. After the experience of the Somme in 1916 and Passchendaele in 1917, each of them battles of massive size and duration, Haig had apparently failed to grasp the amount of time required to prepare a big battle, the relation between the size of an attacking force and depth of likely penetration as well as the basic principles of troop disposition and the relation between the furthest position finally reached and the likely German response. It would be difficult to write a worse end-of-term report.

THE ATTRITION PERIOD:
HAIG'S WEAKNESSES

8

The Tool

Whatever Haig's deficiencies as a battle manager, fighting was only half a Commander in Chief's job. In December 1915, when he took over the BEF, it numbered a million men. By December 1917 it had doubled in size, generating a mass of frictions and procedural difficulties in the process. Man management was therefore an important facet of Haig's job and one which offered an intriguing escape route. If he could only get the organizational side right, the quality of his tools might even compensate for a poor grasp of battle dynamics.

What then of Haig's achievement as an organizer of armies? Were the best men selected for command and staff positions? Did staff work lubricate frictions and liberate talents? Were men trained in a way best suited to the realities of the battlefield? And were the most effective weapons systems cobbled together to maximize the BEF's punch?

The Canadians had already demonstrated that these were crucial questions. Their Corps had begun the war as a disorganized rabble at 2nd Ypres on April 1915. Skilled management by Byng and Currie transformed it. By mid-1917, the Canadian Corps had become much the most effective unit in the BEF, demonstrating the fact by the style with which it captured two of the Western Front's toughest defensive positions in 1917 – Vimy Ridge in April and Passchendaele village in November.

On a larger scale, the Germans showed the same progression. Their attacks during 1st Ypres in October 1914 had been marked by colonels on horseback leading frontal attacks into the gun barrels of the Old Contemptibles. On the Somme, two years later, the Germans had become masters of defence in depth, of rapid counter-attacks delivered by highly trained *Stosstruppen* and of integrated machine-gun and artillery fire. So what was Haig doing meanwhile? And were there signs of the BEF following the same path as the Canadians and Germans?

Getting the best men into the chief jobs was always the best way of increasing efficiency, and in this area Haig had a free hand. The fact is not easily demonstrated from British records today, but the Americans unearthed it during the war when Washington asked John Quekermeyer, a liaison officer, to research and report on Haig's appointments system.[1] The analysis he sent back explained the mechanics at length and drew particular attention to the fact that all promotions above battalion level were controlled by GHQ. At three-month intervals, commanding officers at all levels drew up lists of men suitable for promotion and passed them to GHQ for final selection. In theory, the job was done by Haig's Military Secretary, but since he had deliberately chosen a nonentity of low rank there was no check to his will. In theory, too, all appointments were subject to the Army Council's approval in London, but again, although it examined Haig's choice for army command (his personal choice for 1st Army command was once rejected and he was given three names from which to make his selection), its supervision went no further down the hierarchy. As Quekermeyer put it, 'The home authorities never refused the Commander in Chief's recommendations.' This meant that Haig could sack any man who failed to match up to his requirements and replace him with any man he chose.

Checking Haig's criteria for those selections proves a surprisingly easy business, since all his corps and army commanders were pre-war professionals. It was a remarkably narrow circle, and even Borden, Canada's stolid Prime Minister, was startled by the fact when he first came to Britain. 'Attended a conference with overseas Ministers,' he wrote. 'Discussed conditions in the British Army and the amazing influence of the Old Army.'[2]

Just why the selection of leaders from pre-war professionals was likely to produce a rich crop of mediocrities had been exposed a decade earlier. A Royal Commission had probed defects highlighted by the Boers and its conclusion on the overall quality of the professionals and the sort of men who became officers in the first place was squeezed into a single paragraph: 'The pay of an English officer in the lower ranks is poor. In the days when trade was thought derogatory to a gentleman, young men of good position had little choice of a profession but now it is open to anyone to become a civil engineer, to go into the City, the wine trade, the motor car business or any of the hundred and one means by which money may be earned by hard work. The Army, on the other hand, has so far been looked upon as a profession in which money will be spent rather than gained but one in which the work is light and the amusements many. It has consequently chiefly attracted young men whose inclinations were towards an easy, pleasant life.'[3]

Put bluntly, the nobility and gentry used the Old Army as a dumping ground for their stupid children, and Edmonds endorsed the point cheerfully – off the record. After a lifetime in the Army, he was closely acquainted with most of its leaders and retained few illusions: 'It must be admitted that very few of our best brains go into the Army,' he told the Australian official historian. 'The financial prospects are too poor. Dr Weldon of Harrow said to me forty years ago, "No clever boy goes into the Army" and that is fairly true. Our Staff Officers at the beginning of the war had not more than a couple of dozen really competent men amongst them.'

Once these second- and third-rate men joined the Army, they were enveloped by an atmosphere of militant anti-intellectualism graphically described by Field Marshal Ironside after the war. 'The cult of the practical soldier was at its height,' he said of his early days in the Army. 'He was held up to be a man who did not avoid service with the regiment. Many of us knew the amount of work that was done in our regiments before the Boer War and after it! The life of a soldier in those days was a very happy one, for war was really more of a sport than a business. I myself remember when I was a horse artilleryman in 1907 lying in hospital, my Colonel came to see me and saw two military books on my table. He said to me, "What the devil are you reading those for? You are a horse artilleryman. What more do you want?" Many had a similar experience and were discouraged from going up to Staff College as I was. The idea then prevailed that staff work was too much routine. Many officers did not want to do it, not because it was beneath the dignity of a British officer but because it was regarded as not being in his line since he was a fighting man. Many men said to themselves, "All right. When the moment comes, inspiration will come upon me and I will do the right thing because nature has made me a fighting man."[4]

Few old soldiers were willing to break the professional soldier's code of silence, but Edmonds supported Ironside's assessment in a confidential note. As a Staff Officer with a division from 1911 to 1914, he had made a point of questioning all the officers and found out that 95 per cent had never read a military book of any sort.[5]

The Army's system of professional education might have counteracted this sluggishness. It conspicuously failed to do so. John Gellibrand won the Sword of Honour in his year at Sandhurst, passed out first from the Staff College and commanded an Australian division with distinction during the war but he could find nothing to say in support of his Army education. 'Sandhurst was not a success,' he recalled. 'Nothing would make the cadets work, keep sober or behave.' The Royal Academy at Woolwich was, if anything, in even worse shape. Describing his time there in a letter to Edmonds after the war, Brigadier Monkhouse remarked: 'We never worked as they work now. We hunted six days a week. I once hunted seven.'

From Sandhurst or Woolwich, the best men went on to the Staff College. 'What actually happened in the first year,' wrote the acerbic Edmonds, 'was that we sat at a few lectures, the good boys in the front row, the idle asleep in the back row, and heard what amounted to no more than the reading of some paragraphs of the regulation books – mostly out of date. There was a written exam at the end of the first year but nobody regarded it seriously. I was trying to help a lame duck, a nominee, when the invigilator came up. I expected trouble. All he said was, "It's no use prompting him. You must dictate to him," and proceeded himself to do so. Colonel Henderson, best known as the author of *Stonewall Jackson*, gave some excellent lectures on military history but Hender, as we called him, was rather lazy and did not make many criticisms of educational value. He accused me on one occasion of using too many commas. Of staff duties and military administration we were told nothing of value.'[6]

Edmonds might have added that the attachment to other arms for three weeks during the course was far too short to be of any realistic value. 'One may not have learnt very much,' he concluded, 'but one had made the closest and most enduring friendships of one's life.' Whether he thought that was sufficient preparation for British generals who took up the chief commands in the Great War he did not say.

Annual manoeuvres represented the practical side of the Army's training programme and they compared badly with their continental counterparts at the time.

Young men starting their military service in Europe joined *en masse* on the same day each autumn. British soldiers, on the other hand, joined the ranks or returned from overseas duty at any time of the year. A commander might therefore handle 500 men one year and 1,000 the next, all of them at different stages in their training. Nor did the tactics used bear much relation to what was likely to happen in any conceivable European war. General Langlois, attending British manoeuvres on behalf of the French in 1910, was astonished at what he saw – two tight-packed lines of men advancing, without reserves and without orders differentiating between woodland and open ground. 'The idea of occupying points of support or of keeping the intervening ground clear of troops and swept by fire is still foreign to the instincts of the British Army,' he concluded.[7] The first day of the Somme was just six years away.

Though he was too tactful to say so in print, Langlois must have been even more astonished to watch skirmishers who were forbidden to kneel or even take cover and machine guns carefully hidden away so as to conserve their eighty-round allocation for riflemen over the rest of the year. Military bands inevitably advanced with the first wave of the attack and battles stopped for lunch each day. As a Frenchman, Langlois may have appreciated the musical arrangements and relished a leisurely midday meal. As a soldier, he would have thought British practice bad preparation for a European war.

When the annual rite came to an end, few of the commanders who took part were much the wiser, since the printed report got no further than Divisional HQ. The Earl of Cavan, who commanded

British forces in Italy during 1917 and was mentioned in the Cabinet as a possible replacement for Haig in 1918, drily remarked in his memoirs: 'It was not until 1910 and the conference of John French and Horace Smith-Dorrien that I learnt the art of war and of handling divisions. It is a general belief that it is unnecessary to tell the fighting units anything of the plan of campaign. The annual report on manoeuvres certainly never reached me when I was commanding the 1st Battalion of the Grenadier Guards.'[8] Aylmer Haldane had already put the point into a broader perspective at the 1907 Staff College conference when he complained that 'All the practical experience of the British Army was hidden away inside the heads of its leading soldiers.'

The quality of generalship developed by such an amateurish, haphazard apprenticeship was as one might expect. In the Official History, Edmonds formulated an official view which has been regurgitated ever since when he wrote: 'In every respect, the Expeditionary Force in 1914 was incomparably the best trained, best organized and best equipped British Army which ever went forth to war.' His real opinion was safely tucked away in a private letter to Charles Bean, who knew too much from direct observation over four years to be taken in by humbuggery. 'In viewing 1914–16,' Edmonds told him, 'you must remember that from the highest to the lowest, we were all amateurs. The generals and staffs of the regular Army, though professionals in name, had never been trained to fight continental armies or deal with such masses of troops.'

Despite this dead weight of ill-trained mediocrity at the top end of the BEF, the means of improvement lay to hand throughout the war and had been identified indirectly by the Committee of Prime Ministers, established later in 1918 to find out why the 5th Army had collapsed in March of that year.[9] 'Every post should be held by the best man available,' it concluded, 'irrespective of whether he is a professional or civilian soldier.' It was a point well made, and if it had been acted on the result would probably have been startling, since Haig's Army had an abundance of capable men, with some of the best professional soldiers.

Despite the taboo on professionals writing books or leaving their private papers to posterity, names like Jacob, Haldane, Du Cane, De

Lisle, Fuller and Maxse indicate the presence of first-class command material.[10] But just as one convention operated to hide their names from outsiders (when Lloyd George asked Henry Wilson in May 1918 whether incompetents had been weeded out, even Wilson was obliged to reply that neither he nor the Secretary of State knew who the good men were since they were dependent on written reports), so another rigid convention made it quite certain that the stupid stood a better chance of promotion than the able.

Cuthbert Headlam, a civilian soldier who became the *Army Quarterly*'s first editor after the war, identified that convention with characteristic pungency when he wrote: 'It is to my mind quite criminal that men like Watts or our ass from here [Hunter-Weston] should be given commands. If it is left to our people to administer the *coup de grâce*, then we shall be here for many years yet. Why should good men's lives be sacrificed unnecessarily by putting them under incapable leaders? There are lots of capable men fit to command brigades or divisions but no, they are too junior.'[11] Frederick Oliver, Milner's close associate, made the same point more suavely when he wrote: 'Seniority puts a cataract over the eye of efficiency.'

Headlam and Oliver were, of course, referring to the Old Army custom of promoting men on the cab-rank principle of longest in, furthest up. The same two men went on to note how the clannish conventions of the Old Army operated to reinforce the weakness of the seniority system by supporting commanders, however incompetent. As Frederick Oliver put it, 'There is too much old chappery in the Army. The principle is you mustn't turn a rotter out till you have found a fatter billet for him elsewhere.'[12] Headlam's witness was the more damning, since he observed the BEF from high staff positions within it. 'If by any chance failures are sent home,' he told his wife, 'they are put in charge of new divisions and re-appear in a few months to do further damage.'[13]

The Kitchener Armies provided a second source of capable commanders, and it was a source completely ignored throughout the war. No Kitchener man ever commanded a corps and one professional soldier who served with Plumer commented sharply on the fact. 'You avoid all criticism of operations and the higher leading,' he told Edmonds in a confidential letter. 'My impression is that our higher leadership was sadly lacking in the ability to cope with the changing conditions of the campaign as it developed. We had the best brains of the Empire at our disposal and we failed to make the best use of them. Officers of the New Armies and of the Dominions resented so much the domination of Regular Army officers with pre-war ideas of warfare. I have heard them at first hand and they have made a deep impression on me.'[14]

Cuthbert Headlam was one of these resentful Kitchener men and spoke for all of them when he complained: 'One has learnt one's work. That is what the regimental professionals cannot grasp. To them it is out of the question that a man who has not been at Sandhurst, lived for years in a battalion and been to Staff College can ever grasp the intricacies of soldiering. In fact, two years' experience is enough for any man of average intelligence. It is amazing to me that after three years there should be practically no non-Regular generals unless they happen to be Canadian. The old regimental Army is a very close trade union.'[15]

If the selection of commanders from the Old Army exclusively, together with promotion by seniority, underpinned the rotting head of the BEF, what had Haig's policy been?

On the Old Army–Kitchener Army point, Haig was unbending. He explained his position in the course of correspondence during January 1918. Lord Derby started it by taxing Haig with reluctance to promote New Army men.[16] Haig replied that, although many temporary officers had been considered, few were 'qualified'. He underlined the word 'qualified' heavily.

When Derby continued to press the matter, Haig explained himself at length: 'I assure you it has been my unceasing effort to bring merit and brains to the front from wherever they can be found. Our experience of war, however, has shown that brilliancy in any one of the learned professions or possession of high business capacity do not in themselves constitute all the qualities necessary for a first class officer. Indeed, I venture to think that character is more important than any other quality for success as a commander in war. Moreover, those officers of the New Army are brought into competition at once with a number of other officers who are themselves the fittest survivors of a great number. These latter have graduated in the regular forces and have for ten, twenty or thirty years devoted all their energy to the study and practice of war. All have had a careful education before being accepted for the Army and during their period of service before the war, the most searching tests have eliminated all who did not possess qualities *above the average* youth of their age standing. Some of their number, too, have foreseen this war coming and devoted their lives and energies to preparing themselves for it. Can it be questioned that many regular officers have started in this great war with very great advantages over the brilliant-brained civilian who had devoted his talents to other types of life? If this were not the case, what would be the object in maintaining in peace our Staff College course or Hythe or Woolwich or even an Army at all?' [17] It was a good trade unionist's answer.

If Haig was unyielding on the need to keep New Army men well down his batting order, he was equally stubborn on the *ancien régime* principle of promotion by seniority. 'Promotion is to be by selection,' ran one of his directives during the Somme, 'but seniority and service record are to be considered. If the recommendee is not the senior officer, then a list of seniors is to be appended.' A year later, and with Passchendaele behind him, Haig still saw no need to change his position. 'Went into recommendations for the Gazette with the Military Secretary and Kiggell,' he wrote in his diary. 'It is impossible to promote many of the most capable without doing an injustice to some officers of good ability and record.' For Haig, the odd blood bath was apparently a small price to pay for the trade-union principle of the closed shop.

Haig's criteria for promotion are best shown by his choice of corps commanders, since (as Derby pointed out in correspondence with him during January 1918) the War Office never interfered with his personal selection at that level.

There were certainly able men among the corps commanders. The quietly competent Claud Jacob was picked by Haig when the War Office ordered him to Mesopotamia in 1916. Maxse and De Lisle were likewise promoted even though Haig disliked brash, self-confident men and later registered the fact in abrasive comment appended to both names when he re-wrote his diary after the war. But able men were always the exception, and when at the start of 1918 the Cabinet insisted on a purge of the more obviously incompetent, half of Haig's nominees were swept away. Even so, the quality of three who managed to cling to command makes sufficient comment on the rest.

Aylmer Hunter-Weston, a Scottish friend of long standing, was always a laughing stock in the British Army, and Cuthbert Headlam, who served on his staff, frequently pondered the question of whether or not his chief was sane. Hamilton Gordon, on the other hand, was sane beyond doubt, but since he had commanded nothing bigger than an artillery battery before taking command of a corps, his credentials were closely examined by rivals who could only put him down as another of Haig's Scottish friends.

GHQ's Deputy Chief of Staff was another friend whose promotion was noted in Haig's diary. 'Butler spoke to me about his position and of how much he had lost in the way of money and promotion by being deputy chief. He was very nice about it and said he would go on doing it at GHQ as long as required but I think it right for him to be appointed to a corps.' To promote a man to the command of the basic unit of battle on financial grounds looks preposterous, and so it proved. Butler broke down before the battle of Amiens in 1918 and, though he kept going on barbiturates, he made a complete mess of the left flank of the battle. A few weeks later, his corps failed to capture the vital jumping-off position for the Americans in front of the Hindenburg Line, with the result that when the Americans attacked they were cut to pieces.

Even though the field command of the BEF was stuffed with men of this quality, the worst blunders might still have been prevented if capable Staff Officers had supported them from the rear, but, as one might expect, the men chosen for the chief staff positions were picked in the same way as the field commanders.

Lawrence Burgis frequently commented on the level of expertise which resulted.[18] As the man entrusted with Esher's personal cipher and a future Cabinet Secretary, his judgements carry the weight of an intelligent outsider at the heart of Haig's headquarters. 'In GHQ,' Burgis once wrote, 'the regular officer is a tin God and intelligent civilians in uniform are treated with contemptuous indifference. We are not allowed to Mess with the Regulars but a Regular Officer was put in charge of *our* Mess. My opinion of the mental calibre of the Regulars was low indeed till the Second World War. Many green-tabbed officers [Intelligence branch] were professional and business people of the highest capacity but they were regarded as dirt.'

The same narrow clique dominated staffs at all levels below GHQ, even if Borden was the only leading politician willing to say so openly and damn the fact.[19] Addressing the Imperial War Cabinet in July 1918, the Canadian Prime Minister first registered his disapproval forcefully, then went on to indicate what Haig should have done. 'At the outbreak of the war,' he said in minutes recently added to the Public Record Office's collection, 'Canada had a small permanent Army. What would have happened if we had laid down the principle that no man should fill a higher position than that of brigadier unless he had been a member of the standing Army? If we fail to use the brains of the nation for the best purpose, we cannot have much prospect of winning this war. Let me give an example with respect to organization. General Jack Stewart is a Scotsman. He came to Canada about thirty years ago. He is as good a railway builder as any man in North America. I understand he is now under the direction of officers who know nothing about railway construction to which he has devoted his entire life. I understand that he could carry on his present work if he were given charge with 40 per cent of the men presently employed. He was asked to build a railway for the construction of which French engineers estimated six weeks, British engineers three weeks. Stewart examined the ground and reported he could build it in six days. He actually built it in four.'

The consequence of inadequate fighting generals was immediate and indisputable. Blood baths like Neuve Chapelle, Fromelles and Bullecourt were as visible to soldiers during the war as to historians after it. Inadequate Staff Officers, on the other hand, made a less immediate impact, but burgeoning bureaucracy, an immensity of superfluous red-tabbed Staff Officers and the disappearance of fighting soldiers in an increasingly ill-managed BEF were symptoms as obvious to the knowledgeable as the sound of death watch beetle to a church warden.

Esher was among the first to draw Haig's attention to the fact that something was amiss with the BEF's staff work. In February 1917 he wrote to Haig, remarking that 'A division of responsibility which did not exist in December 1915 has grown in proportions that might be fatal if you soon get a move on.'[20] He went on to suggest that Haig could probably sack 10,000 Staff Officers without any loss of efficiency, but if Haig recognized the problem Esher described he seems to have done nothing about it. When the War Office examined the situation at the end of the war, its finding was that staffs at every level had doubled in size during Haig's command proportionate to the growth of the BEF as a whole.

The weight of these bloated staffs was felt most immediately in two areas. The more obvious was described by Lt.-Col. Head in a book which carries the authority of a dedicated professional soldier with experience going back to 1877. 'At night through the mud would come the day's official correspondence,' Head wrote. 'It made a goodly pile of orders, returns, reports and questions of great variety, all requiring some hours to deal with. As officials multiplied, correspondence swelled accordingly. When I visited my French neighbour [near Guillemont on the Somme] to take over his premises, I found that a small sheet of paper would contain all the writing he had to do, and we could play bridge for the rest of the evening at which game he and his adjutant were usually the winners. But the number of clerks employed in the British Army to deal with its enormous mass of correspondence must have been prodigious.'[21]

The paperwork described by Head pinned commanders to their dugouts when they should have been walking their lines, but it was only a symptom of something even more damaging. Too many paper-generating drones meant blurred responsibilities, the BEF's use of manpower being a graphic example.

Winston Churchill was the first to identify the problem when he declared that half the BEF was being wasted on the lines of supply in May 1916. In the manner of grave scandals, the most discordant statistics were then scattered about in defence of the *status quo*. Cowans, the War Office's able Quartermaster General, thought 20 per cent a safer figure and Haig countered with 6 per cent in a letter to the king.[22]

A committee of inquiry was quickly established to resolve the matter.[23] It reported that only three divisions, or 5 per cent of the BEF, were employed in back areas, but that conclusion was little more than a cover-up. Esher was usually in a position to know the facts and he told Haig that although the French had 300 per cent as much front line, they used only 50 per cent the number of men in the rear.[24] The British were therefore 600 per cent over-provided behind the firing line and wasting the equivalent of seven divisions. When Haig made his most strident demands for reinforcement, he was therefore wasting more men on his own lines of communication than he ever demanded from the government.

The scandal surfaced again early in 1918. Increasingly suspicious of Britain's claim to be running short of men capable of military service, the French sent a team of investigators under a certain Colonel Roure to investigate the matter. The conclusion of Roure's report caused the British Cabinet considerable embarrassment and resulted in a Cabinet paper which remarked that if the British employed soldiers in the same front line to support troops ratio as the Germans, they would have been able to put an extra twelve divisions into the front line. In other words, Haig was wasting 20 per cent of his men.[25]

Milner came to Haig's defence, pointing out in another Cabinet paper that the Germans could use POWs and forced civilian labour in a manner not open to the allies, but in private he conceded the point: 'I am satisfied there is great waste in rear services. One cannot begin late against an atmosphere. A Hercules is required at GHQ.'[26]

What then were Haig's views on the quality of the staff work within his command? If surviving documentation is representative, he appears to have found nothing amiss. Only when the condition of the BEF was all but terminal at the start of 1918 did Haig offer a few tentative ideas in a circular ('For Army commanders only') which drew attention to bloated staffs. Haig put this down to three causes: 'The production of non-essential statistics, returns, summaries and pamphlets. The abnormal development of luxurious [*sic*] institutions behind the lines like bath houses, theatres and laundries. The tendency of commanders from brigade upwards to concern themselves with details which are the proper province of subordinate commanders.' Haig went on to outline the critical manpower situation and concluded: 'The Army must be freed from the accumulations caused by three years of immobility and over-centralization.'[27]

Haig's response to outside criticism on the other hand was dismissive. He therefore protested vigorously when the War Office suggested a full-scale inquiry into GHQ's staff work just after the Armistice: 'The work of the General Staff during the war was accomplished with remarkable success. It afforded strong evidence of the soundness of doctrine in the antecedent period.'[28] The inquiry, so Haig suggested, should therefore be suspended *sine die*.

He was overruled, and eighty-four senior officers were summoned to give evidence before the Braithwaite Committee. Only the most fragmentary set of conclusions has been allowed to filter into the public domain, but these are sufficient to indicate the report's indictment.[29] Too many Staff Officers, though too few to represent the artillery, engineers or machine-gunners. A promotion system under two men hopelessly junior in rank, one a close friend of Haig from his Oxford University days, the other his golfing partner in France. Above all, the damning absence of a senior officer to integrate staff work in France.

Generalship and staff work were thus of poor quality, but what of the fighting soldiers and their organization?

The answer is suggested by a single fact. Whenever Haig planned a breakthrough or came upon a particularly obdurate German position, British units were pushed aside and Dominion troops put in charge. Messines had been planned as the starting point of the big British attack in July 1916, and when the Somme was bogged down at the outset the Anzacs were sent from Messines and set against Pozières, the highest point on the battlefield and the key to the first month's fighting. 1917 meant Vimy (Canadians), Bullecourt (Australians) and the capture of Passchendaele (Canadians and Australians). 1918 included 8 August (Canadians and Australians) and the breaking of the Hindenburg Line (Australians and Canadians at the two strongest points).

The use of Dominion men as storm troops roused strong feelings at the time and all the more when the British press during the war and the British Official History after it tried to cover up the fact.

Monash's pungent wartime letters were typical of Dominion feeling: 'Some of these Tommy officers [in spring 1918] are not worth the money it costs to put them into uniform. You can no doubt read between the lines in all I have written in the past – bad staffs, bad commanders. The only war correspondent who has dared to hint at the truth is Philip Gibbs (see the cutting of the *Daily Telegraph* dated 3.4.18 which I enclose).'[30]

The Australians and Canadians were not alone in their criticism. During the war, Cyril Falls served on the staff of the Ulster Division. After it, he wrote the Official History dealing with the first part of 1917 and went on to take up the Chair of Military History at Oxford University. His judgement, off the record, was that 'Our Army was the best disciplined and least effective in the war, though one can't say so in the Official History.'[31]

Were the men who made up that army therefore inferior, man for man? Were they less brave, less intelligent, less enduring than Dominion soldiers? Since about 60 per cent of the Canadian Corps had been born in Britain, and most of the remainder only a generation removed, that can hardly have been the case.[32] What in fact transformed first-class fighting men into second-rate soldiers was the training system over which Haig presided and to which he consistently gave his benediction.

Ivor Maxse, widely regarded as one of the finest trainers of troops in the Army, believed that '80 per cent of the work we do in battle is carried out in training before the battle. That battle is won or lost by arrangements made beforehand. We have learnt that from personal experience.'[33] After watching nearly all the big battles through a telescope from the front line, Bean agreed with Maxse. Comparing the Australians of Pozières in 1916 with the same units in the final push of 1918, Bean reckoned that the Australians of 1918 achieved more at 25 per cent the cost in casualties. 'One never realized before what a difference training has made to the Australians,' he concluded. How then did the training system of the British Army fit the harsh requirements of the Western Front?

Haig offered the rope to hang himself here during January 1918 when he stated that British recruits required nine months of training in Britain and six months in France before they were ready for battle.[34] The French at that time gave their recruits only three months' training in basics and another three in battlecraft, yet in Maxse's judgement still produced soldiers superior to the British in both technique and performance.[35]

That difference was the result of oversights and miscalculations which began when the British soldier joined up. One would have thought it a basic requirement that training in Britain would be integrated with training in France, yet through the war the War Office and GHQ printed separate training pamphlets as if they were fighting different wars. The practical consequence was that what novices learnt in Britain was quite unrelated to the requirements of the Western Front. Taking the introductory programme alone, half a recruit's time was spent on drill and physical training, so that, as one soldier bitterly put it, 'We sloped, ordered, presented, trailed, reversed and piled arms and did everything possible with them except to fire them. With rifles we marched and counter-marched, wheeled right and left, inclined and formed squads and about turned until we were streaming with sweat and weak in the knees with exhaustion.'

When the training programme turned belatedly to practical work, it bore little relation to skills necessary in France. The formation of skirmishing lines which leapfrogged forward in alternate sections and paused to attach bayonets 200 yards from the enemy line represented a style of attack obsolete by the end of the Boer War but basic to the War Office's programme into 1918. Milner summarized these failings in a terse memorandum written in 1918 as Minister of War. Drafts sent to France were ignorant of how to site trenches, conduct a night relief of the front line, attack in open-war style (which was predominant for most of 1918) or consolidate a captured trench.

Once these under-trained men got to France, GHQ took their preparation in hand. By 1917 there were central training schools in each of the five armies and nineteen corps – on paper at least. In practice, as Du Cane told Henry Wilson, no integrated training system ever existed.[36] Guy Dawnay supported that judgement in his capacity as GHQ's Deputy Chief of Staff when he wrote in 1918: 'There is no doubt that our training system is neither perfectly coordinated nor evenly distributed through the armies. I am constantly being told by divisions moving from corps to corps and from army to army that they are being taught different doctrines as they move from one command to another.'

Ivor Maxse quantified this astonishing incoherence in a confidential conclusion to GHQ's internal inquiry after Cambrai. Thirty divisions had passed through his own corps. Two had been well trained. Twelve were trying. Sixteen were without training of any sort. It was a remarkable state of affairs in an army which had been at war for three years.

As if dissatisfied with this disgracefully inadequate training, GHQ went on to destroy any *esprit de corps* which might have developed in its recruits. It did this by adopting what Trenchard's RAF called the principle of the full breakfast table. It was based on the belief that units had to be kept at full strength at all times. Drafts were thus sent as individuals to the first unit calling for men – a practice which effectively destroyed any comradeship which might have developed during training.

Just why this was an error of judgement had been identified forty years earlier by that remarkable analyst, Arand Du Picq. As a Crimean War veteran, Du Picq reckoned that the volume of modern firepower subjected a soldier in five minutes to the quantity of fear which Turenne's men had experienced in an hour on the battlefields of Marlborough's wars. Trembling due to fear had therefore to be taken into account by modern commanders, and men were most effectively kept to their duty, Du Picq argued, by the mutual supervision of comrades long acquainted.[37]

Colin was another French theorist widely read by thinking professional soldiers at the time. A generation after Du Picq, he noted that modern firepower broke up the massed attacks which had for centuries sustained the courage of individuals. The only practicable counter, he argued, was to fuse infantry into teams, using familiarity as the bonding force.[38]

By the time Haig became Commander in Chief, the reasoning of Du Picq and Colin had been made many times more relevant by the escalation of firepower and that increased sense of isolation which was its direct consequence. At the start of the Somme, British soldiers had advanced in lines with men spaced at one-yard intervals. When the battle ended four months later, those lines had been thinned to a man every six yards. The confidence given by long acquaintance had thus become even more important – as Dominion troops showed. All their reinforcements went to units built round areas of recruitment. Wounded soldiers returning to action always went to their old units. It was simple, it was obvious and it may well have been the strongest single factor behind the superior performance of the Australians and Canadians. Even Edmonds acknowledged that possibility: 'Homeland divisions suffered many disadvantages,' he admitted to Bean. 'It was the fault of our military authorities that *esprit de corps*, such a vital quality, so strongly developed in Australian forces, had suffered badly because recovered sick and wounded were not sent back to their old units and drafts, e.g. Irish and Cockneys were sent to Scots units and Lancashire drafts to Yorkshire battalions and so on. Thus officers and men hardly knew each other and there was little to bind them together except common cause.'

Inadequate training. Men and units shuffled round like cards in a pack. There was one final handicap imposed on British fighting soldiers and it related to the tools of their trade – as demonstrated by comparison with the French in spring 1918.[39] Though the two armies were of equal combatant strength, the French had three times as many light machine guns, four times as many heavy machine guns, two and a half times as many heavy guns/howitzers and one and a half times the number of light field guns/howitzers.

The discrepancy was further underlined when the Supreme War Council produced a check list of automatic weapons per division in May 1918.[40] It read damningly:

	Per division
French	972 (1 per 12 men)
Canadian	1,557 (1 per 13)
American	963 (1 per 27)
British	244 (1 per 61)

These statistics emphasize the reluctance of British professional soldiers to acknowledge that revolution in firepower which had transformed the battlefield. Monash usually claimed an originality which went well beyond the facts, but in a book describing the exploits of the Australian Corps in 1918, he outlined how the British should have used the new machinery. 'The true role of infantry was not to expend itself upon heroic physical effort nor whither away under merciless machine gun fire nor impale itself upon hostile bayonets nor tear itself to pieces on hostile entanglements but on the contrary, to advance upon the maximum possible protection of the maximum possible array of mechanical resources in the form of guns, machine guns, tanks, mortars and aeroplanes and to be relieved as far as possible of the obligation to fight their way forward.'[41] Monash noted too that automatic weapons allowed units reduced by casualties to retain combat effectiveness. When Rawlinson expressed anxiety over dwindling Australian numbers during the final advance, Monash replied that his battalions would even benefit from being 25 per cent under strength as long as they kept to establishment in Lewis and Vickers guns. In other words, same firepower, smaller units, greater flexibility. It was a fact the Germans had appreciated for years. Between October 1916 and May 1917, they cut their rifles on the Western Front from 1,300,000 to one million and increased their machine guns from 7 to 12 million. By the middle period of the war, they were therefore coming to rely increasingly on automatic weapons rather than the rifle.

What then of Haig's position on the preparation of infantry and the weapons systems which were to support them?

His reluctance to appoint a strong man to take charge of training is sufficient comment on the first point. Although Haig accepted Maxse as Inspector General of Training in July 1918, he had done so only after intense pressure from London (so Maxse bitterly told his wife) and without the slightest intention of using him.

Haig's interest in developing weapons systems to help his men forward was on a par with the low value he put on the personal skills of his infantrymen and on their spirit of cooperation. An exchange of letters with Winston Churchill in 1918 makes the point well. It began with Churchill's memorandum which suggested re-structuring the

BEF round machinery.[42] As Minister of Munitions, Churchill wanted to abolish the cavalry, reduce the infantry and artillery by 5 per cent and increase tanks, machine guns and aeroplanes as counter-balance.

Before Haig sent his reply, he circulated copies of Churchill's memorandum to each army commander for comment.

Horne, the 1st Army commander, was the first to reply with the opinion that, no matter how weak the infantry became, artillery and machine guns had to be kept up to strength. He particularly requested that his men should be provided with machine guns on the same generous scale as the Canadians.

Plumer protested his ignorance of tanks but urged that 'machine gun power must not be decreased with manpower'.

Rawlinson concluded this unwelcome batch of replies with the blunt assertion that the British were under-equipped with automatic weapons in comparison with all other armies and that this was due not to inadequate production but to prejudice against change of any kind from commanders in the Army.

These weren't the sort of letters Haig liked to read, and Rawlinson was crisply told that his proposals would either reduce the Army by six divisions or cut battalion strength to 820. Haig sent a dismissive reply to Churchill anyway.

The Army Haig sent into battle was therefore as badly organized as most people came to suspect in the post-war period. Poorly trained and ill equipped, supported by staff work of low quality and commanded by generals inadequate to the task, the BEF under Haig was, indeed, the bluntest of swords.

9

The Execution

Most analyses of Haig as a director of battle follow the agenda set out in two sources. The first is *Haig's Command*, a two-volume study sponsored by Haig in 1922; the second, Haig's own diary. In both, the blame when things went wrong is invariably ascribed to French generals or British politicians jostling Haig aside and interfering in areas where Haig was the man best able to judge.

Since the most important documents on the episodes in dispute were locked away for nearly fifty years after the war, those who defended Haig's performance were able to stand their ground, citing the Commander in Chief's own writings in support. Today, with the archives open, an alternative view can at last be put and it is one which rightly puts Haig back centre-stage where he had been throughout the years of the Somme and Passchendaele. More particularly, the documents suggest three basic weaknesses during those years: a faulty selection of battlefield, an inability to break the crust of the enemy's defensive position at the outset and a failure to exploit such fleeting opportunities for breakthrough which appeared.

Haig's unerring instinct for choosing the worst place to launch an attack is a matter of record. The main thrust on 1 July 1916 was against Pozières, the most strongly fortified part of the German position on the Somme. In spring 1917 he launched a frontal attack on the Hindenburg Line, putting Australian infantry against Bullecourt with minimal artillery support and sending massed cavalry against the machine guns of Monchy les Prœux. Three months later, the main axis of Passchendaele was laid across the Steenbeek valley, marshiest of all the valleys in the Salient, and at Cambrai, against all advice, Haig ordered an attack through the neck of a bottle.

His second weakness was shown in a repeated failure to smash the enemy's defensive crust. The reasoning behind this defect was exposed in Haig's address to junior commanders on the eve of the battle of Loos. 'I expect the greatest initiative from subordinate leaders,' he told them. 'Knowing the immediate objective of each phase of operations, the leaders of corps, division and brigade must decide themselves on the best direction and choose objectives which will lead to the most decisive results. The density of attacking waves must depend on a study of the ground and of the nature of the enemy's position.'

It was a fundamental error. The Germans demonstrated time and again in 1918 that if decentralization was right for the second phase of a breakthrough battle, the crust had to be broken first and that meant a centrally organized initial phase, planned down to the last detail.[1] Haig never understood the fact, even though by autumn 1916 several of his best commanders had done so.

The events of September 1916 offer a perfect illustration of Haig's obtuseness in the area of breakthrough as well as a first-class demonstration of what he should have been doing.

After the initial failure on the Somme, a second big attack was scheduled for 15 September. Haig was again closely involved in the planning, but his contribution stopped short with a general outline of what he wanted, which in its chief features was nothing more than a replay of 1 July. Rawlinson's plan was once more rejected as 'too unambitious'[2] and Haig again gave orders for complete penetration of the German position on the first day. 'Risks must be minimized, not by declining to accept them but by skilfully handling the reserves,' he explained. Quite what Rawlinson made of that obscure directive remains unclear.

Haig next ordered the same gun densities as on 1 July. Then, there had been a field gun every 18 yards and a heavy gun or howitzer every 48. In September, the figures were 29 and 59 respectively. Once more, too few guns were being ordered to disperse their fire ahead of an infantry mass scheduled to get right through the German crust in a few hours. It was as if Haig had been asleep for two months.

Ivor Maxse made the strongest possible contrast with Haig in these matters. His particular task was to organize an attack on Thiepval, the last strongpoint on the Somme with observation over the British rear. The attack was scheduled to begin ten days after Haig's September push and only a few miles away. Maxse would have had few illusions. Thiepval had resisted the fiercest attacks for twelve weeks with a garrison of ten Württemberg battalions pledged to defend it to the last man. The vigour of that defence is marked by a cemetery close to Thiepval. The gravestones are laid flat on the ground because the earth was so pulverized in 1916 that no stone would stand upright for long. Even seventy years later, aerial photos reveal concentrations of chalk outlining Thiepval's trenches as if the war had only recently ended.

Confronted by this intractable position, Maxse drew up his plans in the spirit of a conductor weaving together the diverse instruments of an orchestra to achieve harmony. As the thinking man's bulldog, he made no attempt to hide his guiding principle: 'The secret of successful attack in modern war may be summed up in two words – previous preparation. With sufficient time to prepare an assault upon a definite and limited objective, I believe that a well-trained division can capture any "impregnable" stronghold.'[3]

Maxse worked systematically. Prisoners were interrogated and a map compiled on which he marked all the enemy's machine guns and artillery positions. The officers of the attacking division were next brought up sixteen days in advance of the attack for a briefing and were taken by bus to see the position for themselves. When they got back to HQ, they were immediately set to work. The minutiae of the assault had to be planned down to the smallest detail, so artillery and infantry staffs were put in adjacent rooms. Bitter experience by that stage of the war had already shown that messages telephoned or written rather than spoken were the source of many of those misunderstandings which murdered soldiers on the battlefield.

Five days before zero, all plans had been made and a last conference was convened at which all were free to ask any question or raise any objection. Better to risk leaks than ignorance when finalizing an operational plan, Maxse insisted.

He had meanwhile been preparing his own 18th Division. 'Teach, drill and practise a definite form of attack so that every man and officer shall know it thoroughly,' Maxse ordered. 'On the basis of knowledge common to all, any commander varies his attack formation to suit any condition which may be peculiar to his front and objective. With our New Armies formed of men of a very intelligent class on the average, I am in favour of explaining the reasons for adopting certain formations rather than others in the specific attack which they are to carry out. Certainly they require definite methods. Inexperienced men cannot be fed on general principles.'

Assured that a third of his own division's casualties on 1 July had been the direct result of faulty training (he had been given only a week to prepare), Maxse had based his training ever since on the principle that all battalions must be allowed to keep a tight hold on their sixty-four sections and resist the demands of fatigue parties, specialist training schools and leave rosters. Maxse's highly trained and coherent sections were finally brought to the trenches facing Thiepval ten days before zero to get the feel of the terrain.

Their assault enjoyed no overwhelming material advantage. Though they outnumbered the defence four to one, the Germans were equal in machine guns and little inferior in artillery. Maxse preferred to put his faith in the degree of force and energy he could inject into the first attack, reinforcing it with the key element of surprise. Previous attacks had been at dawn from the west. Maxse ordered his attack for midday from the south, with a creeping shrapnel barrage moving at 100 yards per two minutes (double the normal speed) and an overhead machine-gun barrage beating the ground 300 yards ahead of the shrapnel. The first infantry wave was to be issued with 250 Lewis guns, each gun supported from a hip sling and directed against machine-gun posts carefully pinpointed before the attack. By way of contrast, Rawlinson's orders for the 1 July attack had contained the bewildering instruction that German machine-gun nests were not to be shelled during the preliminary barrage and that Lewis guns were to be issued only in the second attacking wave.

Press correspondents were finally brought to Thiepval just before zero, placed in armchairs, issued with binoculars and plied with whisky. The attack they witnessed was, of course, a complete success and supplied a textbook demonstration of how force was best applied to break the crust of the strongest defensive position. Centralized control and the integration of all resources were the key. Thiepval hinted, too, at what might have been achieved if Army promotion had favoured front-line commanders who perceived and acted on the realities of the battlefield rather than those most likely to stick fast to the claptrap of the 1909 edition of the *Field Service Regulations*.

The contrast between Haig and Maxse is striking. The difference in centralization of command is the obvious difference, but a comparison between Haig's and Maxse's harmonization of weapons is equally important.

From September 1916 until Cambrai, Haig relied on the ponderous, predictable pounding of artillery. The outline of his battles changed little. Maxse, on the other hand, always tried to combine force and surprise in equal measure. He had shown the way at Thiepval. St Julien a year later provided an even better example of what Haig might have done had he been capable of lateral thought into the possibilities opened up by modern weaponry.[4] St Julien is an example the more striking too from its setting in the Ypres Salient, that most unpromising of battle locations.

For most of August 1917, the Passchendaele battlefield had been a bottomless bog on either bank of the river Steenbeek, with Gough and Haig trying to prise the German defensive position apart with mallets. All the while, a simple can-opener lay to hand which Maxse proposed to demonstrate with a plan he submitted on 18 August. The fortified village of St Julien was his objective and surprise was to be his chief weapon, achieved by the latest technology deployed in the simplest harmony.

Maxse proposed a combination of 20 per cent smoke shells (to blind enemy machine-gunners) and 80 per cent simultaneously fused shells (to cut barbed wire without cratering the ground) as a preliminary bombardment. The first attacking wave was to consist of tanks, preceded by low-flying aircraft to destroy field artillery which had been identified on oblique photos taken from other low-flying aircraft. A second wave of infantry was to advance at the double behind the tanks and be deployed as 'waves in front and worms behind'.

To Gough's credit, Maxse was given his head. He was, after all, the captor of Thiepval, related to Milner by marriage and had Leo Maxse – spokesman of the prehistoric Right in the press – as a brother. Once he had been given the six battalions he requested, Maxse informed Gough that if those battalions were used in the manner recommended by GHQ, he would lose 1,200 men. Employing flexible formations, Maxse's men advanced 500 yards on a front of one mile. St Julien was captured at the cost of fifteen casualties.

Writing to his wife with typical immodesty, Maxse was triumphant. 'For the first time in the war Kiggell telephoned to ask "How it was done". As if one could explain common sense down a telephone to someone who has never commanded a humble company!' He might have added that both Thiepval and St Julien offered Haig classic examples of the key elements of battle management – centralized control, the harmonization of weapons and a fierce initial punch.

The final phase in any battle was the exploitation of success. Haig's failure to sustain momentum is the final weakness in his direction of battle. There are many examples. After a surprise barrage upset German equilibrium at Neuve Chapelle, huge traffic jams petrified the advance. At High Wood on 14 July 1916, open country beckoned in vain after the system for issuing orders broke down. The following year, a cavalry force reached Cambrai railway station on 20 November 1917, drank German brandy and smoked German cigars – then returned to base. At Amiens, on 8 August 1918, armoured cars would race about the German back area with impunity, then return like the cavalry at Cambrai.

Haig's battles were fought over terrain and against enemy defences which put the BEF at a disadvantage even before the fighting began. The energy of its initial attack was then diffused by chronic lack of coordination and, finally, if by chance the enemy showed weakness, poor staff work and inadequate training precluded exploitation.

10

The Common Denominator

One response to a list of Haig's deficiencies as a director of battle is to link him with Marshal de Saxe's mules, which campaigned often and learnt little. But was Haig alone responsible for the blind spots?

He had been a professional soldier before the war and his rapid promotion indicated, among other things, that his views reflected a large and influential section of the Old Army. Most of his weaknesses were therefore Old Army weaknesses and, with the advantage of hindsight, it can be seen that the doctrine of war inculcated at the Staff College and codified as *Field Service Regulations* on the eve of the Great War was the key factor linking Haig's weaknesses and offering an explanation of them.

This doctrine was the outcome of prolonged analysis during the Edwardian period and took the best military thinking of the time into account. A reader has only to check the minutes of Staff College conferences or run an eye over military books published by specialist houses like Gale and Polden or Hugh Rees in the twenty years before the war to confirm the point.[1]

When war broke out, it therefore brought few surprises for the professionals. Trench warfare and the empty battlefield, 30 per cent casualties and battles lasting weeks had all been frequently discussed in the decade before 1914. There was general agreement that the next European war would be on a massive scale, with big armies fighting on extended fronts. In 1912, for example, the French analyst Colin predicted that armies numbering three million would be distributed along a battle front of 400 km.

Confronted by the probability of battles on a scale so much larger than anything the British Army had known in the past, the great problem appeared to be how these huge battlefields could be controlled. Or, as the soldier charged by the War Office with the task of finding a solution put it, 'The great question is how to secure combination. Until we have a doctrine, initiative may result in disorder. We must all have the same tactical ideas, understand one another's tactical methods and put them into practice in a common-sense way in the field.'

The solution chosen by the War Office was a manual which was to have biblical authority in the Army and serve for doctrine in the style of Prussian practice. That manual was called *Field Service Regulations* (*FSR*) and the key edition was that of 1909, which had been compiled under Haig's supervision.

Battle lay at the centre of *FSR* and its specification was straightforward. Action had to begin with a short, sharp artillery bombardment which would upset the enemy's equilibrium and prepare for an assault by the infantry. That assault would be delivered in lines, each line pressing the one in front and filling the gaps as men fell. Rifle fire was maximized in this way and it was the function of the rifle – not the artillery piece – to beat down the enemy's counter-fire and prepare for a bayonet charge to cut through the enemy's line. When the gap had been made, the decisive phase could begin, with cavalry pouring through it and cutting the enemy's supply line and reinforcements. His front line would thus wither and military victory ensue.

A *FSR* battle was thus a finite proposition, as easy to grasp as it was simple to execute, and Haig never surrendered its vision. As late as September 1918, he supervised full-scale cavalry exercises in person, making sure that his horsemen were in a fit state to dash through a gap which Dominion infantry and his new mustard gas shells were to blast in the Hindenburg Line.

FSR also implied a style of command at each level and a relationship between commanders and commanded which fixed the shape of the British Army throughout the war and explains many of the features which blunted the cutting edge.

The role of the Commander in Chief in particular was conceived as passive through much of the battle. Although he had to choose the battlefield, *FSR*'s emphasis on human factors like élan, courage and the charisma of command meant that humdrum elements like topography, water tables, enemy defensive systems and the like were given a low value in that selection. Nor was the Commander in Chief expected to busy himself with detail. That was the job of the man on the spot. Haig often quoted Lee, the old Confederate chief, in support: 'During the battle my direction is of more harm than use. I must rely on my division and brigade commanders. I think and act with all my might to bring up my troops to the right place and at the right time. After that, I've done my duty.'

On the other hand, physical inactivity never meant sloth. The Commander in Chief's function was quite precise and Haig explained it at length at one of his pre-war Staff Rides.[2] 'The principle is that men who have been engaged for a long continuance of time are more or less like dead cinders. Their ammunition has been consumed. They have melted away to a certain extent. Physical and moral energies are exhausted. Perhaps their courage is exhausted as well. Such a force, irrespective of their diminution in numbers, is a very different force from what it was before the combat and thus it is that the loss of moral force may be measured by the reserves that have been used, as it were, by a foot rule.' What Haig meant by this principle is straightforward. In the first phase of any battle, the Commander in Chief's job was to study the enemy's condition closely. Hence Haig's obsession with the details of German troop movements and with anecdotal evidence on their morale. Likewise his lack of interest in the enemy's steadily improving weapons systems and battle tactics.

When Haig decided from a combination of statistics and information from prisoners that the enemy had become 'a mass of dead cinders', his inactivity was transformed into more conventional command with the task of breaching the line at the 'decisive point' using GHQ's reserve. Exactly how that was to be done Haig explained at length in his address on the eve of Loos: 'Anything I now say regarding the scope of forthcoming operations is based on a study of the map and on the principles which were taught by the late Colonel Henderson at Camberley. It is not enough to gain tactical success. The direction of our advance must be such as will bring us upon the

enemy's rear so that we will cut his communications and force him
to retreat.'

The Commander in Chief's task was, in other words, to identify
the moment when a small addition of force would turn the scale. He
had then to exploit it with his reserve and finally clinch the victory
by using his cavalry against the enemy's reinforcements and his communications.

With the Commander in Chief waiting on the moment of decision
in a headquarters far from the battlefield, subordinate commanders
were meanwhile working to bring that moment about. To an
outsider, the prescription of this hands-off role might seem the best
way to increase disharmony in the hierarchy of command. For two
reasons, that wasn't how Haig saw it. With all his juniors thoroughly
marinated in the spirit of the *Field Service Regulations* of 1909 by a
lifetime's professional training, Haig assumed that harmony would
be automatic even if commanders were out of touch with each
other. Shared principles simply meant they would perceive the same
events in the same way and respond in the same manner.

Haig's second assumption was that a handful of men controlled all
that happened in battle, thus further simplifying the problem of
coordination. A letter written by Haig in August 1916 brings the
point out. 'After tales of the uselessness of the New Army at
Gallipoli, I was a little anxious about their fighting value, but with a
fairly good staff and careful training they have come up to all my
expectations. After all, it is not the division which really fights well
or ill but the officer who commands it.'[3]

By that stage of the war, few fighting commanders would have
agreed with Haig on this matter. Men like Maxse and Haldane were
not only selecting commanders at every level with scrupulous care;
they were training their units in the knowledge (painfully acquired
in two years of campaigning against men rather than principles) that
success depended on skill and cooperation at every level within every
unit.

And what of the infantry, hardly mentioned in *FSR* and to whose
training Haig gave such a low priority? It is self-evident today,
as it was to the Germans and French by the end of the Somme,

that the Western Front required a thinking army capable of infiltration in small units. Why did Haig discount an arm capable of self-propulsion?

His reasoning went back to the dilemma confronting a tiny professional army before 1914. If Britain had to send a large force to Europe, how could civilian soldiers be used to take on soldiers who had already acquired the basics of soldiering from military service?

Britain alone depended on civilian soldiers. For Haig's generation, the only guide to the battlefield strengths and weaknesses of civilians was the American Civil War, in which civilians had formed the infantry mass, commanded by professional generals. It followed that the best guide in these matters was the one British soldier who had studied the American war in depth and had published work on it. He was Colonel Henderson, charismatic Staff College lecturer and guru to Haig and his generation from their Staff College apprenticeships.[4]

Henderson was pessimistic on the whole subject of civilian soldiers. For him, the chief lesson of the 1860s was that civilians began battles with dash but were liable to panic and unable to endure heavy losses. He believed that only the most fiercely disciplined drill could supply a corrective, because 'No Army was ever efficient until obedience has become an instinct. This is a long process if the men in the ranks have been accustomed to thinking for themselves.'

Henderson's gloom would only have been reinforced by the sort of men who joined the British Army as infantry in his own day. 1 per cent came from the servant-keeping class. 7 per cent were shopkeepers. The rest, a mass of unskilled labourers. One notable study of the pre-war Cameronians suggested an average mental age between ten and thirteen, which meant that men going on leave had to be marched to the station and put on the right train.[5] Left to themselves, the difficulty of travelling between barracks and home would have been quite beyond them. Fuller summed up the situation in his own wry way with the observation that the Navy's way of breaking the spirit of a particularly stubborn sailor before 1914 was to force him to perform sentry duty with a handspike as if he was a soldier.[6]

The Old Army's method of turning civilians into infantry who would behave more predictably than the civilians of the Union or

Confederacy followed Henderson's advice. Recruits, according to his *Principles of War*, had to be drilled until a disagreeable tendency to think independently had been bludgeoned out. Obedient robots could then be handed over to an officer and used as an extension of the commander's will.

Set against *FSR*'s views on battle, command and the infantryman's role, Haig's weaknesses begin to make better sense. *FSR* explains the selection of commanders from the professionals alone, the low regard for machinery, the denigration of the infantryman and the retention of a great mass of cavalry. Much of what Haig tried to do at the start of 1916 was therefore taken straight from the book and he wasn't alone in this. Most armies were led into the first year of the war by colonels on horseback, stuffed with a philosophy which bore no relation to the age of barbed wire and machine gun. Where Haig's Army differed – and increasingly so as the war went on – was in its inertia. The French and Germans changed tactics and organization continuously, searching for the best shapes. The BEF alone remained substantially the same. After the Somme, for example, Maxse and Currie were both sent by their army commanders to report on how the French had altered their procedures during the Somme. Both were astonished by the quantity of change and the improvement in quality produced by it. Cuthbert Headlam was equally impressed by improvements in French staff procedures and compared them with his own army. 'Why can't we learn also?' he asked his wife plaintively.

How can Haig's inertia be explained? How was it possible for a commander to follow the precepts of *FSR* long after war had exposed the inadequacy of its principles at every stage? The solution was discovered by 'Boney' Fuller, the Tank Corps' Chief Staff Officer during the war and one of the most acute military analysts after it. In a review of Duff Cooper's *Haig*, Fuller concluded: 'Haig was supported by the conviction that his strategical opinion, based upon the ceaseless study of a lifetime, could not be wrong. He was, in fact, the incarnation of *Field Service Regulations* in the 1909 edition. He fought by a book of rules. His mind ran on rails.'[7]

It was a remarkably perceptive conclusion and one which should have been perceived even before the war by those who appointed high commanders and should therefore have studied the writings of possible candidates. Before the war, Haig was quite sure he had uncovered all the rules of war ('The fundamental principles of war are neither very numerous nor very abstruse'[8]). He was equally certain that these rules had to be accepted as dogma and not weakened by debate ('The development of the General Staff will be thrown back years,' he told Kiggell, 'if you leave your present job. With so many talkers at the War Office, Aldershot and Camberley who know not what war really is nor Clausewitz's fundamentals, the whole show may be wrecked unless you are in a responsible position to be able to put a stopper into the wind bags' mouths'[9]) and that any change in *FSR* was unlikely ('From time to time, the progress of military science necessitates amendment of the law but the advantages of continuity of policy are so great that no change can be sanctioned without the greatest deliberation'[10]).

With military dogmas cut and dried before 1914, Haig felt no need to study the details of his profession, and many competent judges were astounded by the gaps in Haig's knowledge relating to the most elementary aspects of soldiering. Monash was one of them. In a letter to his wife he wrote: 'Haig was, technically speaking, quite out of his depth in regard to the minutiae of the immense resources which were placed in his hands. I was at first quite dismayed to find that he obviously did not know in detail the composition of his formations, as for example when he criticized my dispositions just before the battle of Messines of the heavy and super-heavy artillery which, of course, I had nothing to do with. On a later occasion in 1918, he appeared to blunder badly and be out of touch with the details of the situation when he came to discuss with me how best to exploit the great victory of 8 August before Amiens.'

Edmonds made the same point more brutally: 'Haig knew nothing about infantry or engineers and could not understand artillery.' Nor indeed did he make the slightest effort to find out. Desmond Morton, one of Haig's ADCs, commented on the latter's 'utter dislike of new ideas' which might disturb the threadbare dogmas he took into the war.[11]

Haig's routine might almost have been devised to distance him from disturbing evidence that *FSR* and the principles of his youth had been found wanting.

Charteris commented, for example, on how little Haig read during the war. 'All the threads led direct to one large room in the Chief's HQ where, at a desk on which there was hardly ever a single paper, he controlled the whole vast and intricate ramifications of the growing British Army. Seldom was any matter brought to him and not immediately disposed of. Very seldom did he find it necessary to retain memoranda or other statements for further perusal before giving a decision.'

Nor did Haig discuss military problems, even with close colleagues. 'He could talk on certain subjects which had nothing to do with the war,' Morton wrote. 'But what he was thinking about the war as it stood on a particular day no one, not even his Chief of Staff, could fully make out.' Kiggell would certainly have agreed with Morton's assessment. In a letter to Edmonds ten years after Cambrai, Kiggell recalled Haig's decision to put the emphasis on Bourlon Wood rather than Cambrai. 'He had, of course, as always been thinking much about it himself and saying damn little.'

In briefing sessions, Haig always reduced the airing of contrary opinions to a minimum. 'He would never argue,' wrote Edmonds about Haig's morning sessions with GHQ's section heads. 'If any attempt were made to prolong discussion beyond a reasoned statement, he would bring the conversation to an abrupt conclusion, saying, "I don't want to hear anything more about that."' In the weekly conferences with his army commanders Haig went further. He simply read a prepared paper, then took a solitary lunch from the lunch box his wife had given him at the start of the war. As he explained to his wife, he did not want the weekly conferences to degenerate into convivial luncheons. With Haig at the head of the table, it is hard to believe they ever could have done so.

These symptoms of a man avoiding situations which might challenge his own rigid conceptions of command were accompanied by a disturbing change in Haig himself. Before the war he seldom went to church, preferring to spend the Sabbath on a golf course. War changed this habit of mind, but during his command of first a corps, then an army, Haig makes few references in his diary to Providence or religious matters of any sort. As soon as he became Commander in Chief, however, a religious dimension appears. God, to be sure, was never mentioned by name, and Haig's denomination seems almost to have been chosen as a result of a particular preacher's good looks, youthful energy and simple sermons, but December 1915 Haig's writings make frequent references to a Providence, not the less re-assuring for its devotion to *FSR* and its corresponding approval of most of Haig's military decisions.

It was an unhealthy development in a man already tending towards delusions of infallibility and a sample of his writings during the war makes the point clearly:

'I do feel that in my plans I have been helped by a power that is not my own, so I am easy in my mind.'

'As to the battle of Arras, I know quite well that I am being used as a tool in the hands of the Divine Power and that my strength is not my own.'

'M. Albert Thomas was a Professor of Socialism [*sic*] before the war and has spent several years of his life in Berlin. His age is 39 but he looks older, he is so covered with hair and spectacles. But a fine, energetic man. I quite liked him and felt that Providence had sent him to meet me alone and discuss several problems affecting the British Army before Lloyd George arrived.'

'I feel I am only the instrument of that Divine Power who watches over each one of us so all the honour must be His.'

Many of Haig's weaknesses derived from this cast of mind. Caught in a time warp which froze his mind in 1909, Haig required the re-assurance of juniors at GHQ and seniors in Heaven as well as high battlements and deep moats, divinely sanctioned.

Was Haig therefore unaware of his weaknesses? An ironic and rather perplexing postscript would suggest otherwise. It derives from notes written in Haig's own hand for the guidance of those selected to draft his final dispatch as Commander in Chief.[12] The great interest of those notes today is Haig's exclusive concentration on all the weaknesses later generations were to find in his command.

'Certain proceedings of the war have been the subject of adverse criticism,' Haig began. 'It seems desirable to place on record the views of myself and my staff of the more important points and justify the actions taken.' Haig's admission of 'justification' was naturally omitted from the final document.

Each paragraph then selects a particular weakness. Thus 'discipline – very remarkable and reflects great credit on the nation. In the past, new armies lacked confidence in their officers. The regular soldier and officer were looked on as "wooden headed" and "stupid". In our New Army, we have been very free of these views(!)'.

The Old Army's monopoly of high office was obviously a sensitive area. Haig's defence of his own *ancien régime* attitude combined self-justification with a desperate search: 'Company commanders have commanded divisions and brigadiers have risen to command armies with great success. This shows that pre-war training was on sound lines. The principles of command and staff work have stood the test of war and are quite sound. The Military Secretary should be given information on the subject of new officers and of ranks to which very humble men have risen, e.g. a signalman of the North Western Railway to be a lieutenant-colonel etc.'

The rest of Haig's notes sustained the high-wire act, stating the weaknesses and discounting them with a combination of self-righteousness, bluster and astonishment that anyone might even doubt the practice of an Old Army man. Thus:

'. . . The value of mechanical contrivances. We are frequently told that this or that would "win the war", e.g. machine guns alone would win! Aeroplanes and bombs ditto! That a tank with six men was equal to a battalion! Mechanical contrivances have been greatly exaggerated in comparison with the value of infantry. There must also be artillery and cavalry!'

'. . . Cavalry have been pronounced useless in modern war!'

'. . . Organization generally. Previous organization should be upset as little as possible in war. Each war has certain specific conditions so some modifications will be necessary but if our principles are sound, these will be few and unimportant. The same remarks apply to training and education. The longer the war has gone on, the more satisfactory do the principles of our training manuals appear! The war has been won, in great measure, because of the good work done by our Staff College during the last thirty years. The educated (militarily) officer has counted for so much. (signed) D. Haig, 7.1.19.'

These notes underline the mind of a commander whose thinking had stopped in 1909. Haig's rigidity had been a serious liability throughout 1916–17, but these had been years of German passivity. 1918 would be very different. An enemy long dormant then launched a series of massive assaults and the war became fluid, trench warfare becoming a thing of the past. How would Haig react to a situation for which *FSR* gave so little direction? Cast off from his moorings, would Haig perhaps make that quantum leap into flexible thinking which was so long overdue?

1918:
A YEAR OF MOBILITY

11

March 1918:
The German Offensive

Just before dawn on 21 March 1918, 4,000 German guns opened fire on the southern part of the British front. It was one of the fiercest barrages of the war, and Winston Churchill described the overwhelming impact it made on him. 'The night was quiet,' he recalled. 'There was a rumble of artillery fire, mostly distant, and the thudding explosions of aeroplane raids. Suddenly the silence was broken by six or seven very loud explosions several miles away. I thought they were probably twelve-inch guns but they were probably mines. And then, exactly as a pianist runs his hands across a keyboard from treble to bass, there rose in less than one minute the most tremendous cannonade I shall ever hear. It swept around us in a wide curve of red flame, stretching to the north far along the front to the 3rd Army as well the 5th Army front to the south and quite unending in either direction.'[1]

After a few hours of softening-up, German infantry penetrated the British front line through the holes blasted by their artillery to such effect that the British were driven back twelve miles, losing 600 guns and sustaining 40,000 casualties in the process. A week later, the Germans were still advancing. The British had been forced back forty miles, and twenty-five of Haig's sixty divisions had become little more than skeletons.

It was the biggest defeat suffered by an army on the Western Front up to that moment, but it was something more. The Germans had shut up shop in the West since December 1914, concentrating their efforts against Russia. During these years of passivity, the

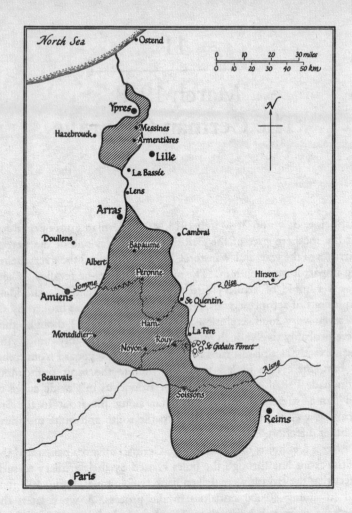

8 GERMAN TERRITORIAL GAINS, March–May 1918

The German advance was made in three bursts. The first, in March, pushed the front to Montdidier; the second, in April, to Hazebrouck; the third, in May, south from Soissons. Important as these gains were for the Germans in acreage, the chief threat to the allies was psychological. Mutual suspicions were increased, enmities deepened both between allies and, within each country, between the war and peace factions.

British exhausted themselves in a series of battles in which they were lucky to advance more than fifty yards a day after the most prolonged battering. Now, in a single week and without warning or apparent effort, the Germans had broken right through a carefully prepared defensive position with the ease of British regulars cutting Dervishes, Ashanti or Aborigines to pieces. The impact was therefore as much psychological as physical, and the diary of the 5th Army's chief gunner indicates the impact on the British high command.[2]

24 March: Men utterly worn out. Marvellous how they hang on. News during the day that the 3rd Army on our left has been driven in. A day of great crises. Looks as if the fate of the whole world will be decided in the next four days.

25 March: Hanging on by our eyelids all day. Lt.-Col. Harvey ordered to see Gough in the evening on behalf of his commander General Carey. He went in his pyjamas and was told by Gough that there was nothing between the Germans and Amiens. All they had to do to capture the place was to walk straight ahead.

The response at GHQ was little different. Henry Wilson noted Haig's mood on 25 March with his characteristic mixture of accuracy and malice: 'Haig is cowed. He said that unless the whole of the French Army came up, we were beaten and it would be better to make peace on any terms we could.' Nor was Haig the only man knocked off balance at GHQ. 'I went into the Commander in Chief's bedroom in my pyjamas,' Edmonds wrote, 'so that he should regard the visit as wholly unofficial. Had he noticed that one of his senior Staff Officers had gone off his head and another seemed to have senile decay? His reply was that their speech seemed odd and incoherent but he attributed this to his own deafness. He asked me what he should do. He couldn't send them home in the middle of a crisis. "Well," I said. "As regards M, it doesn't matter. He has done nothing for days but drive, night and day, carrying trifles from one railhead to another, but N is responsible for ordering and allocating engineering stores. This must go on so it would be best to order Colonel S to help him." Three days later, having shaved and had his bath, M dressed himself in his best uniform and shot himself in an armchair.'

Once the initial panic had passed and men began to take stock, two big questions were asked. If the British had been unable to break the German front after two years of bloody attrition, why had the Germans managed to achieve the impossible within a week? And how had Haig performed during the crisis? Strong doubts about his competence had been raised by Passchendaele and Cambrai. Had he shown himself a better man in defence than in attack perhaps?

The Commander in Chief's initial response to the first question had been contained in a dispatch for the Cabinet: 'On much of the front, the German advance was checked at the first line of the battle zone. In spite of constant pressure, our units kept together to a wonderful extent and repulsed the enemy by constant counter-attacks' – and so on in the same absurd vein.[3]

Within a couple of weeks, GHQ replaced this stop-gap with a cover story which has been fiercely debated ever since and remains today's orthodoxy, less a few chips in the veneer.[4] The crux of it was that Lloyd George had starved Haig of reinforcements after Passchendaele, then forced him to take over more front line from the French. Inadequate manpower was thus doubly diluted – or so Haig maintained.

The real facts were more complex and were rooted in the final months of 1917. Seen from the Cabinet room, the most important requirement after Passchendaele and Cambrai had been defence. Only when the Americans arrived in force could the British resume the offensive and fight a decisive campaign of 1919. Defence was necessary too, Lloyd George told Hankey in October 1917, so that Britain might remain a match for the Americans at the peace conference. The Prime Minister's view might seem pessimistic in the light of what came later, but at the time it was supported in one of the longest Cabinet papers Balfour ever wrote and no student of the period has ever accused Balfour of extreme or hasty judgement.

Ironically, the same Americans Lloyd George feared offered him the means of pursuing the cautious policy favoured by the Cabinet. In autumn 1917, Washington promised that twelve double-strength divisions would be ready for action by the end of March 1918. It must have seemed a providential intervention, since it allowed recruiting to be eased back on a restive home front. British divisions could

16 Haig, surrounded by his army commanders. From left to right, they are Plumer (2nd Army), Byng (3rd Army), Birdwood (5th Army), Rawlinson (4th Army) and Horne (1st Army).

17 Sir Hubert Gough, 5th Army commander and an important figure in the Somme and Passchendaele offensives. He was sacked after the débâcle of March 1918.

18 Sir Ivor Maxse, one of the finest commanders on the Western Front. He rose to take charge of a corps before being made responsible for training in France.

19 Moving up to the line. The ruined tower of the Cloth Hall at Ypres is in the background. The town's wall stretches across the photograph in the middle distance. Where the road cuts it, the commemorative Menin Gate was to be built after the war.

20 Paul Nash's painting 'The Menin Road, 1919' had a special meaning to Nash's generation. Through the bloodiest months of Passchendaele, the Menin Road had formed the battle's chief axis.

21 Paul Nash's painting 'Ypres Salient at Night'. It brings out better than any surviving photograph the feeling of the front line between battles. Night was the period of watchfulness; day of rest. Star shells burst to illuminate no-man's land, each side checking the 100 or so yards between opposing front lines for night patrols and raiding parties – or just from nervousness. With water so close to the surface, trenches in the Salient were usually built above ground, not below it.

22 Men advancing into battle in tight-packed lines led by their officer, whom enemy snipers easily picked out by his distinct uniform and the pistol in his hand. The sandbags in the forefront might be used for carrying rations, grenades, trophies or fragments of dead bodies.

23 Primitive apparatus, the quantity of shells and the emptiness of the period's battlefields mean that very few battle photographs have come down to us. In this photograph of the battle of Albert, the British are seen attacking near Mametz on 1 July 1916, the first day of the Somme. The white lines are excavated chalk from the German first-line trench systems. The second line lies just over the crest on the reverse slope. The black smoke is characteristic of bursting shrapnel shells.

24 German trenches seen from the Somme front line.

25 A German machine-gunner lies dead beside his weapon. The heavy Maxim, mounted on its robust iron sled, could spray up to 1,000 rounds a minute with the greatest accuracy, killing attackers and, in combination with barbed wire, funnelling them to areas where heavy artillery could complement their work.

26 A captured German trench, Puisieux, 1917. Its width and the wooden frame show that a dugout had been blown up here. Few prisoners were taken in the heat of battle. The occupants would therefore have been killed. Australian soldiers called the process 'ratting'.

27 The desolation of a Great War battlefield, with five soldiers using duckboards to cross the crater field of Passchendaele.

28 The Somme battlefield looking towards the Butte de Warlencourt, a famous landmark and furthest point reached by the end of 1916.

29 Passchendaele village before and after the battle of 3rd Ypres (known at the time as the battle of Passchendaele). At a conservative estimate, half a million shells have burst in the area shown on the second photograph. It covers about half a square mile.

30 'The Wine of Battle, October 1917' by Will Dyson, the
Australian artist. Haig gave statistics to this theme in a speech he read
before the British Legion after the war. His notes run, 'One million
British dead; 2,120,000 wounded; 400,000 widows and orphans;
600,000 wound pensions'.

31 John Singer Sargent's famous oil painting 'Gassed' shows groups
of men led towards casualty clearing stations after being temporarily
blinded by mustard gas. Parties of six were led by an orderly. When
the sketch was made, there were several hundred men waiting and
being led. Haig watched Sargent working on the painting and, rather
curiously, approved Sargent's theme.

also be reduced from twelve to nine battalions in anticipation and still keep the BEF's framework intact despite heavy casualties in 1917.[5] The assumption here was that the Americans would be fed into British divisions and bring them up to strength before serious fighting was resumed after the winter break. Even the stubborn Pershing gave the scheme his support at the start of January 1918. If, in the event, no American division was fit to fight when the German attack came, that could hardly have been foreseen at the end of 1917.

Lloyd George's position therefore made good sense, and it contrasted starkly with Haig's at the start of 1918. One would expect the British Commander in Chief to have been warning the government and clamouring for men after Passchendaele. He did the exact opposite in fact. The crucial meeting in which Haig made his position clear came on 7 January, when he was invited to appear before the Cabinet.[6] The session began with the politicians asking Haig for an opinion on what would happen in 1918. Would the Germans attack and, if they did, would the BEF be able to stand its ground?

Haig's account of what followed was disdainful. 'I spent the day with the War Cabinet,' he told Kiggell. 'All were particularly friendly but many stupid questions were asked. I did my best to answer them.' And so he did, but if Kiggell had been present he would have been surprised by many of Haig's statements. Had the British really defeated 131 German divisions with half that number in 1917? And did the British suffer 600,000 casualties to the German 900,000 in doing so? If Haig was right, his conclusions followed and the BEF's superior fighting ability would allow him to discount the increasing number of German troops on the Western Front. If on the other hand he was wrong, the consequences of a German victory in Russia might be as grave as the Cabinet had feared in September 1917. The War Office preferred the gloomier line, or as Henry Wilson put it, 'Robertson called Haig a fool. Haig told the War Cabinet that he was quite confident he could hold his own and never insisted on the necessity of being supplied with men.'

If Haig's view on the 7th come as a surprise, his correspondence offers a simple explanation. After the Somme and Passchendaele, Haig never believed that Ludendorff could launch an attack different in style from the long-drawn-out pounding of his own. Haig's policy was therefore to hold men back for the difficult times later in 1918. As he put it to Sir George Greaves just nine days before the German attack, 'England is able to run the show herself if our government will only give us more men *before the autumn* [Haig's emphasis]. That may possibly be the anxious time for us.'[7]

It was obviously a point of view well understood at the War Office. A week before Haig's letter to Greaves, a War Office memorandum sent to GHQ stated that 85,000 front-line soldiers would be sent to France during the next three months and an extra 74,000 for work in back areas.[8] More men were available, the War Office wrote, but on Haig's assurance that he could hold off a German attack for eighteen days, 12,000 men were kept in Britain as a strategic reserve. In other words, Haig believed he would have time to control the pace of an attrition battle and feed in drafts as required. For that reason, he rejected a mass of men classified B1 at the start of January and went on to take a phlegmatic view at the Cabinet session of 7 January.[9] Only after strong War Office pressure did he request reinforcement. The letter he wrote with its crossings-out and alterations can still be read, attached to the formal Cabinet minutes today.

The story behind the extension of the British line was equally paradoxical. Though Haig liked to give the impression it had been forced on him by a devious, unsupportive government, the truth was that he had known for some time that an extension would take place. In July 1917 he was already writing in his diary that a four-division sector would have to be taken from the French later that summer.[10] Passchendaele delayed the transaction and, when serious negotiations began, Lloyd George supported Haig's determination to keep the sector as small as possible. In the event, it was only the threat of resignation from Clemenceau which forced a six-division frontage on the British. The traditional picture of Haig fighting his corner alone is therefore a fable. The soldiers and politicians had been united.

Nor was the sector in a bad state of repair as we have been led to believe. Gough's initial inspection made that perfectly clear. Reporting back to the army commanders' conference of 20 November,

Gough described the first line as complete and the second line as half finished. Both had artillery emplacements every 150 yards, with more observation positions than Gough could man. The rail system, too, was of such density that Gough told his audience that no further building was necessary. As he put it, 'The French have left us 230 km of light rail which makes an excellent system together with the excellent roads.'

The one deficiency Gough recorded was in the third line, but since GHQ's defensive scheme visualized a rear position much further back than anything conceived by the French, that was not considered much of a handicap.

GHQ's defence of its position in March 1918 was thus inadequate to explain the depth and speed of the German breakthrough. Men had been offered and rejected. The line taken over from the French had been pending for half a year, which had given Haig enough time to make detailed provision for when it was formally handed over. So what had gone wrong and to what extent was Haig culpable?

Once the episode is placed against available documents rather than the lies and half truths which have been hawked for so long, it is the number of important decisions Haig got right rather than his errors of judgement which stand out.

For a start, Haig decided early on that there would be a German attack and though he told his wife, 'One is so in the dark what the Boche means to do,' he began to plan his defence on 7 December 1917. On that day, army commanders were ordered to build a defensive system similar to the one described in the German hand-book of March 1917.[11] From bitter experience, Haig could tell his commanders: 'It embodies the lessons of two years' defensive experience and is thoroughly sound.'

Where would the attack come? In January, the British team on the Supreme War Council expected a small strike against La Bassée in the north, with the heaviest attack against Paris and the French.[12] By the end of the month, their views had changed.[13] Lloyd George was given the new assessment and he ordered that it should be passed on to Haig, with Leo Amery the go-between. Amery later recorded: 'Haig said many stupid things – that the French were no use; that he was able to hold the line against the Germans; that he was not going to divert troops to help the French.'[14] Lloyd George was furious and he ordered Haig to attend a formal briefing at Versailles by the British experts of the Supreme War Council.

The Commander in Chief had no choice, but registered his resentment openly, 'twiddling his moustaches and studying a paper he was to read that afternoon,' as Du Cane noted. The same evening, Haig described the lecture for Kiggell with a wearied pen: 'I thought it rather a waste of time. Their conclusions were most impracticable.' And yet Haig had obviously pondered the lecture because he quietly accepted all the War Council's conclusions. They had picked the Cambrai–St Quentin sector as the weakest point, with the flanks of the Cambrai Salient particularly vulnerable, since the Germans enjoyed rail superiority of 25 per cent in the vicinity. Haig was bound to acknowledge common sense of that sort.

He listened to the lecture on 30 January. A fortnight later, he told his army commanders to expect an attack between Lens and the Oise in March and a second blow against Ypres in April.[15] By 2 March, Haig had narrowed it down. The attack would be on the 3rd and 5th Army fronts with a view to cutting off the Cambrai Salient and drawing in British reserves – which was indeed the underlying purpose of Ludendorff's strategy.

Haig was also right on the sort of attack the Germans would deliver. Stealth in preparation combined with a violent first strike came as no surprise, because the War Office had sent him detailed German orders for the battle of Riga,[16] a gem fought on the Eastern Front in September 1917. Assault troops had de-trained seventy miles from the point of attack and marched by night to escape aerial observation. Artillery had been moved up in the same way and set in place a few days before zero in the knowledge that the first shot would be accurate. New developments in the calculation of muzzle velocity made this possible and allowed the correct muzzle elevation to be set by a quick calculation on paper rather than by ranging shots (as hitherto) which would have betrayed everything. A heavy six-hour bombardment was thus able to blast gaps which small groups of storm troops could penetrate and create panic in.

Haig never contemplated an attack in this style himself, but he had made a study of similar tactics used against the French in summer 1917[17] and GHQ's Intelligence branch confirmed his wisdom in January 1918. Beverloo, the German Army's chief training school, was reported to be working on infiltration in hilly, wooded country. The southern part of the British line matched Beverloo's choice exactly.

Haig's prediction of date was equally accurate. His Intelligence chief and the experts at Versailles agreed in January that a German offensive could be mounted on 1 March, even though the Germans would stand inferior in artillery and have an advantage of only twenty-two divisions. (1 May appeared to suit them better and summer weather would allow an extension of the battle front south across the Alps and north into Flanders.) On 16 February, Haig therefore told his army commanders that the Germans would probably attack first in March and again in April, before making their chief attack in May.[18] Ten days after that conference, the French passed on information from their spies in Switzerland.[19] The Germans would attack on 10 March. Haig – correctly – preferred his own projection of a date between 15 and 25 March.

Haig had thus got the date, place and attacking style right. Why then did the front collapse so completely? Or, put another way, why did Haig give Gough half Rawlinson's men and guns in proportion to his length of front if Rawlinson was in untroubled Flanders and Gough was where Haig expected the attack to come? The answer can be discovered in the conjunction of two factors. The first was Haig's adoption of a defensive scheme which asked too much from his own poorly trained men; the second, an error he shared with Pétain as to how Ludendorff would attack.

To grasp the defensive scheme concocted by Haig and Pétain necessitates going back to July 1915. Anticipating an attack to separate the British and French, the War Office had been alarmed at GHQ's response. Sir John French declared an intention of fighting his way back to the Channel ports. Robertson, his Chief Staff Officer, favoured staying put and maintaining the French link at all costs. Faced with this disagreement, Asquith invited written analyses from all army commanders in France.[20]

Haig's analysis began by trying to anticipate what the Germans might do. An advance on Paris he discounted because of the strength of successive defensive lines and an expectation of continued resistance even if Paris fell. Deep penetration along the Somme past Amiens looked more dangerous, but would compel surrender only if U-boats controlled the Channel or if British industry proved unable to sustain an encircled British Army. 'If neither condition pertained, then the position of Germany would be one of great danger. The force cut off would become increasingly strong and would threaten German flanks.'

By elimination, Haig came upon the option he feared most – a direct attack on the Channel ports. Weighing up marshy ground, rail configuration and canal systems, Haig selected Messines–La Bassée as the danger zone and all the more because German communications in the Lille area allowed thirty-one divisions to attack on a twenty-mile front there.

How should the British respond to such an attack? Haig was unequivocal: 'For reasons given in the former part of this paper, there is little doubt that retention of the coast is the more advantageous course' – in other words, the British should fall back on the Channel ports if attacked. Rather unexpectedly, Joffre agreed with Haig's analysis when it was shown to him. The ports were so important, he told Asquith, that the British must base their plans on them. The French would support the British meanwhile by counter-attacking the southern flank of the advancing Germans.

Haig and Pétain picked up this old analysis at the start of 1918 and began to coordinate the details in earnest. British army commanders were kept in touch with this planning through January, and when the scheme was finalized they were fully briefed in mid-February.[21] The crux of the final Haig–Pétain scheme was that if the British alone were attacked they would fall back on the Channel ports, and if the French, they in turn would retreat south-westwards.

The detailed application of this policy in the field was dictated to Gough when Haig met him on 9 February. The most important directive Haig gave him (in the light of what was to happen when the offensive began) was that, if the 5th Army were attacked, Gough should make a big jump all the way back to the Somme so as to dislocate the German offensive.[22] It was a startling and dangerous brainwave on Haig's part. A fast coordinated movement by an entire army needed a level of training and quality of staff work far beyond the BEF. Gough seems to have welcomed the idea nevertheless and gave journalists an outline of these tactics which Bean summarized for his record. 'If the Germans break through, even to Calais, our routes of retirement right back to the sea are already laid down and our plans prepared.'

Lloyd George was later to criticize Gough for employing only 8,000 men on building defences after his allocation had been increased from 24,000 to 50,000 in the seven-week period before the attack. But why waste labour building defences for a position which was to be evacuated at an early stage? Better to use it for getting men down from the sensitive Flanders region if they were needed – and that is what Haig did. An order of 4 January, marked 'Very secret', answers a question which has bothered historians for two generations. Where were the missing labourers and what were they doing? 'For adequate and efficient lateral movement in the rear of the battle zone,' ran Haig's secret order, 'and for rapid movement of reserves, Sir Douglas Haig has decided that a light railway system of two north–south lateral lines, connected at intervals by cross lines, will be built. The material and labour is not available to construct these lines concurrently with an expansion of existing system in forward areas . . .' The wording explains both the missing labourers and the discrepancy in resources between Gough and Rawlinson. The work of one was planned to shift the surplus of the other as circumstances required.

All these schemes and preparations might seem purely defensive, but that wasn't the case. The only point of going back was to lure the enemy into a trap and set him up for a counter-strike from whichever army was under less pressure. The size of the counter-attacking force was set at six divisions and detailed preparations were made to move forces of that size. When the news broke of a German attack concentrated on the British alone, those in the know were therefore jubilant. Bean happened to be passing the Ministry of Information in London early that morning at the very moment John Buchan was coming down the steps. 'Good news!' Buchan said to him cheerfully. 'The Germans have fallen into every trap we have laid.'

Buchan went on to tell Bean that a rapid retreat to the line of the Somme and St Quentin canal had been part of Haig's plan from the start. So what went wrong, and how did the Germans manage to get through a revolving door held open for them with sufficient force to burst the door clean off its pivot?

The answer lies in a single factor – Haig's miscalculation of force. On 7 January, he had described the attack he visualized to the Cabinet and Derby later sent him a querulous note about his address: 'Every member of the Cabinet was under the impression you had stated a belief that the Germans would make no great offensive on the West Front but might attack on the Cambrai scale . . .'

Haig's reply is not available, but Derby's understanding was correct. Addressing army commanders on 16 February, Haig confirmed that fact when he said: 'The Germans must be expected to follow sound principles. They will try to wear us down before the main attack.' In other words, Haig expected a light initial attack which would give ample time for the Haig–Pétain scheme to be set in motion. More particularly, Haig anticipated that the Germans would disperse their attacking forces, allocating them to a ten-mile sector near Verdun, a thirty-mile one near Reims and at odd points on the sixty miles between Lens and the Oise.

Two items in the Haig papers show that Haig's assessment remained the same to the end. In one of them, Haig expressed satisfaction twenty-four hours before the German attack that six divisions promised by the French could be concentrated near Amiens within six days of his own request. The French would therefore be ready to begin fighting at Péronne within eleven days. It was clear proof of the degree of underestimation in Haig's calculations, since the attack, when it finally came, required the French to be fully prepared for battle within three days.

The same point was made in a letter Haig sent his wife on 20 March. Although his son had been born five days earlier, Haig explained that the enemy were rather threatening and he therefore thought it better to delay his visit to London for a week and sent soup instead: 'The cook is making some soup for you and I am arranging to send it by King's Messenger on Friday . . . My actual presence in France at the moment of the attack is not necessary. All the reserves and other questions such as moving up troops in support have already been settled. But, on general principles, I ought to be with the Army when the battle is active.' There could be no better proof of Haig's certainty that the German attack would be a small-scale affair.

The offensive actually began the day after Haig wrote that letter and Gough's army moved back on Péronne without disturbing Haig. 'I am glad the attack has come,' Haig wrote. 'It was a case of kill, kill, kill all day so the enemy must have lost very severely.'

Disillusionment came soon enough, and the second major question arising from the great German offensive poses itself at this point. How did Haig perform under the stress of a massive attack which had destroyed three months of preparation within hours? The custom has been to give him high marks, using a narrative based on his diary to do so, but there is a major problem here because Haig's handwritten diary differs widely from the typed version which historians have always used for the examination of this controversial period. The best way to clarify the discrepancy is to tell the story twice over, using the typed diary first and following it with an account based on the handwritten version, bearing in mind that the handwritten diary pre-dates the typed and is therefore likely to be more reliable.

The traditional story begins with Haig meeting Pétain on the afternoon of 23 March. According to the typed diary, signs of vacillation were already apparent in Pétain. As Haig put it, 'In reply to my request to concentrate a large French force about Amiens, Pétain said he was anxious to do all he can to support me but he expected that the enemy is about to attack him in Champagne. Still, he will do his utmost to keep the two Armies in touch. If this is lost and the enemy comes between us, then probably the British will be rounded up and driven into the sea. This must be prevented even at the cost of drawing back the north flank on the sea coast . . .'

Haig and Pétain met again during the evening of the 24th. 'Pétain struck me as very much upset and anxious. He had directed Fayolle, in the event of German advance being pressed still further, to fall back south-west towards Beauvais in order to cover Paris. It was at once clear to me the effect of this order must be to separate the French from the British right flank and so allow the enemy to penetrate between the two. I at once asked Pétain if he meant to abandon my right flank. He nodded assent and added, "It is the only thing possible if the enemy compelled the allies to fall back still further." From my talk with Pétain, I gathered that he had recently attended a Cabinet meeting in Paris and his orders from his government were "To cover Paris at all costs". So I hurried back to my headquarters at Beaurepair Chateau to report the serious change in French strategy to the CIGS and the Secretary of State for War and ask them to come to France.'

In his diary of 25 March, Haig went into more detail on the message he had sent to London. The gist, he said, was 'to arrange that General Foch or some other determined general who would fight should be given supreme control of operations in France' and from that moment, according to the traditional story, events revolved around Haig's proposal.

On the 26th, high-level discussion of Haig's request took place at the celebrated conference of Doullens, leading soldiers and politicians meeting in the local Town Hall and Haig recording the chief speeches at length in his diary.

The chief exchange, according to the typed diary, began with a French suggestion: 'It was proposed by Clemenceau that Foch should be appointed to coordinate operations of an allied force to cover Amiens and ensure that the French and British flank remained united. This proposal seemed to me quite worthless, as Foch would be in a subordinate position to Pétain and myself. In my opinion, it was essential to success that Foch should control Pétain so I at once recommended that Foch should coordinate the action of the allied armies on the Western Front. Both governments agreed to this. Foch seemed sound and sensible but Pétain had a terrible look. He had the appearance of a commander who was in a funk and has lost his nerve.'

From Haig's point of view, this narrative does him proud. Pétain had panicked at an early stage. Haig took control and produced the best solutions at every point and makes a strong contrast with dithering, panicky Pétain. March 1918 thus appeared to bring out the John Bull in Haig. But what of the alternative account in the handwritten diary?

The traditional story emphasizes Pétain's funk. The new dispensation starts by emphasizing the vigour of his initial response. Haig's private secretary told Esher that 'Relations with Pétain were very different from those with Foch when it was like drawing an eye-tooth to get assistance' and Haig's handwritten diary confirms the point. When Gough told Haig that the Germans had got through his reserve line about 8 pm on the 22nd, Haig immediately contacted Pétain, only to discover that Pétain had that morning given the order on his own initiative for three divisions to move up at once. 'The situation is better tonight,' Haig concluded. 'The French are said to be moving up quickly.'

When Haig and Pétain met on the 23rd, GHQ's minutes remarked on Pétain's calm and set out his position.[23] 'Pétain attaches great importance to the maintenance of the connection as the enemy is sure to try and drive between the two Armies.' These minutes go on to describe French efforts to maintain the link and record a French assurance that six of their divisions would be concentrated at Amiens within six days. Both the quantity and the timing were exactly those which had been agreed between the two Commanders in Chief in February.

In his typed diary, Haig described Pétain's intention of deserting the British, hence the message to London. The handwritten diary makes no mention of any of this, and when Duff Cooper came to the period in his research of Haig's official biography he was evidently disturbed by the discrepancy and queried it with Edmonds – who in his turn admitted that he had been unable to trace any evidence of the supposed telephone call. 'It seems to me the later message I mentioned in the Official History must have been telephoned, but no copy or confirmation is to be found in the files. I had a long search some months ago. I thought the message was mentioned in Haig's diary. There is not the least doubt what Haig's sentiments were at the time.'[24]

In fact, as Edmonds well knew, the message requesting Wilson's presence in France had been written in Haig's room at 5 pm on the 24th and telephoned to the War Office at 6 pm. It was confirmed at 6.35 pm and can today be found as message 7734 in the War Office's cipher book.[25] There never was any later message. Milner's journey to France and the conference at Doullens which followed therefore owed nothing to Haig and everything to Clemenceau's wire to London expressing concern with the orders Haig was issuing.

When Haig's 6 pm message had been phoned through ('Situation is serious. Morval Ridge [on the old Somme battlefield] lost so 3rd and 5th Armies are separated. Junction with the French can only be re-established by vigorous offensive action of French while I do all I can from the north in conjunction with them. I meet Pétain tonight') Haig set off for his late-night meeting with Pétain.

The British party consisted of Haig, Lawrence and Sidney Clive, the GHQ liaison officer with Pétain. Despite the claims in Haig's typed diary, Clive found nothing disturbing to record after a supposedly critical conference. His diary concluded with Pétain's cheerful, 'I shall sleep better tonight than I have done for many nights.'

Haig was less cheerful. Earlier that evening he had handed a personal letter to Foch's Chief Staff Officer stating: 'It can only be a matter of time before the French and British Armies are driven apart. It becomes necessary to take immediate steps to restore the situation and this is only possible by concentrating immediately astride the Somme, west of Amiens, at least twenty French divisions to operate on the northern flank of the German movement against the British Army which must fight its way slowly back, covering the Channel ports. Any delay in deciding upon this plan may make the situation critical.'[26]

This determination on Haig's part to get back to the Channel ports was repeated a few hours later when he met Byng: 'Haig made it quite clear,' Byng recalled, 'that the BEF had now to safeguard itself and no help could be expectd from the south. Further withdrawal must now be to the north-west with the 3rd Army safeguarding the right flank of the BEF by swinging back its own right. Haig took for granted that no help was to be expected from Gough.'[27]

With the British running away to the north, an allied conference became vitally necessary. Retreat to the Channel ports had certainly been part of the Haig–Pétain plan, but it was always assumed that any movements backwards would be part of a policy of coordinated counter-attack. The French share in the plan was being carried out to the letter (and since they were not under attack, Haig's later claim that the French proposed to retreat south-westwards was pure invention), but the sheer size of the German attack meant that a counter-attack by six divisions had become inadequate. The Haig–Pétain plan had to be completely re-structured. Hence the conference at Doullens.

Exactly what happened at that conference remains unclear. Montgomery-Massingberd, Rawlinson's Chief of Staff, took notes on behalf of GHQ, but when Edmonds approached him for the full story in 1924, Montgomery-Massingberd could only point out that the language used was French, that discussion had been split between a number of groups and that he had been stuck in a corner of the room.[28] At the end of the conference, his own record had anyway been amended by Haig in person before being filed away as GHQ's record. Montgomery-Massingberd concluded that his written account was likely to be as suspect as his own memory.[29]

The Cabinet's record might seem a better source, since Milner was involved in the negotiations throughout and went on to write the Cabinet's official account.[30] But he only put pen to paper twenty-four hours after the event.

The best transcript is probably Montgomery-Massingberd's original draft, discovered by Lloyd George's secretary in 1934 during research for the latter's memoirs.[31] In this draft, Haig's ambivalence on the vital rail junction of Amiens comes across strongly, indicating that his position had changed little since the panicky note to Foch on the 24th. Montgomery-Massingberd recorded Haig's stance in these words: 'It is vitally important to hold Amiens but there must be no break between the 1st and 3rd Armies. This is more important than holding Amiens. All available reserves are therefore to be sent to the 3rd Army. We will cover Amiens so long as possible but will then fall back on the Arras–Doullens line.'

In the second session at Doullens, Amiens was again the chief object of discussion, and Haig budged from his determination to fall back on the Channel ports only at that point. As Montgomery-Massingberd's notes put it, 'Haig pointed out the absolute necessity of pushing troops up from the south. After some discussion, it was agreed unanimously that the important thing was to cover Amiens. Pétain explained how long it would take his troops to arrive.'

The conference then broke up into several groups. Everyone

appeared to be talking at once, but the principal discussion was between Clemenceau and Milner. The latter gave an opinion that Foch was the man most likely to deal energetically with the crisis. Clemenceau took the idea to Haig and Pétain, and the discussion between them (in Milner's presence) lasted thirty minutes. Milner told his private secretary later that Haig's first reaction had been to assert that he would take orders only from his sovereign, but British dependence on the French made the final decision inevitable. As Montgomery-Massingberd said, 'After much private discussion, a resolution by Clemenceau was drawn up and read out. This amounted to a decision that General Foch would be placed in a position to coordinate the action of the Commanders in Chief.'

In his Official History, Edmonds took the story a stage further by asserting that Haig intervened to increase the scope of Foch's authority, but this seems to have been a characteristic act of faith on Edmonds's part rather than a statement of historical fact, and Montgomery-Massingberd was unable to confirm it when Edmonds checked it with him in 1925.[32] Nor is it easy to believe that an eyewitness acting as GHQ's secretary would have missed an interjection of such importance by his chief – if that interjection was ever made. The outcome of Doullens was anyway what mattered, and there was never any doubt about that. The British retreat to the Channel ports was stopped and Haig had to surrender much of the independence he had fought so long to retain.

Summarizing the story of March 1918 as told in Haig's handwritten diary, the traditional narrative is almost reversed. In place of Pétain's funk and Haig's magisterial calm, it is now Pétain who keeps his head and Haig who panics when the Germans force their way between the 3rd and 5th Armies. Rather than Pétain threatening to desert Haig, it is Haig who actually deserts Pétain, scampering away to the north with little thought for the consequences. The Doullens conference, too, was the result of a move by allied politicians, Foch's appointment being secured over Haig's opposition. It makes sad reading for Haig's supporters, and the actual situation on the battlefield during these tortuous proceedings gives a final piquant twist.

*

The Germans began the offensive with 195 divisions on the Western Front. Ludendorff had reserved sixty-three for the attack, with eleven to hold the line beforehand. The first six days of battle had consumed seventy-three divisions. The next four, another ten. Success had therefore stretched the Germans to the limit and practical problems were mounting all the time. On the 21st, each infantryman had been given a single iron ration plus food for two days, two water bottles of coffee and 150 rounds of ammunition. The usual difficulties in replenishing those items were compounded by having to carry them across the wilderness of the old Somme battlefield, itself further devastated during the German retreat of spring 1917. Herbert Uniacke, chief gunner in Gough's 5th Army, noted in his diary that the enemy's difficulties with thirst, hunger and fatigue were increased by an abrupt change in the weather on the 26th from high summer temperatures to equally unseasonal wintry conditions. For attacking troops pushed to breaking point, the change must have come as a body blow.

Sidney Clive meanwhile wrote with enthusiasm about the French. 'French rail and lorries working magnificently. 160 to 180 trains arriving daily and with twenty-five divisions coming by lorry.'[33] This optimism on Clive's part was confirmed by an American observer on the 29th, writing to the President: 'French reserves arriving in such numbers as to arrest the German advance. Amiens in less danger than on 27th. German communiqués less confident. Thirty British and seventeen French divisions now face seventy-eight.'[34]

What of the 5th Army, which had borne the brunt of the attack?

Emilio Kinkhelm was well placed to gauge British morale. As an attaché for Argentina in Berlin, he had been brought to the front with the other attachés to witness the fall of Amiens, planned for the 30th. In his report (intercepted by British Intelligence), Kinkhelm wrote that the 5th Army had been severely mauled. Though ninety prisoners he checked had all been captured in a single wood, they came from four separate divisions. It was an indication of the degree of disintegration within the 5th Army. The common feeling of German soldiers on the spot was nevertheless that the British had fought bravely. Watching prisoners going to the rear, Kinkhelm noted their phlegmatic calm with surprise. One soldier in particular he picked out as typical. He was a young man whose face seemed to have been split right open to leave an eyeball dangling on his cheek. The man was quietly smoking a pipe and when Kinkhelm asked him about the battle, he spat out the words, 'Dirty Germans!' If there had been radio news or printed information sheets giving a bird's-eye view the 5th Army might have panicked, but with each man's vision limited to a tiny area, retreat had been a low-key affair for the most part, and there was little enough evidence of a significant breakdown in morale.

All this evidence of stalemate, rapidly developing, meant that if allied politicians had not intervened to stop the British Army running away to the north, Haig would have presented the Germans with an important victory against the facts of the battlefield. The conference at Doullens and the events of the 26th were therefore of the greatest importance in the history of the war – but for reasons very different from those usually put forward on Haig's behalf.

12

August 1918: A Turning Point?

August 1918 remains a month of critical importance for any assessment of Haig and the reason is simply stated. According to the usual scenario, the Germans exhausted themselves in a number of massive attacks between March and July 1918. The allies recovered slowly meanwhile and, after snuffing out the last German offensive near Reims, counter-attacked and took the Germans by surprise in the battle of Amiens on 8 August. From that moment, the German Army was forced back, its morale steadily declining, its organization crumbling, its reserves railroaded backwards and forwards the length of the Western Front in a despairing attempt to plug holes punched by rampant allies.

The standard British view gives the British Army the lead role in this performance and gives Haig star billing. He was the first to foresee the victory. Amiens was Haig's battle. The strategy which kept pressure on the Germans was Haig's strategy. The winning conception of a concentric advance to maximize the punch of the allies was Haig's conception. There is only one possible conclusion. Whatever the shortcomings of the apprentice, the final phase was managed by a master at the height of his powers.

It all makes pleasant reading for patriots, and there was little criticism of this traditional overview until documents made available in the 1960s were set against it. Discrepancies then appeared at every point. German military weakness on the Western Front became hard to find and the French and British were discovered anxiously debating the possibility of their own military defeat well into July 1918.

About that time, the documents show Foch taking hold of strategy, with Haig restive in a subordinate position and playing little part in strategic planning from July until the end of the war.

The narrative of Haig's command for 1918 must therefore be restructured so as to match the documentary record, and the German offensives in the early spring of 1918 make the best starting point.

During that period, the Germans made two massive attacks on the British front, the first in the south on 21 March, the second on 9 April against Armentières, directed against the Channel ports. The savagery of these attacks has never been fully grasped, but 300,000 British casualties in the four weeks after 21 March record it with the precision of a seismograph.[1] Those figures mean that British losses in those four weeks were similar to Passchendaele's — which lasted nearly five times as long. If British writers after the war failed to see what the figures meant, Foch was under no illusion at the time. 'It is undeniable that the British Army is exhausted,' he remarked at a conference in May.

Had the Germans directed their next attack at the British, it is quite probable Haig's Army would have been defeated. That was the opinion Rawlinson gave Du Cane after the war, but for reasons imperfectly understood, Ludendorff turned his attentions elsewhere and created one of the few complete surprises of the war. On 25 May, Haig asked Foch through Du Cane whether another attack was imminent. 'I don't think so,' Foch replied. Forty-eight hours later, the French were hit by forty-two divisions and 4,000 guns on the Chemin des Dames. There was no greater crisis in the war.

In an unpublished draft of his memoirs, Pershing described Foch panic-stricken and confused, striding back and forth at a secret session of parliament, flinging his arms in wild gestures and shouting, '*La bataille, la bataille, il n'y a que ça qui coûte.*'[2] Foch had gone on to issue preliminary orders for what the 3rd Bureau called 'The Big Plan'.[3] This involved pulling back from the flanks of the Western Front and fighting a massive battle in the open to defend Paris as a battle of last resort. Sidney Clive probed the French mood at the time and got an opinion at Pétain's HQ that if this battle were lost and Paris fell, the war would have to be ended. He immediately checked that dire assessment with the War Office's Director of Intelligence and McDonogh confirmed it.[4]

The Cabinet's reaction underlined the scale of the crisis. On 5 June, their discussion concerned the speed with which the British Army could be pulled out of France, and a little later Leo Amery was asked to work out the details of a 'Dunkirk' operation.[5] Realizing meanwhile that the loss of France as an ally required a deepening of alliances and understandings elsewhere, the Imperial War Cabinet was summoned and Milner briefed Lloyd George on the tone of his opening address. The gist of his advice was that the Dominion representatives had to be carefully prepared for the worst, with Italy and France beaten and Germany left 'in control not only of Europe and most of Asia but of the whole world'. In that situation, Milner suggested, Britain would become 'an exposed outpost' dependent for its survival on trade with Australia and India. Milner concluded: 'If our bonds with the USA and Japan were really tight, we could win through but our position would be one of constant and immediate peril.'

Milner handed these notes to Lloyd George on 11 June. The British were critically short of men at the time and the French within a whisker of defeat. What of the Germans? After three massive attacks, did they still have the manpower to convert an edge into a victory? The facts as Lloyd George and Haig knew them were ominous indeed. When they had attacked on 21 March, the Germans had 195 divisions on the Western Front. In June, they had 207, each with battalions at their full strength of 850 men.

It seemed that the Germans had victory within their grasp. The British and French were disunited and on their knees. The Germans appeared to have enough men to finish the job, but again they hesitated. It may have been the tactical difficulty of fuelling a big attack at the end of a deep salient. It may equally have been a quarrel between the Bavarian Crown Prince in the north and the Prussian Crown Prince in the south over the best place to commit German reserves (French Intelligence briefed Pershing's representative to that effect). Either way, the Germans failed to follow up their advantage by transferring the point of attack to the north, where their manpower was sufficient to have a good chance of breaking through to the Channel ports while the French were still shaken – or so Rawlinson thought and Haig feared. By the time the Germans were ready to attack again, they did so on 15 July in the same region as in May (forty-three divisions and 5,000 guns near Reims, hoping to take Paris itself) and were themselves surprised. The attack hit an empty position. The French counter-attacked. The Germans were sent into full retreat. It was their first major setback of 1918.

The impact of this counter-attack was graphically recorded by Pershing's liaison officer with Pétain. 'The babel of voices in the office was great. Everyone's face was creased with smiles. One would impersonate Ludendorff at the phone receiving news of the counter-attack and, in mingled French and German, give the conversation. Two others would impersonate a meeting between the Crown Prince and Ludendorff and convulse the audience with their gesticulations. Another would pretend to be the Kaiser and so on. Between laughs, they would read the latest message, mark it on the map and shake my hand. Several have said that without the United States, this would not have been possible.'[6]

When the celebrations died down, the traditional view of the war has it that the British attacked on 8 August and broke the stalemate. Eleven divisions and 400 tanks had been brought to the front using methods learnt (at last!) from the Germans, and on the first day of the battle alone the British advanced six miles and took 12,000 prisoners and 200 German guns. It was a British triumph.

Even Ludendorff admitted the importance of that day. 'August 8th was the Black Day of the German Army,' he wrote in his memoirs. 'It marked the decline in our fighting power and, the manpower situation being what it was, it robbed me of the hope of discovering some strategic expedient that might once more stabilize the position in our favour. The war would have to be ended.'

Haig's protagonists were naturally quick to link their man with the trenchant victory and with the triumphs which seemed to follow hard upon it. Duff Cooper, Haig's official biographer, went so far as to claim the whole conception and all the credit for his man. 'In view of the decisive effect which was produced,' he wrote, 'it is important that the credit for its conception should be justly assigned.' Foch's original plan had envisaged only a small British offensive near Armentières – or so Duff Cooper claimed. Haig's breadth of vision had been necessary to persuade a timid Foch that a combined offensive at Amiens offered exciting possibilities. 'The plan had been Haig's from the first,' Duff Cooper concluded. 'He had thought out every detail of it and British forces were to be mainly responsible for its execution.'

So much for the claim. What of the facts? On the point of conception, Bean settled the matter conclusively in a masterly chapter in the sixth volume of the Australian Official History. Foch had planned a surprise counter-strike at Amiens within days of taking up his coordinating role in March 1918.[7] When the German thrust at Armentières subsided, Foch again pulled the Amiens project out of his files, specifying tactical elements very similar to those adopted in August – twenty divisions, 200 tanks and a barrage held back until zero.[8] Once more, a German offensive intervened, but by the second week of July and with events moving in his favour, Foch again took his old idea out of its pigeon hole and gave it to Haig on 11 July in the form of a directive.[9]

What was Haig's response? Contrary to accepted wisdom, he was openly pessimistic, and with good reason. The Germans remained very strong, the allies correspondingly weak and jittery. Eleven days later, Haig told the War Office that he still expected to be attacked in Flanders.[10] If he wasn't, the best he could offer Foch was a small attack near Arras. Only if he was given incontrovertible evidence that German reserves in Flanders had been depleted would he consider a battle at Amiens, and then using only Dominion troops. The job of the French in that area was to be a passive one, defending the line beforehand so that Dominion men could pass through them to deliver the attack. It required a personal visit from Foch on 23 July to break down Haig's resistance and cajole him into actually starting his preparations for a battle at Amiens.[11]

Although there is nothing explicit on record, the reason for Foch's success in converting Haig was one which gave Foch the whip hand over Haig at the time, explained his ability to anticipate the July attack with such accuracy and was to give Foch an edge over Haig to the end of the war. It was a breakthrough in Intelligence work comparable in importance to breaking the Enigma Code in the Second World War.

The story goes back to August 1917. The Germans that month suddenly silenced the richest source of allied Intelligence with an electronic breakthrough noted in American Intelligence bulletins. 'The newest German wireless sending stations are now making use of automatic controllers which continually and automatically vary wave lengths. Receiving stations are provided with these controllers which automatically adjust themselves to the lengths of the waves, however much they vary.'[12] This bombshell was reinforced by a complete change in German codes on the eve of the March offensive. The combined effectiveness was clearly demonstrated by the degree of surprise achieved by the Germans in their big attacks of 21 March, 9 April and 27 May. But this German advantage was to disappear as suddenly as it had come and by July, the wheel had turned full circle. American archives show that the French had acquired the ability to brief liaison officers with an unbroken sequence of high-grade information reaching from Ludendorff's headquarters right down to each German Army Group on the Western Front.[13] Whether this breakthrough was the result of improved electronics or, as seems more likely from the reports of the American Paul Clark, through well-placed spies or informers, remains unclear. Either way, it was a development which was to have a decisive impact on the strategy of the war's last hundred days.

The British had their first hint of this breakthrough four days before the July battle, when Foch's representative in London met Lloyd George and told him that the Germans would attack four days later at a particular spot (indicated on a map) and that five days later Foch would counter-attack on the flank at another spot (also indicated on the map).

This foreknowledge of German intentions was to prove a crucial factor. Haig had asserted his unwillingness to make any commitment to Amiens unless he was given indisputable evidence that the Germans would not attack in Flanders. On 23 July, Foch not only gave him that assurance but threw in a detailed outline of the enemy's strategic intentions for the rest of 1918.[14]

The Germans, said Foch, would retreat. Their aim, as in spring 1917, would be to frustrate the attacking schemes of the allies and safeguard their own centres of communication. Foch went on to list those centres, suggesting that the Germans wanted to keep the allies at least 20 km from each and would therefore force them to cross 50 km of devastated ground to reach them.

At the end of his briefing, Foch passed a map to Haig. The successive lines of retreat Foch predicted showed that although the Germans could surrender their 1918 gains without strategic disadvantage, they were bound to keep firm hold on the lateral railway line which skirted the Ardennes and passed through Lille, Hirson, Mézières and Metz. If the Germans failed to keep hold of it, their Army would be split in two. Foch's advice was therefore to press the enemy with advanced guards, keep in touch and harass the German retreat with the aim of knocking the German timetable off balance. The time to attack seriously, Foch suggested, was spring 1919. Before that, the allies should just keep shoving as hard as they could.

Haig was converted by the quality of Foch's information and from that moment he was content to slot into that battle at Amiens which Foch had been preparing since April. That at least was the surface appearance.

Even after getting Haig's agreement, Foch had in fact much work still to do before Haig would agree to make Amiens a substantial battle. Lloyd George recalled Foch's difficulties during a meeting with Smuts and Hankey on the treatment of that period in his memoirs.[15] 'I got the facts from Henry Wilson,' Lloyd George recalled. 'Foch went there and found Haig arranging for an ordinary attack on 8 km. Foch said "You must make this 30 or 40 km." Haig replied, "I have no troops." "What?" replied Foch. "Have you no troops in your trenches for 20 km to your left?" Haig replied in the affirmative. "They will do. And what of Debeney? He is on your right. He has troops in the trenches. I will order him."' Hankey expressed surprise at Lloyd George's story, but the documents usually support Wilson's testimony despite its sneering tone, and Rawlinson's diary for 26 July adds extra weight with its entry – 'Foch insists on going jointif.'

Though he might agree to widen his frontage, Haig's reservations remained as strong as ever, and during the conference with Rawlinson on 29 July Haig ordered a short advance no further than the outer defences of Amiens and, even then, spread over forty-eight hours.[16]

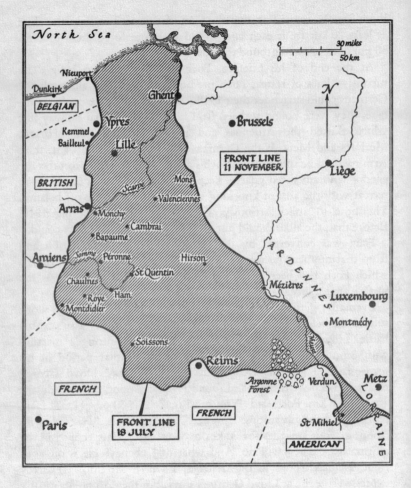

North Sea

Nieuport
Dunkirk
BELGIAN
Ypres
Kemmel
Bailleul
Lille
BRITISH
Scarpe
Arras
Monchy
Cambrai
Bapaume
Amiens
Somme
Péronne
Chaulnes
St Quentin
Roye
Ham
Montdidier
Soissons
FRENCH
Paris
FRONT LINE
18 JULY

Ghent
Brussels
N
Liège
FRONT LINE
11 NOVEMBER
Mons
Valenciennes
Hirson
A R D E N N E S
Mézières
Luxembourg
Montmédy
Reims
Argonne
Forest
Verdun
Metz
FRENCH
St Mihiel
AMERICAN
L O R R A I N E

30 miles
50 km

9 ALLIED TERRITORIAL GAINS, July–November 1918

The last stages of the war have usually been treated as a walkover for the allies. But comparing the German front line at the end of hostilities with Foch's analysis in July 1918 (Map 3, p. 71), it is clear the Germans kept hold of most of the ground they required in the south even if they were forced to surrender more than was tactically comfortable north of Mons. By 11 November, the allies had anyway outrun their communications. The Germans meanwhile had salvaged most of the equipment necessary for resuming the war in spring 1919.

Next day, when Foch heard of this, he came down hard on Haig. 'Go as far as you can on the first day. Go again on the second day and the third before the enemy can concentrate his reserves. After that, you will certainly have to pause but you may succeed in going so far that the enemy will have to clear out of the whole Amiens Salient. Renew the attack as soon as you can and you may force him over the Somme.'[17]

Once again, Haig appeared to accept Foch's gingering, and in the final British conference on 5 August he told his commanders: 'If all goes well, other French troops will cooperate south of Montdidier and it is probable that the operation will develop into one of considerable magnitude. To take full advantage of this, three divisions will be in general reserve close behind the front. Our first objective will be the outer Amiens defence line. Our second objective will be the Roye–Chaulnes line, then pushing on to Ham to aid the French.'[18]

These may have been Haig's final words. They weren't his final orders. Twenty-four hours before the battle, Haig issued fresh orders, marked them 'Very secret' and scaled down the battle's scope.[19] The outer defences were again specified as the final objective of a very limited advance (they were to be reached for lunch on the first day) and there was to be no further movement after that first day. Put more bluntly, Haig was sabotaging Foch's battle.

Why was he doing it? The most immediate explanation is in the advice GHQ's Intelligence were tendering that the enemy could reinforce the area with four divisions in twenty-four hours and another five in ninety-six. A strong counter-attack might therefore be expected with some confidence, and at that stage of the war the German capacity to embarrass British offensives outweighed any edge Foch could offer. Haig's 'Very secret' orders therefore concluded with further emphasis on Dominion troops capturing the German gun line and going no futher. 'In no circumstances' were they to exploit success.

These secret orders meant too that Haig was giving his army commanders on the spot very different instructions from those he passed on to Foch. Edmonds endorsed the fact indirectly when he later refused to give Bean a copy of GHQ's operations diary for 5–7

August even though he probably suspected that Bean was too good a historian to be bamboozled – and so it turned out. Three days before the battle, Bean interrogated Monash and he already had all the chief facts before the fighting began. As Bean put it, 'I asked Monash if his objective was to be unlimited. "Strictly limited," he said. He had warned Lawrence that if he wanted to exploit his success, he must have troops already there beforehand and all the arrangements made – that it could not be done offhand by troops they happened to have on the spot. Lawrence said that it had been decided on no account to go beyond the objectives. We are going for the enemy guns. We are not to trouble about the infantry in a few villages on the edge of the old Somme battlefield and we do not intend on any account to go into the old Somme battlefields themselves. I asked Monash why they did not think of exploiting the success themselves if they achieved it. He said, "They don't want to dissipate the Australians." He has obtained a promise from General Lawrence that if the affair goes well, the corps will be drawn out of the line for a spell.'

Lawrence had been content to acquiesce in Haig's caution. Davidson, Haig's Director of Military Operations, expressed dissent as forcibly as on other occasions and sent a blunt note to Haig: 'If the battle goes well and the troops reach the Red Line early, we may gain further objectives on the first day. Our reserves should be pushed up on the 8th and Rawlinson told by 11 am else there will be a repetition of Loos.'[20]

If Haig read Davidson's advice, he ignored it and gave GHQ's reserve strict orders not to move into the battle area before the second day, and only then if they were urgently needed to meet a German counter-attack.

Rawlinson summed up Haig's thinking at this time in a letter to Henry Wilson on the evening of the 8th. 'I think we have given the Boche a pretty good bump today. Resistance will stiffen. After tomorrow, we may expect counter-attacks. Haig has sent five divisions from GHQ's reserve so I am quite secure against accidents.'[21]

The story of 8 August is therefore that of a battle conceived by Foch, initiated by him and following the format he had worked out in May 1918. Haig's contribution was to drag his feet and do all he could to undermine a bold counter-stroke. It should therefore come as little surprise that a check on the degree of blackness in the German Army's 'Black Day' produces another bagful of surprises.

Although he had little advance warning of Amiens, Bean knew all about German retreats on the eve of battle. He had already seen them in advance of Haig's attacks at Messines and Passchendaele. Guessing the Germans might do the same ahead of the battle of Amiens, Bean took a position high above the battlefield before dawn on the 8th and described what he saw from the escarpment of the river Somme. 'I looked into the valley. It was deserted with scarcely a trace of German occupation. They had retreated before we attacked. No dead Germans. No dumps. No wire. No reserve trenches. I am convinced our men are only encountering rear guards.' When Bean questioned prisoners later, they confirmed the fact of retreat but said they had gone back only a couple of miles and were surprised that the allies had pushed so far.

Bean pursued the matter after the war, requesting his researcher in Berlin to find out if the Germans really had been rattled by the Amiens attack. The answer would not have surprised him. The allied advance went rather deeper than the Germans had expected and the unnecessary panic of men suddenly attacked affected the Germans quite as much as the allies previously. Army Group records thus show a degree of agitation at midday on the 8th and Ludendorff was informed of an intention to retreat all the way back to the Somme — a major pull-back. But, Bean's researcher went on, 'It is extraordinary how as soon as they saw we were carrying out separate actions instead of a second attack which they feared for the 9th, the whole tone of their reports to Army Group HQ changes.' More precisely, Ludendorff was told at 5 pm on the 9th that, since there was no sign of an allied reserve, further retreat was unnecessary. So much for the 'Black Day' and Ludendorff's post-war inventions.

The phase between the Amiens battle and the decision to make a coordinated attack on the Hindenburg Line is another for which great claims have been made on Haig's behalf. It runs from 9 to 27 August and the key proposed in Haig's typed diary is that he first defied Foch, then won him over to his own scheme. It is a story which begins with another of those heated meetings between Haig and Foch, this one on 9 August.

According to Haig's diary, Foch began by urging Haig to go on battering away beyond the outer defences of Amiens. Haig refused. 'I spoke to Foch quite straightly and let him understand that I was responsible to my government and fellow citizens for the handling of the British force. Foch's attitude at once changed and he said that all he wanted was early information on my intentions so that he might coordinate operations of the other armies and that he now thought I was correct in my decision not to attack the enemy in a prepared position. But notwithstanding what he now said, Foch and all his staff had been most insistent for the last five days that I should press on along the south bank [of the Somme] and capture the Somme bridges above Péronne regardless of German opposition and British loss.'

In place of Foch's unimaginative bullocking, Haig subsequently produced an alternative and explained it to Foch on the 10th. 'We must expect the German reserves to arrive very soon in order to check our advance. My plan is to advance on my left on Bapaume and Monchy . . .' In other words, Haig was proposing to close down the Amiens sector and open a new front which would outflank German resistance at Amiens. It was a classic example of the 'indirect approach' as advocated by Liddell Hart between the wars and all the more impressive because (according to Haig's typed diary) it had been planned three weeks in advance.

The only problem with this claim is that it fails to fit either the available documents or even Haig's own handwritten diary. For a start, Haig's intentions throughout were to concentrate the main British effort in Flanders. On 14 June, he had written to Pershing urging him to concentrate the chief American force in Belgium.[22] He followed this with another letter on 1 August deploring Pershing's decision to remove all American troops from the British sector ('I trust events may justify your decision') and went on to say that although the British intended to fight in Flanders whatever he did, a small advance there would free Dunkirk from the danger of German shelling and open a port which could handle 50,000 tons daily.[23] Haig's conclusion was that the Americans should therefore consider a rapid change from their bases at Nantes and Bordeaux. 'A change at the decisive moment would have decisive results in 1919,' Haig concluded. Pershing's reply has not survived, but a crisp negative can be assumed.

The events of 8 August seem to have made no difference to Haig's determination to go north. As the reliable Du Cane put it in an unpublished book on Foch, 'Haig wished to bring the Somme operations to an end on the 11th and begin preparations for an offensive at Kemmel in Flanders. These preparations, said Haig, would take three or four weeks and if the Amiens attack was not ended at once, it would not be possible for the British to attack again in 1918.'

This means that the traditional picture of Haig showing Foch how best to exploit the success at Amiens is incorrect. What Haig really wanted was to use the French as bait and Byng as a diversion to pin down German reserves pulled south from Flanders, then break out of the Ypres Salient.

More particularly, the claim to have planned Byng's thrust as a major attack to shift the angle of attack and threaten the German flank fails to survive a check against the facts. On the 9th, Haig's orders required Byng to send out cavalry scouts near Bapaume and ascertain German intentions. Only on the 12th was Byng given a sizeable force (four infantry divisions, the whole Cavalry Corps and some tanks). Even then, his instructions were not to attack before the 21st and to do so only with the greatest caution. 'There are reports of withdrawal south of the Scarpe so there will be little resistance in the early stages. Push forward strong advance guards.' These were tentative orders indeed.[24]

Byng followed his instructions closely, and when the advance guards were at last sent forward they halted within two miles. Pershing's liaison officer described the reaction of Pétain's 3rd Bureau chief when he marked Byng's advance on the map. 'The British affair today is only a raid. Do they think they can win the war by such timid offensives? For three months they have done nothing but rest and now look at them! It is only the French and Americans who are fighting.'

The fact that Haig had little interest either in Byng's push or the offensive on the southern part of his line was underlined by the progress report he sent to the War Office on 26 August. 'Our spirits are high but exhaustion from the long advance is starting to tell. Our casualties since 8 August are over 50,000. Our resources do not permit a battle from the Somme to the Scarpe. Our aim is to attack the hinge of the Scarpe–Bapaume front and develop a new offensive on a fresh section of the line so the 3rd Army cannot be reinforced. This means action between Bailleul and Ypres.'

In the third week of August, Haig was therefore scaling down in the south and preparing for a final push in Flanders before the winter rains, despite Foch's pressure to mount vigorous attacks on the Somme. This course committed Haig to deception. A fine example of this is to be found in orders written on 23 August and invariably quoted by historians: 'Risks which a month ago would have been criminal to incur ought now to be incurred as a duty. It is no longer necessary to advance in lines and in step. On the contrary, each division should be given a distant objective which must be reached independently of its neighbours even if one flank is thereby exposed.'

As they stand, the orders suggest an ebullient, confident Haig, transformed into the soul of attack by Amiens. But these much-quoted orders weren't the only ones issued on the 23rd. Another set, written for army commanders alone, pointed out that since enemy defences were arranged in depth, a breakthrough was to be expected only in very exceptional circumstances.[25] The first set of orders was for junior commanders, journalists and posterity; the second for the men who actually had to conduct the operations and confront the facts.

Such evidence of dithering on Haig's part, together with his determination to fight a big battle in Flanders at the end of the year, brings the story to the point where Haig is supposed to have made his third and most decisive intervention in August 1918. In place of a strategy which amounted to little more than blind, opportunistic hammering in the spirit of that Foch catch-phase, '*Tout le monde à la bataille*', a single letter from Haig to Foch on 27 August supposedly concentrated the attacking energies of the allies by directing them concentrically against key rail junctions like Cambrai, St Quentin and Mézières.[26] Two days after he sent that letter, Haig registered his personal triumph in a letter to his wife. 'As regards our future plans, he [Foch] is in full agreement with me.'

Put more bluntly, Haig was claiming that he had taken charge of operations, dictating the timing and direction of those attacks which led directly to the Armistice. As Lord Blake expressed it in his edition of Haig's typed diary, 'On 8th August, Haig launched the highly successful offensives known as the battle of Amiens. There is no need to describe the series of victories which followed. The most deadly blows were struck by the British Army which was indeed the only really effective fighting force on the allied side, for the Americans, though courageous, were still inexperienced and the French were now in an exhausted condition. Foch prudently interfered but little with Haig's plans. Unity of command, however much it may have pleased – for different reasons – the French and British governments, had little effect on the strategy of victory. This was mainly conceived by Haig and carried out by the British Army.'

Lord Blake is here expressing an orthodoxy which has become so deeply entrenched by repetition over three generations that it has acquired the authority of a religious incantation. But is it right? Does it stand up to the documents we can read today and is Haig's role quite as central as the history books would have us believe?

There is no doubt that a radical policy change took place at the end of August 1918. Clark (Pershing's representative with the French) and Benson (Haig's man) were both re-assuring their respective HQs on 24 August that Foch intended to pressure the Germans for only three more weeks and then dig in for the winter. A decision to carry on to the Hindenburg Line within the week was thus a major change. Haig's share in it, however, can be quickly discounted.

In the third week of August, he had written Foch a furious letter demanding a cut of 18,000 yards in the British line if the Americans left his zone – as they were about to. He then went to see Foch personally, reporting to his wife on the 24th: 'I saw Foch yesterday. He is arranging for the Americans to take an active share in the fighting. It seems quite wrong that they should be merely looking on.' Closer inspection of Haig's well-known letter to Foch on 27 August in the light of his preoccupations at the time thus alters our understanding of it. The traditional view was that Haig took hold of allied strategy, transforming Foch's blind banging into a coherent concentration of effort against the decisive point – the German rail system in the neighbourhood of Mézières. In fact, all he was doing was drawing Foch's attention to the relatively minor matter of how best to use the Americans, Haig suggesting a 50/50 split between the British and French.

The reason for Foch's change of strategy must therefore be sought outside Haig's letter, and the conjunction of two crises offers the best explanation.

The first involved the British Cabinet or, more precisely, Milner's suggestion to the Imperial War Cabinet on 31 July that the British should bring fifteen divisions back from France for use as a mobile reserve which could be sent anywhere in the world.[27] There is little in the documents to explain the context, but presumably it fitted in with British strategy announced at the end of 1917, devised to maximize British manpower as a bargaining chip at the peace conference. Whatever the motive, Milner's proposal was adopted by a new executive body called the Committee of Prime Ministers (formed as an *ad hoc* pacifier after Dominion protests over the conduct of Passchendaele) on 14 August. If implemented, it would have effectively prevented any more allied operations in the autumn of 1918 and taken the sting out of prospective attacks in spring 1919.

Here indeed was a crisis for Foch. He was already well aware of Haig's mounting bitterness and, almost certainly, Haig would have informed him of the Cabinet decision on 14 August to add weight to his own complaints. An entry in Leo Amery's diary suggests he did so – 'telephoned the War Office to stop Haig telling Foch of the Army Council decision to reduce the BEF to thirty-two divisions on 1 November'.[28]

Alarming news from the American front added to Foch's problems at this moment. After a meeting with Pershing on 14 July,[29] Foch must have believed that he had reached an understanding. The meeting had begun with Foch's observation that since the Americans had half a million men in France, it was right they should be given an army sector in October; but, until then, 'The French and British divisions should be supported, reinforced if necessary by American infantry. There should be assigned to this, infantry without their artillery and other divisional elements.' For the moment, Foch gave the Americans a temporary sector near Reims, instructing them to make limited attacks in July and September and use St Mihiel to the east as a rest area.

Foch went on to outline his own strategy at that meeting. His big offensive was scheduled for 1919. Arras and the Argonne Forest were to form the extremities and the American contribution was to be delivered in the Reims–Argonne sector on the right flank. 'The objective of the offensive is naturally the rail network as far as the *voie de rocade* [trunk line], Mézières via Cambrai towards Valenciennes and the north. Success in reaching this railway line would throw the bulk of the enemy's rail traffic through Liège and would, in addition, force a considerable part of his Army against the Ardennes.' The conjunction of these pressures, Foch suggested, would drive the Germans right out of France and from a large part of Belgium too.

That had been Foch's strategy in July. In August, Pershing tossed Foch's plans aside and began to make detailed preparations for a major offensive of his own in the 'rest' area of St Mihiel. Both Clemenceau and Lloyd George were furious when they heard what Pershing was up to and, as Derby told Balfour on the 27th, 'Clemenceau told Foch that the time has come when he must give Pershing orders and if they were not obeyed, then he would wire President Wilson himself.'

Confronted by Haig's recalcitrance, an angry British government and American freelancing, Foch saw a way out of his problems in the conjunction of two other factors.

The first was the state of the German Army. In late summer 1918, the enemy was temporarily short of men as a result of the gamble of throwing the whole '1919 Class' into the 21 March attack. A direct consequence was that the Germans hit an acute short-term manpower shortage in September. The 3rd Bureau confirmed this fact on 24 August, telling the Americans that one of their spies had attended a conference of Bohm's Army Group on 8 August and discovered that though half a million recruits from the '1920 Class' were being rushed through German depots, they would not arrive at the front until October.[30]

The second factor was the rapid growth in American numbers, noted in Borden's diary on 23 August. 'The victories of the last four weeks would have been impossible but for the Americans. One million have arrived since I left Ottawa on 24 May.'

Foch was therefore confronted by a crisis and a solution which would satisfy American ambitions, pressure the British government into keeping its Army up to strength in France and, by throwing the Americans into action, placate Haig. Within twenty-four hours he had made that decision. Firing off a broadside at London to start with ('Foch insisted on the necessity of keeping up our sixty-one divisions and we could do it and if we did not he would resign,' wrote Henry Wilson in his diary[31]), Foch next contacted each Commander in Chief. The directive he gave to each of them has not come down to us, but it can be inferred from an early draft of Pershing's memoirs. Pershing's typescript refers to a conference on 30 August: 'In the conference, Foch indicated a definite decision to execute his 1919 plan in 1918 and therefore extend the attack from the Argonne Forest to the Meuse.'[32] That same day, Haig met his own army commanders and 'told them of the general plan decided on by Foch yesterday. The enemy was to be engaged on a very wide front from now on and there was no risk of any counter-attack from the enemy.'

It will be noticed that, in all this, Foch originated and Haig followed – and necessarily so. However loudly Haig might proclaim the British Army's share in what followed (and he was much assisted by the fact that the British sector contained a lot of ground which the Germans could afford to give up without a fight), he was well aware of his own Army's fragility, so that when Lawrence advised an immediate deployment of cavalry on 1 September, Haig gave him a firm refusal. 'The decisive moment will arrive when the Americans attack in force,' he explained. 'The British Army must still have the means of exploiting the victory.'

Two days later, Rawlinson and Byng began competing with each other in their advance. Haig again stepped in briskly. 'No deliberate operations on a large scale will be undertaken for the present,' he told the two men. 'The troops are to be rested as far as possible with a view to resuming vigorous offensive in the near future in conjunction with operations to be carried out on a large scale by our allies.'[33] Haig was certainly aware of his status as a single cog in a larger attack, whatever claims his advocates made later.

Early in September, Haig was finally able to brief his army

commanders on the exact shape of the attack.[34] Dawnay, his deputy Staff Chief at the time, was under no illusion at the conference. Writing to his wife, Dawnay described the integration of five separate attacks as 'Foch's great battle', extending the length of the Western Front in the course of a fortnight.

16 September: Preliminary operations.
26 September: French and American assault on the Hindenburg Line.
27 September: Assault by the British 1st and 3rd Armies.
28 September: Plumer and the Belgians to advance in the Ypres Salient.
29 September: Assault by the French 1st and British 4th Armies.

Foch's own explanation of the strategy behind this crescendo was characteristic. 'I met him almost every morning that summer,' wrote the American liaison officer at Foch's HQ. 'I would be on my way to his HQ; he returning from the village church where he had been to say his prayers. One day as I saluted him, he paused as though inviting me to speak. I ventured the remark that the Germans seemed to be getting more than they could stand. He came up close to me, took a firm hold of my belt with his left hand and with his right fist delivered a punch at my chin, a hook under my ribs and another drive past my ear. He then shouldered his stick and without a single word, marched on to the chateau, his straight back and horseman's legs presenting as gallant a sight as one could wish to look upon.'[35]

What Foch was conveying to Bentley Mott in his own characteristic way was a strategy remarkably like Ludendorff's earlier in the year. Probe here, pound there and seek to destabilize rather than break through or try for a decisive victory on the battlefield.

Professional and discreet as he always was, it is unlikely that Foch told Mott about Haig's contribution, which had been to attack as little as he could with as little force as he could get away with and with as much complaint as possible − or so it must have seemed to Foch. What conclusion the Frenchman drew remains equally unclear. Did he attribute Haig's mulishness to bloody-mindedness? Was he aware of British ambitions in Flanders? Or would he have put Haig's position down to simple caution after the ferocious pounding the BEF had taken earlier in the year and recalled German skill and strength and his own panic in May 1918? Unlike other Commanders in Chief, Foch never addressed those questions either in speech or writing later. Nor did he leave any thoughts on whether or not his decision to launch the 1919 attack in 1918 had been the right one.

What assessment would Foch have made of that crucial decision at the end of August 1918? If he had been alive in 1940 to witness the German invasion, would Foch have shown the jauntiness Mott described? An offensive in 1919 would have been reinforced by a huge American presence and a much stronger British effort than was possible in autumn 1918. Churchill fleshed out that point in a paper for the Imperial War Cabinet, dated 12 July 1918, describing work in progress at the Ministry of Munitions. This aimed to equip the BEF with 4,800 tanks early in 1919. One third of its shells would then be mustard gas ('Ace of trumps' Foch always called them). Sixteen-inch howitzers would meanwhile deliver one-ton shells with enough accuracy to hit a single room in a targeted house. The British munitions industry would have been capable, in other words, of delivering a crushing blow.

Foch's decision was therefore a gamble. He must have known that the combination of a temporary troop shortage with political dissatisfaction and economic hardship in Germany might smash the enemy. If it didn't, the commitment of raw Americans together with news of heavy casualties without discernible advantage in war-weary Britain and France might well force that premature peace which Kitchener feared in 1916. Kitchener had gone on to predict that a compromise peace would mean the resumpton of war within twenty years, with the British and French fighting at a disadvantage. Events were to confirm Kitchener's (and the Committee of Imperial Defence's) far-sightedness, but little blame attached to Haig. The crucial error of attacking six months early was Foch's. Since March 1918, Haig had merely been the tea boy to Foch's managing director.

13

The Last Hundred Days: An Advance to Victory?

The last hundred days of the Great War have always been presented as a triumphal march towards an inevitable victory. This was certainly the official view, and General Maurice set it out in a slim volume which was rushed into print shortly after the Armistice.

His scenario was simple. The Germans had been stunned on 8 August, punched against the ropes during their retreat on the Hindenburg Line and finally knocked out when revolution inside Germany reinforced disintegration at the front. It was a view which made sense when compared with what ordinary soldiers at the front had seen or people at home had been told, and when the official histories were published in the thirties and forties, they appeared to support Maurice. If there were any who had a hunch that the official view was flawed, they could do little, since there were no documents available for reference.

The problem with Maurice's interpretation is that while it may have suited British governments in the twenties and thirties, when war with Germany remained a constant possibility, it bears little relation to documents now available.

At the start of September, for example, the old view would suggest that far-sighted men like Haig had the scent of victory in their nostrils – and why not, with only ten weeks of war left? But an examination of what allied leaders were actually writing at the time reveals a uniformly gloomy state of mind, and with good reason. All allied Intelligence passed through the Supreme War Council, and with the best information in front of them the Council saw little cause for optimism. One particularly detailed paper noted how well the Germans were conducting their retreat. Five hundred trains were passing daily between Germany and the front line over a rail network described as 'excellent'.[1]

Ivor Maxse had the same impression at GHQ and set it out in a letter to his wife on 8 September. 'The British have been fighting strong rearguards since 21 August. Half the generals don't know what is happening to the Hun. According to their several temperaments, they think either that the Hun is about to collapse and chuck it in or that he has got something cunning up his sleeve and will let it out at the right moment. The nearer you get to the battle front and the further from the cages in the rear or hospitals containing wounded prisoners of war, the more convinced you become that the Hun has got away most of his stuff, most of his heavy guns, nearly all of his light guns, practically all of his rearward dumps of ammunition and all of the vast array of engineering materials which modern armies require. We have not captured the half.' There was certainly no thought of chasing a defeated enemy. At the end of August, the Canadians reported ferocious German resistance near Arras, thus supporting the common feeling of allied GHQs that German morale remained high along the whole front.[2]

Germany's ability to replenish her front line was just as worrying.[3] At the start of September, the Germans still had 120 divisions in the front line and seventy-three in reserve — quantities comparable with their position on the eve of the year's great spring offensives. Nor could the allies take comfort in those 1,300,000 casualties sustained by the Germans earlier in the year. The '1920 Class' would add 450,000 men in October and 70,000 patched-up wounded returned each month in the normal order of things. On top of this (and a particularly tough morsel to digest) one hundred divisions would be freed by shortening the line in a comparatively short retreat to the Meuse. The end result of this combination, according to the War Office, was that spring 1919 would find the Germans with a million fresh troops ready for action.

There was even anxiety over whether or not the Germans could still launch a major counter-attack. Information from French spies suggested that Hindenburg was gathering thirty divisions for a counter-offensive in Lorraine at the end of August[4] and the French high command took that view seriously. Its Intelligence branch had sources deep in the German command system and an attack in Lorraine seemed a possible explanation of that scarcity of enemy reserves in August for which there was no explanation in necessity.

The War Office was thinking along the same lines. An MI3 paper forwarded to the Cabinet suggested that the enemy's '1920 Class' was being gathered for an invasion of the Netherlands. The aim, so the War Office thought, was to lengthen Germany's coastline in preparation for a big U-boat offensive in 1920.[5]

Analysis of this sort reads strangely today, but with so many German soldiers mislaid, Intelligence seized on small leads and filled in with informed speculation where facts were missing. As late as 7 October, James Marshall-Cornwall at the War Office was preparing a paper on how Germany would counter-attack with those twenty fresh divisions which were being gathered.[6]

Lloyd George summarized these various sources of anxiety in one of the regular letters he sent to Dominion premiers over the last months of the war. 'In German morale,' he wrote on 12 September, 'there has been considerable weakening but nothing to show breakdown in the Army. It is impossible to forecast military events over the next two months.'[7]

September had thus been a gloomy month for the allies, but the October documents must surely indicate an abrupt change in their fortunes. With so little time left for fighting, how could it be otherwise? The breaking of the Hindenburg Line at the very end of September certainly seemed to offer the perfect springboard for an acceleration. Haig's official biographer, for one, claimed that as a fact, and he was only expressing post-war orthodoxy when he wrote: 'When the month of September ended and the Hindenburg Line had fallen, the war was in fact finished, although for six weeks the fighting continued while the facts were slowly being realized by the soldiers and statesmen on either side.'

Unfortunately for Duff Cooper's assessment, the documents give little support. The Germans, to be sure, entered a short period of crisis. Ludendorff's order of 28 September stated: 'In view of the lack of reserves in fighting condition and of the crucial rail situation,

Army Groups cannot reckon on receiving reinforcements.' Two days later, he ordered a stand to be made on the next prepared position for 'as long as possible'. Things looked tricky, and a report from the Supreme War Council on 12 October suggested the Germans might reach a critical point in a very short time.[8] They hadn't reserves to counter-attack nor could the next prepared position be held by defensive tactics alone, since the Germans had lost 20 per cent of their artillery and a quarter of a million prisoners since July 1918. If only the weather stayed fine, the Germans would be forced to retreat over four weeks and take prohibitive casualties – or so the Supreme War Council believed.

The moment passed. On 13 October, the 3rd Bureau told their American liaison officer: 'A few days ago we thought the enemy would crack but he has shown skill in extricating himself without great disorder. His well conceived retirement using rearguards was working well. He showed no signs of any marked reduction in morale. He was not now in a state of defeat.'[9]

When the Cabinet telegraphed fresh orders to Haig on 15 October, they therefore instructed him to 'continue fighting day and night to the utmost limit of your capacity', but Haig was doubtful and sent a paper by return which his Chief of Staff read to the Cabinet three days later.[10] It is a paper of critical importance which must be compared not only with the edited version in Haig's diary but with the traditional picture of a Commander in Chief confident of imminent victory.

'The German Army,' ran Haig's paper, 'has been badly beaten but has not broken up. It is still capable of serious resistance. There is no evidence of the disorganization which is supposed to follow a decisive defeat and it is certain, in my opinion, that the German Army is quite capable of making an orderly retreat to a pre-determined line of defence and of holding that line against equal or possibly superior forces. I do not exclude the possibility of an offensive by eight or ten divisions made for the purpose of gaining time. The situation of the allied armies is as follows. The American Army is disorganized, ill-equipped and ill-trained. It must be at least a year before it becomes a serious fighting force. The French Army is thoroughly worn out and capable of little offensive action this year. The British Army is the most formidable fighting force in the world but there seems to be no prospect of its strength being maintained. There is no reason to suppose that the German Army cannot make a perfectly orderly retirement to the line of the Meuse. This would not be the case if the French and American Armies were capable of a serious offensive this autumn. But they are not and the fact must be reckoned with. The British Army is not large enough on its own or sufficiently fresh to force a decision. In the spring of 1919 the allies will have a very formidable task before them but will probably succeed in forcing the line of the Meuse and driving the enemy back upon the line of the Rhine. In 1920, the real crushing of Germany will be possible, always provided that the British Army is kept up to its present strength. It is well to remember that the American Army, being fresher, will be the decisive factor . . .'

The conclusion Haig drew has been cut by the British censor, but American historians were allowed to make a full copy and it can be read in Washington today: 'As to the political situation,' Haig wrote, 'it might be assumed that provided the settlement following an armistice assured the world freedom from the German menace for the next two generations and an admission of failure in their plan of world conquest, that is as much as can be attained at the present moment.'

Haig's pessimism might surprise readers brought up on the fictions of the twenties and thirties, but it was based on two harsh facts which left their stamp on everything the allies did over the last two months. The parlous state of allied communications, due to the enemy's destruction of roads and railways as he retreated, was the most immediate of those facts. The Germans had already shown their ability to create chaos during their spring retreat to the Hindenburg Line in 1917. Now they repeated the performance, and Currie's diary recorded the effect: 'The fact is the enemy is making a very orderly and practically unmolested retirement. Our trouble is that the troops are very tired and we are too far ahead of our railheads.'[11] Those words were written at the end of October.

The Supreme War Council backed Currie with an assessment of its own a few days later. 'The Boche is yet far from beaten. He is hard to follow because of our rail problem' – and problems were increasing all the time. By 5 November, Rawlinson was able to measure thirty miles between his own front line and the railheads supporting it.[12] He concluded that a week's preparation would be necessary before his advance could continue, and a week later he was even gloomier. 'It is a physical impossibility for the British Armies and, I think, the armies of any nation to continue their advance in strength rapidly. If they do so, they will starve.'[13] Or, as Edmonds put it that same day at GHQ, 'The enemy is going back so fast that cavalry and cyclists have to be sent forward to discover his position. Few think the end near.'

With peace only a few days away, this coagulation of movement was scarcely credible after the war, even to those closely involved in the final stages. While gathering material for his biography of Haig in 1922, even Charteris seems to have shaken his head in disbelief. He checked his recollections against those of Haig's Chief Staff Officer. 'One of two things was certain that first week in November,' Lawrence confirmed. 'Either the Germans would throw in their hand or there must be a delay of at least a month before we could fight another battle on a big scale. The destruction of road and rail made this inevitable, hence my worried visit home.'[14]

The second reason for the great German escape was the disastrous military performance of the Americans, though one would read the massed bulk of American publications in vain to find serious treatment of the fact.

Although much had been hoped of fresh American troops in double-strength divisions, their preparations had gone askew from the start. In part, this followed inadequate organization before the expeditionary force even left America. Lecturing on the eve of the Second World War, General Marshall looked back on his experience of 1917. In 1940 he was the American Chief of Staff; in 1917, he had been a humble Staff Officer. 'General Harbord went to France as Staff Chief of a force devoid of material,' Marshall recalled. 'We embarked with a part of an entirely new division of which I had never even seen a photostat of the organization until we were aboard ship. I then discovered – and I was a member of the General Staff of that division – that we had units in the division of which I had never heard. There was very little literature on the war as it was then conducted. We had one small English pamphlet, a single copy of which we studied conscientiously. Landing at St Nazaire, I was immediately sent on a circuit of the division. I discovered that of the 200 men to a company, approximately 180 were raw recruits. I found that some of these new units not only did not have their weapons but the men themselves had never heard of them.'

The same rawness was evident when the fighting began. A confidential report on the Americans who stormed the Hindenburg Line at the end of September noted many of the faults which characterized the British Army on the Somme.[15] Divisional commanders and their staffs had been rooted in headquarters twelve miles from the front line. Brigadiers had been in their dugouts meanwhile, trying to find out what was going on by telephone. So it was now with the Americans. Bean gave a splendid example of this state of affairs when he described the 27th American Division's HQ during operations. 'Lewis seemed a kindly old chap,' wrote Bean. 'He was rather like an old English gentleman called on to manage a war and managing it from his library. He ran in and out whenever a message was received but not with any obvious grip on what was happening. Not obvious to the outsider anyway. One of the US divisions was in difficulty with its rationing arrangements. I put the matter to Lewis. "Rations!" said the old chap. "Don't talk to me of rations. I've got a battle on!" It seems almost unbelievable to our people yet I think they might almost have done the same thing years ago. Perhaps not. We always had a pretty good appreciation of the importance of Q work.'

Ivor Maxse made similar notes after visiting the American 2nd Corps. 'Platoon commanders never took their men out to practise handling them. They admit their heavy losses in recent operations were due to "bald-headed tactics" and the desire on the part of everyone to rush through, regardless of cost. They admit that their support, reserve and front line units were all mixed due to reinforcing every check in the line. Their Q work was poor with orders received late or not at all.'[16] On the supply side, Maxse's report noted a complete absence of medical provision and a breakdown of supply arrangements ahead of battalion HQ. With regard to individuals, Maxse's observation on brigadiers was terse and to the point –

'Impossible. Too old.' Below brigade level, he added, 'The officers with few exceptions knew nothing and would learn nothing.' Privates, on the other hand, were 'keen and brave' and their custom of ignoring their own officers and seeking practical advice from Australian veterans ('Say, what's the dope on this joint?') was tacitly approved.

The human cost of such ignorance was all but overwhelming. Bean's photographer gave him an example from the front line. 'Wilkins found the Americans sitting in the bottom of a trench thinking that the exploding grenades they heard were shells. A Lewis gunner was cleaning his gun. Wilkins asked him why he was not firing. He replied that he didn't know there was anything to shoot at. Wilkins said that unless he used his gun, he would never be able to use it again. The Germans were within ninety yards in the same trench, throwing potato mashers with an officer directing from a shellhole outside the trench. Wilkins got them to snipe at the officer. He thought they seemed completely ignorant of danger or how to face it. The Lewis gunner was killed by a machine gun and Wilkins was shot through the sleeve, losing his gas mask below the chin to another bullet.' Bean concluded with a delightfully dry aside: 'There was obviously nothing more to be photographed in that direction so he worked round on the right.'

American weakness unfortunately went deeper than faulty organization and inexperience. Both would improve with time. Rottenness at the head was another matter; and when President Wilson gave Pershing virtual *carte blanche* at the start of 1918, the way was open for errors in strategy which could not be redeemed.

The whole idea of rushing a homogeneous national force into major battles was probably mistaken. To have then dismissed all French instructors in August and ignored advice from French 2nd Army staff who knew the Argonne battle area intimately certainly was. Indeed, the way in which Pershing proceeded to plunge into a double-headed battle after rejecting all the advice offered by an experienced ally almost beggars belief. Foch urged an offensive for the third week of September. Pershing stuck fast. He wouldn't forgo the attack already prepared for St Mihiel at the start of September. The end result was a compromise which Pershing described with appalling candour in the early draft of his memoirs. 'We had undertaken to launch within the next twenty-four days two great attacks on battlefields sixty miles apart with practically the same army.'[17]

The consequence was that a quarter of a million men and 1,000 guns had to be moved from one battlefield to another in three weeks using only three roads and at night. The men supervising this elaborate transfer had no previous experience of war operations, were unable to call upon French experience as a result of Pershing's decisions and had only 20 per cent the numbers which the French would have used to handle movements of comparable size.[18] If a German general had been put in charge of the Americans, he couldn't have created greater confusion if he had tried.

The twin battles which followed can be briefly described.[19] After the first day at St Mihiel, the American supply line jammed as solid as Haig's on the Somme in July 1916. The American advance came to an abrupt halt and the presence of 200 corpses on the battle front showed that the Germans had been given ample warning and enough time to retreat. The Americans had simply punched empty air at great cost.

Things went little better in the Argonne. On the first day, the Americans advanced six miles. Over the next twenty-one days, they managed just three miles and, once again, transport arrangements broke down. Charles Grant travelled widely in the battle zone on behalf of British GHQ and saw for himself the state of the back area. He described cookers being looted. He heard of 400 American troops dying of starvation and wounded men dying because they couldn't be got back to casualty clearing stations.

So what did Pershing make of it all? An entry in his private diary on 14 October indicates the quality of his understanding: 'I hope for better results tomorrow. There is no particular reason for this hope except that if we keep on pounding, the Germans will be obliged to give way and for the fact that this particular manoeuvre has been carefully studied out.'

All these things were widely remarked on at the time. When Lloyd George urged Foch on 7 October to appeal directly to the American President for Pershing's removal, Foch replied that he was already working on it. Henry Wilson's attitude was characteristically caustic: 'The state of chaos the fool has got his troops into down in the Argonne is indescribable.'[20] The conclusion was clear to all, and even if Pershing had been sacked on the spot the damage was already done. As Lloyd George wrote on 21 October, 'All the information reaching me is that the American failure completely upset Foch's great strategical plan of 1918. There is a first-class military scandal brewing since the facts are becoming known even in American circles in London.'[21]

The combination of breakdown in transport and the American failure in battle meant that, right up to the moment of Armistice, well-placed observers despaired of finishing the war in 1918. On 27 October, for example, Lord Derby noted Haig's opinion that if the Germans got back to the Meuse, they would save eighty divisions by the reduction of their frontage and 'would then have the whole of the "1920 Class" to prolong the war for a year and even longer'. On 31 October Haig added a comment of his own: 'Byng, Horne, Rawlinson and Birdwood are all agreed that from the military standpoint, the enemy has not yet been sufficiently beaten to cause him to accept an ignominious peace. The enemy is fighting a very good rearguard.' There could be no stronger evidence of British pessimism.

Although the end of the war was only a fortnight away, Haig's pessimism was shared by his allies. Pétain's 3rd Bureau told Clark on 1 November: 'The Boche knows the military game from A to Z. There is not a single place he falls back from unless he wants to. He is retiring to shorten his line and create two or three masses of manoeuvre.'[22] The Americans supported that assessment from their own observation, and next day the President was informed that 'the morale of the enemy is apparently improving. A larger part of their heavy artillery and munitions have been successfully withdrawn to Germany. Three American officers who have recently escaped from a German prisoner of war camp after a month's confinement state that they have found that the discipline of the German troops in France is still very good and though their rations are poor, the soldiers do not complain. Without exception among rank and file, it is thought that the war will be over in two or three months but officers are convinced that it will take six months. They are confident that, if necessary, they can hold out for two or three years. It is reliably reported that the allied victories have not made nearly the impression on the German mentality which might have been expected.'

President Wilson was given an equally gloomy briefing on 9 November.[23] Strong German counter-attacks were reported at the key rail towns of Hirson, Montmédy and Mézières and he was told: 'Collapse of resistance has yet to be accomplished. Discipline is beginning to break but the enemy can still retreat in good order.' There followed a statistical breakdown of the number of rest days given to fifty of the best German divisions. In comparison with the March–June period in 1918, the allocation of rest in July–October averaged only one day less at ten days. Bearing Maxse's rule of thumb in mind that a fortnight was sufficient for a division to recover its fighting force after a battle and adding the facts that the Germans had re-opened home leave for front-line troops and kept 337,000 new recruits in their home depots during discussions over the Armistice, the pessimism of allied Intelligence reports can be seen to have had a firm grounding in fact.

When the news of the Armistice percolated back to the various HQs, a sense of astonishment was therefore widespread. Grant recorded a mood of 'subdued joy and bewilderment' at Pétain's HQ.[24] Clark noted the 3rd Bureau's opinion that the turn of events was beyond belief.[25] The member of staff who gave Clark this information added that he had to keep pinching himself to confirm the shock of such rapid and unexpected developments.

Haig's HQ appears to have been equally stunned. As late as 19 February 1919, when Edmonds dined at Haig's London home and studied the situation map for 11 November, Haig asked him quietly, 'Why did we win the war?'

In the front line, the after-taste seems to have been one of sourness rather than bewilderment. The enemy might have acknowledged defeat, but men who had watched the war from close quarters found little to savour when the end came. There had been no clearcut victories in battle. German retirement had been comparatively unmolested and the enemy's country was reached only after the Armistice, and when the troops finally got there they were disturbed by what they found. The Canadian press published many letters from the occupying Army, most of them remarking on orderly civilians, smoothly functioning bureaucrats and disciplined German troops marching back to be demobilized from where they had joined the Army. Above all, the Canadians reported a pervasive feeling within Germany that their Army had never been defeated.

Even the widely held view that the Germans had suffered severe food shortages was found hard to substantiate. President Wilson was told in a report dated December 1918 that food was plentiful in Germany and that, although stores had been distributed to the Reserve Army during the final period, an excellent harvest in 1918 had replenished all deficiencies. The report concluded that German civilians had generally eaten better than civilians in the allied countries, particularly away from the big towns.[26]

Such a state of affairs was poor reward for years of hardship and a blood cost set out by Haig in his notes for a speech in 1926: five million soldiers enlisted, 20 per cent killed, another 40 per cent wounded. It amounted to an overwhelming price to pay for a war which had stumbled to such an indecisive conclusion.

With large-scale unemployment ahead, a time of questioning was bound to follow. Had there been negligence? Incompetence perhaps? If so, where did the blame lie? Was the Old Army culpable, or just Haig? And what of the Cabinet's role? Or, putting the matter more cynically, if Haig, the Old Army, the War Office and the Cabinet had all been remiss, what measures would be taken to re-write the history of the Great War and falsify the public's understanding of it?

FALSIFYING THE RECORD

14

Haig's Fictions

When Duff Cooper's official biography of Haig was published, the *Daily Mail* approached Winston Churchill for a review.[1] His own book on the war (*The World Crisis*) had been an attractive mixture of passion and inside information. A newspaper hostile to Haig since 1917 must therefore have hoped for waspish indiscretion. They were to be disappointed. Churchill's review was tempered by the moderation of a man still hoping for high office. It drew particular attention to two well-publicized facets of Haig's retirement.

The first of these was ostentatious neglect by the government of the day. 'Titles, grants and honours of every kind, all symbols of public gratitude, were showered upon him but he was given no work. He did not join the counsels of the nation nor was he invited to re-organize its army. He was not consulted upon the treaties. No sphere of public activity was open to him. It would be affectation to pretend that he did not feel this. He was 58 – an age at which Marlborough still had four great campaigns to fight.'

The second aspect was Haig's response to the government's neglect. He might have been expected to make a bid for public acknowledgement in the style of Sir John French's post-war writings. He maintained instead the dignified reticence of an old warrior, living out the remainder of his life in the ancestral home of Bemersyde on the river Tweed. 'The years passed,' wrote Churchill. 'People began to criticize his campaigns. As soon as war censorship was lifted, pens ran freely. There was no lack of material. There was deep resentment against the slaughter on a gigantic scale alleged upon notable occasions to have been needless. All this will long continue to be debated. However, Haig said nothing. He neither wrote nor spoke in his own defence. Some of his Staff Officers, without his knowledge, published a controversial rejoinder. The volume was extremely ill-received by the press and public. But neither the serious criticism nor the unsatisfying defence extorted any public utterance from Haig.'

These phrases have an elegant ring and were in line with majority opinion at the time, but, as Churchill must have known, they bore no relation to the facts. In his capacity as Minister of War, Churchill had himself given Haig the job of organizing the occupation of the Rhineland in 1919. When a number of riots broke out among soldiers awaiting demobilization, it was Churchill again who put Haig in charge of the home army. Once those threats passed, Haig was offered the Governor Generalship of Canada and Viceregency of India. He rejected both.

Churchill's 'shower of honours' gives an equally false impression. The period after the war was, in fact, a time of wounding squabbles and petty spite, beginning at once with the Victory Procession in November 1918.

When he discovered that he was to be placed in the fifth carriage of a special train from Dover to London, Haig's response was furious. 'I felt this was more of an insult than I could put up with, even from the Prime Minister.' Haig went on to assert that he had effaced himself for years for the sake of the alliance and 'in consequence patiently submitted to Lloyd George's conceit and swagger. Now the British Army has won the war in France in spite of Lloyd George, I have no intention of taking part in any triumphal ride with Foch and a pack of foreigners merely to add to Lloyd George's importance and help his election campaign.'[2] In a letter to his wife next day, Haig continued to rumble. 'I enclose yesterday's diary from which you will see the extraordinary behaviour of Lloyd George to me. He seems to be determined to go to the end in the same spirit as he has treated me all along. I can't think what his object is in trying to belittle the British Army except he is afraid that it might interfere with him and his schemes of revolution and Bolshevism.'

That same month, Haig fought another battle, this time over honours. The point of contention was stated by Milner in a letter to Lloyd George: 'The king wants a viscountcy for Haig. Plumer is a bit different to the other commanders regarding length of service and, on the whole, better. So a peerage for Plumer and for the others a GCB?'[3]

Haig naturally found the offer unsatisfactory, pointing out that 'When Field Marshal French was recalled from commanding armies in France for incompetence, he was made a Viscount.' He therefore put in a bid of his own. Philip Sassoon, his private secretary, was sent to London with two messages – one, a blast against the title on offer; the other, a demand for a cash gratuity of £250,000. Even Lady Haig protested at the crudity and greed of this double-barrelled discharge, but without effect. 'I only want sufficient pension to enable me to live in a simple way without monetary anxieties for the remainder of my life,' he explained.[4]

The result of this dutch auction was that Haig gained in title but lost in cash. An earldom replaced the viscountcy, but the £250,000 requested by Haig was knocked down to £100,000. Even so, it should have been enough to remove Haig's financial anxieties at a time when an ordinary man could live adequately on £2 a week and very comfortably on £4.

Once the basics had been settled, Haig continued to discover slights and insults in the round of ceremonies which accompanied victory. It was almost as if he regarded himself as the sole architect of that victory and resented sharing centre-stage with anyone else. When the Australian Corps marched through the City of London, for example, Haig sourly commented that the event had only been contrived by the Australian Prime Minister 'to let off a few speeches and glorify his own deeds'. A little later, Beatty, the First Sea Lord, was given the Freedom of the City of London and Haig complained in the same resentful spirit. Though his own carriage had been put behind Beatty's in the procession – not unreasonably one might have thought – 'there was no doubt in the hearts of the people I came first as was made evident by the tremendously enthusiastic welcome.' Following the Beatty affair closely, Allenby was given the same honour as London had given Beatty. 'I had to attend,' Haig muttered angrily into his diary. The only saving grace was that after the mayor proposed Allenby's health, Haig was able to get away with 'a few words from the soldier's point of view so that only civilians eulogized him'.

Haig's attitude in all these matters showed an acute concern with worldly honours, whatever Churchill professed to believe. Nor was it likely that a man always anxious to get his own achievements into print would leave the history of the war to soldiers junior in the service or, worse, to those civilian intellectuals he despised so fiercely. Nor did he.

From the Armistice through to his death in 1928, Haig worked ceaselessly in his own cause, the Official History being his most immediate concern. For a generation at least, access to a full range of documents was the official historian's prerogative. That privilege put him in a unique position to establish an authoritative framework of events – and reputations. When the first-choice official historian was sacked shortly after the war, Haig therefore put in a proposal that Boraston, his own private secretary, should be appointed.[5] The suggestion was rejected, but Edmonds, a Staff College colleague and member of GHQ's staff during the war, was probably a very acceptable man from Haig's point of view.

When work began on the Official Histories, Edmonds always sent drafts to Haig. These were studied closely and returned with long comments in the margin. Writing of his corps in 1914, for example, Haig pointed out: 'They had nearly three months' hard experience of the war and had beaten the Germans every time we met them, notably on the Chemin des Dames when we forced the passage of the Aisne in the face of the 3rd Corps, probably their most efficient taken all round.'[6]

Off the record and in private correspondence, Edmonds cheerfully ridiculed Haig's timidity on the Aisne.

Of Neuve Chapelle in spring 1915, Haig asserted: 'It was in fact a wearing-out battle. The situation was in some respects similar to that of April 1917 after we had taken Vimy and Monchy. We had to go on attacking in order to prevent Nivelle and company from saying that the British had not held the German reserves so the French attack was not successful.'[7]

Edmonds had a copy of Haig's orders and was able to check them against the size of his attacking force. He therefore knew very well that Neuve Chapelle had been planned as a breakthrough battle from the start.

The Official History went on to support Haig's conduct in the battle of Loos. 'My dear Archimedes,' purred Haig. 'Your account of the Loos operations is extraordinarily accurate so far as I can check it by the reports which reached me. To think of these "reserves" at Loos is a nightmare. The terrible results of keeping reserves too far back was clear to me when Lord K. visited us in August.'

As Edmonds well knew, those reserves had in fact been placed exactly where Haig had requested them.

In his correspondence with Edmonds, Haig was responding to the work of others, but to anyone who knew him it was unlikely he would be content to leave it at that. After previous wars, Haig's practice had been to publicize his own contribution. The Sudan had thus given rise to an anonymously published book and the Boer War to unit war diaries presented to the Staff College. Critics might raise an eyebrow over Haig's urge to get into print and his oblique way of going about it, but there was nothing unusual in his conduct. Few high-ranking British commanders since Wellington have resisted the temptation to use journalists and ghost writers as a means of supplementing income and reputation. Haig's actions thus fitted a well-established tradition – but one with a necessarily furtive façade, since generals, like other professionals handling dead meat – surgeons, undertakers and the like – were under the same conventional requirement to refrain from direct advertisement.

Haig's own publications began within a year of the Armistice and involved the dispatches he had sent to the Cabinet. Published in the *London Gazette* during the war, their obvious function had been to highlight the good and omit the bad for the sake of the war effort. Haig now published the lot (Lord Birkenhead remarked at the time on the peculiarity of Haig's retention of copyright), saying that he had done so 'as a tribute to the valour of the British soldier and the character of the British nation'.[8] He also hinted at an alternative explanation when he added: 'They [the dispatches] are at the moment the only available account of a most splendid and most critical period in our national existence.'

It is difficult to see how the Commander in Chief's dispatches could pay tribute to a common soldier conspicuous for his absence in them. An account in Haig's own words of his own battles, culminating in the full-blooded forty-nine page apologia of his final dispatch would, on the other hand, have done his personal reputation no harm at all.

Haig's next project began just as work on the dispatches was being concluded. It took the form of a seventy-five-page 'Memorandum on Operations on the Western Front 1916–18', placed in the British Museum during 1920 with instructions that it was not to be published before 1940.[9]

The text of the Memorandum had little to do with battle. A single page of the seventy-five covered the Somme, Messines, Passchendaele and Cambrai. What did concern Haig was the bloody stalemate of 1916 and 1917, the débâcle of spring 1918 and an advance to victory under French management. The obvious excuse for such an embarrassing progression was to blame the French at all times and the British government when foreigners failed him as credible whipping boys. Haig undertook such work cheerfully.

The end product was thus a document heavily skewed against the French, with sixteen pages devoted to the Nivelle 'plot' and another thirteen to the establishment of the Supreme War Council and extension of the British line during the winter of 1917–18. Comment in these sensitive areas ruled out publication ('Of course, no full statement could be published before our next war with the French,' was Kiggell's comment after he had polished the Memorandum), but publication had never been Haig's purpose. Knowing that several substantial histories were in the course of preparation, his intention was to distribute his own potted version of events, and this he did to such effect that when a suspicious George V checked up, he was shocked to discover that eight copies had been sent out with propaganda in mind.[10] Among the recipients were Conan Doyle ('Tell him not to quote from it'), Charteris, Buchan, Gough, Davidson and Spender of the *Westminster Gazette*, whose copy is displayed as the Haig Memorandum in the British Museum today.

While the finishing touches were being added to this Memorandum, Haig was well into a larger statement of his own case. This took the form of the two volumes titled *Sir Douglas Haig's Command 1915–18* and rushed into print to embarrass Lloyd George's election campaign of 1922.[11] John Boraston and George Dewar were the authors credited, but Esher and Lawrence (Haig's former Chief of Staff) wrote chapters anonymously, Haig's being the guiding hand throughout. The Field Marshal would probably have preferred to keep that hand concealed but was unable to do so. Maxse for one was well aware of Haig's role and told Liddell Hart in the twenties that his acquaintances all knew that Dewar and Boraston was 'really by Haig'.[12] Charles Bean was another who came to the same conclusion. In his notes, Bean always referred to the two volumes as 'Haig and Boraston'.

Letters recently available support Maxse's assertion and show Haig supervising every stage of *Sir Douglas Haig's Command* with personal visits to the authors and letters nudging them in the right direction. 'I am very glad to see you well employed today,' he told Boraston on one occasion. 'I only hope it will be the first of many profitable visits to your office.'

Haig went on to correct the drafts. After reading the chapter 'Unity of Command', which had been written by Lawrence, Haig sent a querulous letter. 'Dear Lorenzo, I still maintain – and in this I am supported by a note in my diary – that Pétain *warned* the French divisions collecting about Montdidier that their lines of retreat would be south-west in the event of a German advance on Amiens continuing. So I have struck out your last two lines and added in their place about the line of retreat given to the French divisions on our right.' (Lawrence had obviously doubted Haig's scapegoating of Pétain in his own draft!)

Haig also lent his wartime diary and a selection of letters to the authors. Boraston later denied this in a letter to *The Times*,[13] but as an official historian Cyril Falls would have known the facts when he wrote: 'This book [Dewar and Boraston] has a certain importance owing to the fact that the authors were allowed to use the late Lord Haig's diaries and correspondence.'[14]

Haig's most direct intervention in the book came in the first two chapters, and a personal voice can be clearly heard.

'As to the Nivelle episode, that was hateful ... I have, since learning the facts, often turned it over in my mind, looking at it from various standpoints but failed to see it in a redeeming light.' The personal 'I' supplies the key here.

Referring to the lessons which could be drawn from the dispatches at another point, the author observes: 'It is fortifying for those amongst us who never wavered in the conviction that the costly offensives in 1916 and 1917 were necessary ...'

The Haig exclamation mark makes a frequent appearance in these chapters. On Nivelle's casualties, for example, the text remarks: 'Somebody at GHQ announced that the French stated their casualties at 120,000. In fact, those appear to have actually been the figures of GQG [French GHQ]. The Commander in Chief remarked, "Halve that number." Later it was almost halved!'

Despite personal direction and the loan of private records, Haig's authors proved to be more than ciphers. Boraston's chapters in particular are notably calm and judicious in documentation as well as being the only ones invariably signed by the author. Lawrence's response to Haig's suggestions and pressure was also less than whole-hearted. 'Haig was given most distinctly to understand from Pétain ... There is not the slightest doubt of this ... In fact, the orders were actually issued ...'

One author went so far as to ignore Haig's guidance. The chapter covering the Calais conference in February 1917 rejects the view that the proceedings had been 'the plot' described in Haig's introductory chapters. The author went on to display notable independence of judgement throughout. Who was he? Latin tags, Dryden squibs and lengthy quotations in French from confidential French documents betray the hand of Lord Esher, and the similarity of this chapter to its counterpart in Esher's anonymously published book *The Pomp of Power* supports that identification.[15]

The Dewar and Boraston volumes were anyway something of a mongrel, as was their reception. 'Lord Haig stands behind the writers,' ran a typical review. 'That at once raises the book to the first rank of importance. While this is the most fascinating of war books that has yet appeared in England, it is about as safe as a Mills bomb with the pin out. Explosions must follow.'[16] And so they did, but with a majority verdict that Haig had wounded his own cause more deeply than his opponents'. This feeling must in part have been due to a strong revulsion against all war books immediately after the Armistice, but there was also a body of criticism which detected self-satisfaction and paranoia, never far below the surface in Haig's personality. Cyril Falls – by no means an opponent of the Army or its commanders – put that point bluntly in a review: 'The writers' aim and object is the glorification of the British Commander in Chief and they continually overreach themselves in attempting to prove too much. As a consequence, their references to the French are frequently unfair and sometimes almost ludicrous.'

There is no record in the Haig papers of a personal response to this mixed reception, but Haig's continuous tinkering with his wartime diary suggests a lingering sense of unease over his own place in history.

The diary had been written by hand each night during the war, the top copy going to Lady Haig via the King's Messenger and the carbon copy being kept in its binding for Haig's record. The point of this exercise, so Haig told the king in 1914, was private (to serve as a daily record 'for my wife's information' and 'for my own recollection in days to come')[17] and that gloss was underlined after the war by the dedication Haig wrote in the dispatches presented to his wife: 'To my wife Doris. In grateful recollection of all she was to me during the Great War. Although she regularly received instalments of my daily diary, yet no one has ever been able to say, "Lady Haig told me this."'

When Lord Blake was chosen to edit this diary in the early fifties, he was impressed by what he read. The diary was, he suggested, a unique record. Other generals wrote memoirs long after the event. Haig alone set down his recollections at the time. 'As a result,' wrote Blake, 'it has the advantage of being a fresh and vivid record written before he had time to forget or need to invent.'

If Blake had enjoyed the benefit of documents opened in the 1960s, he would probably have reconsidered his judgement, for though Haig was technically correct in stating that no one could say, 'Lady Haig told me this,' his choice of words was deliberately misleading. When Haig wrote that curiously stilted dedication to his wife in the dispatches both of them knew very well that long extracts of the diary had been circulated on at least two occasions – as Haig's own private papers demonstrate.

The first was in that troubled period following Loos. 'I have taken on myself to do a bold thing,' Lady Haig wrote to the king's secretary, Stamfordham, on 1 October 1915. 'Douglas makes me his secretary and sends me his private diary to type for him. He trusts me with it implicitly and knows I keep it under lock and key and *do not talk*! From time to time, he has given me permission to send extracts of his diary to Colonel Wigram [the king's assistant secretary] of past events. I typed yesterday an extract which struck me as so *important* that I have taken upon myself to send it to you *privately* to read with also former extracts dealing with present operations. I trust you to divulge (if it will do any good) privately what you consider right but I hope you will keep secret the source of information. These are such critical times we are going through that I felt obliged to take this action.'

Stamfordham's reply makes it clear that the 'critical times' related chiefly to her husband's promotion prospects. 'It makes one sad to feel that had the urgent entreaties of the General of the 1st Army [Haig] to have the reserves close up been attended to, the splendid attack made under his command might have been carried to a completely successful issue.'[18]

During the Somme, another thick packet of diary extracts was sent to Buckingham Palace. Again, the motive was support for Haig at a critical time. 'I would like to get these precious documents back to you as early as possible,'[19] Wigram wrote to Lady Haig. 'If these politicians would only leave the military alone, all would be well. This is where we miss Lord K. He would not have been working behind Sir Douglas's back.' This was written in September 1916, when an influential group led by F. E. Smith and Churchill were vehemently criticizing Haig's conduct of the Somme, assisted, so Haig believed, by Robertson.

There is another type of leakage, at a lower social level than these two but suggesting that many other individuals received portions of diary during the war. Although the Haig papers make no mention of the fact, Conan Doyle's papers register him picking up a complete copy of Haig's 1914 diary from Lady Haig in person – which poses a vital question. If Haig knew that Conan Doyle was preparing a full-blown war history with the benediction and active support of the Committee of Imperial Defence[20] and if he knew, in addition, that a garrulous monarch was privy to his diary, how candid was an ambitious soldier like Haig likely to be in reconstructing the events of the day? Reviewing Blake's edition of the diary, Lord Geddes, for one, expressed strong doubts. As a man who had served on French's staff and worked later with the War Cabinet, Geddes wrote: 'Many of the important men and episodes were known to me personally but I do not recognize the picture presented.'[21]

The circulation of Haig's diary during the war and its use for propaganda poses a second question. If this diary was written to bend history in the writer's favour, was Haig ever likely to reproduce assessments he had jotted down in the heat of action which might read unflatteringly if published after the war?

The text in the Scottish National Library certainly indicates post-war tampering, together with plenty of crystal-ball passages which have the smell of addition long after the event. A sample from a very large selection illustrates the point.

In May 1917, Haig went out of his way to give the 66th Division 'a splendid character' – an unusual thing for him to do in the diary. The 66th were later given a key role in the assault on Passchendaele and failed disastrously. Haig must have expected post-war recrimination from the Australians who were advancing next to the 66th, all the more since Bean had witnessed the storm which blew up between the Australians and GHQ at the time. A pre-emptive strike therefore?

A month after praising the condition of the 66th Division, Haig recorded a meeting with Gough on the eve of the battle of Passchendaele, during which he 'urged the importance of the right flank [the Passchendaele–Gheluvelt area]. The main battle will be fought for . . . the Gheluvelt Ridge.' In correspondence with Edmonds after the war, Gough denied that such a meeting had taken place and surviving documentation fails to support Haig's claim. According to most documents, the main battle was planned for the Houthulst–Thourout axis, which lay well to the west of the Gheluvelt Ridge.

Haig's entry would, on the other hand, allow him to transfer the blame for August 1917's disasters on to Gough's shoulders.

The lead-up to the German offensive in 1918 offers another crop of improbabilities which go against the grain of contemporary documentation. Five weeks before the 21 March attack, for example, 'I reminded Gough that whenever we attacked, we had been able to break the enemy's front and advance well into the German system of defence. We must expect the Germans to do the same if they attack in force.' The British had, of course, never managed to penetrate in depth and Haig's planning at the time was for Gough to give up a large slice of ground at the start of the battle.

A fortnight before the first attack, the diary records Haig giving Maxse exact details of the attack he was likely to face, and three days before the second German offensive on 9 April the diary gave a repeat performance in prophetic accuracy. Both predictions are at odds with all contemporary documents which have come down to us.

Once the German attacks had been made, criticism of the British response grew fierce. The Canadian Prime Minister was particularly bitter, one of his charges being that Gough's front had been in-adequately prepared for defence. Another more specific accusation was that the British use of barbed wire had been scandalously deficient. Again Haig is covered by his diary. The entry on 8 March comments on the poor defences inherited from the French (a point contradicted by Gough's own report to GHQ) and on the insufficiency of Gough's labour force (Haig was in fact using the men to build a railway linking Ypres and Amiens). On 21 February, the diary states that 20,000 tons of barbed wire had been used during that month alone, but that is the only reference to barbed wire in the diary and only makes sense in relation to a charge made by the Canadian Prime Minister – in June 1918! And so it goes on.[22]

Post-war amendments like these would have involved extracting and re-writing awkward entries. Did Haig's original diary allow him to do this? Paper for the re-write would have presented no great difficulty. The notebooks he used came from Hugh Rees of Regent Street and were readily available. Water-marking posed more of a problem, since each leaf was marked with the name of the papermaker and the year of manufacture, but Rees sold diary books of similar size which were unwatermarked and as a man with previous experience of re-writing a field diary ('How did Oliver get an incorrect version of Douglas's Sudan diary?' runs a letter by Haig's sister in the Haig papers. 'He must say it is incorrect in his office . . . A very misleading copy'[23]) Haig would probably have kept extra copies of virgin books, suitably watermarked.

The carbon copies offered more difficulty, since Haig had kept them firmly bound in the Hugh Rees covers. The simplest solution, if any top copy had to be destroyed and re-written, was to cut the carbon copies from their binding. This Haig did. Nor is it easy to see why he should have done so unless he intended to tamper with the top copy.

Why did Haig do it? Why make alterations which later research would be almost certain to detect?

Psychological factors offer one explanation, and Lord Geddes noted one of them in his review of Blake's edition: 'At the core of Haig's being there was a sense of the existence of powers opposing him. He had a persecution diathesis, not a persecution mania, and was always suspicious that someone was plotting against him.'[24] Haig's purpose in re-writing was, in other words, the preparation of defensive positions in anticipation of attack.

Lady Haig offered a more specific explanation in an address she delivered at a Foyle's literary luncheon in 1936. As the person most likely to know the truth of the matter, she stated: 'Two years before my husband passed away, he told me that he had heard that Mr Lloyd George was going to bring out some terrible reminiscences of the war and that Douglas felt that it was his duty to the Army – not for himself – to get together a story from his diaries in order to be ready to neutralize any harm that might ensue. He did not live to accomplish this. The work on his diaries and letters after Douglas's death took me three years to accomplish.'[25]

As it stands, Lady Haig's explanation presents practical difficulties. Although Lloyd George signed a contract to write his war memoirs in 1922, the outcry against an elected war leader making £75,000 in that way led to the contract being annulled almost immediately. Nor was there any indication that Lloyd George was about to resume work on his memoirs until the early 1930s.

Churchill's *World Crisis* certainly bothered Haig a little later and led to a lengthy exchange of letters, Haig sending Churchill a substantial quantity of extracts from his diary.[26] But by 1926 Churchill's book was near completion. If Haig had wished to counterattack with a re-worked diary, he would have been considering publication long before 1926, the date specified by Lady Haig.

This leaves a much simpler explanation. Kenneth Rose's recent biography of George V mentions a conversation in which Haig told the king that he had been offered £100,000 for his memoirs.[27] The king objected strongly, citing Repington's memoirs ('A cad and a blackguard') and Bacon's book on the battle of Jutland (which had disgusted him). Rose gives no date for this conversation but publication dates for Repington and Bacon put it after 1925 – which would fit Lady Haig's recollection of a project taken up suddenly in 1926. It suggests a motive as well. Though Haig was comfortably off, he was by no means rich by the standards of the day. Little of the family's whisky money had filtered into his side of the family and a large slice of the £100,000 voted by parliament had been spent on Bemersyde because public subscription ('A personal gift from the people of the British Empire in recognition of his brilliant service' ran the circular soliciting contributions) fell far short of the sum demanded by the member of the Haig family who had owned it previously. The money offered for Haig's memoirs was, in other words, security for his wife, son and two daughters.

Haig thus devoted much time and energy in his declining years to bending the historical record, but did it matter? Was it of any importance what an old man did with the history of those years which had been the pinnacle of his career? Generals from Caesar through Wellington and Napoleon to Montague did as much with more lasting effect. But where Haig's tricks differed was in the dilemma he presented to his employers. He had rushed a complete and personalized history of the Western Front into print before the official historian had even begun to assemble the govenment's point of view. Could that government afford to go against Haig and contradict his line on important matters?

The dilemma is briefly stated. In a war which lasted four years, killed one million Britons and wounded another two and a half million, few of the original problems had been resolved. Above all, the German Army had not been defeated in the field. Both the Cabinet and the War Office expected a resumption of the same war with the same allies within twenty years. Could the British professional Army be discredited? Was it wise to bring out the antagonisms between the British and the French or between Britain and her Dominion contingents?

And there was a domestic dimension as well. In 1919, Britain was the same fragile, bitterly divided country as it had been when the war began. Party animosity, trade-union bitterness and Irish dissatisfaction could all have led to civil war and gave Britain the appearance of disintegration on an almost Habsburg scale. If the country was to be held together, the credibility of authority had surely to be maintained, and that was not easily done in November 1918. The war had ended unsatisfactorily. Social division had been exploited by the various factions to manipulate the press throughout the war, while military deficiencies had been appallingly clear to many of the five million who had worn khaki and returned in a disgruntled, unsettled state of mind.

Here was a dilemma indeed. Was there to be a candid statement of the facts, followed by hard, critical analysis with a view to improving matters? If so, Hankey's objection to Lloyd George's memoirs hinted at the dangers. 'Is it really to the public advantage that our national heroes should be hauled off their pedestals? It has somewhat the same effect as would be produced if some distinguished churchman were to marshal the historical evidence against the Saints.'

And what of Haig's pre-emptive fictions? Were they to be disowned, ignored or reinforced? And if accepted, what of Haig's disruptive attitude towards the French or towards his own political masters? The answers would lie in the directives given by the Committee of Imperial Defence to the official historian.

15

The Government's Support of Haig

Haig's fictions and the war's unsatisfactory ending posed few problems for the government in the short term, since it held almost all the evidence and was in a position to overwhelm critics with a mass of documents, selectively edited or even written after the event and pre-dated if need be.[1]

This was the result of the Committee of Imperial Defence's far-sighted arrangement to corner the chief documents, made in August 1914 when 'young Oxford graduates holding a commission in the Reserve Army' had been sent to France for the purpose of gathering sensitive material.[2]

The decision to use these documents was also made at an early stage.[3] The spur here was the historian at Joffre's headquarters, who had begun to publish narratives hostile to the British Army at the start of 1915. The British government made their counter-move later that year by setting up two separate historical projects. The first ('A popular history to counter distorted versions now appearing', the CID put it) was to be written in patriotic style. As Esher told Hankey, 'The popular history will be like Amery's history of the deeds of valour by the British Army' in the Boer War. Kitchener's demand for plenty of coloured illustrations underlined the market contemplated by the government.

The CID went on to advise Asquith that the selection of an author was 'a most sensitive matter'.[4] The confidential nature of the documents involved and the need for publication as soon after the war as possible required a 'reliable' writer. As founder of the CID's

Historical Section, Esher was duly consulted and he put forward the name of Sir John Fortescue, who was Royal Librarian during Esher's time as Royal Archivist. Esher's judgement carried weight and as courtier and author of the highly respected, multi-volume history of the British Army, Fortescue seemed an ideal choice, sound to the point of tedium.

The second series of histories was to be 'a detailed staff history with special reference to the west front'. Because analysis which was intended to educate an army had to bear some relation to the truth, a first-class military brain was required and there were few obvious contenders. With Maurice and Macdonogh serving at GHQ, James Edmonds became the almost inevitable man as the most brilliant examination candidate of his generation, the founder of MI5 and an old CID hand. He had taken up residence at GHQ early in 1915 to vet and classify all documents passing from the Western Front to London. The man and the location were obviously ideal for an official historian and, camouflaged by low rank and a job definition which changed chameleon-like in about every Army List that was issued, Edmonds began his work.[5]

With matters of authorship settled, the CID recorded their own thoughts on the big history and there was general agreement that Edmonds's work couldn't be released for forty years. The explanation formally offered for the long delay was a curious one – the need to withhold information from the French and Germans. The parallel requirement of keeping blunders from the British public seems to have been taken as read by all concerned.

The popular history, with its breezy, broad-brushed treatment and earlier publication date, proved a much more ticklish matter. The first volume produced appeared in a final draft late in 1918 and the response was incredulous. The CID had made it clear that propaganda was required.[6] Against all expectations and after studying a wide selection of unit war diaries, Fortescue was beginning to write something of a very different sort. According to his narrative, the government had failed to prevent the war when it had the power to do so. Haig panicked during the retreat from Mons and deserted Smith-Dorrien during the battle of Le Cateau. Sir John French had been reduced meanwhile to the role of a passive, bewildered spectator, quite unable to grasp events.

Faced with revelations like these and the prospect of more to come once this appallingly frank historian got into his stride, Haig should have been a worried man. After reading Fortescue's manuscript for the first time shortly after the war, 'Tavish' Davidson certainly was and sent a worried letter advising speedy counter-measures. Haig remained imperturbable. 'I have no doubt that the official historian will do full justice to us all. Let us leave it at that.'[7] Knowing Haig's concern over matters of reputation after three years of daily contact, Davidson must have been surprised by his chief's calm, though he probably guessed that Haig was privy to confidential information and that Edmonds as official historian was the source of that information.

Edmonds had returned from France in February 1919. He had taken up a position as Director of the Official Histories. Atkinson, an Oxford don whose father lectured at Sandhurst, had been filling the post in Edmonds's absence. He was now relegated to the menial work of sorting unit war diaries and Edmonds set about the serious work of silencing Fortescue. In a secret memorandum for the CID dated February 1919, he suggested killing him off within a year and, though the CID's reply isn't on record, the setting of a Byzantine trap suggests approval by Edmonds's employers.[8]

Anticipating indiscretion (a colleague wrote in the *Dictionary of National Biography*, 'Fortescue held very definite views and never hesitated to express them, sometimes rather more forcibly than the evidence warranted') Fortescue was invited to review Sir John French's notorious book, *1914*. He did not disappoint. In the pages of the October 1919 *Quarterly Review*, Fortescue slaughtered his text. On French at Le Cateau, for example, he wrote: 'The fact, we fear, is that on the 26th Lord French and his staff completely lost their heads and in a vain endeavour to conceal this, he has taken leave of all sense of accuracy.' Fortescue followed up with more in the same robust vein before concluding: 'A worse example to young officers than is to be found in this book we cannot imagine. We entreat them to avoid it or, if they do read it, to study it for warning against what is wrong . . .' and so on.

Through the twenties and thirties, Edmonds supported most of Fortescue's strictures in correspondence and conversation, but ritual murder had been his purpose in 1919 and Hankey, the Cabinet Secretary, was brought in with the government's solicitor to search the law for suitable weapons. A summary of their plotting un-expectedly survives and registers disappointment that Fortescue had cited no confidential material in his review or committed an offence against the Official Secrets Act. Their conclusion was that the angle of 'controversy in public' should be pressed and a case made that the impartiality of the Official History had been compromised. Fortescue was anyway sacked and duly returned to the Royal Library with an honorary Fellowship of Trinity College, Cambridge, to stop his mouth. Edmonds took over Fortescue's position and immediately scrapped the popular history in favour of a hybrid project of his own which would combine the popular history and the staff history, covering the Western Front in ten volumes and following the style of the Prussian Official History of the Franco-Prussian war – a volume which carried almost divine authority with Staff College men of Edmonds's generation.

The débâcle had thus produced a conclusion in best Gilbert and Sullivan style. The public was to be given a 'Popular' history which was unreadable; the staff were to get a history propagandist to the point of uselessness. But Haig at least could breathe more easily. As a loyal Army man and an acquaintance of long standing, Edmonds's definition of his brief would have reinforced Haig's relief. 'My volumes,' he told the CID in June 1919, 'are to be dispatches expanded by the use of corps and divisional reports.'[9] That same month, the man chosen to work on the Gallipoli volumes was given more precise guidance. He had to avoid critical and controversial matter and follow 'the spirit of official dispatches on the operations'. What this meant for Haig can be put very simply. The Official History was being committed to the defence of generals by making high-command narratives written during the war the guideline for writers in peacetime. When Haig's widow expressed anxiety about the Official Histories in preparation shortly after the death of her husband in 1928, Edmonds was therefore able to re-assure her: 'You may be quite sure that I shall endeavour to write the history of his command as he would have wished.'[10]

A second upheaval which further defined and narrowed the scope of the Historical Branch's work arrived in 1922. According to minutes in the Public Record Office, the origin of the storm lay in that torrent of books which flowed from the pens of high-ranking military men and busybodies with insiders' information. No previous war had seen anything like it and if CID minutes are accurate, the authorities had not visualized publication on such a Protean scale nor did they have any counter-measures immediately to hand.

The Branch's secretary sourly suggested that 'Such books owe their popularity to the amount of secret information which they divulge and the extent to which they enter into personal controversy.' He had the wit to realize that expressions of disapproval were futile and added an opinion that counter-measures should be taken since 'it would be morally wrong to leave the public or armed services to such guidance'.

Hankey had always been uneasy over the possible storms government-sponsored history might generate. Now he joined his colleagues in favour of a counter-strike in the shape of an official account. 'It would serve as an antidote to the unofficial histories which habitually attribute all naval and military failures to the ineptitude of the government,' he explained. 'To say nothing of the accounts of individual officers, frequently ill-informed and partisan in character, which are apt to mislead the public as well as the service.'

Though CID minutes for 1922 survive in surprising detail in the Public Record Office,[11] there is no mention of the books which caused the institution such concern.[12] Apart from Peter Wright's *At the Supreme War Council* and C. E. Montague's *Disenchantment*, there are no obvious villains. On the other hand, 1922 was the year in which Maurice's incendiary pamphlet and Haig's Dewar and Boraston volumes were published. These offerings, little read today, would have posed a real dilemma at the time. Was the history to follow the distorted scenario sketched with such vigour by a former Commander in Chief and by the CIGS's right-hand man? Or was it to state the facts and destroy the credibility of those high-ranking soldiers?

There is no record of what must have been a stiff debate, but the final decision was probably inevitable. Edmonds had been instructed to follow Haig's dispatches on important issues. Now he was told to defer to the CIGS at every point and, more particularly, keep his treatment of the stalemate period (December 1914–January 1918) short and delay publication as long as possible. From Haig's point of view, of course, the less said about Neuve Chapelle and Loos, the Somme and Passchendaele the better.

Discussion in this crucial meeting ended with the selection of an author for the 1918 volumes – always a potential powder keg, incorporating as they would the March débâcle, Foch's takeover and an Armistice without a victory. The final decision was in keeping with the mood of a session determined to cut out any public spectacle of friction in high places. The War Office wanted Maurice (thus showing their support of his 1922 pamphlet). The CID's sub-committee rooted for Aylmer Haldane, a former corps commander and Edmonds's closest friend. In the end, the two groups agreed on a line which indicated tacit support for the Dewar and Boraston volumes when they left the decision on the 1918 volumes to Haig. He put up Kiggell, and Kiggell got the job.

Once these key decisions had been taken in Haig's favour, procedures for organizing and writing the histories were set up which allowed Edmonds and the CID to control every stage of production and exercise strict control over writers at all points.

The process started as soon as public records returned from wartime storage in the tin mines of Cornwall.[13] To make room in the Public Record Office, all Army documents were sent to Edmonds at 2 Cavendish Square and stored in the basement. For three years he read and sorted everything. Documents considered unimportant were sent for storage to St Nicholas's School, Isleworth. The remainder stayed in the basement and were sorted into 25,000 box files covering over 2,000 yards of shelving. 280 drawers of maps supplemented the documents and together these sources comprised 25 million sheets of paper.

More important than taming this mountain of paper was the separation Edmonds made between the daily narrative of the unit war diaries and the messages, orders, reports and field telegrams which formed the appendix of each diary. Edmonds extracted the latter and filed it separately under the classification number Cabinet

70. Official historians of friendly governments who were given limited access referred to this holding as 'The British Master File' and the immediate result of separating it from routine war diary material was to give Edmonds the means of controlling access to almost all the most important documents.

When Edmonds's Nibelung hoard was ready for transfer to the Historical Section's base on the Victoria Embankment in 1923 (the *Daily Mail* printing plant on one side, the presses of the *Evening News* on the other and the Metropolitan railway running underneath and shaking the building with each passing train), Edmonds laid it down that no civilian was to be given access to documents higher than those of division level. Serving officers might read specific documents above that level but only on condition that writings based on them were submitted for censorship before publication. Even the historians in Edmonds's team were restricted and given only the minimum documentation necessary to support the official line at each stage of preparation.

The first of those stages was the production of a simple narrative.[14] Edmonds always referred to the compilers as 'hacks' and, advising his successors on how 'hacks' should be selected, he cautioned against employing 'men leaving jobs because they can't fit in. Avoid men under a cloud in their careers or men of idiosyncratic temperament or character.' In other words, Edmonds opted for conformist non-entities to extract a factual narrative from the war diaries of lower formations. The instruction given to the 'hacks' was that they were to use the Commander in Chief's dispatches to get the general shape of their story ('Their only use for the historian,' as Edmonds drily remarked).

The narrative produced by this scholarly underclass was then chopped into compartments by date, area and unit without regard to style. 'The object of the first narrative is to present history with all the facts,' wrote Edmonds. 'If in doubt, include too many.'

The specific purpose of the narrative ragbag was twofold. On the one hand, it was to provide a basic record which would be 'kept permanently in the Section' and serve as a quarry for historians certified reliable by the CID. On the other, it provided the text which Edmonds had to send serving officers by the terms of his contract. It is sometimes assumed that the official historian canvassed veterans to enrich his narrative and make it truer to the facts. That was never the case. Edmonds's story line was pre-determined. He simply went through the motions to meet his obligations. He certainly never sent whole chapters or fragments of any length for comment. Participants, like 'hacks', were given only as much as was considered necessary. No outsider was ever permitted to wander through whole chapters or threaten security by getting a preview of the Official History's line of argument or points of emphasis. Even so, Edmonds impregnated his colleagues with deep awareness of original sin. 'Don't ask officers for their version of events. Give them a narrative to chew on. There is great value *after* they have read it in chatting over luncheon.' In other words, the more that got on to paper, the greater the danger of leaks.

A final narrative with comments attached was then passed either to Edmonds or to the historian chosen for the main draft. A wide range of documentation became available at this stage, and Edmonds listed it in a departmental memorandum. It included War Office branch diaries, the correspondence of the Army Council, the Prime Minister's minutes, the Secretary of State's correspondence, the minutes of the Chiefs of Staff Committee at the War Office, and Defence Committee minutes. It was a rich diet, and modern researchers will note that none of these items is in the public domain today.

Edmonds's own first draft had a limited circulation, going only to the Army Council, representatives of the major government departments and a handful of high-ranking generals. Few examples of their comments or of the alterations they imposed have been allowed to filter through to the Public Record Office, but those which have suggest careful scrutiny and a resolute determination to impose interpretations favourable to established authorities.

An example on the military side which relates to the first volume for 1916 is a set of instructions from the Army Council.[15] Since Edmonds had been instructed to defer to the CIGS, the gist of those instructions was duly incorporated into the final text, even though Edmonds knew well enough that the Council's views bore little relation to the facts.

Referring to Churchill's recent book *The World Crisis,* the Army Council began by noting 'the misleading impression of unthinking stupidity in the British higher command conveyed by the picturesque phrases of Mr Winston Churchill'. It suggested that Edmonds insert a paragraph to counter the charge that Haig had chosen the strongest part of the enemy line for his own attack. 'Before the attack, allied commanders were not and could not have been aware of the elaborate nature of concealed German defences' – a line which Edmonds knew from his own records to be false. The Army Council went on to suggest that responsibility be fixed on Joffre by bringing out Haig's preference for a battle in Flanders – which Edmonds again knew to be false from documents he had recently sent out to Bean in Australia. The final request was that responsibility for the 7.30 am kick-off be placed firmly on French shoulders – again wrongly, as Edmonds knew.

There are no records showing a Foreign Office blue pencil on Edmonds's drafts, but letters in the private papers of Gallipoli's official historian suggest that the Foreign Office was no less energetic in distorting history to its advantage.[16] A word sent for Aspinall's 'private ear' in 1931 provides a good example. Because a copy of the finished work would be sent to Atatürk, the Turkish head of state, the Foreign Office was anxious to please the Turks. At present, it was noted, Aspinall's text omitted the Hamlet of the play. Couldn't Kemal's name be inserted in the epilogue? As a divisional commander, Kemal had surely acted at three critical moments, and since it could be safely assumed that jealousy existed between Turkey and Germany, couldn't this be exploited? By such means, an unimportant junior commander was transformed into a military hero, his fictitious role written into all subsequent histories of the Gallipoli campaign.

The Foreign Office's stand over Ian Hamilton's reputation was equally revealing. In 1927, it wrote to the secretary of the Historical Branch, who in turn passed the letter to Aspinall. 'Although Hamilton may not be unduly sensitive as to how his reputation appears in history, there is a public side as well as a private one. Many French troops were under his command and, what is of greater importance in this connection, many Dominion troops. Is it not therefore politic that the Official History, so far as is compatible with historical truth, endeavour to present the Commander in Chief in a favourable light? You may well think this suggestion impracticable if I appreciate aright the hint in your previous letter that the key to much that is not clear in the direction of this campaign lies in the relationship existing between the Commander in Chief and Lord Kitchener and this is a factor which cannot be discussed at the present time.'

When Edmonds had received his instructions and woven them into his text, the final version went to two men. The Germans used the historian Delbruck and the soldier von Kuhl to make a last judgement on intelligibility and style. Their British counterparts were two Oxford dons – Atkinson and Wood.

Once they had given their benediction and the draft had gone off to the government's printers, Edmonds had to make quite sure that troublesome researchers wouldn't be able to undermine the sacred text. With this in view, all drafts and narratives were retained by the Historical Branch, guaranteeing that outsiders would be denied both the detail of the original narratives and references to particular documents which were in the margins of those narratives.

One more stage remained, and that the most sensitive of all. The documents themselves had to be processed in such a way that evidence for accounts different from those of the Official History was removed. Edmonds was therefore given personal authority to go through all documents bearing on the Western Front and divide them between those for burning, those for retention by the CID and a small quantity which could be safely passed to the Public Record Office, selected and arranged so as to guide researchers towards conclusions which had been built into the Official History.[17]

In this sensitive work, Edmonds had the assistance of only one higher clerical officer and three clerks, which means that his sifting took four years. It was a price Edmonds and his employers were willing to pay. The fewer the eyewitnesses and the less their grasp of what was going on, the better.

But the official historian's work wasn't at an end when his volumes were written and the documents thoroughly sifted. The CID expected their man to take offensive action against any author whose work might carry weight with the public and whose line might be contrary to the wishes of the authorities. Today, work of this sort is delegated to MI5's F branch. In Edmonds's time it fell to the official historian in person.

Retired generals were seldom much of a problem to him. Appeals to professional loyalty or threats in respect of club membership and City directorships seem to have been all that was required. When Plumer's former Chief Staff Officer, Charles Harington, undertook a biography of his old commander, for example, Edmonds encountered no difficulty over treatment of the controversial Passchendaele period. Harington simply inserted an article written by Edmonds for the *Journal of the Royal United Services Institution* in February 1935. That article may indeed have been written with Harington's schedule in mind.

Sacked army commander Hubert Gough, with his burning sense of grievance, was more of an obstacle. When Gough suggested that Shaw Sparrow, the journalist, should write a sharp introduction for his book on the 5th Army and its troubles, Edmonds sent a brisk letter with a characteristic threat in the tail.[18] Despite the 'silly' Dewar and Boraston book, it was wrong to discuss Haig's errors in public, Edmonds wrote. Haig had been greatly handicapped by the enmity of Lloyd George and the intrigues of Henry Wilson. Charteris's poor Intelligence work had been another burden. Haig would have protested at having to take over more line from the French if he had not been misled on enemy strength. 'Your policy should be to show that, given Haig's total force, the 5th Army was bound to be weak as a blow against it could produce no result. The 5th Army was never broken but stemmed the advance.'

Edmonds then turned to a brisk offensive. Why had Gough's defences lacked depth? Why had the causeways across the Somme not been cratered? Why had Watt's 19th Corps been given so many men? Why did soldiers dislike being sent to the 5th Army? 'All these points are debated by your friends and the last one is the damning one,' Edmonds concluded. Though he held a complete copy of his army's war diary and should have been able to meet most of Edmonds's points with ease, Gough declined to do so. Perhaps the example of General Maurice, with highly paid press work, a chair at London University and an honoured position in London's clubs, provided an attractive example of the rewards awaiting sacked generals who sang the right tune.

Edmonds had less leverage over civilians who stood outside the patronage system of the establishment. To deal with potentially damaging criticisms from that quarter, Edmonds developed the smear into a fine art.

Gough was an indispensable butt in this regard and usually available, since Haig's practice had been to employ the dashing cavalryman at the spearhead of all his most controversial offensives. 'In Flanders in 1917, Gough showed too much cavalry spirit,' Liddell Hart was told in a typical Edmonds letter. 'Earthworks protected by barbed wire cannot be taken by a general charge any more than permanent fortifications by the chests of grenadiers, as Napoleon told a marshal. Gough complained of lack of blood lust among the troops and one day when I was having tea in the staff Mess of the 5th Army, he burst into the room almost yelling, "I want to shoot an officer." There was an awkward pause till the APM arose and said apologetically that there were no officers under sentence. To this, Gough rejoined that he knew that but he wanted to get hold of an officer whom he could shoot as an example to the others. He did get hold of one who had momentarily failed and he was shot. It was said that Gough in a bowler was a very different person to Gough in a brass hat.'

Was Edmonds telling the truth? Haig's Routine Orders name a single officer shot in 1917. That man was a temporary sub-lieutenant of the Royal Navy's Volunteer Reserve and he was executed on 5 January. Edmonds's credibility is further dented by the fact that, when he repeated the anecdote to Wynne, who was writing the Official History's Passchendaele volume, Edmonds wrote that two officers had been shot, on Gough's orders.[19]

Byng was another of Edmonds's butts. When Sylvester was researching the background of Cambrai for Lloyd George, Edmonds told him: 'Byng was not called to the Cambrai inquiry or he would have been sacked. Byng has never been a great soldier. He is a great man of the world and has the reputation of being the readiest liar in the British Army. He later resisted Haig's suggestion to evacuate the Cambrai Salient in 1918.'[20]

Byng's share in the failure at Cambrai was, of course, substantially less than Haig's, and Haig's orders to Byng early in 1918 had been to hold the Flesquières Salient as a false front for as long as possible.

Two civilians always needed more than those throw-away lines
and gratuitous slanders which were Edmonds's stock in trade, and
these two men were the best informed of all civilian outsiders –
Winston Churchill and Charles Bean.

In his dealings with Churchill, Edmonds always approached with
the exaggerated courtesy of a mongoose stalking a particularly
deadly cobra.[21] Referring to a draft of *The World Crisis,* he suggested: 'In view of your high and esteemed position in the hearts of
your countrymen, I think you might cut out some of the sarcasms
about the military leaders.' Churchill responded with a courtly bow:
'This Somme chapter certainly requires a strong addition showing
the undoubtedly deep impression made upon the Germans by the
wonderful tenacity of the attack. If you have anything that bears on
this, perhaps you could bring it along with you.'

Writing to Bean two years later about these exchanges, Edmonds
remarked: 'I read Churchill's typescript and galley proofs. I dripped
acid on them and spent several weekends with him, talking things
out.' The result seems to have satisfied both parties. 'I find nothing
against the general line of argument,' purred Edmonds after reading
the final version. 'But on no account should my name or mention of
the Branch appear. We should have all sorts of people clamouring
for help apart from possible trouble in parliament.'

Bean himself proved a much tougher nut. As a result of a Cabinet
promise to the Dominions in 1916, Bean had enjoyed access to the
war diaries of all units fighting on either side of the Australians and
of all headquarters (including GHQ) which had given orders to
Australians. Even though the CID had stonewalled for six years and
held back what they could, Bean's clerk had still been able to spend
three years in London and copy a mass of documents. This meant
that no other war historian outside the ranks of the CID – Liddell
Hart included – had access to more than a small fraction of Bean's
riches.

Bean's stubborn independence reinforced the sensitivity of the
material he had acquired.[22] There was never anything in him of
those run-of-the-mill academics who gladly castrate their critical
faculties for the sake of a university chair. Indeed, Bean's stubborn
attitude towards hints and heavy-handed requests from GHQ had

already led George V to deny him the decorations requested by the commander of the Australian Corps on two separate occasions during the war.

Bean therefore represented a potential danger of considerable magnitude – as Edmonds frequently reminded the CID. 'The general tone of Bean's narrative is deplorable from the Imperial standpoint,' he said on one occasion, quoting the opinion of the British commander in Egypt. 'Murray's view was that Bean was beyond teaching [*sic*] and had better be left alone. At any rate, I have given him our point of view.' And what a fascinating point of view that was for the 1916 volume under discussion at the time.

In the course of correspondence, Edmonds made it plain to Bean that he had begun his own work on the Somme with a preconceived view. 'I hope to show and prove from German sources that the Somme was the turning point of the war since most of the best of the Germans were killed off. This could not be done without losing the flower of our manhood. Future generations, I feel sure, will regard Haig and his commanders as the Americans do Grant, Sheridan and Sherman although the clamour against the latter was shrill enough in the 1860s from uninstructed critics. They won the war and wars can only be won when the forces are evenly matched by the drive of commanders.'

Edmonds went on to re-assure Bean on points of detail – that GHQ's Intelligence work had been first class; that the breakdown of transport stemmed from Rawlinson's expectation of reaching German roads within a few days; that the absence of a protective creeping barrage at the start of the battle had been due to shortage of shells; and that Buchan's statement to Bean on Haig's intention to go on until he had lost half a million men was not to be seriously regarded. 'On the few occasions Buchan appeared at GHQ, he was not persona grata. He and Gibbs were the most gullible of the publicists.'

Edmonds wrote a good deal more in the same vein, unaware of the range and depth of Bean's fieldwork. During the war, Edmonds had been stuck in GHQ, classifying documents on behalf of the CID. Bean, on the other hand, had moved freely between the front line and corps headquarters. He had talked frequently with Birdwood and Monash. Montague and Lytton gave him inside information from GHQ. Keith Murdoch had passed on confidential snippets in his capacity as go-between for the British and Australian Prime Ministers. Bean therefore knew that Buchan was a personal friend of Haig and had written most of Haig's dispatches during the Somme. He was certainly aware that Gibbs had been the best informed of the British correspondents, personally consulted by the War Cabinet on occasion. From documents copied in London during the 1920s, he would have known that Haig's intention had never been to break through on the Somme and that Charteris's work had been widely regarded as suspect throughout the British Army. From his own examination of the British officer in charge of Australian artillery, he knew only too well that the absence of a desperately needed creeping barrage had little to do with a shortage of shells and much with technical backwardness and the absence of those skills which were required to fire a creeping barrage.

Edmonds's correspondence with Bean on matters of detail and interpretation was a massive one, running through the 1930s and covering all Bean's Western Front volumes. The quantity of deception and downright lying dealt out by the British official historian makes astonishing reading today. Referring to the Nivelle period, for example, Edmonds's final judgement was that 'The personal relations between Haig and Nivelle remained excellent as soon as they both realized that they were being deceived by the lying politicians who wanted to get them at loggerheads so as to get control of the military operations.'

Another gem from Edmonds was the story that Lloyd George had deliberately withheld reinforcements from the Western Front at the end of 1917 because he 'refused to be Haig's butcher'. When Bean asked for the source of that much-repeated story, Edmonds gave him the name of Whigham, Robertson's deputy at the War Office, but when the Cabinet Office vetted Edmonds's own one-volume history of the war, he had to agree to cut the story out. 'I had my doubts about Haig's butcher,' he admitted. 'It was Churchill who told me of this outburst and I had his permission to quote it. It does not appear in any of Winston's writings.'

The end product of Edmonds's work was therefore an Official

History which presented a fraudulent account of the Western Front, supported by documents mischievously selected and leaks maliciously planted in the path of writers pressing too hard on the truth. But there was never anything personal about it. Edmonds had been given very precise instructions on method and story when he began his work, and when the work was completed thirty years later that commission had been faithfully executed.

Despite all efforts, the government still found itself in difficulty almost as soon as Edmonds went into retirement. The lapse of the fifty-year safety period in 1968 meant that a quantity of documents would have to be made available to the public and two books gave an early warning of the problems lying ahead. Leon Wolff's *In Flanders Fields* (1958) described the Passchendaele campaign in vivid detail and, by achieving best-seller status, indicated an unexpected revival of interest in the Great War. In the late 1930s, war books had been lucky to sell more than a few hundred copies; in the fifties, the paradoxical effect of the Second World War seemed to have been a sharpening of public dissatisfaction with the miserable amount of nourishing information provided by the CID between the wars.

Alan Clark's *The Donkeys* (1961) made an even stronger impression. Based, according to Liddell Hart's information, on notes and documents provided by a renegade official historian, Clark's book gave a remarkable picture of feeble British generalship during 1915 and remains the single most accurate book in print on any Western Front campaign, desite systematic attempts to discredit it. At the outset, Haig's solicitors had threatened legal action for 'defaming the Field Marshal's heirs and successors'. Publish and be damned, Beaverbrook advised the author. Clark was fortunately able to take the first point of his advice and avoid the second.

With servants criticizing gentlefolk and civilian intellectuals toying with revisionism, the authorities sensed danger. What was to be done?

One possibility was to come clean. The issues involved had already been aired by the sub-committee supervising the Official Histories back in 1928.[23] Milne, the CIGS, taxed Edmonds with being too kind to generals. Edmonds replied that he was inclined to hint at things rather than state them baldly. 'We do not want everybody to see the troubles we had and the mistakes we made,' he added. Churchill chipped in at once: 'Nor do we want our children to make the same mistakes. They must be brought out.'

Thirty years later, these opposing viewpoints confronted the authorities but with a vital difference. The indecisive result in 1918 had been clarified in 1945. The central powers had lost. The Entente had won. There was therefore no justification for subterfuge. Weakness in the British Army could be candidly confronted and old allies insulted — if that was the best course. A blunt statement at the outset of the necessity of using the Official History as a weapon in the lead-up to the Second World War would also have carried conviction — if it had been openly made in the 1950s.

The opportunity was missed. The short-term, shortest-sighted way out of an immediate difficulty was chosen and that was to scapegoat Edmonds and treat him as if he alone had been responsible for past distortion. His coffin was therefore dug up, his corpse gibbeted. Translated into modern practice, this involved placing a carefully vetted selection of Edmonds's private papers into an archive to create the image of Edmonds as a latter-day John Aubrey, a garrulous old gossip. That was the first step. The second was to stamp Edmonds's professional work as unreliable and thus distance the CID and Cabinet Office from the chosen historian.

The job was done by placing in the Public Record Office a file which had the same function as those carnivorous plants which entice with the scent of rotting flesh, then snap shut on their victims. In this case, the scent was supplied by a file carrying the irresistible title of 'Passchendaele'. Its contents were, in fact, a tiny fragment of the correspondence related to that particular volume in the Official History and, even then, correspondence which covered only a handful of the less controversial chapters.[24]

The strand which drew the selection together was Edmonds himself and the gist was that an increasing number of people were beginning to doubt Edmonds's judgement. In pride of place was a lengthy letter from Sir Norman Brooke, Cabinet Secretary at the time. 'I am not happy,' he wrote 'at the thought of leaving Edmonds to revise the volume as he thinks fit, without the restraints imposed by the criticisms of a colleague. I fear that whatever restraint he has exercised in his past writings, he has not always been able in recent years to resist the temptation to introduce strong personal views into his historical work.' Since the procedures imposed on Edmonds involved vetting by the chief departments of state and deferring to the War Office at every point, Brooke's assertion was preposterous. But the Cabinet Office was receiving unpleasant messages and expecting worse. It therefore shot its own messenger.

This course of action deferred criticism in the short term, but was it really to the advantage of the armed forces to support the palsied structure of its *ancien régime* period? And was it in the public interest to underwrite a falsified version of the war, circulated by an inadequate Commander in Chief?

The sharpest comment on these matters was passed by Major-General Walter Lindsay, who had commanded the 50th Division during 1914 and 1915, writing to Edmonds during the 1930s. 'The battles of the Ancre (late autumn 1916) made the most tremendous impression on my mind . . . I have always looked on them as the most frightful indictment of our methods of command at the time. They were characterized by a futile waste of life, materials and morale arising from the fact that the battle seemed to be fought by directors with little appreciation of the conditions prevailing. Most of the mistakes were repeated at Passchendaele. It really was reluctance to write this sort of thing at all that made me delay my answer as I felt that it was so long ago that what did it matter? Yet the more I wondered whether I should write what I thought or not, the more I felt that unless our history of the war gives us an official criticism of the methods employed and points out the disastrous results of those methods that were wrong, we shall not be able to profit from our past experience.'

BIOGRAPHICAL
SKETCHES

Addison, Christopher 1869–1951
In peacetime, a Professor of Anatomy and editor of the *Quarterly Medical Journal*, war saw a remarkable transformation when Lloyd George put him first into munitions, then made him Minister of Reconstruction. One of Lloyd George's greatest contributions to government was to demonstrate a principle once stated by the steel-making pioneer Henry Bessemer: 'I had an immense advantage over many others dealing with the problem inasmuch as I had no fixed ideas derived from long-established practice to control and bias my mind and did not suffer from the general belief that whatever is, is right.'

Albert 1875–1934
King of Belgium from 1909. Bespectacled beanpole of a man with the wit to state the military case against Passchendaele at length from the start of 1916. Had a son at Eton and in the same house as Ivor Maxse's boy.

Allenby, Edmund 1861–1936
3rd Army commander 1915–17, commander of the Egyptian Expeditionary Force 1917–18 and a trencherman of massive bulk. His irascibility was legendary. Corps commander Haldane gave an example. 'He damned an officer on a trench round. "Very good, sir," said the officer. "I want none of your bloody approbation!" Allenby retorted. It is better not to answer him when he is bullish.' Allenby was a shocking horseman and a great lover of flowers. He once stood for a quarter hour in front of 'a really lovely carved church door', humming the Emperor Concerto as he examined it minutely. As a soldier, his Staff College report can't be improved on: 'So long as the situation falls within his knowledge of it, it is rapidly and thoroughly dealt with. In matters with which he is not so conversant, he is not very good in working into detail. He has energy and the power of exerting influence on others and getting work out of them.' But as T. E. Lawrence told the American military writer De Weerd, Allenby was bigger in personality than in intellect and he was a big enough

man to know it. 'You know I ought to be Adjutant General,' he told Grant, one of GHQ's liaison officers. 'I should have made a damned good one.' Allenby was a man of the greatest integrity and would allow no criticism of GHQ or of colleagues at his own headquarters.

Amery, Leo 1873–1955

MP 1911–18 and Assistant Secretary to the Cabinet 1918. Special adviser to the Cabinet on European affairs. Lady Carson wrote of him: 'Amery really tries to think that Lloyd George is almost an honest man and is all for Henry Wilson and seems to think we had better fight on as many fronts as possible. Of course, he is an awfully clever little man but he gets ideas into his head and nothing moves them. I think he is selfish and greedy. Little men generally are. He piled on jam and ate it on his cake and everything sweet is so difficult to get.' Amery had in fact the 'awful cleverness' of a Fellow of All Souls. Often right, his lack of tact undermined his influence in council. 'I think Leo must be the cleverest bloody fool alive,' Balfour once observed.

Arthur, George 1860–1946

Kitchener's private secretary 1914–16 and ranking with Esher as confidential adviser to George V. Haig wrote to Arthur regularly on the understanding that such letters would be passed on to the king. None of these is in the public domain today.

Aspinall-Oglander, Cecil 1878–1959

Staff Officer with Hamilton at Gallipoli and chief planner of the Anzac landing. Joined Haig's GHQ subsequently. Wore corsets and high-heeled boots but wrote an outstanding official history of the Gallipoli campaign – despite Edmonds's blue pencil, which cut about one third of it.

Asquith, Herbert 1852–1928

Liberal Party leader 1908–26. Prime Minister 1908–16. Calm and urbane with the temperament of a judge. Birkenhead remarked that he fought cleanly, winning without insolence and losing without rancour. A consummate advocate, he lacked talent for chairing Cabinet meetings. Idle or wasteful discussion went unabridged. Lloyd George once remarked that men were like army lorries marked 'load not to exceed three tons'. 'They can carry any load up to three tons safely and well. Give them a load in excess of that and they will break down.' The mounting problems of the war, the loss of his son Raymond on the Western Front and of Venetia Stanley to Montague, his colleague, took Asquith's loading to over three tons and prepared the way for his replacement by Lloyd George.

Baker, Newton 1871–1937
Secretary of War for Woodrow Wilson from 1916. A self-declared pacifist, Baker's chief qualification for the post was that in the presidential election of 1912 he had swung crucial votes for Wilson.

Balfour, Arthur 1848–1930
Prime Minister 1902–5. 1st Lord of the Admiralty 1915–16. Foreign Secretary 1916–19. With his turned-down collars, large ties and gentle manner, Balfour kept the curiosity and vulnerability of a small child to the end of his life. He protected himself with 'old-fashioned' charm. Some thought Balfour's excessive courtliness compensation for lack of heart. As a holder of fifteen honorary doctorates, he was incomparable in argument, but a man who stayed in bed until midday whenever he could was intolerable as a departmental chief. For him, important state papers were regarded with the same indifference as daily newspapers. 'News is either important or unimportant. If it is unimportant, I don't want to know about it. If it is important, someone is sure to tell me about it.' He used to address the Imperial War Cabinet on the state of the world from notes jotted on the back of an old envelope, omitting whole continents. Most damning of all, as Lloyd George told Riddell, was that his whole mind was opposed to action. Balfour, of course, passed this failing off with charm. 'Balfour made us laugh in describing his failing memory. What constantly happens is that some difficult foreign problem arises. His officials place the problem before him from every point of view, put their advice clearly and then leave him to prepare notes for a speech. "What I always forget is the decision come to. I can remember every argument, repeat all the pros and cons – can make quite a good speech on the subject – but the conclusion, the decision, is a perfect blank in my mind."' Much of this was play-acting, of course. As founder member of the Committee of Imperial Defence, he was one of the most influential men in Britain and was bound to have a place in any Cabinet that was set up during the war.

Bean, Charles 1879–1968
Australian-born and English-educated, Bean was the official Australian war correspondent and writer of six massive volumes of Official History after

the war. Bean witnessed every major Australian battle and talked constantly with men at GHQ, corps headquarters and in the lower commands. After the war, he obtained access to a great mass of British war records not available to researchers today. Adding to such resources the most meticulous and painstaking scholarship, Bean bequeathed some of the most valuable writings on the Great War and certainly one of the richest collections of private papers.

Beaverbrook, William Max Aitken 1879–1964
Wealthy Canadian businessman turned MP 1910–17. Took charge of recording the Canadian war effort on the Western Front while pushing the fortunes of fellow Canadian, Bonar Law. Minister of (dis)Information 1918, subsequently keeping his hand in as proprietor of the *Express* newspapers. Frederick Oliver once remarked that Beaverbrook 'looked like a human toad' and so he did. But he was an intensely able toad. His books on the politics of the war sparkle with the intelligent malice of a latter-day John Aubrey. He circulated the first of these books in typescript during 1917. Balfour pronounced it accurate. Bright young historians make small reputations by professing otherwise.

Beddington, Edward
Staff Officer to Gough's 5th Army.

Below, Otto von 1857–1944
Opposed Haig at Arras in April 1917 and supervised the remarkable *Blitzkrieg* victory over the Italians at Caporetto that autumn before taking charge of an army in the March 1918 offensive.

Benson, Rex 1863–1939
Served under Clive on GHQ's mission with Pétain. Together with Paul Clark, his American counterpart, Benson enjoyed the privilege of being able to open any drawer in the French 3rd Bureau (Operations section).

Bertie, Francis 1844–1919
Career diplomat who filled the Paris embassy with Palmerstonian dash from 1905 to 1918. As a Foreign Office man, he fought Esher and the CID, disliking Haig as an Esher man. Though critically ill during the war, his private papers are always informative and usually well balanced, but scholars who dislike Bertie's conclusions emphasize the conjunction of lechery and cancer.

Birch, (James) Noel 1865–1939

Artillery adviser at GHQ from the Somme onwards. Knowledgeable soldiers often cited Birch as an example of the Old Army's preference for second-rate men from the Royal Field Artillery or Royal Horse Artillery over first-rate gunners from the Royal Garrison Artillery. Broad acres and fat wallets counted for more than professional skill, and the obtuse barrages of 1917 were a direct result. In his favour, Birch gave unwelcome advice to Haig without hesitation.

Birdwood, William 1865–1951

Commander of the Anzac Corps till summer 1918. Often in the front line and known to all his command by sight, Birdwood had severely limited military ability. 'He never drew up the plans for an operation,' his Staff Chief told Bean. 'It was not an element in his capacity. He was not an organizer. When Birdie went out for the day, he never brought back with him a reliable summary of what he had seen.' Fair-haired, blue-eyed and physically trim, those qualities had led to him becoming private secretary to Kitchener in the Boer War period, with consequent promotion far beyond his true level. But, as Maxse pointed out, 'Birdie's way was to shake hands with everyone and by the time anyone had found him out, thousands more had been won by handshakes in arithmetic progression.'

Blamey, Thomas 1884–1951

Chief Staff Officer to Monash's Australian Corps in 1918.

Bliss, Tasker 1853–1930

Pershing's Chief of Staff. Subsequently American delegate with the Supreme War Council at Versailles.

Bonar Law, Andrew 1858–1923

Leader of the Conservative Party 1911–21 and Lloyd George's right-hand man in the War Cabinet. Haggard, unassuming, careworn, Bonar Law never lost his temper, facing criticism as leader of the Commons either with the face of gloom (his normal expression) or with deprecatory smiles and gestures. Derby truly remarked that, though a first-class debater and 'with all the qualities of a leader, Law had no personal magnetism and could inspire no man to real enthusiasm'. Lloyd George added: 'He would never decide things. He was admirable in the second place but hated supreme responsibility.' Master of the depressive throw-away – 'Well, there's lots of trouble ahead' was a favourite dampener – Bonar Law was equally master of the dry and caustic aside. Thus Lloyd George: 'I always feel inclined to throw away my notes but I find if one trusts the audience, one is apt to be led astray and say foolish things on the spur of the moment.' Bonar Law: 'If you don't mind me saying so, I think that fact has contributed in large measure to the success of your speeches.' Compulsive pipe smoker and chess player, Bonar Law had seen his wife die just before the war and was to lose a son on the Western Front.

Boraston, John 1885–1969
A barrister who joined the CID's Historical Section in 1915 and was sent to GHQ to serve under Edmonds during 1916. He was Haig's private secretary for a short time after the war and wrote Haig's Memorandum on Western Front operations during that time.

Borden, Robert 1854–1937
Canadian Prime Minister 1911–20. Riddell noted a remarkable absence of either charm or enthusiasm, but as spokesman for the most effective formation in the British Army, Borden's criticisms always carried more weight than those of Australia's firebrand 'Billy' Hughes.

Braithwaite, Walter 1865–1945
Chief Staff Officer to Hamilton at Gallipoli. Divisional commander on the Western Front, promoted corps commander in autumn 1918. An active spiritualist after the death of his son.

Broad, Charles 1882–1976
Staff Officer to Uniacke, who commanded the 5th Army's artillery.

Bruchmuller, Georg 1863–1948
Chief gunner in Hutier's German 18th Army. Perhaps the most skilled and innovative gunner of the war. Master of those abrupt and massive bombardments which took the allies by surprise in 1918 and paralysed both reinforcement and counter-fire.

Buchan, John 1875–1940
Composed GHQ's dispatches during the Somme before becoming subdirector of the Foreign Office's Department of Information. Wrote *Greenmantle* and a volume of poetry in those years. As Burgis remarked of Esher, his patron, and Edwardian society generally, 'These sort of people had an

extraordinary amount of leisure. Even during a political crisis, they seemed to have so much time.'

Burgis, Lawrence 1892–1972
Esher's private secretary from 1909 to 1913, at which point he joined the Black Watch. Handled Esher's private cipher at GHQ before taking the position of Cabinet Secretary in 1918.

Butler, Richard 1870–1935
Served on Haig's 1st Army staff and followed his master to GHQ. Haig wanted him to be Chief Staff Officer. The War Office rejected this since Butler was only forty-two years old. An able brigadier, Butler became a poor deputy CGS, with great capacity for causing offence. He rose finally to corps command, featuring in serious setbacks in the preamble to the 8 August 1918 offensive and in preparations to storm the Hindenburg Line.

Butler, Stephen 1880–1964
British Staff Officer attached to the Anzacs and, for a short time, to GHQ. Won golden opinions all round.

Byng, Julian 1862–1935
Cavalryman who rose from Canadian Corps commander to GOC, 3rd Army, through 1917 and 1918. The Canadians regarded him highly. He excluded political interference with robust good sense and took the men into his confidence, lecturing to all units and ordering the issue of 40,000 maps before the classic Vimy operation. A man of intense earnestness, Byng was, in the words of Anzac Staff Chief White, 'An unambitious man without any desire for personal fame – a very rare thing in generals and a very precious quality in the eyes of those under them.'

Callwell, Charles 1859–1928
Director of Military Operations at the War Office for the war's first seventeen months. He was sacked for leaking information during the Dardanelles inquiry period.

Carson, Edward 1852–1935
Attorney General 1915. 1st Lord of the Admiralty 1917. Member of the War Cabinet without Portfolio 1917–18. Though a powerful Protestant war lord in Ulster, Carson was curiously ineffectual away from his power

base. Singularly effective in covering his constant intrigues against Lloyd George from the eyes of posterity.

Castelnau, Édouard de 1851–1944
Commander of France's eastern group of armies under Pétain. Maxse commented on the impact his simplicity made. He thought it comparable to Roberts's. Fathered thirteen children, three of whom died at the front. A fourth was a prisoner of war. Maxse noted that baffling combination of decision and ability within his profession, limitation and slowness in every other area.

Cavan, 10th Earl of 1865–1946
Commanded the Brigade of Guards, a corps and the 10th Italian Army on the Piave front in 1918. Of his ability, Henry Wilson remarked, 'Mr Cavan doesn't see very far but what he does see, he sees very clear.' Known as 'Fatty' in the army.

Cavendish, Frederick
Liaison officer with the French armies from 1915. Answered to the name 'Caviare'.

Cecil, Edgar 1864–1958
Son of the 3rd Marquess of Salisbury, thus guaranteed a comfy billet in the public service. Under-Secretary for Foreign Affairs 1915–16. Assistant Secretary of State, Foreign Affairs, 1918 as well as Minister of Blockade 1916–18. One of the front runners among the anti-Bolshevik scaremongers.

Chamberlain, Austen 1863–1937
Secretary of State for India 1915–17 and member of the War Cabinet 1918.

Chamberlain, Neville 1869–1940
Mayor of Birmingham 1915–16. Director General of National Service 1916–17. Lloyd George told Riddell that Chamberlain represented one of the few ministerial pigs he took from a poke, 'and I am not very sure of my pig'. The degree of disorganization in recruiting would, however, have defeated far abler men.

Charteris, John 1877–1946
Director of Intelligence at GHQ 1916–17. A soldier with unusually diverse

experience. Fluent in French and German, Charteris was an FRGS and had reported the Balkan wars for *The Times* in 1912. His father had been a professor at Glasgow, his brother was to be one at Sydney. Esher captured his two sides well when he characterized him at once as 'cleverer than most soldiers' and 'a pushing, untactful person'. The latter quality combined with rapid promotion entirely dependent on Haig's favour made him widely unpopular. So, too, his absurd battle with War Office Intelligence. But such papers as have reached the public domain strongly suggest that his own Intelligence work was first-class and his present reputation (he is not in the *Dictionary of National Biography*) is due to a deliberate decision to sacrifice him.

Churchill, Winston 1874–1965
1st Lord of the Admiralty 1911–15. Lieutenant-colonel with the Royal Scots Fusiliers 1916. Minister of Munitions 1917–18. Esher once commented that Churchill's 'power for good or evil is very considerable. His temperament is of wax and quicksilver and this strange toy amuses and fascinates Lloyd George, who likes and fears him. He handles great subjects in rhythmical language and becomes quickly enslaved by his own phrases.' Lloyd George also discerned the flaw: 'His mind is a powerful machine,' he wrote. 'But there lay in its makeup some obscure defect which prevented it from always running true. When the mechanism went wrong, its very power made the action disastrous to the cause and the men with whom he was cooperating.' The reference was to Antwerp, the Goeben, Coronel, Gallipoli. Riddell once said to Lloyd George, 'Winston's mind is concentrated on the war,' to which Lloyd George replied, 'Yes. But it is more concentrated on Winston.'

Clark, Paul
Pershing's liaison officer with Pétain and a most valuable historical source.

Clausewitz, Carl von 1780–1831
Entered the Berlin War College 1801. Chief of Staff to a Prussian corps in the Waterloo campaign and wrote his seminal *On War* as head of the War College 1818–30. Died of cholera.

Clemenceau, Georges 1841–1929
Prime Minister of France 1917 to the end of the war, Clemenceau was a French Lloyd George. A fierce orator and radical outsider (Lloyd George

said of him 'He loves France and hates all Frenchmen'), Clemenceau embodied resistance to the invader. When it was suggested in 1914 that the government should leave Paris, his characteristic reply was, 'Yes, I think you are right. We are not near enough to the Front.' During the war, a front-line soldier gave him a bouquet of dusty flowers. These were always on his desk and were buried with him. During the intrigues against Lloyd George at the start of 1918, Clemenceau leaked confidential information furiously to Pepington and Maurice – for which service Haig wrote glowingly of the Frenchman in his diary re-writes.

Clive, Sidney 1874–1939

A professional soldier who served as a liaison officer with the French. High-level approval was later indicated by a fusillade of Mad Hatterish titles (Extra Equerry to the Queen and Marshal of the Diplomatic Corps). But his value is not in these baubles but in a diary he kept during the war. It is lengthy, well informed, intelligent – and indispensable.

Cowans, John 1862–1921

The War Office's Quartermaster General throughout the war. Cowans looked like a prosperous corn merchant and kept all his records in a large pocketful of grubby notebooks. And yet, as Lloyd George remarked, 'Whatever doubts and grumbles there were about the deficiencies of other war leaders, there was never a murmur from any quarter as to the efficiency with which Sir John Cowans did his work. When I came to know him better, I realized that under his rough exterior and stolid look there was a simple and kindly nature and an inexhaustible fund of good humour and joviality.'

Currie, Arthur 1875–1933

Commanded the Canadian Corps from Vimy to the end of the war. Currie remains the most successful allied general and one of the least well known. Immensely tall, pot-bellied and with the appearance of a company cook in his characteristic dress of shirtsleeves and braces, what little dignity Currie had was blasted away by his equally characteristic bad language. But he had a great capacity for war. Currie's Chief Staff Officer recalled his general devouring every military tract available, questioning every good soldier he could find and displaying 'intense interest' in the war. His guiding rule was stated in his diary – 'Thorough preparation must lead to success. Neglect nothing.' His style of command was admirably summed

32 Aerial photographs of Falfemont Farm taken during the battle of the Somme showing the effect of intense bombardment. *Top*, 26 April 1916, *middle*, 28 July 1916, *bottom*, 1 September 1916.

33 The British 60-pounder could fire up to 300 shells daily into an area a hundred yards or so square. The bombardier on the left makes final adjustments to the fuse. The two men on the gun alter elevation. The NCO to the right clasps the delicate sighting mechanism used to lay the gun for indirect fire. The shell had a range of eight miles – equivalent to a shot from Epping Forest dropping into Trafalgar Square.

34 Tanks and reinforcements move up to battle.

35 The great mine crater at La Boiselle, blown on the first day of the Somme.

36 Panorama of the Passchendaele area.

37 Destroyed German trenches at Ovillers, looking towards Bapaume Road, July 1916.

38 A British soldier awaiting burial. The soldier's Hadfield steel helmet is standard issue, designed to counter shrapnel shells. His gas mask (together with cigarettes and chocolate) are in the bag round his neck. Missing puttees indicate a rear area. The care taken over a dead body was the norm.

39 British dead awaiting burial in a cemetery near Monchy les Prœux (near Arras) in 1918. By the end of the war an astonishing 20 per cent of British soldiers had been killed, the figure including those who served in relatively inactive theatres, on the home front or as C3 men on the lines of communication.

40–42 'Ruined men, desolated hopes'. *Top left*, a shrapnel wound; *top right and bottom*, limbless men.

43 Joffre, Poincaré, King George V, Foch and Haig at Beauquesne, Haig's advanced headquarters, for the start of the final push. The date is 12 August 1918, just four days after the battle of Amiens.

44 Pétain leaving British Advanced Headquarters, Iwuy, 15 November 1918.

45 Charles Bean was Australia's official war correspondent. In that capacity he witnessed every major battle and interviewed commanders at all levels before and after those battles. He devoted twenty-three years to writing Australia's highly authoritative official history, and his working papers remain a major (and almost unknown) historical source for the Great War. He is seen here with his parents on the eve of war.

46 Brigadier-General Sir James Edmonds, the British official historian.

47 Haig's post-war home of Bemersyde. It overlooks the river
Tweed in the Scottish border country. The British public were
supposed to have bought it as a present for Haig. Most of the cash
came from Haig's acquaintances, in fact, and that hostile branch of
the Haig clan which owned it did handsomely from the transaction.

48 Haig at work in his attic study at Bemersyde in the mid-twenties.
He would have been re-working his diary at the time. After his
death in 1928, his wife set up the study and bedroom beneath it as a
museum but, ten years after the war, public feeling had become too
bitter for such a gesture.

up in *Maclean's Journal*: 'No flashing genius but a capable administrator, cool headed and even tempered and sound of judgement. He has surrounded himself with a capable staff whose counsel he shares and whose advice he takes. He is the last man in the world to stick to his own plan if a better one offers. So far as tactics go, he is the first among equals for such is the way his staff work.' His capture of the Drocourt–Quéant Switch in autumn 1918 remains the British Army's single greatest achievement on the Western Front. The combination of unprecedented densities of artillery and machine guns with flexible infantry sections was the Canadian trade mark under Currie's command.

Curzon, 1st Earl (George) 1859–1925
Elevated to Lloyd George's War Cabinet as its spokesman in the Lords, Curzon was described by Hankey as 'an intolerable person to do business with – pompous, dictatorial and outrageously conceited'. Oliver added a comment on how little Curzon ever grasped what went on in other people's heads and how limited his experience (Lloyd George once bewildered him by asking who Gipsy Smith, Jimmy Wilde and Billy Sunday were). And yet all admitted his credentials. He was tenacious, courageous and immensely hard working (as Lloyd George told Harold Nicolson in 1936, 'He was not perhaps a great man but he was a supreme civil servant'). The disappointments of his youth had purged him and left a man who, in the opinion of Amery and Milner or an observer like Crawford, would have made an excellent Prime Minister. As chairman of the War Committee, men noted his reticence, his control of business, his interventions to cut windbags short and focus the discussion.

Davidson, John 1876–1954
A Boer War veteran with the King's Royal Rifles, Davidson went on to become a Staff College lecturer in 1912 and a Staff Officer when the war began. As the man charged with extracting the Indians from the line in 1915, Davidson managed his assignment with dispatch within ten days, reporting personally to Haig each evening on progress. Haig liked what he saw. Bright, young, handsome, Scottish and with the letters PSC (Passed, Staff College) after his name, Davidson possessed every quality Haig required of personal staff. In 1916 he thus became Director of Military Operations. For three years he posed objections to all Haig's schemes, several times getting to the point of dismissal to a division, yet he survived – the only one of Haig's top aides to do so to the end of the war. The dull,

obsequious book Davidson wrote on Haig at the end of his own life should not detract from his record as Operations Director. The extraction of official papers and low quality of entries in the *Dictionary of National Biography* on staffers like Davidson and Kiggell (no entry at all for Charteris!) have done an injustice to the more capable of Haig's entourage.

Dawnay, Guy 1878–1952

As an Eton and Oxford man with experience as clerk in the Commons, Dawnay was something of a mongrel in the Old Army. Yet connections and intelligence combined to push him into a top staff job at Gallipoli. Since Haig picked up Hamilton's old team almost *in toto*, Dawnay's career prospered and by 1918 he was Deputy Chief of Staff. The highpoint of his career was the mission to London in 1915 when he offered a dagger, reinforcing Hankey's eyewitness report and concealed by the publicity given to Murdoch's unimportant letter, which was plunged into Hamilton's back. A second highpoint was his editorship of the *Army Quarterly* after the Great War. In his time, that magazine sparkled with intelligent, critical comment.

De Lisle, Henry 1864–1955

De Lisle's rise was based on (1) having Roberts as a patron and (2) managing the first polo team made up from infantrymen to win a cup in India. His secret says much about the Old Army. Cavalrymen just hit the ball and chased; De Lisle's men passed the ball like a football. De Lisle was always intensely unpopular with the divisions and corps he commanded. Bean told the story of a German sniper being lynched on capture. He had shot at and missed De Lisle. Ungenerous and abrasive he may have been. He was also an able soldier in the hectoring style of Ivor Maxse.

Derby, 17th Earl of 1865–1948

Director General of Recruiting 1915–16. War Minister 1916–18. British ambassador in Paris 1918–20. A fat, ruddy-cheeked man of the greatest good humour. Brusque, direct and frank, he might have been mistaken for the manager of a cotton mill. As a politician, many expressed doubts. Northcliffe called him 'the great jellyfish' and Haig's diary, in the re-written version, was uniformly rude. Since hostile comment comes just from the compromise peace faction, it is a fair guess that Derby's chief crime was to remain a man of integrity through 1918, opposing the Maurice conspiracy in particular. The matter would be settled by Derby's detailed daily diary. Unfortunately it 'disappeared' while the official biography was being written. Until it is produced, an observation by one of

Asquith's daughters is more suggestive of Derby's political footwork than all the pique of men like Oliver, Haig or Northcliffe – 'Lord Derby is sufficiently clever to pretend to be stupid in order that people may think him honest.'

Dill, John 1881–1944

Like Alanbrooke and Montgomery, Dill learnt his trade with the Canadian Corps and rose to high position in Haig's HQ subsequently. Edmonds remarked that front-line commanders who wanted decisions in 1918 avoided senior men there and went straight to Young Turks like Dill in the Operations section.

Du Cane, John 1865–1947

Held a number of staff appointments during the war before taking charge of the 15th Corps from 1916 to spring 1918. After that and to the end of the war, Du Cane was Chief of GHQ's Mission with Foch and, though he spoke no French, the private diary and unpublished book he wrote on that period remain documents of candour and importance. Pre-war Staff College conferences reveal Du Cane as an able, intelligent soldier and, during the war, there was some talk of Du Cane rather than Henry Wilson taking the position of CIGS.

Edmonds, James 1861–1956

Few official historians have had better brains than Edmonds. His Staff College entry marks were double Haig's and he reckoned to be able to translate military material from any European or Asian language. Bean later wrote, with some awe, that Edmonds seemed able to quote at will from an immense range of reading, and take in a printed page almost at a glance. The CID identified him early and brought him in to set up MI5 in 1904. When war broke out, he was sent to gather documents for the subsequent Official History at GHQ. The position required the supple qualities of a courtier and, for the only time in his outspoken life, Edmonds displayed them. 'I was on terms of friendship with all the British generals from Haig downwards,' he told Bean. 'I never belonged to any party and since I was not competing for promotion, I enjoyed confidences I might not otherwise have had.' The result, as Edmonds later told the Cabinet Office, was that 'Only Hankey knows more about the Great War than I do' – and Edmonds's correspondence bears him out. Only a profoundly knowledgeable man could have produced an Official History so misleading in detail and yet with that ring of plausibility which has led to a general acceptance for so long. The quicksilver, whimsical Edmonds would have been among the first to relish the irony. As he told a correspondent once, 'I have written too much history to believe in it. If anybody differs from me, I am prepared to agree with him.' He finished his historical work in 1947, writing in that year to Bean, 'Bread is rationed. Clothes are at prohibitive prices. Tobacconists have up "Sorry. No cigarettes" and to crown all, coal is running out so that factories are closing down. I believe this is all planned in order to start a revolution, as Professor Laski and the agents of Russia desire. But Providence will look after us and confound their knavish tricks.' Died aged ninety-four. He attributed his own longevity and robust health to the wartime routine of fifty minutes' work and 10 minutes' rest each hour, daily ablutions in cold water and a regular work-out with dumb bells.

Elliott, Harold 1878–1931

Though a barrister by profession 'Pompey' Elliott proved a natural soldier. His command of the 15th Australian Brigade and his own wartime writings are of outstanding quality. Australia's official historian wrote of him, 'Big and burly with an immense jaw, a tuft of iron grey hair stands up permanently on end with sheer energy. He is the living figure of one of those woodcuts of the great old Admirals of the age of Hawke and Rodney. His every utterance if it be but to ask the day of the week, he gives it with a lift of the chin like a challenge.'

Esher, Viscount 1852–1930

Reginald Brett, 2nd Viscount Esher, was an MP from 1880 to 1885. After that, he became a ubiquitous grey eminence, flitting between Court, Cabinet and command HQs in the Army in an unspecified capacity. His position and influence have long been matters of speculation, but much becomes clear if the Committee of Imperial Defence is assumed to be an extra-constitutional organization, established after the Boer War to plan the coming war with Germany. Documents in Australia indicate a CID existence altogether more continuous and influential than documents placed in the Public Record Office are calculated to suggest. The fact of the Cabinet's policy-making Committee being the CID from the outset of the war, staffed by the CID's Secretariat and using CID procedures, and finally becoming the War Cabinet, is a matter of record. Esher and Balfour were founders and guiding hands of the CID. Esher in particular played a key role in establishing MI6 and the Historical Branch, both departments of the CID. His correspondence in the period of influence crackles with intelligence and shrewd comment, but at the end of 1917, when he threw in his lot with the compromise peace faction, he lost influence at Court and was excluded from decision-making.

Foch, Ferdinand 1851–1929
Entered the Army in 1870 when the Franco–Prussian War began and rose rapidly as an artillery expert, Staff College lecturer and theorist with a European reputation. As an Army Group commander on the Somme, he lost his status with the sacking of Joffre but returned as Pétain's Chief of Staff in May 1917. Generalissimo from spring 1918, Foch dictated strategy until the Armistice. Physically small, he was alert in body and mind and with an intensely dignified, masterful bearing. Economical with words, he punctuated silence with a battery of violent gestures which meant that only those who had worked closely with him for a long time could fully understand what he was driving at. Even then, Weygand, his inseparable Staff Chief, was the only man with a full comprehension. Foch worked with a tiny staff of about thirty men and set up his HQs in a sequence of remote, over-heated *châteaux*, filling rooms with the fumes of his cheap cheroots. British liaison officers found him always approachable and never a man to take offence. '*Pas de protocole!*' was a frequent and explosive interjection and the only fixed point in Foch's day was mealtime – midday for lunch and 7.30 pm dinner. Rawlinson commented shrewdly on Foch's strategy in 1918: 'I am overjoyed at Foch's methods and far-sighted strategy. I worked in close touch with him in 1916. He is a better man now than he was then, for his fiery enthusiasm has been tempered by adversity.' Remarking on his intense Frenchness: 'He knew nothing of Britain. The Rhine to him was the river of life and death.' Lloyd George noted, too, Foch's staunch integrity and his uprightness in all dealings. This was reflected in his refusal to produce self-justifying memoirs. One of the ablest commanders of the war, Foch remains one of the least known. His papers are dispersed within the family. No soldier or historian appears to have made the effort to rectify this huge gap in our knowledge.

Fortescue, John 1859–1933
Librarian of Windsor Castle 1905–26 and the historian chosen to write an official history of the war for popular consumption. It was scheduled for publication as soon after the end of the war as possible, but Fortescue was

sacked when his narrative proved unacceptably truthful. Edmonds then rolled the popular and staff history into a single production, combining the worst features of each – the propagandist deceptions of a popular history, the dullness and long delays of a staff production.

French, John 1852–1925
Commander in Chief till December 1915. Subsequently Commander in Chief, Home Forces. In April 1918, French told press proprietor Riddell that the military débâcle that spring had been due to Haig and Robertson. 'Both should be court martialled and taken out into that square [pointing out to Horse Guards Parade] and shot.' It was a characteristically impetuous judgement. And not necessarily incorrect.

Fuller, John 1878–1966
Chief Staff Officer to the Tank Corps, planner of tank use at Cambrai and, between the wars, a leading theorist of *Blitzkrieg*. Respected Staff Officer Lynden Bell ('Belinda' in the Old Army) wrote in 1919: 'Fuller is an officer of quite exceptional merit. In energy, tact and brainpower he is almost in a class by himself.' Like contemporary Leo Amery, he paid the penalty for perceiving solutions too quickly and showing awareness of the same. As Faraday once said, 'The real truth never fails to appear ultimately and opposing parties, if wrong, are sooner convinced when replied to forbearingly than when overwhelmed.'

Geddes, Auckland 1879–1954
Professor of Anatomy at Edinburgh before being seized by Lloyd George's crimps and posted Director of Recruiting 1916–17 and Minister of National Service after the sacking of Neville Chamberlain 1917–18.

Geddes, Eric 1875–1937
Deputy Director Munitions Supply 1915–16. Director General of transport at GHQ 1916–17. Admiralty Board 1917 as honorary vice admiral. Member of the War Cabinet 1918. A politician wrote of him: 'He didn't know anything about politics or parliamentary procedures. He was a complete tycoon. Geddes was very aggressive but was a boyish sort of person. He had all the virtues and vices of youth. On the other hand, he had great ability and drove a path through when he decided on anything, with great vigour. He was very fond of medals and must have been a Godsend to his tailor. Geddes always liked to be dressed in the appropriate

uniform (he was simultaneously an admiral and a general!) which he had gained permission to wear. He wasn't popular because he had no finesse in dealing with people.' Wide as he was tall, Geddes joined Lloyd George's hymn singing with relish. Lloyd George was the baritone and Geddes a bass with the lungs and roar of a bull. Auckland Geddes thought the war period the high point of his brother's career.

Gellibrand, John 1872–1945
Kings, Canterbury, the Manchester Regiment and PSC (Passed, Staff College) before migrating to become an apple grower in Tasmania. Invariably incorrectly dressed, he rose to Australian divisional command. Gellibrand was typical of that great mass of effective junior and middle-range commanders thrown up by the war who had failed to find a place in society before the war and failed to find one after. In Europe, these men were to give Fascism its cutting edge.

George V 1865–1936
Like a painfully conscientious boy confronted by a man's job, George V displayed many of George III's virtues and defects. His strength was in a fixed determination to benefit the whole nation. His stance against the Jellicoe Rump in the Admiralty and the men behind the Maurice conspiracy was of inestimable benefit. At the same time, the king was often too excitable to be effective. One Minister wrote: 'I gave the king a list of orders for Council approval. His eyes fell on a proclamation forbidding the importation of boots. "Why may we not import boots? Don't we want boots? Aren't other countries short of boots and oughtn't we to have as many boots as we can get?" His voice grew louder and louder, shriller and more strident.' The same Minister seven months later noted: 'His voice was rather more strident, his gestures rather more syncopated.' The king was also inclined to be indiscreet and partisan. Desmond Morton, Haig's ADC, wrote, 'The king was remarkably indiscreet at times. He used to refer to Lloyd George as "Thatt Mann", the Germanic pronunciation becoming very strong, and was completely on the side of the soldiers against the Frocks. There was an occasion when he gave me the most violent instructions on the telephone to pass a very rude message to Lloyd George.' Beaverbrook believed that 'George V continually interfered with civilian administration and brought plans to ruin again and again.' Perhaps so, but Pershing was probably nearer the truth when he wrote in his diary during August 1918 (at a time when the king was pressing him to send a sizeable

American contingent to fight with the British), 'I should have liked to argue with the king and set him right but, seeing that he is the king and that what he thinks will have very little influence on the situation, I let it go.'

Gibbs, Philip 1877–1962
The most capable and best-informed of the British war correspondents.

Gold, Ernest 1881–1976
As 3rd Wrangler and a Fellow of St Johns, Cambridge, Gold had written a seminal paper on the effect of thermal winds on Zeppelins. This together with the fact of the president of the Royal Meteorological Society being a man of German extraction led to Gold's selection for meteorological work at GHQ. He began with a staff of three, predicting when the Germans would be most likely to use chlorine gas. By the end of the war Gold had a staff of 120 and was reporting daily on all facets of weather. A colleague wrote of him: 'He was rarely unnecessarily intimate. Slow in speech and deliberate of thought, he had the exasperating practice of keeping silent for minutes. Subordinates with an appointment were kept waiting. He listened to arguments but rarely conceded a point. He was indeed an uncomfortable superior to work with.' Perhaps Gold's profession was in its infancy, but his reports were often little better than hunches and, in the case of Loos and Passchendaele, disastrously wrong.

Gough, Hubert 1870–1963
Commanded the 5th Army 1916–18. Notorious for his lack of understanding of any branch of the service but cavalry. Bean's notes on Gough's approach to Pozières and Bullecourt make horrifying reading today. At Pozières, he had every intention of sending the Australians straight into a major attack without time even for a preliminary reconnaissance. His reputation by autumn 1917 was such that the Canadians even refused to serve under his command. Gough owed his rise entirely to Haig's favour – his fall too. After the débâcle of March 1918, Haig told one of Gough's staff officers: 'After considerable thought, I decided that public opinion at home, right or wrong, demanded a scapegoat and that the only possible ones were Hubert and me. I was conceited enough to think that the Army could not spare me.'

Grant, Charles 1877–1950
Du Cane's assistant in the 1918 mission with Foch.

Grey, Edward 1862–1933
Secretary of State for Foreign Affairs 1905–16. US ambassador Page described him to the President as 'Very natural. A simple and earnest man.' Like Asquith, he regarded politics as a part-time activity. Of the four books he wrote, one was on bird watching, another on fly fishing.

Grierson, James 1859–1914
In charge of the Eastern Command from 1912 and earmarked for high command, Grierson died of a heart attack at the very start of the war.

Griscom, Lloyd
Pershing's personal liaison officer at Haig's HQ.

Haking, Richard 1862–1945
Staff College professor who commanded a corps 1915–18. Would have been given an army but for the War Office veto. One of the men who backed Haig in his manoeuvring against John French. It is not easy to see any other reason for him remaining in France. The bloody reverses at the Hohenzollern Redoubt in 1915 and at Fromelles in July 1916 led to the tag 'Butcher' being linked with his name throughout the Army. Even Edmonds made little effort to back Haking in the course of his copious correspondence with Bean.

Haldane, Aylmer 1862–1950
A corps commander who represented the best type of leader in the Old Army. Haldane began each day with a cold bath and vegetarian breakfast eaten out of doors whatever the weather. Always in a hurry and always on foot, Haldane seemed more Prussian than British in type. As a Staff Officer put it, 'The harsh trials of official business were seldom mitigated by the exercise of charm and humour. The admiration of his staff was greater than their affection.' But a first-rate soldier.

Hamilton, Ian 1853–1947
Commander in Chief at Gallipoli. Evacuation there spelt the end of his prospects.

Hankey, Maurice 1877–1963
Royal Marine artilleryman in 1895. Secretary to the CID by 1912 and Cabinet Secretary in 1916. Short, bald, lean, Hankey was a humourless,

non-smoking teetotaller. Having worked under him for many years. Burgis agreed with Baldwin that Hankey had no bowels. Receiving the telegram of his brother's death at the Western Front, Hankey simply glanced at the message then said, 'Well, Donald has gone. Where was I, Owen?' (his stenographer). Others found a more attractive man. Lloyd George's staffer Thomas Jones wrote: 'It is difficult to understand Hankey until one realizes that temperamentally one is dealing with a man who is still a boy. His clever, quick brain is unclouded by any bias or prejudice. It is the mind of a brilliant civil servant who has no dealing with factions and is unfettered by convention ... He is the prince of secretaries ... If by any chance he should find a rare day at his disposal, he will return with a memorandum written upon some point which is awaiting discussion.'

Harbord, James 1866–1947
Pershing's Chief of Staff. Took command of a division for a time before taking charge of American Expeditionary Force supply in Europe, which was in the most complete shambles.

Hardinge, Charles 1858–1944
Under-Secretary for Foreign Affairs 1916–20, previously Viceroy of India and heavily tarnished by the Mesopotamian scandal.

Harington, Charles 1872–1940
Plumer's Chief Staff Officer and a soldier highly regarded during the war. Bean wrote of him: 'He was clearly not one of those society cavalry generals or hunting squires put in charge of 300,000 men. He has the face and unconventionalities of a scholar. Receding forehead. Rather watery blue eyes, not at all clear, and lips which show his teeth. The type of a university mathematical don very much engrossed in his work.' When Aylmer Haldane praised Plumer in front of Haig, 'Haig fired up at once and said "You would never have heard of Plumer if I hadn't sent Harington to him."' The two men were, in fact, a perfect team, but Plumer was very well able to function efficiently when Harington went to the War Office in spring 1918.

Headlam, Cuthbert 1876–1964
Clerk to the House of Lords 1897–1924. Barrister, Inner Temple. Staff positions at most levels including GHQ in the war. Editor of the *Army Quarterly* 1920–26. MP 1924–9 and Parliamentary Secretary to the

Admiralty for a further three years. Headlam's daily letters to his wife constitute a valuable source on the friction of war as seen from division and corps HQs.

Henderson, George 1854–1903

Professor at the Staff College 1892–9 and author of the seminal *Stonewall Jackson* in 1898. His obituary in *The Times* stated: 'He exercised by his lectures and his personality an influence upon the younger generation of officers to which it would be difficult to find a parallel nearer home than of Moltke in Prussia.' Since 'the younger generation' in question were all the high-ranking generals of the Great War, Henderson's belief that the chests of grenadiers would crush an opponent's firepower can be seen as malign. Had Henderson not died young, the Russo-Japanese war might have caused him to change his teaching.

Hindenburg, Paul von 1847–1934

Served in the Prussian Army in the wars of 1866 and 1870. Put in command of all German land forces in 1916. Edmonds wrote of him: 'One of his pupils at the Kriegsakademie told me that Hindenburg was the only one of his teachers who was human and could see another person's point of view. I met him during the manoeuvres of 1908. He was aboutt fifty inches round the chest, smelt of stale cigars and lager and had charming manners. Apparently the ladies found him charming as well for he had recently been respondent in in an *Ehescheidung* affair.'

Horne, Henry 1861–1929

Commander of Haig's 1st Corps artillery. Promoted to a corps for the initial Somme attack. 1st Army commander 1916–18.

House, Edward 1858–1938

President Wilson's personal representative in Europe from 1914.

Hughes, William 1862–1952

Welshman who settled in Australia in 1884. Organized the maritime unions and became Prime Minister in 1915. Tiny, frail, impulsive, his loud voice and selective deafness made him a formidable proposition in Cabinet. Had he not been confronted by party weaknesses (of his own making through the conscription issue) Hughes might have taken that place in the War Cabinet subsequently offered to Smuts.

Hutier, Oscar von
Commanded the German 18th Army. His startling victory at Riga in best *Blitzkrieg* style in autumn 1917 made certain that he would be at the cutting edge of Ludendorff's March 1918 offensive.

Ironside, William 1880–1959
Staff Officer who commanded a brigade in 1918. A giant of a man, he served as the model for Buchan's more objectionable heroic characters.

Jacob, Claud 1863–1948
From command of an obscure Indian division, Jacob was given a corps on the Somme in one of Haig's more inspired decisions. Maxse wrote that Jacob's character secured the full confidence of all who served with him. Unambitious personally, Jacob was fearless of superiors. 'Essentially a man of practical common sense, receptive to new ideas', he initiated a system of half-hour staff conferences each evening to evaluate the day and plan for the morrow. Would have become Commander in Chief, India, after the war but, faced with two names and knowing nothing of Jacob, the king chose Birdwood, senior by a small amount. Fuller's private correspondence explodes violently on the stupidity of that choice.

Jellicoe, John 1859–1935
Commanded the Grand Fleet 1914–16. 1st Sea Lord 1916 and Chief of Naval Staff 1917 before being sacked later that year. The Admiralty would have mounted a strong opposition but the king stated his position clearly and the danger passed.

Joffre, Joseph 1852–1931
2nd lieutenant in the 1870 war, by 1914 Joffre had become Chief of Staff. A huge, pot-bellied and often speculatively shaven man, Joffre surprised many who met him face to face. As Lloyd George told Riddell at the end of 1915, 'He is alert and vigorous and not at all like the heavy, impassive person he is made to look in his photographs. He is full of vitality, kindly and humane, his face expressing force and steadiness but not great ability.' Edmonds backed Lloyd George in a rare display of admiration for a fellow soldier. 'Joffre was one of the most impressive figures I ever met. Solid and stolid with masterful blue eyes, he compelled obedience.' But as a French colleague tersely remarked, Joffre was morally excellent, militarily a nullity.

Jomini, Henri 1779–1869

A Swiss who served with the French revolutionary armies in 1789. Chief of Staff to Ney in 1813, he changed sides to become ADC to the Tsar. Organized the Russian military academy and advised Nicholas I at the time of the Crimean War. His *Summary of the Art of War* (1838) was among the first serious attempts to provide a synthesis around mathematical rules and one of the chief inspirations behind that near-fatal volume, *Field Service Regulations* of 1909.

Kerr, Philip 1882–1940

Owner of 32,000 acres and a favourite son of the Milner circle. In 1910, he founded the *Round Table*, much the most influential of the journals advocating Imperial unity at the time. In December 1916 he became private secretary to Lloyd George. A good brain and casual dresser. The *Dictionary of National Biography* noted disapprovingly: 'He did not think it incongruous to attend the coronation of his sovereign in an Austin 7.'

Kiggell, Launcelot 1862–1954

Director of Staff Duties at the War Office 1901–13. Staff College Commandant 1913–14. Chief of Staff to Haig 1916–17. Fuller styled Kiggell a 'tall, gloomy, erudite soldier meditating like a Trappist monk at Montreuil' and there was something in the description. Older than his years, in constant poor health and a soldier who had never held a field command, Kiggell was always cut off from the pulse of the Army and its organization in the field. Indeed, he came to France for the first time only in January 1916. Clive was probably about right when he said at the end of 1917, 'The real person who must be changed is Kiggell, straight and charming though he is. He is unknown to the Army. He neither organizes nor assists the work of the staff . . .' Quite why Haig asked for such an inexperienced Staff Chief in the first place is another matter.

Kitchener, Horatio 1850–1916

Secretary of State for War from 1914 until drowned in June 1916 on his way to Russia. His present reputation has been affected by his solitary nature ('K's ingrained habit of trying to keep everything in his own hands,' Milner called it), his secretiveness ('If there were two ways to proceed,' wrote ambassador Bertie, 'one straight, the other crooked, Kitchener always preferred the crooked one') and his inability to work with politicians (his first words to Birdwood when visiting Gallipoli were: 'If you only knew what a relief it is to get away from the politicians. Men who are always at you; to whom you have to explain things as you would to a little child and who cannot understand them even then'). But on the big questions such as the likely duration of the war and Britain's optimum strategy, Kitchener was usually right. As Oliver told Austen Chamberlain, 'Stick to Kitchener. His judgement is usually ten times better than the reasons he gives. Shouldn't we keep him just for grand strategy and training armies?' – this in March 1915. Analysis and suggestion were spot on.

Lansdowne, Marquess of 1845–1927
Conservative Foreign Secretary 1900–1905. Leader of the Opposition in the House of Lords and member of the 1915 coalition government without portfolio through into 1916. His retirement was the reason for putting Curzon into the War Cabinet as government spokesman in the Lords. Lansdowne's open letters in the press served as markers for a compromise peace faction that was beginning to coagulate in the second part of the war and which Haig joined at the end of 1917.

Lawrence, Herbert 1861–1943
Commanded a brigade at Gallipoli and a corps in Egypt before picking up the 66th Division in France. According to the *Dictionary of National Biography*, 'The division was engaged with success in October in the fighting for Poelkapelle.' In fact, the 66th suffered 5,000 casualties from its own guns. It was conclusive proof of his talent in Haig's eyes and he became GHQ's Chief Staff Officer shortly afterwards. A tense, lined, lean soldier, Lawrence resembled Hutier so closely that when he first saw the latter's photo, he asked himself what he was doing in a German uniform. His father was the Indian Mutiny's hero. Two of his sons were killed during the war.

Lee, Arthur 1868–1947
Parliamentary Secretary for the Ministry of Munitions 1915–16. Personal secretary to Lloyd George 1916. Director General of Food Production 1917–18. Lloyd George once asked Riddell why a man as capable as Lee was so unpopular. Riddell told him of Lee's pushy manner and obvious indifference to whom he displaced in his upward progress. Presented Chequers to the nation for the use of future Prime Minsters.

Liddell Hart, Basil 1895–1970
Gassed on the Somme as a young subaltern, Liddell Hart spent the rest of

the war studying tactics. With Maxse as patron, he helped to re-write *Infantry Training* and took up positions on the *Daily Telegraph* and *The Times* which gave him both security and a sounding board. His early works on the war (*Reputations* and *The Real War*) were the first non-fictional examinations of what really happened and still retain their value. There is a question mark against his status. Letters in the Buchan papers during the war, his press positions and the curious fact that he did research for both Lloyd George's memoirs and the Duff Cooper *Haig* pose the question. Lloyd George's memoirs and *Haig* were both heavily vetted by the CID with the authors allowed only a limited number of points to score off each other (necessarily so with Hitler in power in Germany). Was Liddell Hart therefore leaking for the CID and helping to soften their position on the war, with Haig dead and a number of published works beginning to undermine the Official History's position? Such a status would help to explain Edmonds's apparent indiscretion in conversation with him and the presence of both Edmonds's and Liddell Hart's (heavily vetted) private papers in the same archive.

Lloyd George, David 1863–1945
Solicitor in 1884. President of the Board of Trade 1905–8. Chancellor 1908–15 and damned by every man of property and privilege as supposed originator of 'The People's Budget' and the Parliament Act, with its attack on the House of Lords. Minister of Munitions 1915–16 and Secretary of State for War 1916. Prime Minister from December 1916. Some could never forget Lloyd George's past (for Lady Carson he was 'That scum of the earth, Lloyd George'). Many kept their reservations ('Lloyd George is an awful little outsider,' wrote Charteris. 'No knowledge. No depth. No really round judgement but considerable energy and a great flow of words'). But most people backed him, since his qualities matched the majority mood at the end of 1916. Oliver wrote of his 'cyclonic energy' and of his display of 'more drive than any three politicians'. Added to energy, as Birkenhead noted, was a talent for creating an atmosphere of easy bonhomie in which all present would talk spontaneously, and another for instantly sensing the mood of speakers and assemblies, making him 'the most persuasive negotiator in the world'. US ambassador Page described these qualities well for the President: 'Lloyd George is perhaps the easiest man to talk to of all men who hold high places. He has little dignity and no presence except as an orator. He swears familiarly on all occasions. But he has as quick a mind and as ready speech as any man I have ever encountered. He is changeable, mercurial. He reasons with his emotions

and reaches quick conclusions. He has been called the illiterate Prime Minister because he never reads or writes but he is the one public man in the UK with the undoubted touch of genius. An amazing spectacle to watch, he compels admiration but not complete confidence.' Many who worked with Lloyd George styled him a bad administrator, constantly changing his mind, never satisfied, prone to violent outbursts of abuse and slow to make decisions. In Cabinet likewise, he was a poor chairman, wandering away from the agenda, slow to shape a discussion, reluctant to confront inconvenient facts. In a letter to Curzon, Robertson showed this side of Lloyd George perfectly: 'It would be valuable if you would kindly explain to the Prime Minister what the nature of the Balkan country is. He seems quite unable to envisage it ... He seems to think there is a single range of hills between Salonika and Sofia whereas the whole country is a mass of mountains. No amount of argument or heavy artillery will alter that.' Inspirer, skilled welder of diverse men and national spokesman in the style of Palmerston in an earlier war, Churchill in a later, Lloyd George's inability to think in a straight line for a sustained period and come to a clearcut conclusion was a major weakness. It is best seen in committee minutes leading to the uncertain conclusion that Passchendaele was to be fought. Perhaps Lloyd George's courage and steadfastness were sufficient counter-balance. Drinking his own mixture of egg, port, honey and cream each morning, he had the resilience of Jimmy Wilde. When Riddell once asked him if he minded the designation of 'the most unscrupulous and inept Prime Minister in history', he replied that men had been saying the same of all Prime Ministers since the office was created and that he was not in the least disturbed by such vituperation.

Long, Walter 1854–1924

Conservative MP 1880–1921. Shortly before the war, he lost to Bonar Law in the party leadership race and became Colonial Secretary during it. An irascible man from the Jacobite wing of his party, Long displayed equally unsound judgement in first backing French against Haig and then in believing that hampers of premium-quality sherry for GHQ would soften Haig's excellent memory in such matters.

Ludendorff, Erich von 1865–1937

As a humble brigadier, took the surrender of Liège at the start of the war in a daring gamble which linked him to Hindenburg for the rest of the war, first as Chief of Staff on the east front, then as Quartermaster General on the west from autumn 1916. Edmonds set down the accepted British view: 'I met Ludendorff in 1900 at the Berlin Kriegsakademie. He was a nasty, sour-faced fellow with a small, twisted mouth peculiarly like the late, unlamented Sir Charles Douglas in face. Not a "gentleman" even by Prussian standards.' The excellence of Ludendorff's interior economy and tactics together with his willingness to promote and use only the ablest men belies Edmonds's short-sighted judgement. Ludendorff's directives, not easily procured today in Britain, are invariably lengthy, closely reasoned and framed with great courtesy. They supply a better guide to the man. Probably the outstanding high commander of the war.

Lytton, Neville 1876–1947
Professional artist and major in the Royal Sussex Regiment. Wounded in 1916. Lytton joined GHQ's staff to take charge of the foreign press. His job was performed with outstanding success.

Macdonogh, George 1865–1942
A soldier of remarkable intellect, Macdonogh got so many marks in the Staff College entry exam of his year (it was Haig's year) that publication of the list was delayed to spare blushes. Became a barrister in his spare time. Set up MI6 (MIIE as it then was) in 1909. Took charge of Intelligence at the War Office 1916–18 and founded an MI directorate for the world. Wrote a colleague, 'Yes, indeed. Dear old Macdonogh. The depth behind those eyes. The way everything one told him went down and down to be pondered over, digested.' Finding his figures a hindrance to their more quixotic assessments, GHQ made great play of Macdonogh's Roman Catholicism. When Macdonogh's Intelligence appreciations failed to coincide with Haig's, the Commander in Chief assumed him to be a cog in a wider Roman Catholic–pacifist conspiracy. Macdonogh's private papers remain buried treasure, hidden away in the vault of a London bank.

Malcolm, Neill 1869–1953
Chief Staff Officer in Gough's 5th Army. A thinking soldier with military publications to his name, Malcolm's image in the war was that of a man over-worked, irritable, under-achieving.

Masefield, John 1878–1967
Poet. Used by the Foreign Office's Department of Information to write propagandist books on Gallipoli and the Somme. The Department was frustrated. Both works were written without rancour as elegies for men

suffering against the setting of a particular landscape and sketched with the poet's art.

Maurice, Frederick 1871–1951
Director of Military Operations at the War Office under Robertson from the end of 1915 to spring 1918. Though he had previously been unpopular as a lecturer at Camberley Staff College, it was generally admitted that he knew his work. During the war he was a key figure in the military intrigues against Lloyd George. Gwynne's papers show that he organized the leaking of confidential War Office material to the press. In the final shoot-out of May 1918, he was the front man in the 'Maurice debate' which tried to blame Lloyd George personally for the débâcle of March 1918. Foch thought he would be shot and any French general who had acted as Maurice did and sent a signed letter to the press attacking the Prime Minister probably would have been. But as the soldier–intellectual of an influential faction urging a compromise peace to thwart the growth of the leftist opposition, he was well protected. The press welcomed his contributions, even after the notorious 'Maurice letter', and he ended as Professor of Military Studies at London University and president of the British Legion when a financial scandal involving substantial payments to the Haig family (according to Edmonds) needed to be hastily covered up by a reliable man.

Maxse, Ivor 1862–1958
Described by Liddell Hart as 'a soldier version of Lloyd George. He is difficult to argue with as he always wants to do all the talking. Bubbling over with fiery energy. Brilliant surface cleverness. Possibly not very deep but seizes salient points fast. Red hot enthusiast for efficiency. Likes people who show they are not afraid of him.' Deputy Staff Chief Dawnay put the impact more briefly in spring 1918: 'Saw Maxse yesterday. Still arguing.' Turned the 18th New Army Division, then the 18th Corps, into first-class fighting organizations. Generally regarded as the finest troop trainer of his age. Inspector General of Training in the second half of 1918.

Maze, Paul 1887–1979
French liaison officer who served without commission and unofficially with Gough and presented a sympathetic picture of his chief in his *A Frenchman in Khaki*. When Goering stayed at the Château St Georges briefly in the Second World War, he came across a copy and wrote on the flysheet, 'The best book I have ever read on the Great War.'

Mensdorf, Count von
Last Austro-Hungarian ambassador in London before the war and intermediary in the abortive peace talks with Smuts early in 1918.

Milner, Alfred 1854–1925
Brought into the War Cabinet by Lloyd George from outside parliament.
Reputation for extreme right-wing politics but did much first-class work,
as Hankey noted: 'I had quite the wrong idea of "damn the consequences
Milner" . . . He was a solid, patient worker who sat up every night in his
little house behind Westminster Abbey, swotting away at the vast documentation it was my duty to circulate and his, to read. He did not make up
his mind until he had grasped the whole issue . . . My recollection is that
Milner was wonderful in tackling a great variety of jobs . . .' Esher approved
too, though for more Esherish reason. 'Milner alone represents the old
tradition of statesmanship in the War Cabinet. The rest are parvenus with
all the excruciating vulgarity of the race.' Gaunt, restrained in manner,
quiet and deliberate of speech, Milner had the habit of curling up in his
chair like a small child when he was absorbed in conversation. In June 1917
Lloyd George had told Riddell that Milner was 'very industrious and
clever, the most helpful of colleagues'; twelve months later, Milner was
driven by his Bolshevik-phobia to join the peace party and his influence in
policy-making declined progressively. On his death bed, quoted Dante and
the current standing of Rio Tinto shares to the last decimal point.

Mitchell, Charles 1872–1941
A Canadian with a breezy, self-advertising manner, Mitchell was also a
remarkably able Intelligence officer, much consulted by Charteris. During
briefings which lasted upwards of three hours, fellow Staff Officers with
Plumer's 2nd Army commonly downed pencils and went on strike. Mitchell never gave an inch of ground.

Monash, John 1865–1931
Brigadier at Gallipoli, divisional commander in France during 1916–17,
Monash took command of the Australian Corps during summer 1918.
Although his staff work was superb, relations with colleagues and superiors
easy and his powers of exposition unequalled within the BEF, his standing
as a commander in the field remains uncertain. Monash planned battles by
numbers, basing himself on GHQ's tactical pamphlets. He never visited the
front line to check his work, before or after a battle. It was a crucial

omission since (as commanders like Currie or Maxse demonstrated) only there could a general gauge morale, judge the true working relation between units or sufficiently grasp the terrain on which a battle was to be fought. His preparations at Passchendaele were therefore inadequate. The tactics of Hamel, supposedly novel, were in fact copied from GHQ's SS135. At Amiens, he played second fiddle to Currie. Mt St Quentin was unnecessary, since the Germans were about to withdraw. His blundering at Monument Wood and Proyart during the 1918 campaign are perhaps the best illustration of all of Monash's insecure grasp when he took charge of an offensive without time for interminable preparation. Monash's subsequent reputation was anyway largely accidental. Liddell Hart needed a stick to beat British professional soldiers with and Monash's *The Australian Victories in France*, written as it was by a citizen–soldier, served his purpose. Monash's book was, however, grossly inaccurate. It had been drafted during September 1918 with a view to bolstering his post-war campaign to become vice chancellor of Melbourne University (or even state governor!) and the writer had been able to use only the documents he had at the time. So where to rank Monash? Level with Haldane and Jacob perhaps. Below Maxse. Some way below Currie certainly.

Montague, C. E. 1867–1928
Joined the Sportsmen's Battalion from the editorial desk of the *Manchester Guardian* at the age of forty-seven. He was quickly put into GHQ and given charge of leading distinguished visitors on battlefield trips. Intensely reticent during the war, after it he wrote one of the most biting and perceptive critiques of the interior workings of GHQ. His war letters, edited by Oliver Elton, remain one of the least-known classics of Great War writing.

Montgomery-Massingberd, Archibald 1871–1947
Rawlinson's Chief Staff Officer. A handsome man of remarkable height, Montgomery-Massingberd won glowing opinions as a Staff Officer during the war. Wrote Maxse to Henry Wilson in January 1916, 'My chief of staff is M.-M. and a tip-top one too.' Praise from such a quarter was rare indeed.

Morton, Desmond 1891–1971
Joined the Royal Horse Artillery in 1911 and got a bullet through the heart at Arras in 1917. Surviving against all odds, he was taken on by Haig as an ADC and in that position Morton encountered Churchill, who took an

immediate liking to him. Third in MI6's hierarchy between the wars, Morton served as Churchill's personal assistant during the Second World War.

Murdoch, Keith 1885–1952
An Australian journalist who managed the United Cable Service from the headquarters of *The Times* during the war. Northcliffe had secured him the vital position of intermediary between Lloyd George and the Australian Prime Minister which made his personal fortune. Northcliffe went on to give him the Melbourne *Herald* after the war as a reward for his skill and energy as a liaison man. Popular wisdom has it that his Gallipoli letter deposed Hamilton and ended Gallipoli. In fact, the decisions had been taken before Murdoch arrived at Gallipoli on the evidence of Hankey, supported later by Dawnay, one of Hamilton's Staff Officers. Murdoch's letter was simply used to divert attention from a major change of policy. Of his journalistic work, Bean wrote: 'It is an object lesson to see how he handles his work. He knows the right hour to go out; the right hour to be back and get his stuff away; the right people to see and how to get a story out of them – and a fine conception of a story too.' Other Australians preferred to see Murdoch as an Antipodean Repington.

Nash, Philip 1882–1968
Served with the Great Northern Railway and East Indian Railway in his youth before taking charge of shell-filling in 1915 and moving on to transport. From 1916 to the Armistice he was Director General of Transport in France.

Nivelle, Robert 1856–1924
Commanded a brigade in 1914, a corps in 1915 and an army in 1916 before becoming Commander in Chief of the French in 1917. When his big offensive secured less ground than he promised, he was relegated to the obscurity from which he had so rapidly come. Little is known of him today apart from contemporary smears recycled as history.

Northcliffe, Viscount 1865–1922
Newspaperman with the *Daily Mail* and *The Times* as a power base. 'He is a considerable man,' Lloyd George once said. 'He has more than a touch of genius but he is spoilt by vanity and an incapacity to work with equals. Too jumpy and always wants his own way.' Played a key role in first discrediting Asquith, then supporting Haig during the 1916–17 battles.

Ended the war in charge of propaganda and a bitter man. Charteris noted that Northcliffe's first cable on entering GHQ used to read: 'Dear mother. I have arrived safely. My love to you. Northcliffe.'

Oliver, Frederick 1864–1934
Inner Temple barrister who turned Debenham's into a major London store. Served with the Department of Information and was a prolific and brilliant correspondent. As a member of that powerful group which dined together each Monday – Milner, Carson, Robinson of *The Times* and Astor – he wrote letters that are extraordinarily well informed on hidden currents. He was a staunch admirer of Haig, a brother Scot, and took the Bemersyde fund in hand when a grateful nation responded with great indifference to that national appeal for a 'Blenheim Palace' suitable for the great Field Marshal.

Page, Walter 1855–1918
Anglophile American ambassador in London between 1912 and 1918.

Perley, George 1857–1938
Minister of Canadian Overseas Forces 1916–17.

Pershing, John 1860–1948
American Commander in Chief 1917–19 and a soldier of quite remarkable ineptitude. 'The higher command of the American Army has given me much concern,' wrote Lloyd George in June 1918. 'Pershing is very commonplace without any real war experience and is already overwhelmed by the initial difficulties of a job too big for him. It is also doubtful whether he will loyally cooperate with the allied higher command. He could not get together a first class staff either.' Lloyd George wrote to President Wilson suggesting that Pershing be put in charge of rear services. The lamentable performance of the American Expeditionary Force in the final campaign can be seen as the price paid for failing to make a radical change of that sort. In Washington's Public Archives there are many empty boxes with just a single scrap of paper, signed by Pershing and stating that he would be returning the contents shortly. The missing papers invariably cover yet another Pershing blunder.

Pétain, Henri–Philippe 1856–1951
Made a big name defending Verdun in spring 1916 and subsequently took charge of an Army Group before replacing Nivelle as French Commander

in Chief. Pioneer of the limited-objective, set-piece battle dominated by linear artillery barrages. Lloyd George professed to rate Pétain highly: 'He is the incarnation of common sense. In any council dominated by soldiers of impulsive resource, this is invaluable for he has more than a touch of scornful scepticism for all new ideas flung down on the table.' Most were offended by his lack of finesse in personal relationships. American Intelligence reported: 'The General is temperamentally direct, often very brusque and not held to be an adroit politician.' Esher summed him up with his usual sharpness – 'Wully [Robertson] with a dash of Rawly [Rawlinson].'

Plumer, Herbert 1857–1932

Commanded the 2nd Army in the Ypres Salient from 1915 to November 1917 and from March 1918 to the end of the war. In the months between, he commanded the Expeditionary Force. Colonel Blimp to look at but appearances were deceptive. Cuthbert Headlam noted during the Passchendaele campaign: 'Met a Canadian at Army School who told me of the amazing belief every officer and man has in Old Plum. He sees a very large number of officers and men from the 2nd and 5th Armies and says the difference is beyond belief. Everyone believes in Plum and will go anywhere for him which is a great triumph for an amazingly hard-working English gentleman. Seldom has a man come into his own more deservedly without advertisement and in spite of every outside influence.' A Sir John French appointee, Plumer was disliked and slighted by Haig. Plumer wrote no books and left no papers to make sure of his position with posterity, for a reason Montgomery-Massingberd found out to his discomfiture. When he suggested that Charles Fergusson was too much of a gentleman for the post-Armistice job of military governor of Cologne, 'Plumer screwed his eyeglass into his eye, looked at me for a moment and then with a smile said, "Can you be too much of a gentleman?" I was rather non-plussed.'

Rawlinson, Henry 1864–1925

Known in the Old Army as 'the Cad', the Wavell papers hold a typical anecdote. 'At an army commanders' conference I attended, Haig discussed whether it was best to go into a wood or round it. I remember Rawly saying at once, "Certainly, I would go round it." After discussion at which the majority favoured going through it, Rawly said, "Certainly, I should go through it."' Promoted rapidly after a sequence of disastrous battles he supervised through 1915, Rawlinson reached 4th Army command early in 1916. He was a cultured man with a quick mind. Bean was favourably impressed by Rawlinson's proficiency in French and capacity as an artist, and by the fact that almost alone among higher commanders Rawlinson opposed the death penalty. His reaction to the Australians was to present each officer with a copy of Kipling's 'If' with orders to learn it and think it over. Seventy years after the war, there it still no agreement on Rawlinson's military capacity.

Repington, Charles 1858–1925
Entered the Army in 1878 and served in Afghanistan, Sudan and South Africa. Drummed from the service for sexual indiscretion, fanned and trumpeted by Henry Wilson. Repington turned for revenge to journalism, first with *The Times*, then with the Jacobite *Morning Post*. He orchestrated the Shell scandal of 1915 which nearly overturned Asquith's government and the Maurice debate affair, which all but did the same to Lloyd George. The source of his power was the astonishing extent of his knowledge of the most secret war information, based on the freedom he was given to see all documents and meet all people at the War Office. His correspondence with Walter Long in the early days of the war even more than his celebrated memoirs illustrates the astonishing amount of inside information to which he was privy.

Riddell, George 1865–1934
In charge of the *News of the World* and closely associated with Lloyd George. Contemporaries noted a natural aptitude for acquiring news and a mind that worked best in paragraphs. He was tall and haggard, with a stoop, and his clothes used to hang from his frame like a scarecrow's. His country residence was a sparsely furnished room at Walton Heath golf club from which he indulged that passion of the age, golf.

Robertson, William ('Wully') 1860–1933
From trooper in the ranks in 1877, Robertson rose to CIGS in December 1915 before finally reaching the sinecure of peacetime Field Marshal. The clarity of his Staff College lectures was praised even by Edmonds and, with his mastery of Indian languages, indicated a brain of quality carefully camouflaged behind a brusque manner and dropped aitches. Robertson's Achilles heel was identified early by Esher. 'He will find the politicians difficult to cope with, disciplined as he is to the word of *command*.' Robertson's chosen method of dealing with the difficulty caused even the mild Derby to protest. 'The worst of it is that Wullie is one of those men who cannot suffer fools gladly and certainly his manner to the cabinet is, to say the least of it, one that could be improved upon.' Robertson's bloody-

minded abrasiveness was given edge by his temperament. He was often presented as an iron-hard, narrow-minded sergeant major. Oliver was one of the few to spot the real Robertson: 'He has a typical Scotch face, manner and temperament but he doesn't talk the language. He is much more cockney than Scotch. He is by no means the hard, phlegmatic sergeant major type. On the contrary, he is highly strung and eager in manner.' In origins and temperament, he and Lloyd George probably had too much in common. Lover of pipe smoking and apple puddings, Robertson was a gifted mimic. Curzon was his favourite butt – 'that pompous windbag' as he called him. Physically, as Lady Carson remarked in her diary, he was 'too attractive'.

Rosenthal, Charles 1875–1954
Australian architect and artillery specialist who in 1918 took charge of a division. May well have been original of Lawrence's *Kangaroo*.

Rupprecht, Crown Prince 1869–1955
Confronted the British at Arras in 1917 and again at Cambrai and Armentières in the battles of spring 1918. Army Group commander and, as a Bavarian, bitter rival of the Prussian stranglehold at OHL (GHQ).

Sassoon, Philip 1888–1939
MP for Folkestone. Passed from Rawlinson's staff to Haig, who made him his private secretary. Haig explained his reasoning to Kitchener: 'I want an honest, not too clever military secretary because the assistant military secretary is quite able to run the office by himself. The private secretary must be sharp and quick and pleasant to work with.' Sassoon was all those things as well as being bilingual in French and English and an organizer totally lacking a sense of time. He inherited friendships with the Asquiths, Greys and Balfours through his millionaire family. He was an adroit intriguer but, as the family biographer points out, he was also a vital intermediary. 'His soothing manner and flow of chatter rallied Haig from the dour moods which often terrified his staff. Even senior officers began to use Sassoon as a go-between when the Chief was gruff and almost unapproachable.'

Sassoon, Siegfried 1886–1967
Cousin to Philip and a poet who used the family influence to have a statement read in the Commons during April 1917: 'I am making this

statement as an act of wilful defiance of military authority because I believe that the war is being deliberately prolonged by those who have the power to end it.' His poetry proved a more influential and longer-lasting indictment.

Scott, Charles 1846–1932
Editor of the *Manchester Guardian*. Down-market Old Testament prophet and (qualified) backer of Lloyd George.

Secrett, Thomas
Batman to Haig throughout the war. Took his master's name later in life (see the interview in Ronald Blyth's *The View in Winter*).

Sims, William 1858–1936
American rear admiral who took charge of the Atlantic destroyer flotilla 1913–15. Commanded all US ships in European waters from April 1917 to the end of the war. In that role, he was permitted to enter the Admiralty and go through any drawers he wished.

Smith, F. E. 1872–1930
Conservative M.P. 1906–18. Solicitor General 1915 and Attorney General 1915–19. Constant critic of GHQ, he later became Lord Birkenhead.

Smith-Dorrien, Horace 1858–1930
One of the two corps commanders at the outbreak of war. Promoted to the 2nd Army in 1915, Smith-Dorrien was soon removed for non-military reasons and packed off to an East African command.

Smuts, Jan 1870–1950
Bencher of the Middle Temple. Cambridge double first. Supreme commander of the Cape Colony Boers in the South African war. He won golden opinions in that capacity. Those opinions were rapidly dispelled by his flounderings against Von Lettow-Vorbeck in East Africa in 1916–17. Smuts was brought into the War Cabinet in accordance with the non-democratic Empire-oriented procedures of the CID, which took over the Cabinet at the end of 1916. He exercised little influence. 'If only Smuts could restrain his intellectual contempt for his Dominion colleagues as well as for British Ministers, he would carry things a long way.' The writer was Leo Amery, a man well qualified to recognize the defect. In Smuts' case, it went unrectified. An energetic supporter of Haig throughout.

Sparrow, Walter Shaw
Editor of literary journals, chess player and amateur military historian.
When Gough invited him to take up the pen in support of the 5th Army,
Shaw Sparrow did so with enthusiasm and inaccuracy.

Spears, Edward 1886–1974
Head of the British military mission in Paris 1917–20. Rated below Esher
as a source of information in London and GHQ.

Spender, John 1862–1942
Editor of the *Westminster Gazette* and staunch supporter of Asquith, whose
official biographer he became. Through that link, he got to know Haig.
The current Western Front memorandum in the British Museum, filed
under Haig, is in fact Spender's copy, re-bound.

Stamfordham, Arthur 1849–1931
Private secretary to George V from 1910. He had previously been a Royal
Artilleryman and had seen active service in the Zulu War of 1879. His
catapult into Court was provided by Sir Evelyn Wood, for whom he had
been an ADC.

Stephens, Reginald 1869–1955
Corps commander in 1918.

Stevenson, Frances 1888–1972
Private secretary to Lloyd George from 1913 and mistress, subsequently
wife.

Thornton, Hugh 1881–1962
Private secretary to Milner 1916–20.

Thursby, Cecil 1861–1936
Admiral in charge at the Anzac landing 1915. Thereafter steady decline to
command of the coast guard and naval reserve in 1918.

Tudor, H. 1871–1965
Artilleryman and divisional commander in 1918.

Uniacke, Herbert 1866–1934
Chief gunner in Gough's 5th Army.

Wavell, Archibald 1883–1950
Served in France 1914–16. Severely wounded and sent to the Caucasus as
military attaché before joining Allenby's staff in the Middle East 1917–20.

Weygand, Maxime 1864–1945
Reputedly the illegitimate son of Emperor Maximilian of Mexico, he was
known at St Cyr as Maxime de Beaumont. Became Foch's indispensable
Chief of Staff. Wrote Henry Wilson: 'In some ways, he is the best staff
officer I have ever seen but he is a terrible centralizer and every single detail
has to be brought to him.' This was, in fact, the recommended job of a
Chief of Staff as laid down by the War Office committee which examined
the workings of GHQ staff in 1919. Told Grant at the time of the
Armistice that if he had not been married and had a family, he would have
gone into a monastery, as he had seen so much of the littleness of men
during the previous four years.

White, Cyril Brudenell 1876–1940
Birdwood's Chief Staff Officer in the Australian Corps, following his chief
to the 5th Army in 1918. He was offered command of the Australian Corps
on three occasions, once by Haig personally, but his ambition stopped short
of high command and he was content to let Monash take the corps.

Wigram, Clive 1873–1960
Served with the Lancers in India, became ADC to Curzon there before
becoming the king's assistant private secretary in 1910 and marrying
Neville Chamberlain's daughter two years later.

Wilson, Henry 1864–1922
CIGS in 1918, Wilson had qualities unusual in the soldiers of his generation.
Kiggell noted two of them: 'Always jolly and informal, he was the only
general who could meet the politicians on level terms . . . He fascinated the
French and could say outrageous things to them. "We can't trust you
Frenchmen an inch." Coming from him, this caused laughter. Imagine
what the effect would have been coming from Haig!' Additionally to his
social skill with politicians and allies, Wilson had unusual breadth of
imagination, acquired from his early years, so Esher thought. 'Wilson as a
boy was asked by his father if he was doing anything and if not, to "Come
up in a balloon with me." His father would make a world survey in great
detail (politics, flora, animals and so on). This habit remained with Wilson
as a most treasured possession and he used to visualize the war from his

balloon'. Set against these pluses was a quality unusual in soldiers and more typical of the Balfours, Greys, Asquiths and Bonar Laws of the time – failure of nerve when faced with the need to make a firm decision. As Lloyd George put it, 'Much the best brain I met in the upper ranks of the professional Army but he had no decision. He shrank from the responsibility of the final word.' Milner supported Lloyd George on the point during the war, Ivor Maxse after it. A second weakness was sketched by Lloyd George. 'He was whimsical almost to the point of buffoonery. He answered a serious question or expounded a grave problem in a vein of droll frivolity undignified in a man of responsibility. The habit detracted from the weight his position and capacity ought to have given to his counsel.' Hankey thus described him on one occasion chasing the seventy-six-year-old Clemenceau round a conference room like a schoolboy. At another time, he reversed his cap and gave the German point of view as Henry von Wilson. His final weakness was in divided loyalty. Newton Baker, the American Secretary of War, was startled by Wilson's statement that his loyalty to the Orange cause in Ulster was greater than his loyalty to the British Empire. Currie's information, too, was that the basis of the Lloyd George–Wilson estrangement for the war's last six months was the Prime Minister's negotiations with Sinn Fein. From a personal point of view, it was however a stance which gave Wilson the backing of Milner, Bonar Law and Carson. Would he have become CIGS without it? Immensely tall and thin, with piercing blue eyes, deep voice and death's head face, he looked as grotesque physically as he was unmilitary mentally. His death had a flavour all too typical of that generation of high-ranking soldiers. Confronted by a pistol-waving Sinn Feiner and easily able to escape into a private house, Wilson turned to face his antagonist with an absurdly inadequate sword.

APPENDICES,
REFERENCES AND INDEX

Appendix 1

Sources Used: An Evaluation

Because state documents were not opened until fifty years after the Armistice, most books on Haig's command are based on material from a small number of books, endlessly re-cycled. There are advantages, of course. Inevitable anecdotes and well-worn quotations give a sense of security and the impression that most problems have been solved. Minor points remained for discussion, of course – Edmonds's casualty figures, Gough's sacking, the six-week gap between Messines and Passchendaele and so on – but for the most part the basic framework seemed to be in place.

Like the springing of the trap under a condemned man, the unsealing of archives in the sixties dumped military historians unceremoniously on their backsides. New areas of inquiry opened up. Gaps became larger than areas of knowledge. Accepted truths required testing. Where were historians to start?

Cabinet papers were the obvious place, since the Cabinet always dictated British strategy, whatever impression Haig and his colleagues liked to give.

The sheer bulk of these papers is impressive. Asquith's chief policy-making committee had been recorded verbatim from the start of the war by the clerks of the Committee of Imperial Defence, and when Lloyd George succeeded Asquith at the end of 1916, Maurice Hankey and his twenty-four typists did the same job for the Cabinet. The result was fifty sides of close-packed foolscap for each Cabinet meeting throughout 1917 and 1918.

The written account kept by the BEF forms a second major source. The massive size of that holding was the result of a requirement in King's Regulations that all units, from battalion to GHQ, had to keep a daily diary. 'The object of the diary is twofold,' the Regulations explained. 'To furnish an accurate report of operations from which the history of the war

can subsequently be prepared and to collect information for future reference with a view to effecting improvements.'

The Regulations went on to indicate the extraordinary amount of detail expected by the War Office. 'The original copy [of the diary] will be forwarded on the last day of each month to the officer in charge of the Adjutant General's branch. The following points should all be recorded – all important orders, instructions, reports, telegrams issued and received . . .' and so on.

The end product was an archive of 26,000 boxes, stored in the basement of the official historian's London office. Each box measured fifteen by ten by four inches and contained only the more important documents, since 500 tons of paper had already been deposited at St Nicholas's School, Isleworth, soon after the war.

Private collections constitute a third class of fresh evidence and they offer a rich diet because the Edwardian age was the last before telephones and cars destroyed the Victorian habit of letter writing. It came, too, at the tail end of a 300-year period in which the Puritan duty of soul-searching had been reinforced by the Evangelical tradition which made the keeping of a diary an obligation. The example of Lord Derby suggests the quantity of paper which could be generated by that custom. Secretary of State for War and ambassador in Paris, he still found time to write about forty letters daily and fill ten quarto sides of densely packed diary each evening (with a carbon copy sent to Balfour). Nor was he untypical. A modern researcher is astounded by the sheer mass of many private collections. The Haig papers are a good example. That small fraction open to the public today spreads over twenty yards of shelving and incorporates a daily diary for the war period running to three quarters of a million words. The papers of Rawlinson, Maxse and Monash are just as comprehensive and the collections of politicians like Lloyd George, Balfour and Milner at least comparable.

Reading about the cheerful round of gossip, golf and generous lunches which embroider these private collections (four days before the first days of the Somme, Hunter-Weston at one of the corps HQs wrote: 'I shall myself be getting up quietly at the chateau, far away from the sound of the guns and shall have nothing to do with the war until the reports come in') and comparing them with life in the front line (about a million British soldiers killed and two and a half million wounded) a reader is forcefully struck by the obscenity of much in the private record. And yet if any sort of sense is to be made of the Western Front and a better understanding gleaned from these fresh sources, obscenity becomes indispensable.

In quantity and quality, this new material dwarfs the printed sources. Its value is beyond dispute, but there are hidden shoals against which a reader must always be on his guard.

At first sight, Cabinet records have a feel of almost clerical solidity. Massively bound and assembled in series and sub-series, they exude quiet authority and give a researcher the feeling that in the high politics of his work, the decisions and the rough talk leading to those decisions tell the story just as it was – in outline at least.

This surface appearance is deceptive. Cabinet records are not verbatim and Maurice Hankey, who was in charge of producing them, never intended them to be. 'I aim not at an accurate account of what everyone said,' he once wrote, 'but at a general synopsis of expert evidence on which conclusions are based and a general summary of arguments for and against the decision taken, preserving as far as possible the principles of collective security.'[1]

Nor did Hankey send his work to the Public Record Office undiluted, On 15–16 January 1917 the Cabinet discussed the Nivelle offensive. Although the account in the Record Office runs to about six lines for each day, the Lloyd George papers hold a set of minutes for those meetings covering about 160 printed sides. It is a discrepancy which reinforces an impression from other extracts in Lloyd George's papers that the Cabinet Office holds several sequences of Cabinet records and keeps the most detailed transcript safely locked away from public examination.

Deep cuts distort Hankey's abbreviated record further. Though Lloyd George's memoirs claim the Cabinet was never informed of French reservations over the Passchendaele offensive, minutes for 8 June 1917 show Henry Wilson telling the Cabinet that the French had little confidence in the impending battle. In another example, Lloyd George insisted that the final offensive in 1918 was initiated without his knowledge. It was a position which enabled him at the time to work easily with Dominion Prime Ministers who had just come out against further operations on a large scale. But minutes for 24 July give the lie. They record that Lloyd George had been briefed by Henry Wilson well in advance on the battle impending at Amiens. These controversial matters have simply been deleted from minutes made available to the British public, and anyone wishing to check them must go to Ottawa's Public Archives and consult Canadian transcripts, which are often fuller than their counterparts in the Public Record Office.

Other cuts can no longer be tracked down. In September 1917, for example, the Germans offered peace terms so attractive that even Lloyd

George hesitated before pressing ahead with the policy of military victory. The Cabinet's agenda on 24 and 27 September indicates that the German proposal was discussed, yet minutes on the shelves of the Public Record Office relate only to German air raids. In the same way, Hankey's hand-written secretarial notes for 28 December 1917, though consecutively numbered, have pages missing. Broken sentences prove as much, and since the Cabinet's agenda for that day lists a discussion of peace negotiations between Russia and Germany, Hankey's scissor work is exposed.

If Cabinet records require caution, they remain an oasis in a desert in comparison with War Office records. Retention or destruction by the military has been on such a scale that it would be impossible to write more than a brief article from documents about the organization of the War Office during the Great War.

The direct telephone link between the War Office and GHQ in France produces a good example. According to the official historian, the line was used almost daily and he had been able to check transcripts of all conversations during March 1918 in his attempt to establish the information Haig phoned to London. The fact is recorded in Edmonds's private papers, and yet no telephone transcripts have reached the Public Record Office.

Even if War Office records were more widely available, they would obviously have to be studied with considerable scepticism if official tele-grams are anything to judge from. In November 1916, for example, Robertson told his commander in Salonika to send 'personal' rather than 'official' telegrams.[2] 'One must have a little personal communication sometimes,' he explained. These 'private' telegrams were, of course, to be addressed to the CIGS personally so as to bypass the Secretary of State. Robertson's predecessor had been even more oblique. During the Gallipoli campaign, Kitchener instructed Ian Hamilton to send two quite different telegrams each day. He could then produce either in the War Council, as he thought best.[3]

The records of the British Army in France contain just as many gaps and googlies. The most important of these relate to the documentation of GHQ. When American official historians visited London in the 1920s, they were told that Haig's operational records were kept separate from other records and had to be consulted through a card index. Tasman Heyes, transcribing British documents in the mid-1920s for the Australian Official History, used the index for three years (though not without difficulty. Heyes once complained to Bean: 'Edmonds quite intentionally tried to put me off the scent. I know from another source that the papers *are* there'). Today neither the card index nor the files have been handed over for public reference.

The same applies to Intelligence records. Originally classified under four sub-headings, the most important got a 1A imprint. From a small number available in Australia and Canada, it is clear that Charteris's department issued at least 4,000 of these 1A appreciations over two years and, where checks can be made, they usually turn out remarkably accurate. After the first disastrous day of Passchendaele, for example, Gough complained bitterly about the briefing Charteris had given him. Checking the text of the appreciation, Charteris's accuracy on the number and disposition of German forces together with his prediction of a German counter-attack and its probable location is first-class. Unfortunately, the Cabinet Office has done its work well and the Public Record Office holds virtually no 'I' Branch papers today.[4] Nor do the private papers of Charteris or Sidney Clive (GHQ's Intelligence Director during the final advance) offer assistance. They too have been weeded.

War diary material below the level of GHQ is in better shape, but butchery at each stage of the journey which documents had to make from the front line has to be kept in mind.

Pressure of battle or the neglect of a commanding officer at the sharp end of the war could easily reduce the daily record of a unit to a handful of lines in pencil. Military embarrassment might even add a touch of farce. After the chlorine gas attack of April 1915, for example, the 3rd Canadian Brigade's war diary was burnt so that a re-write would exonerate the commanding officer. That brigadier had many imitators at all levels during the war.

There was, of course, no guarantee that orders for battles were actually written before those battles or that post-battle appreciations bore the slightest resemblance to what had actually happened. There are plenty of examples, even from Haig's pen. His OAD90, dated 1 August 1916 and written for the Cabinet during the Somme, gave an appreciation which positively glowed with optimism. Next day, he issued OAD91 to the two army commanders involved, noting that the British had few reserves and that there was a long way to go before the Germans were beaten. The same dualism appears on many occasions during the war. Lies for the Cabinet; candour for generals on the spot, in other words.

Even if a fighting unit handed full and truthful documentation to GHQ at the end of each month – as King's Regulations required – the journey through that place often proved fatal. The 2nd Army's Intelligence Director witnessed many 2nd Army records being burnt and officers from the Canadian War Records Section lamented the fate of 1st Army documents. These were stored in sacks and closed with preservation seals, but still ended their journey in GHQ's furnaces.

Lists indicating the extent of the destruction can be found in the private papers of John Boraston, who served as Edmonds's assistant at GHQ and was given the paradoxical title of Keeper of Records. One of his lists describes a sample of material burnt during March 1918. It covers the battle of Passchendaele and includes all artillery returns, Intelligence information on German artillery and details of Anzac and Cavalry Corps movements and of Intelligence intercepted by the Germans.

Another of Boraston's lists, dated March 1919, includes all situation reports for the Western Front, all tank situation reports and everything to do with the state of training in the British Army. Just how much other material Boraston burnt in the twelve months separating these two lists can only be conjectured, but the indications are of a massive holocaust.

After passing through GHQ, documents were sent to the War Office and there joined 'Specially secret matter' which had been picked out by Edmonds and sent direct, as required by one of Haig's Routine Orders dated May 1916. Once this 'specially secret matter' had been stored in War Office safes, only Edmonds of the official historians was allowed direct access to it. The private papers of Gallipoli's historian gave an example. Had Birdwood wanted to re-embark his Anzacs at the end of the first day of their landing? In 1927, Birdwood and Admiral Thursby assured Aspinall that no exchange of letters had taken place on the day in question. Aspinall appealed through Edmonds for confirmation. The reply came back from the War Office that they held the original telegram signed by Birdwood – 'All available boats required on the shore' – with Thursby's reply – 'Lower all boats and stand by to send them to the beach.' Hamilton's sudden appearance on his flagship put an end to this scheme at a pivotal moment for the campaign, yet Aspinall made no reference to it in his volume.

The last stage in the holocaust came in 1945, when Edmonds began sorting all documents into three piles – for the Public Record Office, for retention within the Cabinet Office and for burning as 'of no permanent value'. The end result was the withholding or destruction of so many orders, reports, maps and conference minutes that any real check on Edmonds's Official History volumes today is all but impossible. The strongest evidence for this fact is in the thickness of war diaries. The rule here is that the more important the unit, the greater the destruction and the thinner its surviving records. Corps diaries are thus about twice the thickness of army diaries – a preposterous state of affairs.

The biggest gaps usually crop up where a reader would expect to find them. The Canadians, for example, had been intended for the spearhead at Cambrai in November 1917. A month before the battle they were sent north to Passchendaele. That move destroyed Cambrai's only chance of success for the sake of a position of limited tactical value in the Ypres Salient. The diary of the Canadian Corps has been gutted for September, when the Cambrai plan and the Canadian role in it were being finalized. Conversely, the diary of Byng's 3rd Army has been cleared out for October, when battle plans for Cambrai were finally cobbled together. The Canadians took Passchendaele village in November after sorting out the chaos Gough and Plumer had got themselves into during the battles of early October. A reader will find neither the chaos nor the operation orders leading to the capture of Passchendaele in the Public Record Office, though a reasonably full story can be pieced together from material in Canada.

Should anyone wish to get the feel of what a full unit war diary ought to look like or get some indication of how much has been extracted by the Cabinet Office elsewhere, Australian records give the best guide. During the war, the Australian government got permission to look after its records in return for a promise to supply London with photostats. As a result, Australian war diaries remain much the most substantial of those available to the public. But there are big gaps even here. Staff at the Australian Corps HQ had the privilege of vetting documents before they went to London, with the predictable result that pre-battle conference minutes and post-battle analyses have disappeared together with about 20 per cent of orders and a similar percentage of battle reports from lower formations. 'Pompey' Elliott, a fiery and capable brigadier, offered a splendid example of this skulduggery. After a chaotic battle at Polygon Wood in the Ypres Salient during September 1917, Elliott insisted on including a report in his unit war diary drawing attention to the incompetence of his own divisional commander and the panic of the Royal Welch Fusiliers next door. Birdwood forbade Elliott to file his report and when Elliott ignored him – as he often did – a Staff Officer was sent to London to destroy the offending report. Fortunately, Birdwood reckoned without Elliott's knowledge of Army ways from his Boer War service. Elliott had taken the precaution of handing a duplicate in person to the man in charge of Australian records.

One final and unexpected stumbling block remains for the optimistic researcher of unit war diaries and that is the speed and quality of the work done by Charles Atkinson as Director of the Historical Section from 1915 to 1919. In that period, he almost completed his task of summarizing all unit war diaries to assist the work of the official historians. Researchers checking unit war diaries today and finding them neatly typed in compact double columns can see for themselves that the Public Record Office has been fobbed off with a good deal of the Atkinson material rather than the originals.

Private collections make up another new category and, like official documents, they need to be read with a cold eye.

Interference with important collections could be sanctioned at the highest level. The Henderson papers serve for example here. Henderson had represented the Labour Party in the War Cabinet for eight months and amassed 2,000 Cabinet papers. Though these are listed in the inventory of the collection, at some stage unknown to the archivist in charge all 2,000 were spirited away.[5]

The Lloyd George collection suffered similar burglary. In July 1947, Beaverbrook paid Lloyd George's widow the then considerable sum of £15,000 for 800 boxes of Lloyd George papers. Between the Lloyd George home and Beaverbrook's front door, a robber who seemed to be wearing Cabinet Office livery got hold of those boxes and extracted sequences of minutes covering the Dardanelles Committee, the War Committee and the War Cabinet. Hankey had a particular interest in the telegrams from Spain which told the embarrassing story of the German peace offer in September 1917 and, despite Beaverbrook's furious protest, these too were taken.

Cabinet Office burglaries are spectacular, but the unromantic tamperings of the donors themselves usually do more damage. The Robertson collection offers a fine example. After writing his memoirs, Robertson admitted to burning half his papers in 1922, presumably for the purpose of eliminating documents which contradicted the line taken in his published work.

The Monash collection is another example. An obsessive recorder of his own life, Monash kept every piece of paper he could, down to postcards from the French prostitutes he patronized and lists he made at regular intervals itemizing the contents of his pockets. On the military side, Messines indicates the scale of his collection. When he sent papers covering the battle for storage in London, they filled a box measuring 15 by 11 by 9 inches. By the end of the war, Monash had gathered 150 of these boxes on military operations alone.

Checking his papers today, it appears that about 90 per cent of this operations material together with the very detailed private diaries he kept during the war are missing. Even the letters to his wife ('I never object to you showing people what I write except when it is marked "Secret". You should advertise my division as widely as possible, not among private people who don't count but among public men like MPs, journalists, the Wallaby Club, university circles. Try to get my messages into the papers . . .') were edited and re-written for publication when the war was over.

It would be wrong to stigmatize Monash for this, since it would be difficult indeed to find a single collection of private papers unscarred by drastic alteration and pruning. The papers of Tory patriarch Walter Long, for example, hold no letters to leading politicians for the duration of the war even though they are abundant for the periods on either side. Northcliffe's weekly letters to his staff on *The Times* are fluent, balanced and informative, but there are none in that newspaper's collection for the period May to November 1917 when he was working closely with Haig. Of serving soldiers, Cuthbert Headlam left a unique record, since he served on the staff at almost every level up to GHQ and sent lengthy, candid letters to his wife each day, and yet his private diaries from 1916 to 1918 have been extracted – the only ones missing in a long sequence otherwise complete.

Diaries usually offer the quickest check on the integrity of a particular collection. The shrewdest manipulators either re-wrote their diaries in entirety (Hankey and Esher of the civilians and Rawlinson of the soldiers, for example) or kept this most contemporary of records well away from public scrutiny. Lloyd George is a case in point. In a conversation minuted by the Cabinet Office, Hankey referred to Lloyd George's diary as even fuller than his own.[6] Lloyd George's second wife mentioned it in passing when she told Beaverbrook that her husband's diary for the latter part of the war was held by 'the family'. Whether she meant the actual family or the Cabinet Office is unclear, but there is no trace of such a diary in the Lloyd George papers today.

Other Cabinet Ministers are only marginally less fastidious. A handful of typed extracts in the public part of the Derby collection are the only snippets accessible to unvetted researchers. Milner, too, bequeathed only a few pages covering the Doullens conference in March 1918, specifically to counter the version leaked to the press by Haig in the twenties.

One diary in particular remains of central importance to the history of Haig's command and that is the Haig original.

The crucial question here is a simple one. If Haig's wartime diary was rewritten to present his own case in the best possible light and the post-war re-write even more so, was there a master diary to keep the truth on record for Haig's private reference? If such a record was indeed kept, the word 'diary' would fit it better than the mixture of fact and fable passed off today as 'the diary'. What is the evidence for such a diary?

On the point of negative evidence, it is noticeable that well-informed contemporaries avoided calling the document edited by Blake a 'diary'. Haig's own practice was to call his writings home each day 'Notes from the diary', thus implying a bulkier parent source. There is frequent ambiguity, too, in his wife's references. She once wrote of 'collecting Douglas's papers together' for publication during 1928 in a context that makes it plain she was referring to the 'diary' currently in the Scottish National Library.

Close associates certainly kept their distance. Esher frequently put ostentatious quotation marks round the word 'diary'. As a well-informed insider entrusted with a hamper of Haig's bound diary volumes when he went home at the start of 1918, Esher presumably knew of Haig's alchemy. The Haig Trustees must have been in the same position in the thirties and they called Haig's so-called diary 'the papers' – as did Blake when he gave a title to his edition in 1952.

The careful ambiguity of men close to Haig points in a single direction, but is there hard evidence for an accurate Haig diary outside the public domain today? The *corpus delicti* can't be produced, but documentation points towards two people and an institution having that diary or a copy of it in their possession.

The first person is Lady Haig, and the presence of two 'diaries' can be inferred from her own description of the transcriptions she made around 1930.[7] Between 1928 and 1930 she worked hard ('I sat up at night with only two hours' sleep, to do the work quickly') to complete a five-volume work, four of which were an almost verbatim copy of the diary which can be seen by the public today. When the Trustees put an embargo on publication, Lady Haig prepared another version of the diary in twelve volumes, all the more striking since she used none of the letters or documents which added considerably to the length of her five-volume manuscript. What had happened to that second manuscript is uncertain. During her convalescence from a nervous breakdown at Hampton Court Palace, Duff Cooper got access to the document cupboard at Bemersyde without Lady Haig's knowledge and took the volumes. From that moment, they have not been seen by outsiders.

The second person who left references to a second diary is Edmonds, the official historian. The most unambiguous references are in his comments about copying the Haig diary for the Historical Section's records. In 1928 he told the committee supervising the Official Histories that Haig had lent him his complete thirty-two-volume diary.[8] A letter from Haig to Edmonds in September 1927 supports this, instructing Edmonds to insert a document in Volume 32. In 1935, however, court proceedings over ownership of the Haig diary stated that the diary had been sent to Edmonds by instalments up to 1930. Correspondence in the Haig papers supports that fact and the two positions are obviously incompatible.

Edmonds offered a second glimpse in 1946. He was in the process of winding up his job and making a final winnowing of the documents. In the course of his weeding he told the Cabinet Office that in addition to the thirty-five-volume Haig diary, he held eleven boxes of other parts of the text, three boxes of Haig's comments on chapters in the Official Histories and three other boxes. His letter ended with a request for permission to burn the eleven boxes of text and the three miscellaneous boxes.[9]

The Cabinet Office was curious and requested further detail. In supplying it, Edmonds transformed his boxes. Eleven changed from a carbon copy of the text sent to Bean into a photostat of the diary from June 1917 to November 1918 which had been made for security purposes. Three boxes changed from a scrapbook, a copy of the Memorandum and correspondence with Lady Haig into three boxes of index. The fourteen boxes, whatever their contents, were anyway burnt in February 1947 and the ashes were probably all that remained of Edmonds's personal copy of the real Haig diary.

The third reference to this other diary relates to the British Museum. In the course of the 1935 hearing at the Edinburgh Court of Sessions, it was stated that 'General Edmonds, with the approval of Lord Haig, caused two typewritten copies of the diaries as submitted to him to be made. One of these copies was retained by General Edmonds. The other was returned along with the typewritten copy which had been lent to him. These two typewritten copies were then lodged by Lady Haig in Harrods stores for safe custody where they remain unseen by her or anyone else until after the serving of the present petition.'[10] There was no doubt here. Harrods was the name. And yet the rumour ran from an early date that the original diaries were held by the British Museum. Northcliffe's *Daily Mail* and Beaverbrook's *Daily Express* stated the point in 1928 and were supported by John Charteris, who should have known if anyone did.

By March 1928, the rumours had become so strong that the British Museum issued a formal denial through its secretary, Arundell Esdaile. At a press conference, Esdaile stated that the museum held two separate[11] sequences of Haig material and that what had been reported as a diary was probably the seventy-two-page Memorandum. There was certainly something in this. A year after lodging his Memorandum, the publication of Milner's version of events in March 1918 drove Haig to produce a counter-blast for the period 21 March to 15 April.[12] One copy was sent to *The Times* through a third party. A second was passed to Edmonds and a third dispatched to the British Museum with a letter of thanks from Haig to the author ('Very many thanks for your "Policy" for the British Museum,' he wrote to Boraston. 'I think you have stated the case well and pointed the right road in almost all cases').

But if the British Museum held two separate Memoranda, one long and one short, that was not to say that the museum classified them under two separate headings, and Edmonds's correspondence with the 2nd Earl Haig in 1949 gives the strongest possible indication of the fact that the second sequence in the British Museum was the real Haig diary.[13]

'I was an old and close friend of your father,' he wrote. 'So close that he gave me a copy of his 1914–18 diary and Memorandum deposited at the British Museum. Soon after the death of the Field Marshal, I told General Du Pree as one of the Trustees that they should withdraw it from the British Museum as, in my opinion, it would not enhance your father's reputation. I am still of that opinion. Do take expert advice. By Army instructions of 1914, keeping of private diaries was forbidden and the diary of the Commander in Chief may be ruled to be an official document.'

Edmonds's wording states plainly enough that the British Museum held a version of the diary. It is also difficult to see why Edmonds would have been so anxious over the publication of a diary already quoted at length by Duff Cooper if the British Museum diary was indeed the same as the one used by Duff Cooper.

In the absence of firm evidence, there is only limited value in speculating on the format of the British Museum's diary, but in a conversation with Liddell Hart in 1928 Edmonds said that he had long held all of Haig's diary and that it was in the nature of a unit war diary. A diary of this sort would have given Haig the best possible factual record and was also the type of documentation which commanders were allowed to keep by King's Regulations.

The most obvious solution to all these conundrums is to assume that Lady Haig's twelve volumes were written in the style of a unit war diary. It would comprise a detailed narrative, supplemented by orders, conference minutes and verbatim records of conversations, recorded by a confidential secretary. There would also be a copy of every letter sent out in Haig's name as well as every inward letter. It would therefore have been a very different animal from the four volumes in Haig's papers today, which were daily jottings written by Haig with propaganda in mind and regularly circulated among a small, influential group during the war.

But whatever the truth of the matter, there is nothing straightforward about reconstructing the facts of Haig's command from documents. The credentials of each letter, diary or set of minutes have to be established and even the most nutritious are like those fish, highly valued by the

Japanese, which kill the unwary. Meticulous processing and the most precise culinary techniques are always required.

MANUSCRIPT MATERIAL USED

OFFICIAL PAPERS

Most were from the Public Record Office. The two chief sequences are War Office and Cabinet Office papers. Canada's Public Archives have copies sometimes fuller than those in the PRO, as do the Lloyd George papers. Through the efforts of Tasman Heyes, the Australian War Memorial's librarian during the twenties, Canberra has a large quantity of GHQ and BEF material withheld from researchers in Britain.

PRIVATE PAPERS (titles and ranks in November 1918)

Commanders in Chief

HAIG, 1st Earl (Sir Douglas): Public Record Office, London; Scottish National Library

PERSHING, Gen. Sir John: Library of Congress, Washington

Army Commanders

ALLENBY, F. M. Sir Edmund: in the Wavell papers, King's College, London

BIRDWOOD, Gen. Sir William: Australian War Memorial; India Office, London

HAMILTON, Gen. Sir Ian: King's College, London

HORNE, 1st Baron (Sir Henry): Imperial War Museum

RAWLINSON, 1st Baron (Sir Henry): Imperial War Museum; Churchill College, Cambridge; Army Museum, London

Corps Commanders

BUTLER, Maj.-Gen. Sir Richard: Imperial War Museum

CAVAN, 10th Earl (Frederick Lambart): Public Record Office, London

CONGREVE, Gen. Sir Walter: private
CURRIE, Maj.-Gen. Sir Arthur: Public Archives, Ottawa
HALDANE, Lt.-Gen. Sir Aylmer: Scottish National Library
HUNTER-WESTON, Lt.-Gen. Sir Aylmer: British Library
MAXSE, Lt.-Gen. Sir Ivor: Imperial War Museum; West Sussex Record Office
MONASH, Lt.-Gen. Sir John: Australian War Memorial; Australian National Library

GHQ Staff

BIRCH, Lt.-Gen. James Noel: in the Rawlins papers, Royal Artillery Institution, Woolwich
BORASTON, Lt.-Col. John: King's College, London
BUTLER, Col. Stephen: Imperial War Museum
CHARTERIS, Brig.-Gen. John: private
DAVIDSON, Maj.-Gen. Sir John: Scottish National Library
DAWNAY, Maj.-Gen. Guy: Imperial War Museum
DILL, Col. John: King's College, London
GOLD, Lt.-Col. Ernest: Meteorological Office, Bracknell
KIGGELL, Lt.-Gen. Sir Launcelot: King's College, London
LAWRENCE, Gen. the Hon. Sir Herbert: Scottish National Library
MORTON, Desmond: in the R. W. Thompson papers, King's College, London, and; the Liddell Hart papers in the same institution

Army Staff

BEDDINGTON, Lt.-Col. Edward: King's College, London
BROAD, Maj. Charles: King's College, London
FULLER, Lt.-Col. John: King's College, London; Rutgers University
HEADLAM, Lt.-Col. Cuthbert: Durham Record Office
MAZE, Paul: King's College, London
MITCHELL, Lt.-Col. Charles: Public Archives, Ottawa
MONTGOMERY-MASSINGBERD, Maj.-Gen. Sir Archibald: King's College, London
RAWLINS, Col. Stuart: Royal Artillery Institution, Woolwich
UNIACKE, Maj.-Gen. Sir Herbert: Royal Artillery Institution, Woolwich
WAVELL, Maj.-Gen. Archibald: King's College, London

Other Staff Officers

BLAMEY, Brig.-Gen. Thomas: Australian War Memorial

BLISS, Maj.-Gen. Tasker: Library of Congress
HARBORD, Gen. James: Library of Congress
WHITE, Lt.-Gen. Sir Cyril Brudenell: Australian War Memorial

Liaison Officers

BENSON, Lt.-Col. Rex: King's College, London
CLARK, Maj. Paul: National Archives, Washington
CLIVE, Maj.-Gen. Sidney: King's College, London
DU CANE, Lt.-Gen. Sir John: Imperial War Museum; Public Record Office, London
GRANT, Brig.-Gen. Charles: King's College, London
GRISCOM, Col. Lloyd: National Archives, Washington
SIMS, Admiral William: Library of Congress
SPEARS, Brig.-Gen. Edward: King's College, London

War Office

KIRKE, Col. Walter: Imperial War Museum
KITCHENER, F.-M. Earl: Public Record Office, London
MACDONOGH, Maj.-Gen. George: Public Record Office, London
MAURICE, Maj.-Gen. Sir Frederick: King's College, London
ROBERTSON, Gen. Sir William: King's College, London
WILSON, F.-M. Sir Henry: Imperial War Museum

British Politicians

ADDISON, Rt Hon. Christopher: Bodleian, Oxford
AMERY, Leo: private
ASQUITH, Rt Hon. Herbert: Bodleian, Oxford
BALFOUR, Rt Hon. Arthur: British Library; Scottish Record Office
CARSON, Rt Hon. Sir Edward: Northern Ireland Record Office, Belfast
CHAMBERLAIN, Austen and Arthur Neville: Birmingham University
CURZON, 1st Earl (George): India Office, London
DERBY, 17th Earl (Edward Stanley): Liverpool Public Library
HENDERSON, Rt Hon. Arthur: Labour Party Archives, Walworth
LAW, Rt Hon. Andrew Bonar: House of Lords Record Office
LLOYD George, Rt Hon. David: House of Lords Record Office
LONG, Rt Hon. Walter: British Library; Wiltshire Record Office
MCKENNA, Rt Hon. Reginald: Churchill College, Cambridge
MILNER, Rt Hon. Sir Alfred: Bodleian, Oxford

Other Politicians

BAKER, Newton: Library of Congress
BORDEN, Rt Hon. Sir Robert: Public Archives, Ottawa
COOK, Sir Joseph: Australian National Library
HUGHES, Rt Hon. William: Australian National Library
KEMP, Sir Edward: Public Archives, Ottawa
SMUTS, Johannes: Cambridge University Library
WILSON, President Woodrow: Library of Congress

Cabinet Office

BURGIS, Lawrence: Churchill College, Cambridge
HANKEY, Lt.-Col. Sir Maurice: Churchill College, Cambridge

Official Historians

ASPINALL, Brig.-Gen. Cecil: Isle of Wight Record Office
BEAN, Charles: Australian War Memorial
DUGUID, Charles: Public Archives, Ottawa
EDMONDS, Brig.-Gen. James: King's College, London; Public Record Office, London

Secretaries

CHRISTIE, John: Public Archives, Ottawa
KERR, Philip: Scottish Record Office
STEVENSON, Frances: House of Lords Record Office
THORNTON, Hugh: Bodleian, Oxford

Press

BEAVERBROOK, 1st Baron (William Aitken): House of Lords Record Office
MAXSE, Leo: British Library
MURDOCH, Keith: Australian National Library
NORTHCLIFFE, 1st Viscount (Alfred Harmsworth): British Library; Times Archive
REPINGTON, Lt.-Col. Charles: Times Archive
RIDDELL, Sir George: British Library
ROBINSON, Charles: Times Archive
SCOTT, Charles: British Library

Miscellaneous

BERTIE, 1st Viscount (Francis Bertie): Public Record Office, London

BUCHAN, John: Queen's University, Kingston, Ontario
ESHER, 2nd Viscount (Reginald Brett): Churchill College, Cambridge
HARDINGE, 1st Baron (Charles Hardinge): Public Record Office, London
HOUSE, Edward: Library of Congress
LIDDELL HART, Captain Basil: King's College, London
PAGE, Walter: Library of Congress
PERLEY, Hon. Sir George: Public Archives, Ottawa
SHAW SPARROW, Walter: British Library
THOMPSON, R. W.: King's College, London

BOOKS QUOTED IN THE TEXT

G. Arthur, *Lord Haig* (Heinemann 1928)
  (ed.), *The Memoirs of Henri Poincaré* (Heinemann 1926)
J. Baynes, *Morale* (Cassell 1967)
Lord Birkenhead, *Contemporary Personalities* (Cassell 1924)
R. Blake, *The Private Papers of Douglas Haig 1914–1919* (Eyre & Spottiswoode 1952)
J. Boraston (ed.), *Sir Douglas Haig's Despatches, December 1915–April 1919* (Dent 1919)
C. Callwell, *Experiences of a Dugout 1914–1918* (Constable 1920)
J. Charteris, *Field Marshal Earl Haig* (Cassell 1929)
W. Churchill, *Great Contemporaries* (Butterworth 1938)
C. Colin, *Transformations of War* (Rees 1912)
D. Cooper, *Haig* (Faber 1935/6)
C. Cruttwell, *A History of the Great War* (Oxford 1934)
G. Dewar and J. Boraston, *Sir Douglas Haig's Command* (Constable 1922)
N. D'Ombrain, *War Machinery and High Policy* (Oxford 1973)
Lord Esher, *The Path to Peace* (Hutchinson n.d.)
  The Pomp of Power (Hutchinson 1922)
C. Falls, *War Books – a Critical Guide* (Peter Davies 1930)
F. Foch, *The Memoirs of Marshal Foch* (Heinemann 1931)
D. Fraser, *Alanbrooke* (Athenaeum NY 1982)

J. Fuller, *The Army in My Time* (Rich & Cowan 1935)

V. Germains, *The Kitchener Armies* (Peter Davies 1930)

M. Gilbert, *Winston Churchill*, Vol. 4 (Heinemann 1975)

Countess Haig, *The Man I Knew* (Moray Press 1931)

J. Harding-Newman, *Modern Military Administration* (Gale & Polden n.d.)

J. Hawkes, *Mortimer Wheeler* (Weidenfeld & Nicolson 1982)

C. Head, *The Art of Generalship* (Gale & Polden n.d.)

G. Henderson, *The Science of War* (Longmans 1919)

R. Holmes, *The Little Field Marshal* (Cape 1981)

D. Kahn, *The Codebreakers* (Macmillan 1973)

H. Langlois, *The British Army in European Wars* (Rees 1910)

Viscount Lee, *A Good Innings* (Murray 1974, ed. Alan Clark)

B. Liddell Hart, *The Real War* (Faber 1930)

A. Link (ed.), *The Papers of Woodrow Wilson* (Princeton, multi-volume)

T. Lupfer, *The Dynamics of Doctrine: The Changes in German Tactical Doctrine during the First World War* (Leavenworth 1981)

F. Maurice, *Intrigues of the War* (reprints from *Westminster Gazette* 1922)

J. Monash, *The Australian Victories in France* (Angus & Robertson 1920)

C. E. Montague, *Disenchantment* (Chatto & Windus 1922)

P. Nordon, *Conan Doyle* (Murray 1966)

A. Du Picq, *Battle Studies* (Gale & Polden 1870)

J. B. Priestley, *Reminiscences and Reflections* (Heinemann 1962)

R. Prior, *Churchill's 'World Crisis' as History* (Croom Helm 1983)

C. Repington, *The First World War 1914–1918* (Constable 1920)

W. Robertson, *Soldiers and Statesmen 1914–18* (Cassell 1926)

K. Rose, *King George V* (Weidenfeld & Nicolson 1983)

E. Spears, *Prelude to Victory* (Cape 1939)

R. Thompson, *Churchill and Morton* (Hodder & Stoughton 1976)

P. Vansittart, *John Masefield's Letters from the Front 1915–17* (Constable 1984)

J. C. Wedgwood, *The Last of the Radicals* (Cape n.d.)

P. Wright, *At the Supreme War Council* (Putnam 1921)

OFFICIAL HISTORIES CITED

AUSTRALIA

Vol. 1: C. E. W. Bean, *The Story of Anzac* (to *4 May 1915*) (Sydney 1921)

Vol. 2: C. E. W. Bean, *The Story of Anzac (4 May 1915 to the Evacuation)* (Sydney 1924)
Vol. 3: C. E. W. Bean, *The AIF in France 1916* (Sydney 1929)
Vol. 4: C. E. W. Bean, *The AIF in France 1917* (Sydney 1933)
Vol. 5: C. E. W. Bean, *The AIF in France 1918* (Sydney 1937)
Vol. 6: C. E. W. Bean, *The AIF in France 1918* (Sydney 1942)

CANADA

A. F. Duguid, *From the Outbreak of War to the Formation of the Canadian Corps, August 1914–September 1915* (Ottawa, King's Printer, 1947)
G. W. Nicholson, *Canadian Expeditionary Force, 1914–1919* (Ottawa, Queen's Printer, 1962)

UNITED KINGDOM

C. F. Aspinall-Oglander, *Gallipoli* Vol. 1 (London 1929)
C. F. Aspinall-Oglander, *Gallipoli* Vol. 2 (London 1932)
J. E. Edmonds, *1914, August–October* (London 1922)
J. E. Edmonds, *1914, October–November* (London 1925)
J. E. Edmonds and G. C. Wynne, *1915, December 1914–May 1915* (London 1927)
J. E. Edmonds and G. C. Wynne, *1915, Aubers, Festubert and Loos* (London 1928)
J. E. Edmonds, *1916, to July 1* (London 1932)
J. E. Edmonds, *1916, July 2 to End of Somme Battles* (London 1938)
C. Falls, *1917, the German Retreat and the Arras Battles* (London 1940)
J. E. Edmonds, *1917, Messines and Passchendaele* (London 1949)
W. Miles, *1917, The Battle of Cambrai* (London 1949)
J. E. Edmonds, *1918, The March Offensive* (London 1935)
J. E. Edmonds, *1918, March–April* (London 1937)
J. E. Edmonds, *1918, May–July* (London 1939)
J. E. Edmonds, *1918 August 8–September 26* (London 1947)
J. E. Edmonds, *1918, September 26–November 11* (London 1949)

UNITED STATES

The United States Army in the World War, 1917–1919, 17 vols. (Washington: Government Printing Office 1948)

RECENT WORKS

Four books stand out for excellence in the use of newly available documents. David Woodward's *Lloyd George and the Generals* (Associated Universities Press 1983) combs the Public Record Office's Cabinet Papers to the last leaf. Its chronological format makes for easy reference. Tim Travers's *The Killing Ground* (Allen & Unwin 1987) has solid essays on important aspects of the Western Front with first-class source references. Dominic Graham's chapters in *Firepower* (Allen & Unwin 1987) are strongly individualistic in their treatment of selected areas of Haig's command but always stimulating. An up-market curate's egg. Geoffrey Serle's *John Monash* (Melbourne University Press 1982) is a mature, well-proportioned book which treats its subject sympathetically. There is still no adequate study of Currie, the Canadian who ranks with Monash in importance (and in quantity of available documentation).

JOURNALS

Two invaluable series are the *Army Quarterly* and the *Journal of the Royal United Services Institute*. Notable articles are G. C. Wynne's 'The Chain of Command' (*AQ*, April 1938) and 'The Development of the German Defensive Battle in 1917' (*AQ*, April 1937). Charles Grant's 'Recollections of Marshal Foch in 1918' (*AQ*, April 1929) is valuable. Guy Dawnay's 1928 poem, written for the *Quarterly*'s issue commemorating Haig's death, adds a pleasant touch of comic relief. The *JRUSI* contains Ironside's address 'The Modern Staff Officer' (*JRUSI*, August 1928) and a remarkably candid analysis, 'British Infantry Tactics, 1914–1918', in the *JRUSI*'s 1919 edition.

BOOKS ON HAIG

Haig seems to have generated more pot-boilers than any other British high commander. Among the few books worth looking at, there is an absolute divide between apologists and prosecutors.

Sharpest and pithiest of the apologists is Frederick Maurice in the *Dictionary of National Biography*. John Charteris's *Field Marshal Earl Haig* (Cassell 1929) retains its value on the personal side. Duff Cooper's *Haig* (Faber 1935/6) pretends to be an official biography but is, in fact, a poorly annotated edition of Haig's typed diary. Whether Duff Cooper did more than lend his name remains a moot point. Letters between Liddell Hart and Buchan in 1932 and 1935 (Buchan papers, Public Archives, Ottawa) suggest Buchan as the real author – which would make good sense. Duff Cooper knew little of Haig, whereas Buchan went to Haig's Oxford college, served with him as an Elder of the Kirk and lived near him on the Borders. There was also good reason to mask Buchan's role, since Lady Haig refused to lend material to Maurice and Buchan, the biographers originally selected by the Haig Trustees. Whoever wrote *Haig*, its text is anyway better studied in John Terraine's *Douglas Haig* (Hutchinson 1963). Terraine used almost identical material but ended up with an apologia more polished and better balanced.

For the critics, Liddell Hart's *Through the Fog of War* (Faber 1938) stands alone. His skill in extracting the last drop of juice from private sources puts his work two generations ahead of his rivals.

Books treating Haig's campaigns show the same absolute divide between apologists and critics. Among the former, Maurice's article 'The Western Front' in the 1926 *Encyclopaedia Britannica* is first-class and the two volumes of Dewar and Boraston have been badly neglected. If not actually ghosted, his master's voice is clearly audible throughout. Blake's edition of the typed diary repays study. Its commentary is elegant and uncritical.

The prosecutors have no comparable volumes. The few men able to bring a sharp eye to the war have generally opted for a broader treatment than opponents, who relate everything to Haig. The single-volume studies of Liddell Hart and Cruttwell remain the best works in the field. Indeed, they stand almost alone in grasp and intelligence. In the fifty years since their publication, attempts to emulate them have been sillier, duller or bulkier. None has been better.

Appendix 2

Haig: A Political Intriguer?

Most historical studies of Haig treat him as a soldier pure and simple. Few mention any political dimension. Yet anyone using documents rather than the usual printed sources finds a surprising number of political references from autumn 1917 onwards. Most of them link Haig with a group which aimed to get rid of Lloyd George, make a compromise peace with Germany and then build up central Europe as a bulwark against Communism. After a lifetime's manipulation of the Army's patronage system, Haig was too canny to leave any direct evidence on paper, so just how strong is the case for the existence of a compromise peace faction and what evidence is there to associate Haig with it?

Desmond Morton's testimony makes the best starting point. After he had served six months as an ADC to Haig, Churchill spotted unusual talent and put him into MI6, where he rose to third in the hierarchy. That position gives weight to his views. In correspondence with the author of a book on his relationship with Churchill, Morton made several revealing comments. 'From neutral, even hostile, Churchill developed a very considerable admiration for Haig,' ran one of these. 'He always admired Haig's obstinacy and had no real objection to Haig's frightful intrigues. After all, Churchill was no stranger to intrigue.'[1]

Morton returned to the subject a few years later with a comment that 'Among Winston's extraordinarily wrong-headed views was the idea that Alex [Field Marshal Alexander of Tunis] was "Cromwell stuff" and would try to seize political power. He was one of those who from 1917 to 1919 – his friend Lloyd George being assured of the same – firmly believed that Haig was intriguing to become Prime Minister of England.'

Most stories of the Great War make no reference to this extraordinary possibility, but it can't be lightly dismissed. Morton is invariably a reliable witness and he must have been able to draw on solid evidence as a key MI6 man. Lloyd George, the other person mentioned by Morton, wins no prizes for reliability, but the quality of his witness is another matter. Esher certainly thought so when he warned Haig in December 1917 that 'Lloyd George's means of information are varied and go deep into the camp of his opponents. Conventions with pressmen, correspondence with Asquith, communications with critics are brought to him by agents. His secret service is undoubtedly well run and is something like Napoleon's.'[2] What danger did Lloyd George perceive and, if Haig was indeed conspiring, with whom and over what issues?

The answer is to be found in attitudes which began to be expressed at the mid-point of the war. Lord Lansdowne, the Tory grandee, established himself as the chief spokesman of an influential minority when he read a remarkable paper to the Cabinet in November 1916.[3] His analysis queried the most basic assumptions of the time. Britain had sustained one million casualties and was paying £5 million daily to sustain the war. Wasn't the price too high? And could the war ever be won? Even if peace was made soon, how many generations would it take to recover from the damage done by war?

Lansdowne had few supporters in 1916, but by the end of 1917 an increasing number of men had come to agree with his reservations in the privacy of their correspondence. Writing to Derby in May 1917, Esher expressed the fears of many acquaintances when he wrote: 'We shall all go down before the new forces that are coming into the war. Thrones, aristocrats, plutocrats and all – even the Girondins who have hitherto led parliament.'[4] The Russian revolution in March 1917 stimulated these fears, and by the end of 1917 Charles Bean was receiving a confidential briefing at Australian Corps HQ to the effect that Haig, Robertson and Henry Wilson all believed that 'the war will end by revolution and they want to see the revolution in Germany come first'.

By the time Lansdowne repeated his views in a letter published in the press at the end of September 1917, many had become sympathetic to his call for a compromise peace and Milner registered the fact in a letter to Carson. 'The situation looks uglier and uglier,' he wrote. 'I thought of you when I saw Lansdowne's letter in the papers. It is just what you foresaw – that one of these days some man of position, not in the government, would say something of this kind which many people must be thinking and set the ball rolling. The position is evidently becoming very critical.'[5]

The crisis Milner feared never involved barricades or guillotines. Men like Lansdowne had no intention of using popular pressure to bolster their cause. In a year beginning with revolution in Russia, the dangers were self-evident. The group's plans were therefore semi-constitutional. Get an *ad hoc* majority in the Commons on an emotive issue, eject the leader of the total-war faction (Lloyd George) and then seize the levers of power. It was an ambitious scheme and an attempt was made to implement it on three occasions.

The first of these followed the establishment of the Supreme War Council in October 1917. The need for a body to integrate the allied effort had been stated by allied generals in a conference during July 1917.[6] Esher had been happy to support them. Without an organization of that sort, he told Haig, the war could not continue through 1918 'because with our present resources and organization, we cannot bridge the gap between our depletion of manpower and the arrival of the Americans'. The Supreme War Council was thus well founded and militarily necessary, as the events of March 1918 were to show, but if the peace faction wanted an issue, the Supreme War Council could easily be dressed up to look like civilian interference in the professional business of war. Given the prestige of generals in the age of Wolseley, Roberts and Kitchener, public support could well swing behind a group which championed the autonomy of the military – or so Lansdowne and his supporters hoped.

The attack took some time to prepare, but in October 1917 Milner was telling his private secretary that by the end of the month either Haig and Robertson or the Cabinet would be on their way out – or both.[7] The climax came on 19 November, Charles Repington covering the critical debate for *The Times*. 'I went to the House of Commons in the afternoon to hear the great debate on the Rapallo Agreement,' he wrote. 'Asquith opened in a speech of great moderation, asking many pertinent questions and Lloyd George replied at once. The House was crammed. I sat at the serjeant at arms' box and had a good view. Lloyd George was at his best. He began slowly and either answered or skilfully evaded all questions. Then he stoked up and began to lay about him using every artifice of the demagogue and play-actor. He played on the whole gamut of human emotions, cajoling, threatening with fierce gestures and rising to a great height of simulated passion. He was humorous too and the whole House rose with him and rocked with joy. What an assembly! Directly the speech was over, everyone flocked out to tea and nobody listened to what followed. Asquith should have put someone else to lead and should have followed Lloyd George.'[8] In other words, the Opposition had taken on Lloyd George in a chamber where he was master and lost. Or, as Balfour put it in private correspondence, 'The Asquith plot bubble is pricked.'

The names of Asquith's supporters remain shadowy, but it was apparent to all near the centre of power that a larger group than Asquith's personal following had been involved.

In a letter to President Wilson dated 3 December 1917, Frederick Lane of the War Department reported a conversation with the British military attaché in Washington on the nature of that opposition.[9] Colonel Harvey had suggested that the Lansdowne letter represented Britain's men of property serving notice that they were looking to diplomats rather than soldiers for victory. Harvey concluded with the prediction that the Tories expected to secure their aims in Cabinet within three months by putting out Lloyd George.

The next crisis came in February 1918, just as Harvey had predicted, the Supreme War Council again supplying a pretext. More specifically, Robertson precipitated the confrontation by insisting that the CIGS alone should give military advice to the Cabinet. The Supreme War Council was, in other words, to be down-graded and Clemenceau was very happy to feed Lloyd George's opponents and the Opposition press directly with all the information they required.

These were powerful interests, and the gravity of the crisis which followed was explained in a letter from Frederick Oliver to Austen Chamberlain. 'This has been the most damnable fortnight in my personal experience of the war. A great deal depends on the attitudes of yourself and Carson, not in terms of ministries but of the fate of the allies in this war. If the present government falls (as it richly deserves to if only its own interests were at stake) Asquith is the only alternative and Asquith clearly has this in mind – we must have peace or we shall have a revolution.'[10] Lloyd George supported Oliver's assessment. 'Have you packed up?' he asked his private secretary. 'We may be out in a fortnight.'

The reasoning behind Oliver's alarm was that Robertson was fronting a loose-knit group which extended well beyond the Asquith faction. Tasker Bliss confirmed the point in a letter he sent to Washington from his position on the Supreme War Council: 'There are three lightning conductor rods erected over Versailles to attract the attacks of men who want to attack not the Supreme War Council but one or other of the prime ministers who constitute it. The controversy over General Robertson has not been carried on by people who care a turn of their hand about him but by people who are seeking the downfall of Mr Lloyd George and his government. I think there is no doubt that the wealthy people of England are, as a class, opposed to Mr Lloyd George. They recognize in him the man best fitted to form a government for the purpose of this war but they dread what he will do when the war is over. These are the people who have attempted to use General Robertson as a club with which to assail Mr Lloyd George.' [11]

Bliss was obviously well informed and he predicted the outcome shrewdly. 'I do not think they have the idea of driving him from power now but of making it easier to do so at a later time.' This proved to be correct, and Hankey was able to re-assure the Prime Minister (in such a state of nervous tension at the time he couldn't concentrate on anything for more than a few seconds) that Robertson's challenge had no substantial force behind it. [12] Three days later, Esher reinforced the point after a tip-off from Spender, one of Asquith's press orchestrators. [13] The message was that Lansdowne and Asquith had agreed to keep Lloyd George in office.

The third confrontation was the most serious of the sequence. It started with an open letter in the press at the start of May 1918 which accused Lloyd George of withholding reinforcements from Haig after Passchendaele and thus putting him in an impossible position when the Germans attacked. The author of the letter was General Maurice, Robertson's right-hand man at the War Office, and the gravity of his charges led to a full-scale debate in the Commons on 9 May. Lloyd George's political existence was again in the balance.

Maurice later claimed that he had acted alone, but documents recently released go against him and indicate the Maurice debate on 9 May as the culmination of plotting which had been actively pursued for a month or so, supported by an influential cabal throughout.

On 15 April, for example, Rawlinson wrote to Derby with the suggestion that Asquith and Robertson would make a better combination than Lloyd George and Henry Wilson. [14] On the same day, he wrote to the king's assistant secretary with the news that Robertson and Gough were supplying Asquith with information for an attack on Lloyd George. Wigram's reply indicates that Rawlinson later withheld a part of his original letter. 'Soldiers and sailors annoy me when they talk of the king turning out the Prime Minister and putting in soldiers and sailors to run the show,' Wigram wrote. 'The people, the press and parliament would not for a moment stand for such an act.'

A week later, Henry Wilson was told that Maurice's letter had been discussed at dinner between the journalists Gwynne and Repington and a military junta comprising Robertson, Gough, Trenchard and Jellicoe. [15] The decision taken at that table may well have been to publish the letter immediately, since Maurice, in conversation with Derby in August 1918, insisted that if only Derby had stayed on as Secretary of State for one more week (he resigned on 19 April), Maurice would have remained in the Army and Lloyd George removed from office.

The affair culminated anyway in a full-dress parliamentary debate, Lloyd George again demonstrating his mastery. 'I knew Maurice to be an excellent Staff Officer,' wrote Samuel Hoare, the banker, 'and went to the House strongly prejudiced in his favour. I shall never forget what happened. Lloyd George made the speech of his life. Maurice stood convicted out of his own mouth and the Opposition was so completely demoralized that although it was expecting Runciman and McKenna to make some kind of defence, not a word was said from the Opposition front bench in reply to the Prime Minister's charges.'

It is clear enough today that a ragbag of titled grandees, disgruntled politicians and disgraced soldiers had been involved in plotting the downfall of Lloyd George, but what evidence is there that Haig had been connected with these schemes of palace revolution? There is certainly no *corpus delicti*. Haig was always careful to work through intermediaries, avoid loose talk and leave nothing incriminating in writing. The case against him is a strong one nevertheless. It begins with the publication of the Lansdowne letter in autumn 1917.

After working closely with the Northcliffe press for nearly two years, Haig turned a somersault at the time of the Lansdowne letter, switching his allegiance to journalists like Spender, Benson, Leo Maxse and Repington, all of them compromise peace men. At the same time, he formed a close link with Asquith, previously a figure of alcoholic fun in the Haig diary.

Haig was a man of the greatest rigidity in daily routines, military philosophy and the selection of friends and allies. A radical change must therefore have taken place in his view of the world for him to have changed his allies at the end of 1917. Northcliffe certainly thought so, and after backing Haig for over a year the proprietor of *The Times* turned a somersault of his own and began to attack him with equal fervour using the Cambrai débâcle as his rod.

By the end of 1917, Haig's transformation was complete and he came out openly in support of Asquith's compromise peace policy, registering the fact in an interview given to Smuts and Hankey during their inspection of Western Front defences in January 1918. 'Haig said he considered that the British Empire had got most out of the war,' Lloyd George was told. 'He doubted whether we would gain more by going on twelve months. At the end of that period, we would be much more exhausted and industrial and financial recovery would be more difficult and America would get a great pull over us. The best policy would be to strengthen Austria, then turn Germany in the direction of Russia for the future. He was strongly in favour of an early peace on these terms.'[16]

Haig played little part in the crisis of February, unsurprisingly perhaps in view of the Opposition's reluctance to press the issue, but he featured in the run-up to the Maurice debate. During April, for example, the British ambassador in Paris told Poincaré that Haig was 'disturbing Lloyd George',[17] and at the end of the month Colonel House gave President Wilson startling news. 'Dear Governor [his usual greeting], one of the ablest men the British have sent over is Major-General Hutchinson, who expects to return this week. He tells me that Secretary Baker suggested you might want to see him. He is in the closest possible touch with Generals Haig, Robertson and Wilson and it might be of some service to see him and give him your point of view direct. He has told me in confidence that he was practically certain that the Lloyd George government would go within a few weeks and that General Robertson would be returned as Chief of Staff.'[18]

After the fiasco of the Maurice debate on 9 May, Rawlinson expressed anxiety that evidence would lead back to Haig — and Haig was certainly keen to distance himself from the affair. 'Reuters states General Maurice has written to the papers,' he told his wife. 'This is a grave mistake. No one can be both a soldier and a politician at the same time. We soldiers have to do our duty and keep silent, trusting to Ministers to protect us'[19] — which was rich indeed coming from a soldier who had intrigued for Kitchener against Curzon, threatened to bring Aldershot out against the government at the time of the Curragh mutiny just before the war and consorted with Northcliffe in the Somme–Passchendaele period.*

George V appears to have thought so too. On 13 May, Wigram wrote to Rawlinson asking, 'Can you find out whether Maurice had been offered employment at GHQ under Haig? There is some heavy lying taking place somewhere. Maurice certainly said that Haig was prepared to give him a job at GHQ but Engelmore goes so far as to say that the War Office had asked Haig whether he would employ Maurice and Haig replied, under no circumstances as he had no use for a fellow like Maurice. All these transactions are supposed to have taken place before the famous letter.'[20]

Was Haig therefore speaking the truth when he referred to a 'grave

---

* The Curragh crisis occurred when an extreme faction in the Army defied the authority of the Liberal government. The issue was whether or not Army officers would obey an order to act against the Protestants of Ulster on the eve of the Great War, and Haig had sided firmly with the dissidents.

mistake', implying his own distance from Maurice? It would have looked suspicious if he had offered sanctuary to the War Office's Titus Oates, and yet Clive's diary for 21 April records Davidson's unequivocal statement that Maurice would be replacing him at GHQ as Director of Military Operations (and that particular diary entry came just a fortnight before the Maurice debate).

From 9 May up to the Armistice, no further political commotions occurred, but Desmond Morton's recollection was of Lloyd George still believing that Haig was after the premiership in 1919. Was there any evidence to support Lloyd George's fears?

Studies of the post-war period invariably stress Haig's noble work on behalf of the veterans and his rejection of any personal reward until the debate over war pensions had been resolved. These studies stress, too, Haig's personal prestige as the crucial factor in getting the disparate veterans' associations to amalgamate into the British Legion. It is a pleasing picture. It does Haig proud. And yet his activities are capable of a very different interpretation.

One easily thinks of Haig's concern spreading over the whole Army like a father's for his children, but his involvement with war pensions was a very specific one from the start and related only to officers. 'Steps have already been taken to meet the case of disabled NCOs and men,' he told the CIGS, 'but the problems presented by large numbers of officers, unable through their injury to support themselves in a style appropriate to their standing in the Army, has not yet received attention.'[21] Haig's suggestion was that £10 million should be invested at once at 5 per cent on behalf of the officers and that residential clubs should be built for these officers.

About the same time, Haig established an Officers' Association of his own. John Boraston, Haig's private secretary in 1919, explained his chief's motives in the *Yorkshire Post* a decade later when he wrote: 'It was Haig's belief that unless the good fellowship between officers and men could be continued after the war, the first few years of peace would see many hundreds of thousands of ex-servicemen disillusioned, without genuine leadership yet with the habits of war not yet shaken off, forming the ranks of the unemployed and turning inevitably to mischief which might end in civil commotion or worse. With this possibility definitely in view, he formed the Officers' Association with the object of keeping some control over the officers of his old Army and, through their influence, over the great mass of demobilized men.'[22]

This was dangerous thinking in the highly charged atmosphere of 1919 and Boraston acknowledged that Haig's attitude could easily be interpreted as the scheming of a soldier with political ambitions. As Boraston put it, 'Short-sighted men of education regarded Haig's plan to keep himself at the head of the ex-servicemen with undisguised suspicion.'

The suspicions of these 'men of education' would only have been increased by Haig's activities in 1919, when the government was drawing up contingency plans to meet a General Strike. Haig's own response to the crisis had been to call a meeting of all military commanders in his capacity as Chief of the Home Army.[23] In that meeting, Haig came out strongly against equipping troops with entrenching tool handles alone, as had been done at Liverpool. He wanted troops to be issued with live ammunition. If the police were unable to cope, bullets and bayonets were to be brought into play and the prospect of civil war squarely faced. Haig was duly summoned to Downing Street three weeks later and in January 1920 was dismissed as Commander of the Home Army. There is nothing specifically on record to establish the connection, but the coincidence of the two events is not easily explained otherwise.

The sacking didn't stop Haig's political activity. That same month Ian Hamilton invited him to join a scheme initiated by the War Office on 5 November. On that auspicious date, the military establishment began its drive to unify all discharged soldiers under a single banner, using canteen funds as a lubricant. By June 1920 that job was completed, assisted by a number of rambling speeches throughout the country. Just why he participated is not mentioned in any of his papers. Patriotism or disinterested service may have been to the fore, as his supporters claimed, but some of his speeches hint at other possibilities. In Wolverhampton, for example, Haig told his audience: 'Short cuts to anarchy are still the fools' talk of unstable intellectuals and the overpaid outpourings [*sic*] of the street-corner agitator. There is all the greater need for men of all ranks to stand stoutly and solidly together. The Legion offers a rallying cry for such men.'[24]

None of this should come as a surprise, for Haig had always been a soldier–politician, involving himself in the Kitchener–Curzon storm and threatening to bring out Aldershot during the Curragh crisis. The chief elements in his rise also had more to do with political chicanery than proven performance on the battlefield and his correspondence throughout the war often reveals political undertones ('Lloyd George would like to make soldiers the scapegoat in the hope of remaining in power a little time longer,' he told his wife on one occasion. 'The fact is that he is afraid of me with the Army at my back . . .').

It was therefore unlikely that a soldier driven for so long by such intense personal ambition would subside quietly into a docile retirement. For three years, Haig's position had placed him firmly on the front page of the world's newspapers. For three years he met a succession of the world's most important leaders, most of whom treated him on equal terms at GHQ, and during that period personal staff had noted the growth of Haig's self-confidence and an increasingly easy relationship with God. Desmond Morton, that sharply observant ADC, uneasily noted an indication of that relationship when he later recalled that from late 1917 Haig always kept three books on his bedside table – a life of Cromwell, *The Pilgrim's Progress* and the Bible. The combination of Christian and Cromwell was one which might have given Lloyd George food for thought.

The case against Haig in this area is unlikely to be decided conclusively one way or the other, but Churchill's suspicion of Alexander during the Second World War, his readiness to sack commanders in whom he had the slightest doubt and his post-war treatment of men like Montgomery and Harris make good political sense when set against Haig's career.

References

2: Personal Credentials

1. Peter Vansittart, *John Masefield's Letters from the Front, 1915–17* (Constable 1984).
2. John Boraston in the *Spectator* 28.11.52.
3. Desmond Morton to Liddell Hart (Liddell Hart papers 17.7.61).
4. John Charteris, *Field Marshal Earl Haig* (Cassell 1929).
5. *British Legion Journal* 1928.
6. Memorandum in the Esher papers dated 20.7.16.
7. Countess Haig, *The Man I Knew* (Moray Press 1931).
8. The Melbourne *Age* newspaper 3.8.32.
9. *National Review*, February 1953.
10. John Russell, *The Haigs of Bemersyde*, reviewed in the *Edinburgh Review*, 1882.
11. Anecdotes on Haig at Sandhurst and the Staff College, in the Edmonds papers.
12. A large collection of anecdotes on a wide range of generals is gathered in the Wavell papers in connection with Wavell's biography of Allenby.
13. Bean diary 27.8.17.
14. George Arthur, *Lord Haig* (Heinemann 1928).
15. Ivor Maxse to his wife 23.7.17 (Maxse papers).
16. Wigram to Haig 17.1.15 (Royal Archives).
17. Viscount Lee, *A Good Innings* (Murray 1974).
18. E. Spears, *Prelude to Victory* (Cape 1939).
19. Thompson to his wife 7.10.15 (E. G. Thompson papers).
20. *Toronto Globe* 7.1.35.
21. Bean's working notes (Australian War Memorial 6673 sequence).

22. Headlam to Charteris 24.11.31 (Charteris papers).
23. Haig to his wife 12.3.18 (Haig papers).
24. Haig to his wife 11.10.16 (Haig papers).
25. Haig to his wife 13.2.16 (Haig papers).
26. Robertson to Haig 1.8.18 (Haig papers).
27. Bertie to Hardinge 17.1.18 (Bertie papers).
28. Haig to Jenty 20.12.17 (Haig papers).
29. Haig to Esher 26.10.17 (Haig papers).
30. Haig to his wife 23.8.17 (Haig papers).

3: *Professional Credentials*

1. Winston Churchill, *Great Contemporaries* (Butterworth 1938). Original in the *Daily Mail* 3.10.35.
2. Noted in George Arthur's *Lord Haig* (Heinemann 1928) and Lord Birkenhead's *Contemporary Personalities* (Cassell 1924).
3. Richard Holmes, *The Little Field Marshal* (Cape 1981).
4. Slotted into Bean's correspondence files on the individual volumes of his history in the Australian War Memorials 7953 sequence.
5. Lord Birkenhead, *Contemporary Personalities* (Cassell 1924).
6. *Quarterly Review*, January 1919.
7. Duff Cooper, *Haig* (two volumes, Faber 1935/6).
8. CAB103/76 dated 10.8.23.
9. WO158/181 covers the battle with the conference in Montgomery-Massingberd's unpublished memoirs.
10. *Army Quarterly*, April 1938.
11. Haig to Kitchener 29.9.15 (Kitchener papers).
12. Robertson to Haig 16.10.15 (WO106/390).
13. Haig to Robertson 21.10.15 (WO106/390).
14. Haig diary 25.9.15.
15. Rawlinson diary 29.9.15 (Army Museum).
16. Robertson to Haig 8.11.15 (WO106/390).
17. French to Kitchener 9.10.15 (PRO30/57/33).
18. Haking to Haig 27.10.15 (WO106/390).
19. The Historical Branch's file on Loos (CAB45/120).

4: *The Somme*

1. Rawlinson to Wigram 27.2.16 (Army Museum).

2. Peter Vansittart, *John Masefield's Letters from the Front 1915–17* (Constable 1984).
3. 29.6.15 (Asquith papers) and November 1915 (Butler papers).
4. Haig's paper 14.12.15 (WO158). Joffre's letter requesting a Somme battle had come on Christmas Day 1915. Haig's reply – the preliminary orders had already been issued. Haig diary 31.12.16 has an interesting flashback.
5. Mitchell papers and Kiggell 22.1.16 (WO158).
6. Haig diary 20.1.16.
7. Clive to Esher 4.7.16 (Esher papers).
8. Army commanders' conference, OAD691 (Mitchell papers).
9. Memorandum F112/179 (Curzon papers). The importance of Verdun was played down at the time. Haig wrote to the king on 15.2.16 that small numbers meant that the Germans had no chance of a decisive victory. On 23.3.16 Grant's diary recorded that the twenty-two-division strategic reserve had not been used by the Germans. On 29.2.16 Haig told the king that Joffre was completely confident of allied victory in the summer.
10. OAD11 (Mitchell papers).
11. Dated 12.6.16 in the papers Heyes copied for Bean.
12. St Pol army commanders' conference OAD912 (Mitchell papers). Also 28.1.16 (WO158) with the specification of three days' preliminary bombardment and fourteen days' battle.
13. Plumer's paper 18.3.16 (Mitchell papers). Sketched in Haig diary 27.5.16.
14. Plumer's report 14.1.16 (Heyes papers).
15. J. Harding-Newman, *Modern Military Administration, Organisation and Transportation* (Gale & Polden n.d.).
16. Charteris's appreciation 5.2.16 (WO158).
17. Haig to Robertson 28.4.16 (Robertson papers).
18. Haig to Esher 29.5.18 (Esher papers).
19. Haig to Bertie 28.5.16 (Bertie papers).
20. Haig to Robertson 3.6.16 (Robertson papers).
21. Haig to Robertson 10.6.16 (WO158/13).
22. Rawlinson 3.4.16; Haig in OAD710/1 on 13.4.16; Rawlinson's map and conference minutes on 15.5.16 in the Rawlinson papers (Imperial War Museum). Also reference in Haig diary 5.4.16.
23. OAD710/1 on 13.4.16 (Rawlinson papers, Imperial War Museum).
24. Haig's directive 8.5.16 (Heyes papers) and OAD291/18 of 15.6.16 in the Canadian Corps's War Diary (Canadian Public Archives).
25. OAD522 on 4.3.16 (WO158).

26. A paper by Foch for G.A.N. 20.4.16 (Birdwood papers).
27. OAD291/18 on 20.6.16 (Heyes papers).
28. Buchan papers (Canadian Public Archives).
29. OAD12 expanded as OAD17 on 21.6.16 (Rawlinson papers, Imperial War Museum) and OAD21 to Joffre on 26.6.16, setting down grandiose objectives of Douai and Cambrai to keep Joffre sweet.
30. Rawlinson at 3rd Army HQ 4.12.15 (Heyes papers).
31. Published as CDS33 by French's GHQ in August 1915 and later by HMSO in 1916. Captain André Laffargue's *The Attack in Trench Warfare*, written in May 1915, went on to discuss the possibilities of small units breaking the line and aiming at deep penetration. This aspect naturally caught the eye of post-war historians.
32. SS494 (Rawlinson papers, Imperial War Museum).
33. Minutes of Staff College Conference, 1911.
34. CAB45/132–3 in miscellaneous correspondence with much detail in Rawlinson papers.
35. Birch to Ivor Maxse 3.11.18 (Maxse papers).
36. 'Artillery Notes', No. 1 (Australian War Memorial 25).
37. 'Artillery Notes', No. 3 (Australian War Memorial 25).
38. Analysis in GHQ's report 27.9.16 with a second dated 14.11.16 (Australian War Memorial 25), together with handwritten reports in Currie and Maxse papers.
39. Manuscript for 4th Army's Red Book in Rawlinson papers, Army Museum.
40. Historical Branch's Somme correspondence file (CAB45/132).
41. Bertie to the Foreign Secretary 7.7.16 (Bertie papers).
42. Robertson to Haig 7.7.16 with reply, OAD51 of 8.7.16 (Haig papers).
43. Haig's instructions from London on his relationship with the French are in CAB63/19 and WO106/298 for 28.12.15 and 21.6.18. Haig diary (WO256) mentions a verbal briefing from Kitchener on 3.12.15.
44. C. Head, *The Art of Generalship* (Gale & Polden n.d.).
45. OAD229 to Robertson on 21.11.16 (Heyes papers).
46. Kiggell to Edmonds in 1938 (CAB45/135).

5: Passchendaele: The Roots

1. C. Cruttwell, *A History of the Great War* (Oxford 1934).
2. G. Dewar and J. Boraston, *Sir Douglas Haig's Command* (Constable 1922).
3. F. Maurice, *Intrigues of the War* (a pamphlet of *Westminster Review* reprints, 1922).

4. Papers by Cecil 27.11.16, Grey 27.11.16, Balfour 4.10.16, Lloyd George 9.10.16.
5. Document dated 8.12.16 with the gist in a letter from Hankey to Robertson 9.11.16 (Robertson papers) and noting the Cabinet's desire for energy on all fronts in 1917.
6. CAB25/1–5.
7. Nivelle's scheme was given to Lloyd George at the London conference by Ribot on 23.12.16.
8. Minutes of Rome conference (CAB28/2/1a).
9. Robertson's notes on the Haig–Nivelle conference, dated 24.1.17 (Macdonogh papers).
10. Haig's views are in his Address to Army Commanders on 3.1.17 (WO158) and at more length in 1A33033 dated 29.4.17, used as Haig's brief for the Paris conference (Heyes papers).
11. Haig to the king 29.12.16 (Royal Archives).
12. The conference of 15 January and Cabinet No. 35 next day are covered at great length in the Lloyd George papers – about 150 foolscap sides against minutes of the same at the Public Record Office in a few lines.
13. Conference 29.1.17 in CAB23/1. Nivelle's point in CAB28/2/1a at Calais. Also Henry Wilson diary 5.4.17.
14. Stamfordham to Derby 15.2.17 (Derby papers).
15. Haig diary 15.2.17.
16. Read by the Secretary of State on 19.2.17 (CAB23/1).
17. Thornton diary in the Milner papers on 13.2.17.
18. Robertson to Esher 14.3.17 (Robertson papers).
19. Robertson recorded as present in War Cabinet 78 on 22.2.17 in Lloyd George papers, G217. Robertson's memorandum to Haig is dated the 24th.
20. Hankey to Stamfordham 4.3.17 (Royal Archives).
21. Haig to the king 28.2.17 (Royal Archives).
22. A chronology of the period in the Lawrence papers.
23. 13.11.16 (WO158).
24. 3.12.16 (WO158).
25. CAB23/13 (Lloyd George papers G249). It bears the classification OAD428.
26. 'A Report on the Chemin des Dames' (undated) in the Macdonogh papers.
27. OAD414 in WO158.
28. Edmonds to Liddell Hart 22.6.34 (Liddell Hart papers).

The whole complex, convoluted business of the Nivelle affair is covered in two first-class chronologies. Hankey wrote a memorandum dated

27.2.17 (CAB63/22). A chronology in the Lawrence papers is re-markably full and includes many documents cited nowhere else.

6: Passchendaele: The Battle

1. F112/179 (Curzon papers).
2. Mitchell papers (Canadian Public Archives).
3. WO153/597 and maps in the Mitchell papers.
4. 1A/33033 produced by GHQ's 'I' Branch for the Paris conference 5.5.17.
5. Mitchell papers. Also G235 in the Lloyd George papers and WO106/407.
6. OAD538 of 5.7.17 (WO158/48), which was the chief Operational Directive for the battle of Passchendaele.
7. 8.1.17 (WO158/39).
8. Haig to Plumer 6.1.17 (Heyes papers). Haig's response to the difficulty was to add an extra army to the strike force by OAD268 (WO158/38).
9. Gas Director's report B412 of 19.7.17 (Canadian Corps papers).
10. WO95/519.
11. OB492 of 16.7.17 (Montgomery-Massingberd papers).
12. Delay mentioned in CAB45/172, Swinton and Bean noting the initial zero on the 19th. Delay to 28th in SG657/54 (WO95/519) and 31st in OAD567.
13. The German withdrawal before Messines is in OAD464 (WO95/275). Also Kiggell's letter to Plumer on 29.5.17 (Heyes papers) and 1A34371 dated 25.7.17 from GHQ's 'I' Branch (Bean working papers).
14. Lillers army commanders' conference 14.6.17, confirmed in OAD291/87 (Bean papers).
15. WO95/519.
16. Robertson to Kiggell 27.7.17 (Kiggell papers).
17. Tim Lupfer's *The Dynamics of Doctrine: The Changes in German Tactical Doctrine during the First World War* (Leavenworth 1981) is an admirable study, but is a year out in its reckoning. A fully fledged German second line is described in CDS303 (GHQ's translation of a German paper dated 4.4.15). Deep dugouts, often supposed to have surprised Haig on the Somme, are described in Rawlinson's diary on 20.10.15. German machine-gun nests are anatomized by Mitchell during August 1915 (Mitchell papers). A fully developed German counter-attacking system, using specially trained squads, is set down in GHQ's CDS85, dated 18.6.15, and in a circular written by Sir John French in person and dated 5.10.15.
18. 'Tactical Notes', 5th Army, 26.4.17 (White papers).

19. OB1919 from GHQ, more formally set out in GHQ's pamphlet SS144. Mentioned in the Haig diary 3.2.17.
20. WO106/318.
21. Bean's working notes.
22. OB2089 of 7.8.17 with Plumer's reply G566 (WO95/275). Rawlinson's reply is in the Maxse papers.
23. Thornton diary 16.2.17 (Milner papers).
24. 11.6.17 (WO158).
25. OAD538 of 5.7.17 in WO158/48.
26. Esher's journals 17.5.17.
27. Sims's comments on Lt. A. Miles's paper 'An Estimate of the Submarine Threat' dated 21.5.17 (Sims papers).
28. Cabinet paper initialled J. R. J. and dated 16.1.17.
29. Cavan to the king, undated (Royal Archives).
30. 1A/33033 of 29.4.17 (Heyes papers).
31. Grey to the British ambassador 9.12.14 (Bean working papers).
32. War Policy Committee 19.6.17 (CAB27/6).
33. January 1916 (PRO30/57/53).
34. Peace offer in Esher 15.10.17 and Pershing's cable to the War Department 15.9.17 (Pershing papers). Item G249 for Cabinets of 24 and 27 September 1917 (Lloyd George papers).
35. Page to Woodrow Wilson 6.10.17 (Wilson papers).
36. Hankey diary 5.11.17.
37. 28.9.17 (CAB23/16).
38. Haig to Robertson 13.8.17 (Robertson papers).
39. Charteris lecture to the National Arts Club, New York, October 1925 (Charteris papers).
40. Kiggell to the king 9.7.17 (Royal Archives).
41. Reference in Esher's journal 19.8.17.
42. Imperial War Cabinet 11.8.18.
43. Timetable in OAD654 of 6.10.17 (Heyes papers).
44. Rosenthal diary (Mitchell Library, Sydney).
45. Ironside to Liddell Hart 29.3.37 (private collection).
46. D. Fraser, *Alanbrooke* (Athenaeum, New York, 1982).
47. Jacquetta Hawkes, *Mortimer Wheeler* (Weidenfeld and Nicolson 1982).
48. OAD703 (Macdonogh papers).
49. 3.12.17 in Hunter-Weston diary.
50. Benson papers.
51. Imperial War Cabinet 14.6.18.
52. CAB103/53.

53. Lt.-Col. A. Burne in CAB103/53.
54. Swinton in G232 (Lloyd George papers).
55. Milner to Lloyd George 18.12.17 (Lloyd George papers).
56. 7.10.17 (WO106/310).
57. IA/40581 from GHQ's 'I' Branch (Monash papers, Australian War Memorial).
58. J. C. Wedgwood, *The Last of the Radicals* (Cape n.d.).

7: Cambrai

1. The genesis of Cambrai is uncertain, but as a rough guide Byng presented his idea to Haig on 6 August. Haig was mildly interested but used the five divisons earmarked for it in Passchendaele a few weeks later. Byng raised the idea again on 5 September and the tanks were earmarked (OAD618 of 11.9.17). The project was formally accepted in a conference on 22 September with a Canadian spearhead. On 7 October the Canadians were sent to Passchendaele. Byng's response was to try to widen the frontage on 18 October, then limit the scope of the battle in his draft scheme of 25 October.

2. The diary index in Box 334 (Haig papers) suggests that Haig accepted the scheme on 15 October after Byng had presented his scheme on 10 October (Heyes papers). Until GHQ's full war diary is put into the Record Office, there will always be uncertainty – the more since a fictitious operation of Lens was used as a cover for the Cambrai scheme from 10 August, clouding much surviving documentation.

3. Byng lecture dated 26.2.18 (Canadian Corps papers).
4. Tandy 4.12.44 (CAB45/118).
5. Draft scheme 1.11.17 in WO95/367.
6. OAD690 in WO95/367.
7. Byng to Haig 8.11.17 (WO95/367) with the reply 11.11.17 as OAD700.
8. Haig's report 23.12.17 (WO158/54).
9. One and a third divisions in Fuller (Rutgers). Four divisions in 1A/40581 from GHQ's 'I' Branch (Monash papers, Australian War Memorial). Five divisions in OAD731 of 24.12.17 (WO158).
10. OAD731/3 of 24.12.17 (WO158).
11. Burn to Edmonds 11.10.44 (CAB45/118).
12. Haig diary 17–18.11.17.
13. OAD690 of 3.11.17.
14. Kiggell's letter during January 1927 (CAB45/118).

15. Staff Rides 1909/1910 (Haig papers).
16. 29th Division war diary (WO95). Weeding may distort here. Night marches in De Lisle diary.
17. Crawford 3.8.44 (CAB45/118).
18. WO158/320, which is GHQ's internal inquiry.
19. Davidson 28.11.44 (CAB45/118).
20. OAD731/3 on 24.12.17 (WO158).
21. 6.12.17 in the Headlam manuscript (Milner papers).
22. GHQ's formal inquiry at Hesdin at the end of January 1918 (WO158/53–5), with Smuts Memorandum (CAB21/22). Lloyd George papers hold a slab of GHQ documents (unavailable elsewhere) in G235. Byng's evidence is particularly valuable.
23. WO153/967.
24. A mass of fascinating eyewitness accounts in CAB45/118. Also two first-class essays in the Staff College library, handed in during 1930 and annotated by Commandant Gwynne. Some of the documents cited in these essays are not in the PRO today.

8: The Tool

1. 28.9.17 in R6165 (American National Archives).
2. Borden diary 16.7.18 (Borden papers).
3. Royal Commission 1904.
4. *Journal of the Royal United Services Institute*, August 1928.
5. CAB103/57.
6. *Army Quarterly*, October 1952.
7. H. Langlois, *The British Army in European Wars* (Rees 1910).
8. Cavan's unpublished autobiography (Cavan papers).
9. William Hughes to Bean in a conversation in 1935 (Bean's working papers).
10. Maxse's bequest is of particular value, its bulk and range apparently a counter-blast to Edmonds blaming him for the German breakthrough between the 3rd and 5th Armies in March 1918. Maxse to Edmonds 7.10.34 (CAB45/184), with Edmonds's reply 7.10.34 (Edmonds papers). The matter obviously disturbed Edmonds, who wrote in self-justification to Bean (13.3.36 Bean papers).
11. Headlam to his wife 2.6.17 (Headlam papers).
12. Oliver to Austen Chamberlain 13.7.17 (Chamberlain papers).
13. Headlam to his wife 21.7.16 (Headlam papers).

14. Col. W. Robertson in CAB45/153.
15. Headlam to his wife 1.9.17 (Headlam papers).
16. Derby to Haig 5.1.18 (Derby papers).
17. Haig to Derby 8.1.18 (Derby papers).
18. Burgis's autobiographical notes (Burgis papers).
19. Imperial War Cabinet 13.6.18.
20. Esher to Haig 22.1.17 (Esher papers).
21. C. Head, *The Art of Generalship* (Gale & Polden, n.d.).
22. Haig to George V 9.5.16 (Royal Archives).
23. Lawson report in WO106/363.
24. Esher to Haig and Kitchener 10.5.16 (Esher papers).
25. Roure report in Du Cane 14.5.18 and at more length in Griscom to Pershing 16.8.18 (Pershing papers).
26. Milner's GT5117 on 15.7.18 and Milner to Geddes 6.8.18 (Milner papers).
27. Haig's paper 28.4.18 (Monash papers, Australian War Memorial).
28. Boraston papers.
29. WO32.
30. Monash to his wife 4.4.18 (Monash papers, National Library).
31. Liddell Hart papers 11/1933/27.
32. Records of Canadian Memorial Tower, Ottawa.
33. Ivor Maxse to Montgomery-Massingberd 31.7.16 (Montgomery-Massingberd papers).
34. Trianon conference 29.1.18 in CAB28/3/1A.
35. Maxse's visit to a French Army training school, December 1916, with Montgomery-Massingberd's about the same time, leading to a report attached by GHQ to their pamphlet 'Offensive Fighting by Small Units', dated 6.1.17.
36. Du Cane to Henry Wilson 8.11.16 (Wilson papers).
37. A. Du Picq, *Battle Studies* (Gale & Polden 1870).
38. C. Colin, *Transformations of War* (Rees 1912).
39. Benson papers (undated).
40. Clark to Pershing 15.5.18 (Pershing papers).
41. J. Monash, *The Australian Victories in France* (Angus & Robertson 1920).
42. Churchill's paper is dated 21.10.17. I discovered references to its date but not to its contents. His GT3835 of 5.3.18 is probably close to it in content. Robertson tipped Haig off on the original paper in 01/211 of 2.11.17. Haig's reply was dated 23.11.17 (Fuller papers). The replies of the army commanders to Haig in June 1918 are in the Rawlinson papers (Army Museum). Lawrence's counter is OB2231 of 23.6.18.

9: The Execution

1. Ludendorff's 'The Battle in the Intermediate Zone', 1.5.18, used as a supplement to US Information Summary No. 140 on 19.8.18.
2. OAD131 (Mitchell papers).
3. Ivor Maxse papers and V. Germains, *The Kitchener Armies* (Peter Davies 1930). Maxse had a wax cylinder cut with his own oral description and presented it to the Bishop of St Albans, but it appears to have been mislaid.
4. Maxse papers and Baker-Carr's lecture 18.3.18 (Canadian Corps papers, Ottawa).

10: The Common Denominator

1. Some of the best are: C. Colin, *Transformations of War* (Rees 1912); De Negrier, *Lessons of the Russo-Japanese War* (Rees 1906); T. McGuire, *The Development of Tactics since 1866* (Rees 1904); Von der Goltz, *The Nation in Arms* (Rees 1906); Caemmerer, *The Development of Nine-teenth-Century Strategic Science* (Rees 1908); A. Becke, *An Introduction to Tactics* (Rees 1909); J. Burde, *Tactical Principles* (Rees 1908); De Pardieu, *A Study of German Tactics* (Rees 1902); F. Maude, *War and the World's Life* (Smith & Elder 1907).
2. Staff Rides were popularized by Haig before the war. They were field exercises, complete with the issue of orders but minus the troops. Haig was obviously proud of them and his papers have the addresses he delivered, in full. Clausewitz is the author most frequently cited, followed, ironically, by Foch.
3. Haig to Harcourt 15.6.16 (Aspinall–Oglander papers).
4. G. Henderson, *The Science of War* (Longmans 1919), includes essays written between 1891 and 1903. Pages 37–8 and 200–212 are of particular interest. Henderson was by far the chief influence on Haig. The ambiguity in Henderson over whether an attack should be frontal or indirect or whether the enemy should be penetrated or pushed back *en masse* is clearly seen in Haig's own divided mind during the pre-Somme conferences.
5. J. Baynes, *Morale* (Cassell 1967).
6. J. Fuller, *The Army in My Time* (Rich & Cowan 1935).
7. *Daily Mail* 7.5.38.

8. Wording of FSR (1909).
9. Haig to Kiggell 14.7.10 (Kiggell papers).
10. One of Haig's Staff Rides.
11. Morton to Liddell Hart in 1961 (Liddell Hart papers).
12. Dill papers.

11: March 1918: The German Offensive

1. Martin Gilbert, *Winston Churchill*, Vol. 4, 1917–22 (Heinemann 1975).
2. Diary (Uniacke papers).
3. OAD188 (WO106/416).
4. OAD843 on 12.5.18 (Heyes papers; noted also in Haig diary WO256).
5. Lloyd George in the Imperial War Cabinet 11.6.18.
6. CAB23/13.
7. Haig to Sir George Greaves 12.3.18 (Haig papers).
8. OB1851A by Fowke (Dawnay papers).
9. Diary 4.1.18 (Clive papers) and Macready to the Cabinet 15.12.17.
10. Haig diary 22.7.17.
11. Doullens conference 13.12.17 and SS561/621, based on OAD291/29, registering the decision taken on 7.12.17 to prepare for defence only. A committee including Edmonds recommended linear defence. Haig overruled them and went for zonal defence.
12. 8.1.18 (CAB25/68).
13. Lawrence's chronology on 29.1.18 (Lawrence papers).
14. Lecture noted in Amery diary 29.1.18 (Amery papers).
15. Doullens army commanders' conference 12.3.18 in OAD291/32/4 (Heyes papers).
16. Registered by the French 2nd Bureau 27.1.18 and passed to London 11.2.18 (CAB25/5).
17. Benson papers, dated July 1917.
18. OAD741 on 7.1.18 (Heyes papers).
19. Clemenceau wired Lloyd George on 23.2.18 according to US War Department records.
20. Haig to Asquith 9.7.15 in CAB17/129, with the Cabinet's decision in French's OAM6044 of 11.8.15 and Joffre's contribution on 13.8.15, both in WO158/13.
21. An order to Gough to prepare the rear defences for the allied counter-offensive is dated 29.1.18 (a chronology in the Lawrence papers). The

Nesle army commanders' conference proceedings of 21.2.18 are in Lawrence's chronology and the Dawnay papers. The order resulting was OAD759/1 of 24.2.18 (Dawnay papers), with the Supreme War Council told much less in OAD770 of 2.3.18.

22. 10.2.18 in the Bean diary and OAD761 in the Haig papers. It is mentioned in a later Staff College tour in WO95/519.

23. OAD785 in the Dawnay papers, with a contemporary comment in Philip Sassoon's letter to Esher reinforcing the point (Esher papers).

24. 25.3.35 in CAB45/184.

25. Cipher book is WO33/920.

26. 25.3.18 in WO158. There are two separate and different documents under that classification.

27. Byng on 25.3.18 in CAB45/192. Congreve's private diary mentions the receipt of two contradictory sets of orders a day earlier in his entry for 26.3.18. In Haig's defence, Lawrence wrote to Byng on 12.2.18 (Heyes papers) stating that if Gough went back to Péronne the Flesquières Salient would have to be evacuated. But there was obviously inadequate provision for Byng to get early warning of that contingency.

28. CAB45/177.

29. CAB45/177.

30. CAB21/41, with supporting detail in the diaries of Leo Amery (Amery papers) and Rawlinson (original version in the Army Museum). Bertie's letter to Balfour on 28.3.18 (Bertie papers) is worth a check.

31. 24.10.34 by Sylvester in the Lloyd George papers. The Montgomery-Massingberd papers also have a copy with GHQ's underlining. The GHQ revised version is classified as OAD795.

32. Montgomery–Massingberd to Edmonds 19.11.25 in CAB45/177.

33. Clive diary 28–30.3.18 (Clive papers).

34. Newton Baker to Woodrow Wilson 29.3.18 (Baker papers).

12: August 1918: A Turning Point?

1. Statistics in Clark to Pershing 19.4.18 (Pershing papers). Also in the Benson papers for the 21 March–5 May period.

2. 1.6.18 in the manuscript of Pershing's memoirs.

3. Clark to Pershing 30.5.18 (Pershing papers).

4. Clive diary 1.6.18 (Clive papers).

5. Amery diary 16.7.18 (Amery papers).

6. Clark to Pershing 18.7.18 (Pershing papers).

7. Grant diary 3.4.18 (Grant papers) and Foch's General Instruction No. 2 in OAD806 of 4.4.18.
8. Unpublished manuscript on Foch (Du Cane papers) and Grant diary 22.5.18 (Grant papers).
9. Grant diary 12.7.18 (Grant papers), with preliminary order in Rawlinson's diary 13.7.18, Davidson's approval (Rawlinson's Army Museum diary) and Canadian involvement in the Currie diary on 20.7.18. Canadian Corps papers have full documentation of the Festubert scheme, showing that a surprise attack by massed tanks, without preliminary artillery preparation, had been thought out in April 1918. Operation Delta was planned 30.4.18 and increased in complexity on 4.5.18 and 13.6.18. Haig finally rejected it on 17.7.18 (WO158/26).
10. 22.7.18 (WO158).
11. Haig diary and OAD900 (Montgomery-Massingberd papers).
12. D. Kahn, *The Codebreakers* (Macmillan 1973), mentions the new code on 11.3.18, with a partial solution by the French on 26.4.18 and a full solution 2.6.18.
13. Clark's letters in the Pershing papers are the best example. Comparable letters from British liaison officers have been extracted from archive collections in Britain.
14. OAD942 in the Dawnay papers and the US Official History.
15. Conversation 22.6.33 between Lloyd George, Hankey and Smuts in the Lloyd George papers.
16. OAD900/3 on 29.7.18 (Dill papers) and Rawlinson Army Museum diary 28.7.18.
17. Du Cane's *Foch* manuscript.
18. OAD900/13 on 5.8.18 (Dill papers).
19. OAD900/18 on 7.8.18 (Dawnay papers).
20. Bean's working papers.
21. Rawlinson to Henry Wilson 9.8.18 (Wilson papers).
22. Haig to Pershing 14.6.18 (Pershing papers).
23. Haig to Pershing 1.8.18 (Pershing papers).
24. 9.8.18 as OAD902/1 (Heyes papers). OAD907/1 on 14.8.18, with the preliminary order 18.8.18 in the British master file (US Public Archives, the American official historian's files). OAD907/10 of 22.8.18 likewise in the British master file.
25. OAD912 on 23.8.18 (Dawnay papers).
26. Letter in WO158/26, with the first Foch reply 28.8.18 (WO158/87) and the second letter with change of tack 29.8.18 (WO158/26). Du Cane's record is on 31.8.18 (WO158/87).

27. Imperial War Cabinet 31.7.18 and the Committee of Prime Ministers' Final Report 14.8.18 (Canadian National Archives).

28. Amery diary 25.8.18 (Amery papers).

29. Fully documented in the US Official History.

30. Clark to Pershing 1.5.18, 4.8.18 and 22.8.18 (Pershing papers), with 3.9.18 in Maxse papers and remarkable manpower graphs in the Milner papers.

31. Henry Wilson diary 1.9.18 (Wilson papers).

32. Pershing's draft report 30.8.18.

33. OAD915 of 3.9.18 (Heyes papers).

34. Haig diary 9.9.18, but OAD916 of 5.9.18 (Heyes papers) notes Plumer being told that he will attack Passchendaele and Rawlinson the Bellicourt tunnel, which means some details were released earlier, if not the full plan, which is in OAD923 of 22.9.18 (Canadian Corps papers).

35. *The Memoirs of Marshal Foch* (Heinemann 1931).

13: The Last Hundred Days: An Advance to Victory?

1. Paper by Nash in CAB45/168.

2. McNaughton's lecture, dated October 1921 (Canadian Corps papers).

3. Macready paper in CAB25/96.

4. Clark 27.8.18 (Pershing papers).

5. 24.8.18 (WO106/327).

6. 7.10.18 (CAB25/79).

7. 12.9.18 (Christie papers).

8. 12.10.18 (CAB45/168).

9. Clark 13.10.18 (Pershing papers).

10. 19.10.18 (CAB23/16).

11. Currie's diary 20.10.18 (Currie papers).

12. Rawlinson's diary 5.11.18 (Army Museum).

13. Rawlinson quoted by Montgomery-Massingberd in *Truth* 7.7.20 (Montgomery-Massingberd papers).

14. Lawrence to Charteris 7.9.28 (Charteris papers). Also Lawrence to Du Cane 20.10.18 (Du Cane papers) stating that, since there was no reason to believe that the Boche was beaten, GHQ had sent Clive to the French GHQ to find out why Foch was so confident.

15. 7.11.18, signed IBA (Uniacke papers).

16. Notes dated 10.11.18 (Maxse papers).

17. The manuscript of Pershing's memoirs is set out in diary form. This

episode is dated 29.8.18. Details of the planned attacks are in the American Official History as the Bombon conference of 2.9.18.

18. 8.10.18 from the French 3rd Bureau (US Official History).
19. St Mihiel is described in WO106/528. The German angle is in a letter from Army Group commander von Gallwitz to the German GHQ on 11.9.18 (US Official History). The Argonne offensive is in Grant's report 26.9.18 (Grant papers); also Mitchell's report (National Archives, Washington) and Clark 11.10.18 (Pershing papers).
20. Henry Wilson diary 7.10.18 (Wilson papers).
21. 23.10.18 (CAB23/17).
22. Clark 1.11.18 (Pershing papers).
23. Report dated 9.11.18 (Woodrow Wilson papers). Grant's diary 6.11.18 noted the orderly German retreat and WO106/318 report dated 1.11.18 comments on fine German discipline.
24. Grant diary 9.11.18 (Grant papers).
25. Clark 11.11.18 (Pershing papers).
26. Report dated 14.12.18 (Woodrow Wilson papers).

14: Haig's Fictions

1. Winston Churchill, *Great Contemporaries* (Butterworth 1938). *Daily Mail* original 3.10.35.
2. Haig diary 30.11.18.
3. Milner to Lloyd George 13.11.18 (Lloyd George papers).
4. Haig to his wife 26.2.19 (Haig papers).
5. Correspondence in CAB103/73 and on the 1918 volume, CAB102/360.
6. CAB45/103.
7. CAB45/183.
8. *Sir Douglas Haig's Despatches, December 1915–April 1919*, ed. John Boraston (Dent 1919).
9. The way in which the Memorandum was put together remains unclear. 1917 and 1918 were written by Boraston, assisted by Davidson (see Boraston in the *Spectator* 28.11.52). Kiggell wrote 1916, working with Haig and a shorthand writer for ten days in November 1919. The first copy (Haig papers) has the pencilled alterations of Kiggell (margin) and Haig (slips of paper). Finished in January 1920, the top copy was sent via Esher to the British Museum, but Esher suggested additional documentation. Dewar and Boraston was perhaps started as a result. Its introduction ('Some Important Events') suggests the possibility. It should be noted that

the Dewar and Boraston introduction answers a question which has always baffled the Haigites – when and why Pétain visited Haig in summer 1917. But it doesn't supply a context for offensive action in the Cambrai–St Quentin region. The answer can be found in various British archives.

10. Wigram to Boraston 17.3.28 (Boraston papers).

11. G. Dewar and J. Boraston, *Sir Douglas Haig's Command* (Constable 1922).

12. Ivor Maxse to Liddell Hart 10.2.28 (Liddell Hart papers).

13. Boraston's letter to *The Times* 19.11.34.

14. C. Falls, *War Books – a Critical Guide* (Peter Davies 1930).

15. Lord Esher, *The Pomp of Power* (Hutchinson 1922), originally published anonymously.

16. A review from *Truth* (n.d.).

17. Haig to Wigram 12.9.14 (Haig papers).

18. Stamfordham to Lady Haig 3.10.15 (Haig papers).

19. Returned by Wigram 28.9.16 (Haig papers).

20. Pierre Nordon, *Conan Doyle* (Murray 1966).

21. Lord Geddes in the *National Review*, February 1953.

22. There are other absurd entries. In the entry for 18.4.17, Haig asserted that only thirty of 5,000 RFC flights had been knocked out and that a French officer had arrived to get ideas on how to organize the French Air Force. In fact, RFC losses during 'Bloody April' were far higher than the worst period of the Battle of Britain and the RFC's organization a disgraceful shambles. An entry on 25.10.17 states that Byng was happy with the men and material he was being given for Cambrai. All documents show him remarkably unhappy. On 29.5.18 Haig wrote that Germany was near the end of her resources. All the facts (he would have known them well) were against that opinion. Haig was simply lying in his own cause.

23. Box 32, Haig papers.

24. Geddes in the *National Review*, February 1953.

25. Speech in December 1936, reported in Foyle's house newspaper 8.1.37, with rather fuller notes by Lady Haig in the Haig papers.

26. R. Prior, *Churchill's 'World Crisis' as History* (Croom Helm 1983).

27. K. Rose, *King George V* (Weidenfeld and Nicolson 1983).

15: *The Government's Support of Haig*

1. B. Liddell Hart, *The Real War* (Faber 1930), was the first serious critical work.

2. Foundation of CID's Historical Section in 1906 by Esher in Daniel's memo dated 14.7.22 (CAB103/62). Same memo on Daniel and Corbett appointed 27.8.14, with Atkinson added for the Army 27.1.15. The dispatch of young officers in Esher to Millerand 23.2.15 (Esher papers). Data on Branch's inception also CAB27/212.

3. Esher to Kitchener 31.7.15 on his fear of Tardieu's work for Joffre (CAB103/69). R. Johnstone, visiting London on behalf of the US Official History in January 1917, was told of the popular/staff distinction and commissioning of Fortescue on 14.2.16. An apologia on Loos had already been placed in the press by the CID's Historical Section.

4. Appointment of a historian in Daniel to Asquith 23.12.15 (CAB103/68).

5. Colonel Daniel (born 1861); Marine, retired 1910; assistant secretary to the CID when Swinton was mobilized) coordinated the three service sections. During the war, Atkinson was in charge of the Army section with Fortescue his historian. Edmonds replaced Atkinson in 1919 with Falls, his historian, in 1922. There were considerable problems with personnel. McMunn was sacked for dissent, Rowan–Robinson and Fergusson for ineptitude. The Gallipoli volumes were held up because the chosen historians (Gordon 1919–23 and Ellison 1923–5) found the task beyond them.

6. Response to Fortescue's first offering in Esher to Hankey 19.6.18 (Hankey papers).

7. Haig to Davidson 12.8.19 and 4.3.27 (Haig papers).

8. Edmonds's first paper 12.9.19 noting friction between Atkinson and Fortescue as well as between Jones and Captain Morris, air analogues. Edmonds's denigration of Fortescue's work to Sandhurst 2.1.20 (CAB103/76) and plotting in CAB103/83 and Minute 1 in CAB635. Fortescue's review in the *Quarterly Review*, October 1919.

9. Original instructions (find facts and criticize as little as possible) in CAB103/97. Instructions to Gordon 30.6.19 (CAB103/97). Expanded dispatch idea in Edmonds's report 30.6.19 (CAB103/97). Use of Prussian history of 1870 war as a model in CAB103/74.

10. Edmonds to Lady Haig 17.2.28 (Haig papers, Box 325).

11. Daniel in CAB103/82. Peter Wright, *At the Supreme War Council* (Putnam 1921). C. E. Montague, *Disenchantment* (Chatto and Windus 1922).

12. The 1922 meeting to discuss the histories is in CAB27/212. Army Council instruction to keep 1915–17 volumes brief and delay publication was at this session. That this was done is suggested by Hankey's remark in the 1929 meeting (CAB103/74) that all histories were

either complete or far advanced. This was confirmed by Edmonds's letters to Bean. In 1927, he stated that the first draft of 1918 was complete, and in 1930 he said the same of 1917. Pigeon-holing allowed work to proceed on a number of in-house Official Histories. Bean was given a list – the Black Sea campaign, Italy 1917–18, intervention in Russia, occupation of Germany 1918–29, occupation of Constantinople. Time was no problem. In the forties, Edmonds told the supervising sub-committee that volumes took two years each. Dispute over an author for 1918 is in CAB27/212 and CAB102/360. When Kiggell disintegrated in 1926, Hyslop took over and was overwhelmed. T. E. Lawrence, Baring and Masefield were all approached and rejected the job. Aspinall then took over in 1928 before being passed on to the Gallipoli series. Edmonds finally took up 1918 after expressing reservations to his supervising committee.

13. Edmonds's takeover in CAB103/97. Visits to Paris in CAB103/69 and 108. Records to own house in CAB103/74. Appendices gutted in CAB103/97. GHQ's card index in CAB102/360. Isleworth repository and fact of full GHQ/Army appendix holding in Heyes essay for Canadian Historical Branch 27.1.28 (Ottawa). Limiting of access in CAB44/428, with Atkinson precis in RG9(3)4722 Ottawa. The fact of no important records being lost in the Blitz in CAB103/18. The fact of Edmonds deceiving even the War Office on what he was keeping secret (including the full GHQ Operations war diary) is in CAB103/58 (correspondence with Lambert).

14. The best treatment of writing procedures is in CAB44/428. The first narrative method is also in Bridges to Cork (CAB103/108) dated 3.4.43. Sample of Edmonds's candour on first draft in 27.7.34 to Macdonogh (CAB45/184). Final draft CAB44/428, with outside readers 14.1.45 (CAB103/108). That each volume took only two years CAB103/108. Edmonds's rationale for his outrageous introductions and conclusions CAB44/428. Edmonds left an essay of fifty foolscap pages on his experience and advice. The Cabinet Office has not passed a copy to the Public Record Office. Records of the US Historical Section have details on the 2 Cavendish Square period.

15. Army Council instructions in CAB103/79. Montgomery-Massingberd's liverish counterpoint on CAB45/132–3.

16. Foreign Office on Kemal 14.10.31 (Aspinall papers) and on Hamilton 28.7.27 (CAB103/78).

17. Edmonds's scheme 8.6.45 (CAB103/21).

18. Edmonds to Gough 10.5.23 (Shaw Sparrow papers).

19. One officer to CB and two to Wynne 17.2.44 (CAB45/33 within CAB45/140).

20. Edmonds to Sylvester 22.3.34 (Lloyd George papers). Maxse was another to find himself scapegoated (Maxse to Edmonds 7.10.34 in CAB45/184, with Edmonds's reply 16.10.34 referring back to 1926 and 1930).

21. R. Prior, *Churchill's 'World Crisis' as History* (Croom Helm 1983), and Edmonds's correspondence with Bean.

22. Edmonds–Bean correspondence is interleaved in the 7953 sequence of files relating to each of Bean's six volumes. The Loos 300 figure is J.E. to C.B. on 19.9.27; the 700 in CAB102/360 and CAB103/82. 'Haig's butcher' is in J.E. to C.B. April 1937 and J.E. to Liddell Hart 9.11.34 (CAB45/184). The retraction in J.E. to Acheson 22.7.50 (CAB103/13). Edmonds's Passchendaele casualty error in CAB103/53. The bizarre statement that the Germans had halved their losses for Passchendaele in a letter to Bridges, 1944 (CAB103/58). CAB45/118 contains the remarkable fact that Edmonds never believed that French weakness was any reason for carrying on at Passchendaele (Davidson's letter 28.11.44). Another gem in the Liddell Hart papers (1944) informed him that readers weren't expected to read appendices; this in connection with a Haig letter to Robertson dated 8.10.17 praising the resilient defence by the French which contradicted the line taken in the text.

23. 9.3.28 (CAB45/241).

24. Passchendaele file (CAB103/112). A rough indication of the date of handover to the Public Record Office is suggested by the latest letter within the file – August 1953. As a postscript to the old chestnuts in CAB103/112, Edmonds told Liddell Hart in 1935 that he was much amused by the colossal ignorance displayed by both sides in the Passchendaele debate, Haig's advocates on the one side, Lloyd George and Beaverbrook on the other.

Appendix 1: Sources Used: An Evaluation

1. Hankey to Austen Chamberlain 10.7.18 (CAB21/97). Also Hankey to Hughes (CAB21/98).

2. Robertson to Milne 7.11.16 (Robertson papers).

3. Pollen quoted in the Aylmer Haldane diary 11.2.18 (Haldane papers). Reference also to other scandalous subterfuges in the Amery diary 10/15.2.18 and Amery to Wavell 18.11.36 (Wavell papers, St Antony's College, Oxford).

4. Reference to the Cabinet Office's 'weeding' instructions for February 1919 (CAB103/97).

5. Reference to Henderson's 2,000 Cabinet papers in CAB63/21.

6. Reference to Lloyd George's diary in the minuted conversations of Lloyd George, Smuts and Hankey on 22.6.33 (Lloyd George papers).

7. The Trustees initially permitted Lady Haig to write a diary-extract life of her husband up to December 1915 (in September 1929) but changed their minds and pegged her back to August 1914 in 1931. At the time there was much controversy over the whole matter of a 'Life'. Edmonds and Boraston turned it down. So, too, did Maurice and Charteris when they were denied access to the diary. Buchan rejected the project after being insulted by Lady Haig, and Trevelyan rejected it without any insults. When Duff Cooper accepted the contract in mid-1933, Lady Haig began her larger book. The five-volume manuscript is in the Haig papers (Box 215–19, with references in Box 334). Reference to the Duff Cooper hijack is in Box 325.

8. 1928 Sub-Committee minutes (CAB103). Haig's letter to Edmonds 22.9.27 and one from Edmonds to Lady Haig 17.2.28 stating that Edmonds was copying volumes 232–34 of the diary.

9. Edmonds's fourteen boxes are in CAB103/55.

10. Final decree in Court of Sessions 30.10.36. Process reference CS275/98/11.

11. Melbourne *Argus* 24.3.28. That newspaper was remarkably well informed on the Haig saga as a result of Sir Henry Gullett's family connections in London. Gullett was a long-time friend of Bean, worked for a time with the *Argus* and wrote the Palestine volume of the Australian Official History. He was permitted to make a selection of passages from Haig's diary for Bean's private use in the 1930s.

12. Steed, editor of *The Times*, tipped off Haig about Milner's press articles (14.11.20 in the Haig papers). Haig's response was a letter to Steed dated 19.11.20, using Davidson to distance himself from the imbroglio. Haig's gloss for the official record is dated 18.11.20 (CAB45/103). The full version is in Box 216, Haig papers, with a letter to Boraston 1.7.21, thanking him for the drafting.

13. 30.5.49 Edmonds to the 2nd Earl Haig (CAB103/55).

Appendix 2: Haig: A Political Intriguer?

1. R. Thompson, *Churchill and Morton* (Hodder and Stoughton 1976). All letters in the Thompson papers.

2. Esher to Haig 2.12.17 (Haig papers).
3. Lansdowne's paper to the War Committee 13.11.16.
4. Esher to Derby 31.5.17 (Esher papers).
5. Milner to Carson 30.11.17 (Carson papers).
6. Supreme War Council 26.7.17 in CAB28/2/1A. Derby to Haig 16.11.17 and Esher to Haig 23.11.17 (Haig papers).
7. Thornton diary 24.10.17 (Milner papers).
8. C. Repington, *The First World War 1914–1918* (Constable 1920).
9. Secretary of the Interior Lane to Wilson 3.12.17 (Woodrow Wilson papers).
10. Oliver to Austen Chamberlain 17.2.18 (Chamberlain papers).
11. *The Papers of Woodrow Wilson*, ed. Arthur Link (Princeton). This letter dated 21.2.18.
12. Hankey to Lloyd George 15.2.18 (Hankey papers).
13. Esher's journal 18.2.18 (Esher papers).
14. Rawlinson to Derby 15.4.18 (Rawlinson papers, Army Museum).
15. Wilson diary 15.4.18 (Wilson papers).
16. Smuts to Lloyd George 22.1.18 (Lloyd George papers G243).
17. *The Memoirs of Henri Poincaré*, ed. Sir George Arthur (Heinmann 1926).
18. House to Woodrow Wilson 29.4.18 (Woodrow Wilson papers).
19. Haig to his wife 7.5.18 (Haig papers).
20. Wigram to Rawlinson 13.5.18 (Rawlinson papers, Army Museum).
21. Haig to Henry Wilson 26.11.18 (Wilson papers).
22. Boraston in the *Yorkshire Post* 31.2.28.
23. Haig diary 26.9.19.
24. Box 334, Haig papers.

Index

Index

FOR THE BEST IN PAPERBACKS, LOOK FOR THE

In every corner of the world, on every subject under the sun, Penguin represents quality and variety – the very best in publishing today.

For complete information about books available from Penguin – including Puffins, Penguin Classics and Arkana – and how to order them, write to us at the appropriate address below. Please note that for copyright reasons the selection of books varies from country to country.

In the United Kingdom: Please write to *Dept JC, Penguin Books Ltd, FREEPOST, West Drayton, Middlesex, UB7 0BR.*

If you have any difficulty in obtaining a title, please send your order with the correct money, plus ten per cent for postage and packaging, to *PO Box No 11, West Drayton, Middlesex*

In the United States: Please write to *Dept BA, Penguin, 299 Murray Hill Parkway, East Rutherford, New Jersey 07073*

In Canada: Please write to *Penguin Books Canada Ltd, 2801 John Street, Markham, Ontario L3R 1B4*

In Australia: Please write to the *Marketing Department, Penguin Books Australia Ltd, P.O. Box 257, Ringwood, Victoria 3134*

In New Zealand: Please write to the *Marketing Department, Penguin Books (NZ) Ltd, Private Bag, Takapuna, Auckland 9*

In India: Please write to *Penguin Overseas Ltd, 706 Eros Apartments, 56 Nehru Place, New Delhi, 110019*

In the Netherlands: Please write to *Penguin Books Netherlands B.V., Postbus 3507, NL–1001 AH, Amsterdam*

In West Germany: Please write to *Penguin Books Ltd, Friedrichstrasse 10–12, D–6000 Frankfurt/Main 1*

In Spain: Please write to *Alhambra Longman S.A., Fernandez de la Hoz 9, E–28010 Madrid*

In Italy: Please write to *Penguin Italia s.r.l., Via Como 4, I-20096 Pioltello (Milano)*

In France: Please write to *Penguin France S.A., 17 rue Lejeune, F-31000 Toulouse*

In Japan: Please write to *Longman Penguin Japan Co Ltd, Yamaguchi Building, 2-12-9 Kanda Jimbocho, Chiyoda-Ku, Tokyo 101*

Death's Men

Denis Winter has taken the First World War away from the politicians and generals and given it back to the men who fought it, and, through their words, to us.

'I would say that it is by a long way the best general book I have read on this war. It tells me a great deal about it that I did not know before and there is nothing in it I would question. I find it amazing that someone who did not experience it should write so vividly and movingly and accurately about it. Certainly every survivor of that distant holocaust should read it' – Gerald Brenan in a letter to the author

'A beautifully organized book' – John Keegan in the *New Statesman*